READINGS FOR LEADERS

Harlan Cleveland

General Editor

Volume IV

SHARED POWER

What Is It?

How Does It Work?

How Can We Make It Work Better?

Edited by

John M. Bryson

and

Robert C. Einsweiler

UNIVERSITY PRESS OF AMERICA

EDUCATION FOR REFLECTIVE LEADERSHIP

HUBERT H. HUMPHREY INSTITUTE OF PUBLIC AFFAIRS

UNIVERSITY OF MINNESOTA

University Press of America®, Inc.
4720 Boston Way
Lanham, Maryland 20706

3 Henrietta Street
London WC2E 8LU England

Co-published by arrangement with
The Hubert H. Humphrey Institute of Public Affairs

Library of Congress Cataloging-in-Publication Data

Shared Power : What is it? How does it work better?
How can we make it work? /
edited by John M. Bryson and Robert C. Einsweiler.
p.   cm. — (Readings for leaders ; v. 4)
Includes index.
1. Public administration—Decision making.
2. Planning.   3. Policy sciences.   4. Power (Social
sciences)   5. Intergovernmental fiscal relations.
I. Bryson, John M. (John Moore), 1947-   .
II. Einsweiler, Robert C.   III. Series.
JF1525.D4S53   1991
350.007' 2—dc20   91-30236 CIP

ISBN 1-8191-8457-8 (cloth : alk. paper)
ISBN 1-8191-8458-6 (paper : alk. paper)

Acknowledgements

Many, many people contributed to the preparation of this book. The editors first of all would like to thank the former dean of the Humphrey Institute, Harlan Cleveland, for his encouragement of our work in the shared-power area, and for authorizing the conference out of which this book eventually grew. We also must thank Nancy Speer, Jane Marecek, and Patti Manske for their enormously helpful efforts in organizing the conference.

Next, we would like to thank all of the participants in the conference. In addition to the authors of the chapters, we would like to thank the following people who prepared papers for the conference: Frederick Norling, Curtis Ventriss, Helen Muller, John M. "Jack" Stevens, Robert McGowan, Barbara Gray, David Robertson, and Mohammed Ahrari. Many other people participated as session chairs or discussants, including: Robert Backoff, Jan Hively, John Brandl, Vera Vogelsang-Coombs, Joleen Durken, Michael Timpane, Nancy Eustis, Barbara Nelson, Thomas Dewar, Laurence Payne, Ira Schwartz, Esther Wattenberg, William Copeland, Charles Krusell, James Bellus, Ray Harris, Barbara Lukermann, Sir James Swaffield, Margaret Dewar, Willis Bright, Earl Craig, Bernard Taylor, Arvonne Fraser, Ian Maitland, Rosita Albert, Susan Geiger, Robert Kudrle, and Roger Williams.

We also would like to thank the staff of the Humphrey Institute who helped prepare the book manuscript. Louise Strauss and Ellen Carlson made major contributions. We are particularly grateful, however, to Donna Kern, without whose help this project never would have reached completion. Finally, the deft editorial hand of Barbara Crosby will be seen in each chapter.

Chapter 8, "Downtown Shopping Malls and the New Public-Private Strategy," appeared earlier in Marshall Kaplan and Peggy Circiti, editors, *The Great Society and Its Legacy* (Durham, NC: Duke University Press, 1986).

Table of Contents

Foreword

The premise of these READINGS FOR LEADERS is not that leadership can be taught but that it can be learned. The largest part of that learning is bound to be "on the hoof," in the practice of leadership in one's own life and work. But it helps to take thought; to know what others in analogous circumstances have faced, what they did that succeeded or failed; to learn how to analyze the constraints and loopholes in the environment for action; to be able to guess where inherited "policy" comes from; to think hard about the future impacts of present actions; and to know by study as well as instinct that everything really is related to everything else. Leaders will do better, it seems, if they reflect on their environment, their purposes and themselves.

A recurring theme in these Readings is that for leaders, uncertainty is somewhere near the center of things. The complexity of relevant factors in any matter touching the public interest, the inherent unknowability of future social and even physical environments, make uncertainty the biggest factor in planning, in decision-making, even in evaluating the effects of actions after the fact.

A program of education for leadership therefore cannot be focussed mainly on how-to-do-it skills, nor can it offer what-to-do prescriptions. Rather, it has to concentrate on helping each leader get used to the assessment of uncertainty, clarify his/her ethical values, and develop for his/her own personal use a comprehensive worldview appropriate for an ambiguous future. More even than practiced skills, leadership is thought-through attitudes, educated instincts.

In the arts and crafts of creating problems that can be solved there has always, as Aaron Wildavsky says, been tension between resources and objectives, between dogma and skepticism, between intellectual reasoning and social interaction. But just now, in the 1990s, the inherent uncertainties of public policy are compounded and our inherited methods for reconciling those contradictions are rusting away.

The reason seems especially to lie in the corrosion of two traditional distinctions that have served us well in the development of modern industrial civilization but are now increasingly indistinct in the world outside our minds. The boundary line between "~private" and "public" has been blurred by both private users of public services and public users of private services. And the line between "domestic" and "international" policies and actions is being erased by an interdependence which has become technologically imperative, culturally compelling, economically embarrassing and politically inescapable.

New "facts"—technologies, migrations, cartels, stagflation, terrorism—keep forcing leaders (in both "private" and "public" sectors) to broaden the categories in which "policy" is formulated and leadership exercised. In economic policy, Keynesian demand management and monetarist doctrines have both fallen short of explaining, much less controlling, global epidemics of inflation combined with global unemployment. The world's many experiments in governance (among the republican democracies, the American experiment has so far been the hardiest) still fall far short of "liberty and justice for all."

In the United States, New Deal philosophy and practice, by which the Federal government served as the drivewheel of social justice, needs reappraisal now that we the people seem to want less government even as we insist on more governance. In the great urban regions where three quarters of Americans live, defining "the city" as a single municipality is clearly too small a view. At the same time, the 20th century assumption that growing complexity requires more centralized systems is in serious question well before the century ends. In international relations, the invention of a new dimension of violence, incinerating millions of people in a few minutes, may have placed a ceiling on the scale of warfare, for the first time in world history. Yet the collision of economic growth with drives for fairer distribution of its benefits, and with resistance from cultural and religious institutions, creates a worldwide turbulence that had very little to with U.S.-Soviet relations even when they were the centerpiece of world politics.

Education for leadership must therefore be an inquiry into the deeper forces at work, an attempt by leaders themselves to connect their small parts of a large complexity with the whole—and thus learn to identify "success" not only with individual or sectoral accomplishments but with general outcomes.

The earlier Readings in this Series are three other books, also published by University Press of America:

The first was POLITICAL LEADERSHIP IN MILITARY DEFENSE, edited by John P. Craven, the ocean engineer and lawyer who served as Chief Scientist of the Polaris project—the submarine missile system that is still, in its later adaptations, the least vulnerable element of U.S. strategic deterrence. Dr. Craven has more recently been Dean of Marine Programs for the University of Hawaii and a Visiting Professor at the Humphrey Institute. He is currently director of the Honolulu-based international Law of the Sea Institute.

The second volume in the series is THE MANAGEMENT OF GLOBAL DISORDER, edited by Lincoln P. Bloomfield, Professor of Political Science at the Massachusetts Institute of Technology and a former member of the National Security

Council staff in the White House, one of the few Americans who has genuinely specialized in global politics and international conflict resolution.

The third volume in the series LAW, JUSTICE AND THE COMMON GOOD, edited by Sidney Hyman, historian of American politics, essayist and biographer, and currently Editor of *The Aspen Institute Quarterly*. It is a succinct review of the best human thinking on these interlinked concepts which are at the core of ethical leadership in every domain.

The launching of the whole project, and the editing and publishing of these three volumes, was made possible by a grant from the EXXON Foundation.

◆ ◆ ◆

The present volume, SHARED POWER: WHAT IS IT? HOW DOES IT WORK? HOW CAN WE MAKE IT WORK BETTER?, started when Professors John M. Bryson and Robert C. Einsweiler assembled at the University of Minnesota's Hubert H. Humphrey Institute of Public Affairs in 1984 a stellar group of thinkers to consider the implications for planning and management of the fact that, in "domestic" as in "international" affairs, we will all be living in a society with information as its primary resource, with nobody in general charge.

To the extent that monopolies of power become impossible, power-sharing becomes the only way to get anything planned, accomplished, evaluated, reorganized, replanned, and accomplished anew. Yet most of our doctrine in public planning and public administration, and in corporate management as well, is rooted in the premise that *somebody* is in charge of mandating and supervising whatever is to be done. The papers written for the Humphrey Institute conference, and the long process of reconsidering and rewriting them thereafter, have produced a set of Readings that directly tackles this doctrinal dilemma.

The first co-editor, John Bryson, has a deep understanding himself of what is involved in bringing about change in a shared-power world. He is professor of planning and public affairs and director of the Master of Planning program at the University of Minnesota's Hubert H. Humphrey Institute of Public Affairs. His interests include leadership, strategic planning, project planning, coordination, implementation, evaluation and organizational design.

Professor Bryson is the author of *Strategic Planning for Public and Nonprofit Organizations* (San Francisco; Jossey-Bass, 1988), named the Best Book of 1988 by the American Society of Military Comptrollers. He has received many awards for his work, including the 1978 General Electric Award for Outstanding Research in Strategic Planning from the Academy of Management, the award for Best Article of 1987 in the *Journal of the American Planning Association,* and the Chester Rapkin Award for the best article in the *Journal of Planning Education and Research* for 1989-90. He is 1990-91 Chair of the Public Sector Division of the Academy of Management, and has served as a consultant to a variety of government policymaking bodies, government agencies, nonprofit organizations, and for-profit corporations.

Robert C. Einsweiler, the second co-editor, is also a major knowledgeable in the world of shared power. He is professor of planning and public affairs. His academic and professional interests include planning and political strategy, managing urban growth and change, environmental and natural resources planning and management, and the role of professionals in government. Formerly director of planning for the Metropolitan Council in the twin Cities, he also has a private planning practice. Einsweiler has served as national president of the American Institute of Planners and the American Planning Association. He is an honorary fellow of the Royal Australian Planning Institute. He has been a consultant to HUD, the National Science Foundation, the Department of the Interior, and the World Bank, other federal agencies, and state and local governments. He earned his M.S. in city planning from the University of Illinois.

Harlan Cleveland
Professor Emeritus and former Dean
Hubert H. Humphrey Institute of Public Affairs
University of Minnesota
301 19th Avenue South
Minneapolis, MN 55455

Preface

Shared power: what is it? how does it work? how can we make it work better? These are the questions the chapters in this book address. The questions arise in the first place because the world has changed. Events are now so interconnected that most important public issues of the day typically arise in settings in which no one is in charge, and in which organizations or institutions must share power in order to address these issues effectively. In other words, organizations or institutions must interact with one another in order to achieve their separate and shared aims. These sharing relationships take many forms, including intergovernmental, interagency, public/private, and joint private arrangements.

Unfortunately, while the world has changed, most of our current theories are geared basically to situations in which a single organization or institution is in charge, or to situations in which individuals (in contrast to organizations or institutions) must share power and authority. Further, the theory development that has taken place typically has had a single disciplinary or topical base that has limited theoretical advance across disciplines and topics. The world of practice, however, can't wait for general theory to catch up. On the international scene, the profound restructuring underway in Eastern Europe and the Soviet Union is but the most dramatic recent example of the emergence of a shared power world in which no one organization or institution is in charge, least of all the various national communist parties. The restructuring of the "Soviet Empire" grows out of failed practice and powerful social movements, but is not guided by a well-articulated theory of how a shared-power world might be made to work better. At home, the world of practice in the U.S. can't really wait for general theory or change in the basic ideology of the country, an ideology that teaches us to think adversarially of public vs. private, state vs. federal, and individual vs. society. As more and more sharing relationships develop out of necessity, there is an urgent need for reflective practitioners and scholars to examine more closely the nature of shared power and how it can be used effectively, efficiently, justly, wisely and with due regard to individual liberty.

Description of the Book

The chapters in this book grew out of a conference on shared power sponsored by the Hubert H. Humphrey Institute of Public Affairs at the University of Minnesota in 1984. The chapters were then revised — often extensively — based on discussions at the conference and commentary provided to each author by the co-editors.

The book begins with an introductory chapter by John Bryson and Robert Einsweiler. The chapter discusses what is meant by shared power and shared-power arrangements; covers reasons for the emergence of these arrangements; outlines the major themes and issues that are found throughout the book; and provides a reasonably detailed introduction to the chapters that comprise the book.

The book's first major section follows the introductory chapter. The section consists of five chapters on major conceptual or theoretical topics that cut across all policy areas and levels of analysis. These chapters focus on: (1) the forces that embed organizations in an increasingly interconnected world; (2) the changes in inter-institutional relations that result; (3) barriers to interorganizational and inter-institutional sharing and how to address them; (4) how to think about power in shared-power settings; and (5) modes of rationality and the preparation of advice for action in shared-power settings.

The book's second major section is subdivided into four policy areas: education, local economic development, industrial policy or full employment policy, and international affairs. These chapters examine power sharing *within* a policy area, so that the general meaning and the limits of power sharing might be addressed *across* policy territories.

In the concluding chapter, Einsweiler and Bryson argue that the lens of shared power provides an extremely useful way of reexamining ideas about how the world works, and of thinking about ways to make the world work better. They use the lens to draw out commonalities and differences across disciplines and policy areas. Power sharing in and of itself is not good; it is simply an observed state of affairs in much of the world. The term prompts an exploration of the conditions that lead to shared power, along with the various shared-power arrangements that organizations and institutions use to cope with shared-power situations. Einsweiler and Bryson end with a number of conclusions organized under the following headings: (1) growing interconnectedness and interdependence; (2) the idea and reality of separation; (3) what is shared and what is not; (4) organization for sharing; (5) new frameworks for analysis and design in shared-power settings; and (6) planning and managing in shared-power settings.

Audience

There are three general audiences for this book. The first is *academics, students, and reflective practitioners who want to understand the new shared-power game better and who want to know how to play the game based on new theory and relevant examples.* These people are generalists who wish to have a theoretical framework or basis for improving their research or practice performance. This group probably would find it most useful to start with the theoretical chapters.

The second audience includes *advanced students and practitioners who want to learn how to play the new shared-power game according to the new rules.* Typically these persons would be specialists who want to improve their understanding and practice in their own domain by learning from parallel, analogous or related experiences. This group also could learn from the theoretical chapters as they apply them to policy areas. This group could start either with the examples or the theoretical chapters.

Finally, the third audience consists of *students and practitioners of planning and decision making who don't understand the new shared-power world.* These people see the world as complex, often chaotic, and frequently indecipherable, and seek some way of gaining intellectual purchase on the new shared-power dynamics. This audience would find it most useful to start with the examples in the policy area section of the book as a way of understanding what shared-power situations are like, before moving to the theoretical chapters.

Academics and students interested in the book may work in several fields and disciplines, including political science, public administration, public policy, planning, management, sociology, organizational design and development, economics, anthropology and history. Specialists in education, local economic development, industrial policy or full employment policy, and international affairs also would be interested. Finally, practitioners interested in the book would include many different kinds of policy makers, government and agency managers and staff members, and policy and planning professionals.

THE AUTHORS

John M. Bryson, co-editor, is professor of planning and public affairs and director of the Master of Planning Program in the Hubert H. Humphrey Institute of Public Affairs at the University of Minnesota.

Robert C. Einsweiler, co-editor, is professor of planning and public affairs in the Hubert H. Humphrey Institute of Public Affairs at the University of Minnesota.

Ernest R. Alexander is professor of urban planning at the University of Wisconsin—Milwaukee.

Richard S. Bolan is professor of planning and public affairs in the Hubert H. Humphrey Institute of Public Affairs at the University of Minnesota.

Barry Bozeman is professor of public administration at The Maxwell School at Syracuse University.

William M. Evan is professor of management and sociology at the Wharton School at the University of Pennsylvania.

Lawrence S. Finkelstein is professor of political science at Northern Illinois University.

R. Edward Freeman is Elis and Signe Olsson professor of business administration at the Colgate-Darden School of Business at the University of Virginia.

Bernard J. Frieden is Ford Professor of urban development at the Massachusetts Institute of Technology.

John B. Harris is staff accountant in the Tax Department of the Atlanta office of KPMG Pat Marwick.

P. Terrence Hopmann is professor of political science at Brown University.

John Kincaid is executive director of the Advisory Commission on Intergovernmental Relations.

Ted Kolderie is senior research associate at the Center for Policy Studies in Minneapolis, Minnesota.

Jeffrey S. Luke is associate professor of planning, public policy and management at the University of Oregon.

H. Brinton Milward is associate dean and director of the School of Public Administration and Policy at the University of Arizona.

Gordon Richards is assistant vice president in the Taxation and Fiscal Policy Department of the National Association of Manufacturers.

Nancy C. Roberts is associate professor of organizational behavior at the Naval Postgraduate School.

Lynne B. Sagalyn is associate professor of planning and real estate development at the Massachusetts Institute of Technology.

David A. Whetten is professor of organizational behavior in the College of Commerce and Business Administration at the University of Illinois at Urbana-Champaign.

George H. Wood is associate professor of Curriculum and Instruction and director of the Institute for Democratic Education at Ohio University.

CHAPTER 1

Introduction

John M. Bryson and Robert C. Einsweiler

Why Focus on Shared Power Arrangements?

Attention to shared power is prompted by the convergence of five trends and the attendant absence of suitable theory to explain what governments and other organizations should do when confronted by these trends. The trends are: (1) Things appear to be increasingly interconnected. For example, occurrences in the natural environment, national economies, and various programs and levels of government all seem to interact. Consider acid rain, the depletion of the earth's ozone layer, and a possible global warming trend—all either affect or will affect most national and local economies and governments. (2) A number of traditional distinctions are blurring to the point of no longer making any sense. For example, the distinctions between domestic and international; between public and private; among federal, state and local; and among various policy areas are all increasingly hard to maintain. (3) The capacity to govern appears to be declining. We have entered an era of "weak regimes" (Janowitz, 1978). (4) "Shared-power arrangements" are used increasingly to deal with these changing circumstances. And (5), a number of questions are increasingly being asked about the effectiveness and desirability of these shared-power arrangements. In particular, many people wonder if shared-power arrangements are contrary to the public interest.

Said differently, the first three trends are forcing a change in how organizations relate to each other to solve problems, make decisions, or pursue projects. The changed relations and behavior embodied in the fourth trend, in turn, are raising the questions noted in the fifth trend concerning how effective these relations are—and whether they *ought* to occur if the public interest is to be served. Judgments about the virtue of shared-power arrangements typically have been based on traditional views concerning appropriate behavior and what is in the public interest, but some people are beginning to question the virtues of the traditional views themselves.

The plain fact of the matter is that the most important public issues of the day typically arise in settings in which no one is in charge, and in which organizations or institutions must share power in order to address these issues effectively. Unfortunately, current theories seem geared primarily to situations in which a single organization or institution is in charge, or to situations in which individuals (as distinguished from organizations or institutions) must share power and authority (as in legislatures). Front-line organizations, however, cannot wait for guidance derived from new theory; they must act. Unfortunately, shared-power actions seem to violate a dominant ideology in the United States that teaches us as citizens to focus on separation—of powers, authority, responsibility and accountability. And the ideology teaches us to think adversarily of public vs. private, state vs. federal, and individual vs. society. Regardless of ideology, however, more and more sharing relationships develop, because they are the only way to obtain action in an increasingly interconnected and interdependent world. Our ideologies—and also our theories—are apparently out of touch with the present reality, and therefore also out of touch with the cutting edge of practice.

Still, we must proceed cautiously since the notion that separation and adversarial relationships are desirable was born in colonial experience with power concentrated in monarchs, and reinforced by later experience with private-sector monopolies, and with the corruption of public and private sector relationships around the turn of the century that gave rise to "muckrakers" like Lincoln Steffens, and the reform movement in government. Separation was written into the Constitution; important adversarial relationships emerged naturally from this separation. Separation and adversarial relationships have been embodied in legislation to correct abuses of power. And they have become embedded in our evolved Western culture that values individualism, equality, autonomy, self-containment, self-sufficiency, independence, capitalism, and democracy (Huntington, 1981; Luke, Chapter 2).

"Shared-power arrangements" is the term we use to focus attention on the emerging relationships and power dynamics among organizations and institutions. These relationships and dynamics go by different names in different settings; the term shared-power arrangements emphasizes the commonalities among them. For example, Kincaid (Chapter 13), Finkelstein (Chapter 14), and Hopmann and Harris (Chapter 15) all emphasize directly or indirectly the importance of "regimes." Milward (Chapter 3) highlights the importance of "policy networks." Whetten and Bozeman (Chapter 4) and Alexander (Chapter 10) explore "interorganizational relations." And Frieden and Sagalyn (Chapter 9) focus attention on "public-private partnerships." Regimes, policy networks, interorganizational relations, and public-private partnerships are all examples of shared-power arrangements; the use of different names in different settings has obscured the extent to which these arrangements represent similar responses to similar conditions. This is *not* to say that there are no differences among these kinds of arrangements and settings; rather, that the habit of focusing on different policy realms using different vocabulary has masked some remarkable similarities across policy realms and organizational responses to environmental changes.

What Do We Mean By Shared Power?

We define *shared power*, following Giddens (1979: 93), as *shared transformative capacity* exercised in interaction between or among actors to further achievement of their separate and joint aims. The actors can be individuals, groups, organizations, or institutions. These aims would include the desire to achieve gains or avoid losses.

Power sharing occurs in a variety of ways. All sharing involves a common or mutual objective between two or more organizations (whether or not the objective is explicitly stated, or agreed upon, or even clearly understood). However, because shared power situations are "mixed-motive" situations, authority is not merged. Participants reserve the right of "exit" (Hirschman, 1970), so that they can make sure their separate aims can be achieved, at the same time as they try to capture the benefits of sharing.

Sharing of course can involve increasing levels of commitment and loss of autonomy. Examples of sharing, going from least to most commitment and loss of autonomy, would include: (1) sharing a common objective toward which organizations work through informal coordination, (2) sharing resources or activities to achieve a common or mutual objective, (3) sharing power, and (4) sharing authority.

This book is focused principally on the third item—sharing power—and the various forms it can take. The book is also concerned with the sharing of resources when that contributes to sharing power—the joint capacity to do more. And it is concerned with the sharing of power as it results *from* or *in* increases or reductions of authority. But the book is *not* much concerned with the first item—informal coordination—as that level of sharing does not affect individual organizational accountability or responsibility, two main triggers of public unease. Further, it does not really address shared authority (or "formal power," as Finkelstein in Chapter 14 refers to it) when that involves the creation of a new organization, agency or unit that has a shared objective as its focus, "contains" or "surrounds" an important problem area, and becomes an organization "in charge." (An example of such a new organization would be a "joint powers" purchasing unit created by two governmental units; the purchasing unit has both the authority and power to act on behalf of its member governmental units. In contrast, many of the organizations discussed by Milward in Chapter 3, Frieden and Sagalyn in Chapter 9, Alexander in Chapter 10, and Finkelstein in Chapter 14 are *new* organizations, but they rarely "contain" the problem areas that are their focus. They either lack the depth of power to produce concerted action or lack sufficient substantive breadth to contain the problem. Thus they are still very much in shared-power realms, even though the organizations occasionally do have some significant authority.)

Finally, this book is concerned mainly with organizational or institutional actors, and with individuals or groups as they relate to organizations and institutions. It is not concerned with individuals and groups in isolation from organizations or institutions.

Viewed another way, shared-power relationships exist in the mid-range of a continuum. At one end of the continuum we find two or more distinct organizations not relating to each other at all, or else relating to one another in a competitive or adversarial way, as in classic economic or political markets (Lindblom, 1977). At the other end of the continuum we find the organizations merged into a new, integrated or unitary organization that "contains" the problem area, and in which presumably we find cooperation and shared objectives.

In the mid-range, we find elements of both extremes: (1) There is no one in charge, as is the case with competitors or adversaries; but there is also direct communication and reasonably shared objectives, as is the case in the merged situation. (2) While the competitors are locked into a win-lose situation, the merged organization expects to be in a win-win situation. The shared-power organizations, in contrast, hope for a win-win situation, but will settle for a reduced win in exchange for a reduced loss (see Hopmann and Harris, Chapter 15).

Shared-power arrangements thus exist in a kind of *tension field* (Wechsler and Backoff, 1987) created by forces external to the organizations. The focus of the book is on this tension region, this middle ground, where the questions of workability and appropriateness mentioned earlier seem to occur. Within this region, the organizations are in a state of dynamic tension owing to the retention of significant autonomy and the ability to "exit." Since autonomy has been reduced, strict accountability and responsibility for actions can no longer be assured. However, joint action allows for joint gains that otherwise would not be possible, while the shared-power arrangements also guard against losses that otherwise might occur.

Selected Examples of "Shared Power" Arrangements
Some examples can enliven this discussion. They are drawn from intergovernmental (including international), interagency, public-private, and private-sector situations.

Intergovernmental. The State of Minnesota created a shared-power "regime" in the Twin Cities metropolitan region centered on Minneapolis and St. Paul. The regime consists of: (1) the Metropolitan Council, a regional planning and coordinating body; (2) subordinate metropolitan commissions in charge of transit, waste control, airports, parks and open space, and sports facilities; (3) local governments; and (4) a set of laws and expectations governing the relations among these entities. These organizations by law must share power in coordinating private sector development and the public sector support functions that enable the private sector to function (Harrigan and Johnson, 1978; Naftalin and Brandl, 1980). Finkelstein (Chapter 14) and Hopmann and Harris (Chapter 15) provide examples of somewhat analogous shared-power arrangements linking national and international levels.

Interagency. As interconnectedness has risen, the number of different government agencies that have an interest in or must approve a public action has multiplied. Until recently, these multiple actions or decisions typically were taken sequentially (see Pressman and Wildavsky, 1973, for an example). Each agency paid attention only to its own concern, and then passed the case on to the next agency for action. Increasingly, agencies with differing functional concerns and from different governmental levels are joining together to take contemporaneous action on proposals in which each shares a piece of responsibility. An example is the Negotiated Investment Project of the Charles F. Kettering Foundation (1982), in which federal, state, and local agencies in several cities worked out a coordinated investment strategy designed to meet the strategic objectives of each.

Public/private. In land development projects, the public and private sectors often create arrangements that go beyond sharing resources to sharing power and even to sharing equity in projects. Frieden and Sagalyn (Chapter 9) describe such arrangements for downtown retail development. As another example, as part of the social contract between business and government that grew out of the economic stresses in the 1920s and 1930s, the private sector was "allowed" to terminate employees in bad economic times. The national and state governments agreed to fashion "safety nets" to catch the dropped employees (Reich, 1987). Freeman and Evan (Chapter 11) and Richardson (Chapter 12) offer further examples of this kind of public/private sharing.

Joint Private. When it appeared that computer research and development efforts needed to be pooled if the U.S. were to remain competitive in international markets, Congress exempted a joint venture of private firms from antitrust laws. Private firms are increasingly using joint ventures as a strategy to pursue their collective and separate aims (Harrigan, 1986). Sometimes these ventures are new legal entities analogous to joint power undertakings in the public sector. But most often they are contractual arrangements fitting our shared power definition.

Recurring Themes in this Book
What can we learn from these and other shared-power arrangements? When does sharing work and when doesn't it? What makes sharing arrangements work and why? How can we improve planning, management, and decision making in shared-power settings? The purpose of this book is to explore these questions and to provide some tentative answers.

A series of themes and concerns weave through the various chapters and provide a basis for comparisons and contrasts among the chapters. While each chapter does not contain all of the themes, each does contain contain enough to produce considerable convergence.

The themes emerge from the juxtaposition of "reality," or the world of practice, with two sorts of frameworks or theories. In the world of practice shared-power arrangements are increasingly used in response to the trends noted earlier. In the world of theory, however, there is often intense debate over the desirability of such arrangements. On the one hand, long-held belief systems that celebrate separation lead commentators to severely critique these new arrangements. On the other hand, some observers—many represented in this book—

argue that these old belief systems act as barriers to understanding the usefulness of shared-power relationships, and go on to propose new frameworks that they believe provide more appropriate approaches for understanding, evaluating, and even promoting shared-power arrangements.

The main themes of the book are: (1) complexity, uncertainty, turbulence, and risk; (2) the blurring and interpenetration of previously distinct realms; (3) fragmentation, division, separation, and the concomitant need for integration; (4) the individual vs. society, and competition vs. cooperation; and (5) the declining capacity to manage and to govern.

Complexity, Uncertainty, Turbulence and Risk

The authors of several chapters refer to the increased complexity of the world in which public and private decisions must be made. Others refer to the uncertainty that occurs because of this complexity. Still others refer to the turbulence of the times, evoking, as Luke (Chapter 2) suggests, a vision of rapid and unpredictable change that produces murkiness or impenetrability. Risk increases for policy makers, decision makers, and managers as a consequence of this lack of clarity and certainty. The risks increase because these people are expected to make good decisions and take effective actions in situations they do not fully (or sometimes even partly) understand or control.

Three basic responses to these complexities and risks are offered by the chapter authors. A number of authors suggest that shared-power arrangements are entered into as a means of reducing risk or sharing risk (e.g., Frieden and Sagalyn in Chapter 9, Finkelstein in Chapter 14, and Hopmann and Harris in Chapter 15). As in many risk-reducing strategies—such as investing in blue chip stocks rather than high growth stocks—the strategy precludes experiencing the lows by forsaking opportunities for the highs. Obviously such strategies may be extremely valuable approaches to handling substantial risks.

Other authors are less concerned with risk, but still see shared-power arrangements as important mechanisms for the management of complexity. For example, Milward (Chapter 3) focuses on the creation and critique of policy networks. Whetten and Bozeman (Chapter 4), Alexander (Chapter 10), and Kincaid (Chapter 13) discuss the creation and effectiveness of interorganizational or intergovernmental relations. And Richards (Chapter 12) argues that macroeconomic and industrial policies should be kept separate because of the different power dynamics at work and purposes to be served.

Finally, Luke (Chapter 2) argues that our current perceptions of the risks and complexities may be more a consequence of an old way of viewing the world than a product of a changed reality. He argues that because people in the U.S. have been taught to perceive and value separateness, autonomy, and capacity for unilateral action, we see the increased *interconnectedness* in the world as troublesome. That is, we see the interconnectedness as increased complexity, uncertainty, turbulence, and risk, rather than as neutral or positive. He argues that several benefits flow from using interconnectedness as a way of viewing the world. First, we can see clearly what now seems cloudy. Second, we can enhance our understanding of what we see to the point that our sense of complexity, uncertainty and turbulence decreases, as does our sense of the riskiness of the world. And finally, increased clarity and understanding increases our capacity to handle the complexities, uncertainties, turbulence, and risk we actually do face.

The Blurring and Interpenetration of Previously Distinct Realms

Four sets of traditional distinctions have been used in the U.S. to establish distinct realms. The four sets are: (1) domestic vs. international, (2) public vs. private, (3) federal vs. state vs. local, and (4) the traditional distinctions drawn among functional programs within governments (for example, among health, education, welfare, transportation, and housing programs). Each of these distinctions, if ever an accurate description of reality, is increasingly less serviceable.

Domestic/international. In the current global economy and marketplace, "domestic" economic decisions often have international repercussions. For example, decisions to subsidize agricultural products or to rein in inflation with tight money and high interest rates rapidly affect international markets for money, goods, and services, and affect "domestic" policy in other nations. Domestic economic policies, in other words, typically fail to stay within a country's borders. On the other hand, a clearly "international" problem, such as the Southeast Asian emigrations to the United States over the last two decades rapidly becomes a very "domestic" problem when, to continue the example, Asian immigrant extended families burden local school systems, or overcrowd single-family housing designed for the U.S. "nuclear family" norm. (See the Richards, Kincaid, Finkelstein, and Hopman and Harris chapters for additional examples of the breakdown of the traditional domestic/international distinction.)

Public/private. When the federal government "bailed out" the Chrysler Corporation, was Lee Iacocca a crafty private entrepreneur, or a highly paid public employee? When local governments take equity positions in downtown retail and office building projects, or when private firms develop weapons systems and collect taxes, where is the line between public and private? (See the Frieden and Sagalyn, Alexander, Freeman and Evan chapters for further examples of the breakdown of the public/private distinction.)

Federal/state/local. Two hundred years ago, the Constitution set out some clear lines between federal and state responsibilities. Over the years, the line faded as more politicians and interest groups at each level became involved in issues at all levels. The metaphor for the federal/state/local relationship evolved, as the relationship changed, from "layer cake" federalism to "marble cake" to "picket fence" to "fruit cake" and now to "policy networks" (see Milward, Chapter 3). All these typifications were based on intergovernmental activity within the borders of the United States.

Kincaid (Chapter 13) now extends the blurring into the international realm as he describes how the various states are becoming more active in foreign relations. Indeed, many of our states seem to make and pursue their own foreign policy, a function theoretically reserved for the federal government.

Functional program lines. Functional program lines or policy areas have been blurring for several reasons. Complex federal programs, such as food stamps (discussed by Milward, Chapter 3), are by law parceled out to the most compatible agency. The Department of Agriculture thus finds itself operating a human services program for the poor, and financial institutions become agents in a public welfare program. Also, old "tools" are being used for new purposes, and old problems are being defined in new ways. Educational reform is now touted as a kind of industrial policy that will help U.S. firms cope with foreign competition. And local mayors see the problem of the urban poor as lack of employment rather than lack of adequate human services or housing. These trends are developing as state and local officials, pressured by declining revenues from higher levels of government, begin to think and plan strategically about their problems and opportunities, and as they analyze the root causes of the difficulties that surround them (Bryson and Einsweiler, 1988). As they try to figure out what they should do, government officials are seeing conceptual and programmatic connections across previously separate functional lines, and are often purposely blurring or bridging previous distinctions in pursuit of desirable objectives. Shared-power arrangements may be both a cause and an effect of these blurred distinctions. As shared power arrangements proliferate, the old distinctions will be increasingly difficult to maintain.

Fragmentation, Division, Sharing and the Concomitant Need for Integration

Throughout the book there is a persistent focus on fragmentation, division, and separation. Sometimes this fragmentation is designed into the world of practice, as in the separation of powers embodied in the Constitution, or the multiple agencies legislatively required to be involved in the food stamp program. Unfortunately, while the Constitution and legislation may divide government authority to prevent the concentration of power or to promote the sharing of power, they typically do not indicate how the world might be made "whole" again, whether through competition or cooperation. The mirror-image, therefore, of the concern with fragmentation is the concern with creating a reasonably integrated whole that is at least the sum of its parts, if not greater than that sum.

These twin themes that are mirror-images of one another appear in several ways in the chapters, and should prompt readers to ask questions about the causes, consequences, and meaning of separation and union. The authors of some chapters assert that the separation is a myth. It may have been an intent, but it does not exist, and therefore is not really a problem. Others find the fragmentation troublesome, if not downright destructive, in some cases. Perhaps what each of these authors sees—whether as Luke (Chapter 2) puts it, they see interconnections or turbulence and uncertainty—is based on each author's attitude about competitive and cooperative relationships.

The basic principle seems to be that division of any authority or responsibility automatically creates the potential for a shared-power relationship when tasks are involved that bridge the divisions. Whether or not such a relationship actually develops, however, is another matter, as is the question of whether such a relationship will result in public benefits.

The emergence of shared-power relationships and the creation of public benefits seems to depend very much on the context, content, process, and the outcomes desired by the parties to such relationships. Somehow structure, action, and communication must be effectively linked if a worthwhile whole is to emerge, a point made perhaps most effectively by Whetten and Bozeman (Chapter 4), Bolan (Chapter 6), Frieden and Sagalyn (Chapter 9), Alexander (Chapter 10), Finkelstein (Chapter 14), and Hopmann and Harris (Chapter 15). The reader must be alert to the situational aspects of the various authors' arguments to understand both the difficulties and possibilities for linking structure, action, and communication in particular situations. Clearly, not all situations are the same when it comes to the creation and effectiveness of shared-power arrangements.

Individual vs. Society and Competition vs. Cooperation
The book's first section on general concepts emphasizes a dual contrast between individuals and society, on the one hand, and competition and cooperation, on the other hand. Additionally, individuals (or individualism) are typically equated with competition, while society is equated with cooperation.

Many chapters refer to modes of cooperative action which would yield higher rewards than competitive approaches. Roberts (Chapter 5), for example, refers to the Prisoners' Dilemma game in which cooperation on the part of the prisoners yields a better outcome for them than competition does. Unfortunately for the prisoners, however, when they are separated from one another and must act as individuals, the likelihood of cooperation decreases and both prisoners are likely to lose. Thus, in the game individuals and competition tend to get equated, as do collective action (or society generally) and cooperation. Further, shared-power arrangements come to be described, almost unthinkingly, as solely cooperative.

One aspect of the discussions of competition and cooperation is that philosophical beliefs about the appropriate weight to be given to the individual or to society are embedded in the discussions. Those who emphasize individuals tend to favor competition, while those who emphasize society tend to favor cooperation (Friedmann, 1979, 1987; Mitnick, 1980).

Another aspect of the discussions is that authors in the first section of the book have difficulty generalizing about the comparisons and contrasts between the paired themes, individual vs. society and competition vs. cooperation. The difficulty arises because an organization may compete at one point and cooperate at another, as

Roberts (Chapter 5) points out, or may cooperate internally in order to more effectively compete externally (Ouchi, 1984). The authors in the second section of the book devoted to policy area applications suggest the choice is not "either-or," but "both-and" in shared-power arrangements. That is, the organizations do not meet as competitively as in perfect competition or in adversarial court proceedings, nor as cooperatively as in a merger of authority. Rather, they compete and cooperate more as in friendly bargaining toward a shared objective.

Declining Capacity to Manage and to Govern
The introductory section of this chapter argues that several trends have reduced the capacity of single organizations to manage and to govern. We have a world in which no one organization is "in charge," or "contains" any important problem, and yet many organizations are involved, or affected, or have a partial responsibility to act on problems that spill across organizational boundaries. Shared-power arrangements typically are designed to increase governance and management capacity in this world that is *functionally* interconnected but *structurally* separated, divided, and fragmented, and in which structural separations are based on strongly held ideological beliefs. Such shared-power arrangements are not seen as "easy" solutions to "easy" problems. Instead, they usually are difficult-to-implement-and-manage responses to very difficult problems.

The authors in the book's general concepts section elaborate the conditions that prompt shared-power arrangements. The authors in the book's section on policy areas discuss ways shared power is or can be used as a governance and management tool to promote desirable outcomes within particular policy domains.

Chapters on General Concepts
These five chapters focus respectively on: (1) the forces that embed organizations in an increasingly interconnected world (Luke); (2) the changes in inter-institutional relations that result (Milward); (3) barriers to interorganizational and inter-institutional sharing and guidelines to address them (Whetten and Bozeman); (4) thinking about power in shared-power settings (Roberts); and (5) modes of rationality and the preparation of advice for action in shared-power settings (Bolan). The perspectives presented in the five chapters overlap in some cases, but differ in others. For example, Luke, Milward, and Whetton and Bozeman rely on background frames of reference that emphasize the structural aspects of systems. Actions by people occur within these frames. Roberts and Bolan, on the other hand, rely on interpersonal-interactive frames to explore how actions are or can be used to shape structure. Collectively the five chapters provide a valuable map to the conceptual territory of shared-power arrangements. Each of the chapters will be discussed in turn.

Luke (Chapter 2) explores several themes: connectedness, uncertainty and turbulence; the blurring of domain lines; fragmentation and separation; and individualism and autonomy. He sums up their contribution to complexity, and the resulting decline in the capacity to govern and to manage. In other words, the consequence of this complexity is that power is dispersed among or shared by a multiplicity of actors, which creates an inability to act unilaterally at the same time it makes multilateral action hard to achieve. (Luke's presentation thus contrasts with Robert's view in Chapter 5 that actors can choose more freely to act unilaterally or multilaterally.)

Luke goes on to argue that while complexity is a fact, uncertainty may be in part the consequence of the lens employed by the viewer. If the viewer does not perceive a *connected* complexity, he or she is more likely to find uncertainty. Luke further suggests that the worst of the current terms, turbulence (with its negative connotations of unpredictability and impenetrability), may *create* perceptions of uncertainty in the eye of the viewer and may result in unwise strategic action. The way out of this situation, he argues, is to adopt the lens of interconnectedness. This eliminates much of the murkiness and swirling uncertainty by focusing on what the complexity truly is and how one might deal with it. He further argues that increasing our capacity for governance depends on: (1) new metaphors and guiding principles to help redefine a variety of political and administrative concepts such as sovereignty, power, citizenship, federalism, and accountability; (2) establishment of new organizational and institutional arrangements; and (3) development of new public policy frameworks and strategies for action.

Milward (Chapter 3) focuses on institutional arrangements and begins with a discussion of four factors that necessitate shared power: (1) institutional overlap, (2) overlapping authority among levels of government, (3) incomplete responsibility of public organizations for program implementation, and (4) public policy instruments that cause fragmentation (e.g. grants, contracts, and subsidies). The necessity to share authority, and therefore the inability to act unilaterally, was one of the founding concepts of the republic. However, things have grown more fragmented over time, and resulting solutions to public policy problems would have surprised the republic's founders.

For example, it is not clear that the founders had in mind the creation of "policy networks," as Milward describes them. Milward observes (based on a case example from the state housing authority in Ohio) that federal government program money provides the glue that holds together actors—public, private, nonprofit— at various governmental levels in a "policy network." The vertical program spine of the network actually contains more power than the horizontal ties in general governments contain. The result is that general governments may more appropriately be seen as holding companies than as the integrated, hierarchically organized governments of conventional wisdom. The "policy network," in contrast to the single organization, becomes a crucial building block of understanding and action in a shared-power world.

Whetten and Bozeman (Chapter 4) begin with an extensive discussion of the barriers to policy coordination in interorganizational networks (or policy networks of the kind Milward discusses). Next, they review the literature on inter-organizational theory and policy coordination. They conclude with five guidelines for enhancing policy coordination.

Whetten and Bozeman write from the perspective of an individual working in an organization trying to make it function effectively. They make several important points relevant to power sharing. First, in the public sector, unlike the private sector, the self-interest of the employee may not correlate with the interests of the organization. This is true for elected as well as appointed individuals. In a situation lacking the narrow focus of a private corporation—in which corporate and individual interests are presumed to overlap to a considerable degree—it is considerably more difficult to command the allegiance of individuals. And, as Ring and Perry (1985) have observed, the incentives often go the wrong way. This is magnified by an authority split in which civil service is a protection against the necessity to respond to the demands of policy makers or management. The consequence for the public sector, the authors argue, is that effective power sharing requires that somehow a persuasive appeal to self-interest must be created.

Second, Whetten and Bozeman also draw on the work of Van de Ven (1976) and others to argue that the degree of sharing is important. Too little sharing among organizations creates too little stake in the joint effort. Too much sharing threatens autonomy. Finally, the cost of maintaining interorganizational relationships is very high. The benefits to be derived from sharing must be clear and substantial.

Roberts (Chapter 5) explores power and decision making. She endorses Bertrand Russell's (1938: 35) view of power as "the production of intended effects." She then draws a distinction between unilateral control, or a distributive or "zero-sum" power perspective, on the one hand; and multilateral control, or a collective, shared, or "plus-sum" power perspective, on the other. The differing resource bases, means and ends of the two perspectives are compared and contrasted. Then Roberts creates what she calls a synergistic model of power; that is, a model that combines the two differing perspectives. She discusses, for the purposes of future research, how one might consider the most appropriate use of unilateral or multilateral action, of distributive or shared power.

While Roberts' model is conceptually neat, she also notes there are some difficulties with it in practice. For example, it may be hard to distinguish between competitive versus cooperative groups. Members of a group may cooperate to compete with others. Alternatively, members of an organization may cooperate at one point and compete at another. The history of cartels presents such alternating episodes of cooperation and competition.

Another point to keep in mind is that Roberts defines power differently than we do in this introduction. We define power as a kind of capacity; she defines it in terms of outcomes. (Indeed, the reader should be careful to keep in mind the definitions authors are using; authors may use the same term to mean different things, or different terms to mean the same thing. These definitional difficulties are a consequence of the newness of addressing shared-power arrangements as a common element of the focus of many disciplines and policy areas.)

Bolan (Chapter 6) rounds out the series of conceptual papers by focusing on planning. His paper really is more general than it might at first appear, however, since it applies to the understanding and preparation of all advice aimed at actors in shared-power situations. His most important contribution is to argue that we must rethink what is meant by rationality if planning (seen as advice for decision making) is to be more effective.

Bolan draws on a variety of philosophical traditions to argue that what we need is what he calls "adaptive rationality." He says that instrumental rationality—the kind typically employed in policy analysis and planning—ignores the problems posed by values. On the other hand, substantive rationality typically ignores the resource limits that condition the technical feasibility of any proposed action. What we need, therefore, is an adaptive rationality that draws dialectically on both instrumental and substantive rationality. Adaptive rationality is needed to mediate between technical effectiveness and legitimacy, on the one hand, and the objective and intersubjective worlds, on the other. Bolan argues that an adaptive rationality would be a more effective rationality for dealing with a shared-power world.

The conceptual papers provide important frameworks from which to look at the world of practice. In the second section of the book, several policy areas are examined to uncover some of the realities of shared-power arrangements in practice.

Policy Areas
Each chapter in the second section of the book examines power sharing *within* a policy area, so that the general meaning and the limits of power sharing might be assessed *across* policy realms. The descriptions of the chapters in this section therefore draw out the authors' findings that relate to power sharing, not policy areas.

Education
Kolderie (Chapter 7) examines the world of local public education as it is currently organized. Some power is shared among school boards, superintendents, principals, teachers, pupils and parents. However, rather than promoting improvements in education, current institutional arrangements have created near gridlock in many school systems. The gridlock is a consequence of student assignment by attendance area to a particular school, the seniority system, and the fact that the public is taxed for the total school system, not what any particular school or teacher delivers.

Kolderie cites the distinction—drawn from Lindblom's (1965, 1977) work—between authoritarian systems (that is, systems run by central authority)—and systems that pursue change through partisan mutual adjustment (that is, systems in which an action by one element in the system triggers responses by others according to their own special interests). Kolderie argues that public schools typically operate managerially in the first mode—the classic public administration mode of central authority and "machine bureaucracy" (Mintzberg, 1979). The organization of most school systems revolves around a central administrative staff and principals (administrators) in each school. Each school, moreover, is divided into subject matter departments. The relationship between management and teachers fits the adversarial model of industrial labor relations. Thus, the conscious divisions within the school, and between schools and central administrations, are somewhat akin to mandated federal-state separations and resulting shared-power relations. The nature of the gridlock in school systems, however, causes the shared relations to reinforce the status quo rather than innovation and change.

Kolderie explores three major proposals to change this relationship. One, called school-based site management, devolves more central authority to the school, enabling the principal and teachers to become a system themselves, to make their own choices and be responsible for them. A second approach is vouchers, a change in which parents as buyers of school services are given greater freedom to allocate their tax dollars to the schools of their choice. The third example is a change in the relationship between management and labor; that is, a change on the seller's side. The teachers would form a professional practice akin to most other professions and contract with the school administration to deliver a course, the work of a school department, or the services of an entire school building. Some of these proposals have already been implemented in various places around the country.

Kolderie draws implications for educational planning from these changes. These altered relationships, he notes, would result in an educational system that may well produce better-educated students than the existing system does. The larger significance of Kolderie's paper, of course, is that it demonstrates that there are many ways to produce coordinated action in a shared-power world that do not depend on large, centralized, cumbersome, and unresponsive bureaucracies.

Wood (Chapter 8) introduces a more fundamental perspective than the interorganizational or interinstitutional perspective. He views democracy as power sharing among individuals and between individuals and the state, and focuses attention on the failure of the educational system to equip individuals to play a truly effective role in democracy. This failure, according to Wood, results from the conflict between inherent contradictions or inconsistencies in attempts to achieve political equality (an ideal of democracy) within the confines of capitalism and the concomitant economic inequality that leads to cultural, social and political inequality.

Wood believes that schools have been the handmaidens of a "protectionist democracy" that has attempted to limit the participation of citizens in the making of decisions that affect their lives. Citizenship in a protectionist democracy is reduced to voting, and politics is reduced to short campaign commercials on television. In contrast, citizenship in a "participatory democracy" is much more active. Citizens are empowered to play a much larger role in the shaping of their lives and the life of the polity. Contemporary education, Wood believes, basically conditions people to be passive cogs in a large machine, the design and control of which they cannot affect in any fundamental way.

Wood goes on to propose a "pedagogy for democratic participation" that would empower and liberate people. "Critical" literacy, "learning by doing," and teachers leading by example would be emphasized to develop students' "civic courage" that would enable them to act democratically and in the common interest. Pedagogy and democratic action would be conjoined.

The significance of Wood's chapter is three-fold. First, he provides an important "base"—individual citizens—for thinking about shared-power arrangements. Second, he emphasizes the value-laden aspects of shared-power arrangements in light of democratic theory. And third, he points out that people—whether citizens, bureaucrats, or policy makers—must *learn* how to share power. Presumably, Wood would argue, there is much that can be *taught* about power sharing to promote democratic values.

Local Economic Development
Frieden and Sagalyn (Chapter 9) focus on sharing between public and private sectors for purposes of central city retail shopping development. The authors contrast the new public-private approaches with those of urban renewal. The urban renewal approach was a contractual relationship in which public and private actions were sharply separated by function and time to minimize favoritism and collusion. The new approaches are much more joint efforts involving shared resources, decision making, and shared objectives.

The chapter also contrasts these new, quite complex undertakings—and the successes resulting from them—with the political science literature on implementation. That literature typically involves the study of complex federal programs and suggests that simplification—for example, smaller, more self-contained projects—is more likely to lead to successful implementation. Frieden and Sagalyn draw an opposite conclusion, and present a set of factors likely to promote success in large, complex projects involving public-private partnerships.

Alexander (Chapter 10) attempts to assess the relationship between the form power sharing takes and its effectiveness in achieving stated objectives. He first examines the conceptual links among coordination strategies, specific inter-organizational forms (that range from strong central control to informal mutual adjustment), and the micro linkages among organizations. Then he assesses the effectiveness of fourteen cases in regional, urban, and neighborhood development in which thirty-two kinds of coordination occur. His measure of effectiveness is the extent to which stated objectives actually were achieved.

Based on the analysis, Alexander concludes that the more "institutionalized" the interorganizational coordination, the more effective it is. Institutionalization is seen as "a process of crystallization of different types of norms, organizations, and frameworks which regulate the processes of exchange" (Eisenstadt, 1968: 414-5).

Institutionalization, in turn, is seen as a surrogate for commitment to effective interorganizational coordination, where commitment includes expectations regarding outcomes and agreements to cover necessary costs and to make necessary adjustments to promote effectiveness.

A cautionary note on Alexander's continuum of interorganizational coordination forms: At one end are informal linkages, while at the other end is the single coordinating organization linking organizations that remain relatively autonomous. When Alexander discusses the single organization as an interorganizational coordination form, he is *not* describing organizations that "contain" the entire problem area. Instead, the single organizations have substantial power and authority to create and regulate interactions among other organizations involved in a problem area. The single organizations are not completely, or even largely, "in charge." They are still basically in the shared-power realm.

In his concluding section, Alexander suggests how his findings may apply to other fields. Indeed, what is striking about the chapters by Alexander and Frieden and Sagalyn is the extent to which their findings are echoed in Finkelstein's and Hopmann and Harris's chapters in the international affairs section to be discussed shortly. In all four chapters, attention is directed to the construction of effective "regimes" to govern interactions in particular policy content areas. And as a result, all four chapters prompt attention to interorganizational design and the construction of regimes as crucial to the creation and governance of effective shared-power arrangements.

Industrial Policy and Full Employment Policy

The two chapters in this section take very different views of whether industrial and full employment policy are—and ought to be—kept separate. Freeman and Evan (Chapter 11) examine public and private-sector relationships from the standpoint of industrial and employment policy. They suggest an alternative to the current public-private relationship in which public regulation or incentives are used to induce socially preferred private behavior. The alternative they explore is the incorporation of the various stakeholders affected by the activity of the corporation into the board and into the decision frame of the corporation.

The authors restate the typical arguments for public intervention as a prelude to proposing their alternative. Public intervention typically is seen as a consequence of normal corporate behavior; that is, private corporations seek to internalize the benefits of their actions and externalize the costs. Government steps in to protect the common resources, or to protect the public from the unacceptable side affects of corporate operations, such as the production of hazardous waste. The public purpose also is to encourage more optimal consumption and production patterns of certain goods and services.

Freeman and Evan argue that if we reframe corporate decision making to focus on *stake*holders, not just *stock*holders, a much diminished role for government would result. Freeman and Evan believe that the inclusion in corporate decision-making processes of those who are affected by the decisions would produce several beneficial effects: The market would become a more perfect market, and the decisions would be more socially acceptable. Thus, less government involvement would be needed. Freeman and Evan's proposal thus stands in marked contrast to most other proposals to promote employment, since these typically rely on increased government involvement. In addition, because all important interests would be represented, there would be no sustainable distinction to be drawn between industrial policy and full employment policy; corporations would behave with due regard to the interests of all their stakeholders. The authors conclude their chapter with an argument that shared power among stakeholders is preferable to the exercise of coercive power by governments.

Private corporate interests are discussed in many of the chapters, but nowhere do they gain the prominence they do in the Freeman and Evan chapter. The authors point out that large private corporations are in effect governments in their own right responsible for major public functions. They are key actors in a shared-power world (Lindblom, 1977) and are themselves arenas for the sharing of power. Another important contribution of the chapter is the introduction of the term stakeholder. The term is synonymous with the "constituencies" or "publics" more familiar to public affairs audiences, and the terms jointly provide a basis for discussing important aspects of public, private and nonprofit organizations and their governance.

In contrast to Freeman and Evan, Richards (Chapter 12) posits that contemporary advanced industrial democracies do and should conduct economic policy at two levels. First, at the macroeconomic level, monetary, fiscal, and in some instances income policies, are used to manage aggregate demand and to stabilize real growth, inflation and unemployment. Second, at the single-industry level, policy is used to achieve structural adjustment in a sector-specific context. The author employs a series of theories drawn from political science and sociology to frame how power is shared in these settings and then to compare U.S. experience with that of Japan and European countries. He draws some conclusions as the basis for further research and for understanding the essential need to see power sharing in a situation-specific context.

The Richards chapter thus emphasizes the need to pay attention to the institutional particularities that make a difference in policy making and shared-power arrangements. While a focus on shared-power arrangements may highlight commonalities across policy areas, one should not let a concern for comparisons mask important contrasts. Richards sees many systems of power sharing that he believes are not particularly connected—and should not be. In keeping with Alexander's view, Richards believes there are many different models of power sharing, and different models may be useful in different circumstances.

International Affairs

Kincaid (Chapter 13) highlights the growing role of the U.S. states in international affairs. He places his discussion within the context of the tension between autonomy and interdependence—and the paradox that more of one seems to provoke more of the other. The rising autonomy *and* interdependence in the world are creating severe governance problems. In particular, state governments feel they are forced to act independently of the federal government in many international arenas in order to cope with a variety of interdependencies that must be managed effectively if the states are to serve their various stakeholders well. In the process, however, states are intruding into areas presumably reserved for the federal government.

Kincaid argues that increasing ethnic, racial, religious, and linguistic forces, along with the growth of strong national governments, are promoting autonomy. On the other hand, interdependency increases with the growth of global communications, commerce, and transportation, and with the growth of regional entities. These regional entities are both a product and producer of shared-power relations.

The author argues that shared power is an alternative to centralized, decentralized, or divided and fragmented power. He then cites the remarkably extensive involvement of U.S. states in international affairs. In effect, the states share sovereignty with the national government in trade relations, foreign policy development, negotiations with foreign officials, and a variety of other efforts. He sees the study of this role of the states and the federal government—as the states seek greater autonomy within a setting of interdependence—as a major potential area of study of shared power.

The importance of the chapter is four-fold. First, the extensive involvement of the states in international affairs is "news" to most people. This information is really eye opening. It alerts the reader to the fact that in the case of shared power we are dealing with a global phenomenon that has local and not-so-local causes and consequences. Second, the chapter highlights specific forces—autonomy and interdependence—that prompt both differentiation and integration at all levels in an increasingly interconnected world system (Wallerstein, 1974, 1980). Third, the chapter causes us to take seriously the notion that indeed there is an emerging world system; that indeed the world, not just the United States, is interconnected across a multitude of issues areas and levels. We all know this intuitively, but there is something about the Kincaid chapter that drives it home with particular force. Perhaps it is simply the directness with which Kincaid demonstrates how simultaneously irrelevant two long-held distinctions can be: namely, the sharp line between domestic and international, and the notion that international relations are the sole province of the federal government. Finally, Kincaid in effect cautions readers not to assume that the best way to govern a shared-power world is to establish some sort of powerful central government for the world. It might be far preferable to stay in the distinctly shared-power realm.

Finkelstein (Chapter 14) addresses the question of power sharing in international organizations. He begins with a conception of power that is reasonably compatible with our own; namely, he sees power as the ability to achieve preferred outcomes in competition with other relevant actors seeking to do the same. He goes on to make the point—and to demonstrate it with numerous examples involving international organizations—that power is specific to specific situations. In other words, power is inseparable from the issues to which it applies.

Finkelstein also defines a continuum for assessing shared-power relations in international organizations. The continuum bears a resemblence to the one we presented earlier to define the location of shared-power arrangements, and to the one Alexander presents to describe interorganizational coordination. Finkelstein's continuum has at one end what he calls a "decentralized unit veto" system where very little is shared other than discussion. At the other end is "centralized majority decisions" where substantial power is exercised in accord with the majority decisions of member states. In between are contests in which the amount of sharing waxes and wanes depending on the issues and the various interests of the international organization's member states.

Finkelstein notes that there are many examples of international organizations moving in one direction or the other over time; the willingness to collaborate, in other words, is not a constant. Based on Finkelstein's presentation, one might hypothesize that the nature of shared-power arrangements at any level might be expected to change over time in response to the perceived interests of the parties involved and their capacities to make changes.

Hopmann and Harris (Chapter 15) are interested in shared power as it affects strategic arms control. As with the other chapters in the book's second section, however, some concepts in the chapter seem to be applicable across policy areas. For example, the concept of *regime* that is so central to Hopmann and Harris's chapter appears to be echoed in other chapters, though different terms are used to label or describe it. Hopmann and Harris rely on Stephen Krasner's definition of the regimes as "sets of implicit or explicit principles, norms, rules and decision making procedures around which actors' expectations converge in a given area of international relations" (Krasner, 1983: 2). The term thus bears a distinct similarity to, for example, "policy networks," "interorganizational coordination," and "public-private partnerships."

As did Roberts in Chapter 5, Hopmann and Harris also rely on the Prisoner's Dilemma to make some important points about shared power arrangements. They note that power sharing occurs in such contexts either to achieve mutually beneficial outcomes or to avoid mutually undesirable outcomes. Regimes develop to facilitate achievements of the beneficial outcomes and avoidance of negative ones.

The authors emphasize several other points found in previous chapters. First is the paradox that the interdependence of shared power results from the existence of at least partly independent actors. Second, shared power seems to apply to mixed-motive situations, in which the interests of the actors are partially overlapping and partially in conflict. Actors in shared power situations thus find themselves working toward mutually beneficial outcomes (that is, the overlapping areas) and away from mutually undesirable ones (that is, the areas of conflict).

Finally, from their specific focus on U.S.-U.S.S.R. arms control negotiations, they note that possible outcomes in bargaining between two nations are substantially constrained by the capacity of each government in its domestic negotiations to arrive at a satisfactory position to carry into the joint bargaining. They then examine the various stakeholders in the domestic game and how they influence the capacity of the U.S. president to formulate an external strategy. The more general point would be that any shared-power arrangements developed in any system would be both enabled and constrained by the interests of the component parts of the system, whether at higher, lower, or similar levels in the system.

Summary

At present most important public issues arise in situations in which no one is in charge, and in which organizations or institutions must share power in order to address those issues effectively. We use the term "shared-power arrangements" to focus attention on the emerging relationships and power dynamics we see among organizations and institutions in a variety of different policy realms in response to similar environmental changes.

Shared power is defined as shared transformative capacity exercised in inter-actions between or among actors to further achievement of their separate and joint aims. Shared-power arrangements exist in the mid-range of a continuum. At one end are organizations that don't relate to one another at all, or else relate in a competitive or adversarial way. At the other end we find organizations merged into a new, integrated organization that "contains" the problem area, and in which presumably we find cooperation and shared objectives. In the mid-range are found elements of both extremes: (1) no one is in charge, but there also is direct communication and reasonably shared objectives between or among organizations; and (2), while participant organizations hope to be in a win-win situation, they will settle for a reduced gain in exchange for a reduced loss.

A number of themes are found throughout the chapters. Many authors cite increased *complexity, uncertainty, turbulence, and risk* as reasons for the rise of shared-power arrangements. Luke (Chapter 2) goes on to argue that if we were taught to focus on interconnectedness rather than separation and autonomy we would see the world as less problematic and would increase our ability to manage the complex-ities and risk that actually do exist.

Many authors also argue that there has been a dramatic *blurring and interpen-etration of previously distinct realms*. In particular, the lines are increasingly hard to draw between what is: (1) domestic and international; (2) public and private; (3) federal, state, or local; and (4) belongs in one policy realm versus another.

Another common theme is that *fragmentation, division, and separation create a concomitant need for integration* when tasks are involved that bridge the divisions. Whether or not such an integrated relationship actually does develop, however, is another matter—as is the question of whether or not such a relationship will result in public benefits. The emergence of shared-power relationships and the creation of public benefits seem to depend very much on the context, content, process and preferred outcomes of the parties to such relationships.

A fourth set of themes has to do with a set of comparisons and contrasts put forward mainly by the authors in the book's first section devoted to general concepts. On the one hand, *individuals typically are contrasted with society, while competition is contrasted with cooperation.* On the other hand, *individuals (or individualism) typically are equated with competition, while society is equated with cooperation.* Authors in the book's second section devoted to policy areas generally suggest that the contrasts do not always hold up in practice—that in practice one can find all combinations either simultaneously or sequentially depending on the circumstances.

The final set of themes concern the *declining capacity to manage and to govern.* Shared-power arrangements typically are seen as ways of increasing governance and management capacity in a world that is functionally highly interconnected, but that is structurally separated, divided, and fragmented; and in which the structural separations are based on strongly-held ideological beliefs. In all cases, however, shared-power arrangements are not seen as "easy" solutions to "easy" problems. Instead, they are often hard-to-implement-and-manage responses to difficult problems.

The authors of the different chapters explore different aspects of these five themes in different ways. The authors in the book's first section explore general concepts related to shared-power arrangements, while the authors in the book's second section explore shared-power arrangements in specific policy areas. In spite of the authors' differences in background and subject matter, they more often than not reach similar, or at least compatible, conclusions. The editors offer several tentative conclusions of their own about shared-power arrangements in the book's final chapter.

References

Bryson, J. M. and R. C. Einsweiler, eds. 1988. *Strategic Planning: Opportunities and Threats for Planners*. Chicago: Planners Press.

Charles F. Kettering Foundation. 1982. *Negotiated Investment Strategy*. Dayton, Ohio: Charles F. Kettering Foundation. (Brochure.)

Eisenstadt, S. N. 1968. "Social institutions: The concept." In *International Encyclopedia of the Social Sciences* edited by David L. Sells. New York: MacMillan-Free Press.

Friedmann, J. 1979. *The Good Society: A Personal Account of Its Struggle with the World of Social Planning and a Dialectical Inquiry into the Roots of Radical Practice*. Cambridge, Mass.: MIT Press.

_____. 1987. *Planning in the Public Domain: Knowledge to Action. Princeton, N.J.:* Princeton University Press.

Giddens, A. 1979. *Central Problems in Social Theory.* London: MacMillan.

Harrigan, J. J. and W. C. Johnson. 1978. *Governing the Twin Cities Region: The Metropolitan Council in Comparative Perspective.* Minneapolis: University of Minnesota Press.

Harrigan, K. R. 1986. *Managing for Joint Venture Success.* Lexington, Mass.: Lexington Books.

Hirschman, A. O. 1970. *Exit, Voice and Loyalty: Responses to Decline in Firms, Organizations and States.* Cambridge, Mass.: Harvard University Press.

Huntington, S. P. 1981 *American Politics: The Promise of Disharmony.* Cambridge, Mass.: Belknap Press.

Janowitz, M. 1978. *The Last Half-Century: Societal Change and Politics in America.* Chicago: University of Chicago Press.

Krasner, S. D. 1983. *International Regimes.* Ithaca, N.Y.: Cornell University Press.

Lindblom, C. E. 1965. *The Intelligence of Democracy: Decision Making Through Mutual Adjustment.* New York: The Free Press.

_____. 1977. *Politics and Markets: The World's Political-Economic Systems.* New York: Basic Books.

Mintzberg, H. 1979. *The Structuring of Organizations: A Synthesis of the Research.* Englewood Cliffs, N.J.: Prentice-Hall.

Mitnick, B. M. 1980. *The Political Economy of Regulation: Creating, Designing and Removing Regulatory Forms.* New York: Columbia University Press.

Naftalin, A. and J. Brandl. 1980. *The Twin Cities Regional Strategy.* Saint Paul, Minn.: The Metropolitan Council of the Twin Cities Area.

Ouchi, W. G. 1984. *The M-Form Society: How American Teamwork Can Recapture the Competitive Edge.* Reading, Mass.: Addison-Wesley.

Pressman, J. and A. Wildavsky. 1973. *Implementation.* Berkeley and Los Angeles: University of California Press.

Ring, P.S. and J.L. Perry. 1985. "Strategic management in public and private organizations: implications of distinctive contexts and constraints." *Academy of Management Review* 10:276-286.

Reich, R. B. 1987. *Tales of a New America.* New York: Times Books.

Russell, B. 1938. *Power.* London: George Allen and Unwin.

Van de Ven, A. H. 1976. "On the nature, formation and maintenance of relations among organizations." *Academy of Management Review* 4:24-36.

Wallerstein, I. 1974. *The Modern World-System I: Capitalist Agriculture and the Origins of the European World-Economy in the Sixteenth Century.* New York: Academic Press.

_____. 1980. *The Modern World-System II: Mercantilism and the Consolidation of the European World-Economy.* New York: Academic Press.

Wechsler, B. and R. W. Backoff. 1987. "The dynamics of strategy in public organizations." *Journal of the American Planning Association* 53:34-43.

CHAPTER 2

Managing Interconnectedness:
The Challenge of Shared Power

Jeffrey S. Luke

Interdependencies are quickly emerging on a global scale, and indicate that complex interconnections have now crystallized to such a degree that it has become the fundamental feature in the environmental context of public administration and political science. The web of interconnections is decreasing our capacity for self-governance as historically conceived. This declining capacity is manifested in a variety of ways:

1. expanding and crowded policy environments in which everything depends on everything else, and power is dispersed and shared by a multiplicity of policy actors;

2. a significantly reduced capacity for any one government jurisdiction or policy actor to effectively act unilaterally;

3. policy formulation and implementation move forward very slowly, unless on rare occasions, they are somehow stimulated by some major event;

4. an increase in slow-acting remedies to important policy issues such as transportation, housing, and economic development; and

5. an inevitable increase in vulnerability and openness to outside influences in that public managers are increasingly dependent on other individuals that they may never see.

Such an environmental context of interconnectedness demands a reexamination of theoretical and conceptual foundations that are based on the background assumption of separation and separateness. Basic concepts such as power must now be redefined in light of the ubiquity of interconnectedness. New institutions and organizational inventions also need to be designed and experimented with in order to remedy the

structural lag that has resulted from the crystallization of global and local interdependencies and the emergence of shared power relationships. Likewise, managerial capacities require enhancement and new policy frameworks, and policy
strategies need to be developed that can be more successful in an interconnected
environment characterized by shared power.

This paper will explore the existence of interconnectedness at all levels of policy
and administration and will consider several of its implications. The first section
provides a very broad overview of emergent interdependencies. The impact of the
interconnected environmental context on the capacity for selfgovernance will then
be discussed, followed by an initial assessment of its implications and a suggested
agenda for action.

Interconnectedness

Interconnectedness may strike one as obvious, but its obviousness in no way
diminishes its importance. Various scholars have noted the increasing interdependencies occurring, from organizational interdependencies (Emery and Trist
1965; Terreberry 1968), intergovernmental interdependencies (Lovell 1981), intersectoral interdependencies (Luke 1984, 1985), to global interdependencies (Keohane
and Nye 1977; Rosenau 1980; Scott 1982). As an analytic concept, Keohane and
Nye define interdependencies as interactions characterized by reciprocal effects
among policy actors. It is thus a situation of "mutual dependence," where the actions
of one actor both impacts and is constrained by actions of another.

They further distinguish interdependencies (high-cost, very important mutual
dependencies) from interconnectedness (low-cost, relatively unimportant mutual
dependencies). In this chapter, no such distinctions will be made for three reasons:
1) interdependencies are often difficult to empirically measure; 2) the relations that
are interdependent are varied, complex and often overlapping; and 3) interdependencies by their very nature require some level of interconnectedness. The
importance of interconnectedness becomes clearer when its definition includes all
forms of interdependencies and dependencies. Few attempts have yet been made to
operationally define organizational interdependencies. The most illuminating is
Astley and Fombrun (1983). Interconnectedness as a description remains operationally ambiguous; yet the metaphor of interconnectedness accurately reflects the recent
changes in the environmental context[1] and frames social reality in such a way that
it reveals new features and relations in that context.

The Shrinking World

In the last two decades, there has been a dramatic shrinkage in international space.
Technology has lessened geographic and social distances, and is rendering the world
smaller and smaller, making the interaction of international, national and local
systems more pervasive and intense. Technology is knitting together cultures,
societies and governments on a global level never before imagined. Many of the

technological developments that are the core of this transformation are less than a decade old. This change did not occur one step at a time, evolving gradually over a period of successive generations in some linear fashion. Rather, it is similar to the process of crystallization, of instantaneous networks forming to link all parts of the globe (Rosenau 1980).

While advances in transportation technology shrunk geographical distance, advances in communications networks reduced social and political distances (Bell 1979). These advances in global communications were not even envisioned 100 years ago, and yet, have now encircled the planet beyond any possibility of retreat into the past. The communications network is the new, central infrastructure tying together the globe.

Natural Resource Interdependencies

Not only has the interaction of the communication, energy and transportation technologies increased the interconnections between individuals and societies, it has facilitated faster economic development and more complex industrialization that results in faster consumption of natural resources. Every government—local, regional or national—now functions in a situation of scarcity in one resource or another. None is self-sufficient and insulated from the outside world. In this environmental context, national and local self-sufficiency is a modern impossibility.

Not only is there interdependence for the production and consumption of natural resources, there also exists an intricate web of connections among the natural resources themselves. There is growing awareness of the interconnectedness of natural life-support systems on the planet, the best example being the importance of phytoplankton in the ocean to earth's oxygen supply. A more recently hypothesized relationship exists between the protective ozone layer in the atmosphere and changes in the world's climate. The concept "eco-systems" captures the essence of this interdependence between various levels of our biological and environmental systems in the biosphere.

Economic Interdependencies

Since World War II, industrialized countries have experienced a gradual but steady escalation of economic and resource interdependencies. Micro-economic interdependence has long been recognized in the industrial organization and economics literature (Ferguson and Gould 1975). Macroeconomic interdependence also occurs, for example, from international trade impacting economic aggregates such as employment levels, rates of growth, and money supply. The technological breakthroughs which accelerated industrialization and the natural, evolutionary development of complex society created the basis for new levels of economic interdependence much beyond Hirschman's (1945) classic analysis of international trade dependence. Where once existed "nearly closed economies" relatively insulated from each other, there now exists one interdependent economic fabric which forces openness in economies and erodes the political independence of national governments (Bryant 1980).

Supranational unions (like OPEC), multilateral trade agree ments and international monetary policies further expand interdependencies among countries. Multinational enterprises, on the other hand, have special impacts that heighten the sense of interdependence between the multinational corporation and the host country, creating a matrix of interconnections and interdependencies between the global private sector and individual nation-states (Veit 1977; Vernon 1977).

Political Interdependencies
International relations scholars agree that the current global system is undergoing a major transformation characterized by increasing interdependencies (Holsti, Siverson and George 1980), although there is no agreement on exactly how this transformation is occurring. All agree that the web of international trade has created mutual interdependence among nation-states. One emergent perspective, the "dependencia literature," for example, generally analyzes the causal effects of foreign economic relations between rich and poor countries. This group of scholars focuses specifically on the tendency of economic development to concentrate in certain growth centers rather than being spread more evenly throughout the international economy, which creates inequitable dependency relationships between nations (Duvall 1978; Caparaso 1978; Seers 1981).

A second theoretical frame of reference has also recently emerged—transnational politics—and assumes that interdependence among nations is mounting, but the nature of the interactions is now expanding to include nongovernmental actors. There are a greater variety and number of significant international actors interacting on the world stage, as well as the regional and local arenas. The sheer number of nation-states has tripled since World War II, and the number of nongovernmental actors engaging in activities across national borders "is so great as to be beyond precise calculation" (Rosenau 1980, 114).

In recent decades, the transnational literature points out, rapid scientific and technological advances have precipitated a proliferation of non-state actors, profoundly changing relations between and within nation-states. The U.S. Embassy takeover by Iranian students in 1979 provides a poignant example. Differentiation must now be made between two types of actors in international affairs: nongovernmental and governmental.

Interdependence stimulates the formations of new nongovernmental actors in the policy arena. Not only are the sheer numbers increasing, but their influence is also growing (Mansbach and Vasquez 1981). Nongovernmental actors are having consequences within countries and across national borders that would have been unimaginable in previous eras.

The Emerging Global Intergovernmental System

Not only are there increasing global interconnections within the three sectors—resource, economic and political interdependencies—there is a growing interpenetration of one with another in the United States. This is expanding the traditional conceptions of intergovernmental relations horizontally into the private sector and the "third sector" at the national, state and local levels. Increasing interconnections between international and local policies are similarly stretching intergovernmental relations vertically into global-local patterns of interaction, rendering traditional conceptions of federalism obsolete.

Old Federalism, New Federalism

Federalism has transformed and subsequently been reconceptualized several times in the last 40 years. Federalism was historically defined as the division of governmental authority between two separate and permanent levels of government, each having a direct relationship with its citizenry, with the functions of each government clearly divided between the two levels. Citizens are thus shared by both levels of government. At the time of Madison, Hamilton and Jefferson, the concept of federalism was extremely new. One hundred years later, Woodrow Wilson concluded in his seminal essay of 1887 that this interlacing of local self-government with federal self-government was still a very "modern" conception.

Defined in these dual federal terms, this "layer cake" conception remained relatively unchanged until the 1940s when the New Deal stimulated irrevocable changes requiring a new conception of federalism to describe these new developments. This new, cooperative federalism was conceived as a "marble cake" (Grodkins 1966), interconnecting all levels of government in a web-like fashion in complex and inseparable ways (Wright 1983). In this intergovern mental web, more colorfully described by Wildavsky (1980, 80) as "fruit cake" federalism, the administrative and political environment becomes more and more interconnected through the growth of multiple and overlapping linkages among public organizations.

The inevitable consequence of this new federalism has been a considerable amount of direct and indirect dependency relationships, characterized by a constant tension between the federal government's goal of addressing national priorities and the state and local governments' need to establish self-determined objectives and priorities (Buntz and Radin 1983). Local governments have always been dependent on the state government; recent changes, however, have complicated, constrained, and further diluted local autonomy. For example, local governments are dependent on the state and federal levels for the provision of fiscal resources (Lovell 1981), shaping local policy agendas and decisional spaces, establishing specific action frameworks and policy options for pursuing certain local policy objectives (Luke 1981), establishing policy parameters for local policy making in politically sensitive areas, and for providing a certain level of certainty and predictability in specific policy areas (Buntz and Radin 1983).

The federal government is conversely dependent on state and local governments. The health of the national economy, for example, is dependent on the local economies of state and cities (N. Long 1979). Mosher (1980) also notes that the growth of federal programs has not been matched by concomitant increases in federal personnel, forcing the federal government to rely on states and local officials to support and administer the programs it helps fund. The picture painted here is one of mutual dependence and substantially reduced functional autonomy that no longer fits the more conventional wisdom of subsystem politics with relatively antonomous units of government.

Three more recent changes have further increased the inadequacies of even the new federalism conceptions. There now exists an interdependence among policy making, administration, and judicial activity resulting in a noticeable blurring of the historical separation of government functions. In addition, the joining of the polity and the economy expands the sphere of intergovernmental relations horizontally into the private sector at the national, state and local levels, creating issues of "intersectoral" relations. Lastly, the increasing interconnections between international policies and local problems stretch inter-governmental relations vertically into global- local patterns of interaction.

Administration and Politics

In retrospect, one finds that it has been very difficult, if not impossible, to separate administration from politics. There are distinct differences in the nature of the task of politics and administration, creating a "profound disjunction" (Waldo 1982) that keeps us from thinking about the two together as one. Yet, without delving into the normative battleground of the politics/administration dichotomy, one must acknowledge their interdependence[2].

Judicial Involvement

More significantly, the courts have now enlarged their influence in policy formulation and implementation, going beyond their historical jurisdiction in determining the constitutionality of legisislative policies enacted through law. Regardless of one's feeling of the desirability or undesirability of this "extravagant intrusion" (Rabinowitz 1982), increased judicial activity in public administration is indisputable (Shapiro 1978).

The emerging interaction among judicial, policymaking and administrative action is characterized by mutual dependence: the judges dependent on policy experts to help formulate court decisions and to monitor its execution, and also dependent on administrators for assuring effective and complete implementation of the court rulings (Horowitz 1977); and the administrators dependent on the courts for framing remedies that are too complex, sensitive or political for administrative action alone (Hartle 1977). The result is an unprecedented expansion of the intergovernmental system into each branch of government, resulting in unprecedented avenues of shared power.

Intersectoral Relations

Recent governmental action now seriously questions the myth of separation between the public and private sectors, further expanding the intergovernmental sphere into the intersectoral arena. One obvious area of interdependency is the public sector's reliance on the private sector and the voluntary, third sector for the production of certain goods and services (Mosher 1980). Other areas of overlap and convergence occur from the application of public policy instruments to handle market failures (negative externalities and "free riders"), the regulatory sphere (where "private" sector action is guided and constrained by federal, state and local laws, regulations and ordinances), emerging public-private partnerships and joint ventures (Kirlin and Kirlin 1982), and government's more recent involvement in directly managing the economy (Kirlin 1982).

No longer can the public and private sectors make highly independent decisions and operate in isolation of each other. Government action not only precipitates from an intergovernmental context, it increasingly emerges from intersectoral dynamics of public-private interaction. Each sector depends on the vitality of the other.

Internationalization of Local Issues

The increasing interconnections between the polity and the economy expand the scope of intergovernmental relations into the private sector at the national, state, and local levels. Also stretching our traditional conceptions, yet somewhat less visible, are the emerging links between international issues (usually considered as "foreign policy") and local problems (typically considered "domestic affairs"). Sufficient evidence exists describing the various interdependencies in national-state relations, state-local activities, and federal-local policies and expenditures. However, this interconnection between global problems and local policies adds a fourth type of relationship, and requires that our modeling of intergovernmental relations be expanded vertically to capture emerging global-local patterns of interaction. As communications and technological advancements shrink the social, geographic and political distances, more and more problems emerge that transcend national boundaries and impact local economies. It thus becomes impossible to ignore the emerging linkages between international policies and local problems.

These new problems are simultaneously and inseparably both international and domestic; hence they are "intermestic" (Manning 1977). There is a growing awareness of the integral relationship between the problems at the local level and problems at the global level. Few problems are isolated. Local unemployment, for example, is not totally resolvable apart from issues of global inflation and trade patterns. The critical issues at the national level (the faltering economy, for example), state level (e.g. reduced tax revenue), and local level (e.g. lack of jobs for local residents) are not isolated problems; rather, they are interconnected and intertwined.

The roots of international issues are often deeply planted in the domestic political soil. The global economic interdependence is now more than international, it is also interlocal. This is an extremely recent development in the history of international, economic relations. Manning (1977) explains:

> Of course foreign affairs and domestic politics have sometimes been visibly intermingled in our national past: the tariff issue is the obvious case. But until recently, such issues were exceptional, while traditional balance-of-power issues made up most of the foreign-relations agenda. *But the exceptional has now become preponderant.* The issues of the new international agenda strike instantly into the economic and political interests of domestic constituencies (p. 309).

It's difficult to deny that global socioeconomic issues are reaching more deeply into the fabric of everyday life. There is also a convergence of findings that strongly suggests the substance of foreign policy is increasingly responsive to internal, domestic issues rather than just international affairs (Rosenau 1971). An "intersocietal web" has thus formed, where foreign policies influence domestic policies, and where domestic variables shape and determine foreign policy.

Declining Capacity to Govern

The increased interdependence at a multiplicity of levels sets new parameters for administrative performance and self-governance, seriously challenging the viability of traditional political jurisdictions and the historical mechanisms of public management and public action. Emerging networks of interconnections limit governments' capacity to perform in old, conventional ways; they tremendously hamper administrative performance and defy traditional assumptions of what is required to "run government." The experience and past working knowledge that public administrators bring to the governing process are increasingly ineffective and even detrimental in many cases when applied to the new interconnected system of governance (Wildavsky 1979). Several constraints now challenge our managerial capacities, institutional designs, and theoretical assumptions.

Aspects of the Problem

First, the interconnected environment generally *reduces the capacity to act unilaterally*. No one person or agency controls the essential elements of a policy-making arena that is now both intergovernmental and intersectoral. The existence, intentions and jurisdictions of other actors substantially reduce functional autonomy and often create a strong sense of powerlessness. Any systematic solution to a public problem now requires public managers to enter the intergovernmental and intersectoral network. Policy formulation and implementation requires multilateral cooperation and the exercise of shared power across traditional boundaries and jurisdictions. There is a significant amount of evidence, much of it precipitating from doctoral dissertations by younger public administration professionals, that concludes that the successful implementation of government policies necessitates the involvement of a large number of relevant actors, both governmental and nongovernmental. Mandel (1981) studying the implementation of the Century Freeway Project in Los Angeles, Reed (1982) identifying the barriers to low-income housing development in Chicago, and Luke (1983) investigating the barriers in stimulating job creation in Southern California provide excellent examples of the difficulties unilateral policy action confronts.

Secondly, public organizations *share their environment* with a multitude of other service providers and beneficiaries. This leads to expanding and crowded policy environments that are not unified, but in which everything depends increasingly on every thing else and where the impact of unanticipated consequences becomes severely problematic. Public managers find it necessary to involve in decisions those individuals who share in the inter-organizational policy-making network (Agranoff and Lindsey 1983). This suggests an increased efficacy in "collective strategies" (Astley and Fombrun 1983) that utilizes a set of public organizations that collaborate in order to pursue specific policy out comes. An individual public manager can now influence policy only slightly, not wholly, and without certainty of outcome. In a shared and crowded environment the impact of any one government on a policy arena declines sharply. The level of interconnectedness in this shared and crowded environment is now a contingency variable that must be assessed by public officials seeking specific policy goals.

Problem solving in a shared and crowded policy environment will necessarily *move forward more slowly,* a third constraint resulting from increasing interconnectedness. Agranoff and Lindsey (1983) have observed that effective multi-jurisdictional problem solving requires

> a large time investment...for development and mutual understanding; that the real political and administrative decision makers must be involved, but the details must be left to the operatives; that the focus must be on the specifics of the issues at hand; that the constant testing and negotiating of solutions are essential; and that eventually the decision makers must reach an agreement, put it on paper, and carry it out through the relevant jurisdiction (p. 236).

Likewise, there will be an *increase in slow-acting remedies* that are merely satisfactory. Each actor will likely have to accept less than an ideal solution, a "satisficing" solution born slowly of an interconnected policy environment.

In addition, interconnectedness inevitably *increases the openness and vulnerability to outside influences* that are out of one's control and difficult to buffer. The impact of corporate disinvestment by multinational enterprises on the economic deterioration of a local economy provides a recent example. This increased openness is a direct outcome of the expanding networks of more complicated cause/effect relationships which causes rapid dispersion of unintended consequences and more devastating non-local effects (Thompson 1973).

As a result of the decreased capacity to control their crowded, shared environment, public administrators feel a strong sense of vulnerability. Many public managers view these new environmental constraints as a source of substantial grief.[3] Any major crisis or problem, however, generates possibilities for new, yet undiscovered opportunities. The increasing interconnectedness is no different; one must view this emergent environmental context as providing a new set of opportunities for public action, with an equally new set of available resources.

Interdependence and interconnectedness provide new resources and new patterns for initiating action in arenas previously thought separate and insulated. This increases the number of potential access points and creates new alternative courses of action available to shape a particular policy outcome. Unfortunately, our lack of sophistication in operating within interconnected environments, our inability to view the interconnected environment as a door opening up new avenues for action, and our delay in utilizing these new opportunities further reduce our capacity for self-governance.

Four Sources of the Declining Capacity

Some argue that the declining capacity to govern is the result of the "human gaps" that occur when public managers and members of governing bodies don't learn as quickly as the environmental contexts and interdependent relationships demand. This causes a gap between the increasing interconnections and a lagging development of managerial capacities. Public officials, a former City Councilman observed,

> have little understanding of the complexity of issue and people interrelations that affect municipal performance...the nature of the context in which they are operating has changed, negating many of the conceptions they have about what it "takes to run a city" (Neu and Sumek 1983).

In an interconnected context, public administrators must be skilled in boundary management, looking outward more, and inward less. Mosher (1980) concludes:

> Most important of all is that our top public executives bring to their work an understanding of the relations and the interdependence of the public sector and the private, and of one level of government with others, both above and below (p. 547).

Others argue that the diminishing capacities to govern result primarily from a *structural lag,* where new institutions are not created at pace with the rapid evolution of global and local interdependencies. At the global level, interdependencies are said to have surpassed the capabilities of the existing international system (Mische and

Mische 1977), and the international institutions and practices are not able to cope effectively (Cleveland 1985). Focusing on the interconnections between foreign policies and local issues, Manning argues strongly that the lack of any institution that links international and local issues is a serious weakness in the U.S. government structure "that is of the most fundamental character" (1977, 323). Similarly, Stephen K. Bailey (1982) contends that "the question of America's continuing capacity to govern" is due to a fundamental crisis of legitimacy of government institutions at all levels. He suggests the creation of new social and organizational inventions that allow "government" to occur as a cooperative effort between public and private institutions. This linking of the two sectors in hybrid fashion "may well be the wave of a fairly long future."

The *lack of appropriate policy frameworks* based on the existence of inter-dependencies may further lessen our capacities for self-governance. Thurow (1980), for example, suggests that the world economy has changed dramatically, but that the American economic policy has not. Bryant (1980) agrees that conventional policy frameworks are inaccurate in an interdependent world economy, and that the basic assumptions governing monetary policy, for example, are now misleading if not flatly wrong. Responding to the new actors, issues and connections emerging from growing interdependence, new government policy-making instruments must be created and new frameworks established that can more effectively guide public action in an interconnected environment.

It may be that we are trying to manage a complex, interconnected society on the basis of a set of *old assumptions, metaphors, and concepts that are theoretically outdated*. Flawed premises inevitably lead to flawed policy. Conventional wisdom may not provide satisfactory solutions to present-day problems. Political and admin-istrative theories have not accommodated quick enough to the shrinking world and the emergence of an inter-societal web, and have failed to integrate the tremendous impact of communications and technological advances since World War II. To merely acknowledge the interdependence of global, national and local systems is not necessarily to make adequate conceptual allowance for it.

Managing Interconnectedness: Agenda for Action
In order to strengthen our capacity for self-governance and to reverse the declining levels of administrative performance due to the crystallization of interconnections, four general areas must be addressed:

1. the articulation of new metaphors and guiding principles in an interdependent, interconnected world;

2. the redefinition of a variety of basic political and administrative concepts;

3. the establishment of new institutional arrangements and organizational inventions that reduce the structural lag; and

4. the refinement of the art of public management and the development
of new public policy frameworks and strategies for action.

The Metaphor of Interconnectedness

Increasing levels of interdependence at a multiplicity of levels—between the public
and private sectors, between one branch of government and another, and between
global issues and local policies—are directly affecting governmental capacity to
perform. What is more problematic, however, is the incongruence between present
interdependencies and the existing theoretical frameworks and their underlying
metaphors and assumptions. Major changes are now required in our most fundamental premises. Any theory of public administration must implicitly assume the
existence of interconnectedness in the environmental context. This basic assumption
and fundamental premise is best encapsulated in the metaphor of interconnectedness.
Unfortunately, our preoccupation with complexity, uncertainty, and turbulence has
monopolized our attention.

From Turbulence to Interconnectedness

Many argue that continuous accelerating *change* is the crucial feature of the
administrative process. This characteristic of most environments scarcely needs
laboring (Emery and Trist 1965). The environment is changing at an increasing rate
towards complexity, with a concomitant increase in relevant uncertainty and un-
predictibility. Everything seems in motion. Constant change and its extreme form,
turbulence, have become the rallying concept for much of the recent education and
training of public managers. Administrators, both public and private, are warned of
the perils of managing in a context of turbulence (Waldo 1971; Drucker 1980).

Others see *uncertainty* and *complexity* as the dominant forces, forcing managers
to learn to cope with ambiguity. The existence of uncertainty in the environment is
suggested by many as the major contextual factor for public administrators. H.G.
Frederickson emphasizes, "Uncertainty is the fundamental problem for complex
organizations and coping with uncertainty is the essence of the administrative
process" (1982, 505). Interesting empirical research is now focusing on effective
public management strategies in a "climate of uncertainty" (e.g. McGowan and
Steven 1983).

A century ago, public administration scholars bemoaned the increasing complexities in governing a democratic society. Woodrow Wilson complained, "There
is scarcely a single duty of government which was once simple which is not now
complex; government once had but a few masters; it now has scores of masters"
(1887). More recently, Beam (1980) suggests that the term "complexity" is the best
description of present intergovernmental reality. Mosher, more troubled by this

reality, argues that this complexity has now grown "beyond the bounds of the most brilliant human minds" (1980, 546).

However, this preoccupation with change, uncertainty and complexity has overshadowed more fundamental underlying patterns that have been emerging. The metaphor of turbulence, an environment full of uncertain, muddy, swirling forces may have clouded our thinking, obscuring more than it clarifies. Within this com-plexity exist overlapping networks of subtle and direct interdependencies and interconnections which can now be recognized, explored analytically, and integrated into governmental policy frameworks. Interconnectedness, not change, turbulence, nor com-plexity, has emerged as the essential feature in the environmental context of public administration, and has replaced uncertainty as the fundamental problem for complex organizations. Managing interconnectedness has emerged as the greatest challenge to public administration in its second century as a discipline. Complexity and uncertainty are major issues; nonetheless, continued focus on them to the exclusion of interconnectedness keeps our attention prematurely fastened to managing the symptoms not the causes. Although turbulence is caused by the complexity and interdependencies of interconnectedness, it is not an inevitable result. Interconnected environments can actually become increasingly stable (White, et al. 1984).

The Importance of Metaphor

In order to develop some sense of direction amidst this complex backdrop of turbulence and complexity, a point of reference or central focus must be provided. This frame of reference is best provided through a generative metaphor (Schon 1979). Although the language of metaphors lacks the precision of scientific language, metaphors play a fundamental role in the development of scientific understanding (Morgan 1980). Metaphors provide a perspective or "frame" that shapes meaning by transforming what is overwhelmingly complex into a more simplified description of the situation, and provide efficient means of transmitting large chunks of information in abbreviated form.

In addition to this framing function, metaphors select certain salient features for attention from what may be a rather complex reality, bringing into focus known features for special attention (Khatchadourian 1968), as well as bringing new features of situations into prominence. Often this results in a reorganization of the foreground and background elements, where the spaces that once had been background, now become foreground. By simply turning our attention to different facts, a metaphor acts as a cognitive instrument which leads us to novel views of a particular domain, giving us new vision or insight (Black 1977).

By *framing* and *focusing attention,* metaphors guide individual and collective action. Perrow argues that such shaping of under lying decision premises is the most powerful, yet largely unrecognized, type of control strategy utilized by managers. These premises are unstated and unexamined assumptions that "direct attention to some stimuli out of the welter that assail us, and evokes particular sets of responses to those stimuli" (Perrow 1977, 41). By socializing organizational members into seeing situations through specific metaphorical lenses or underlying premises, individual decision making is directly guided. This "management of meaning" generates a point of reference that frames and shapes the perceived context of action, and is the primary function of leadership (Smircich and Morgan 1982).

Although we are usually unaware of the metaphors that shape our understanding, Norton Long (1979) argues that this is the most profound type of politics: changing the pictures that are in our heads and providing the definitions of the situation. He stresses that the most important strategy of reorganization is the reorganization of the definitions of the situation (p. 195).

Metaphors create structures of meaning. March and Olson (1983) point out that the essence of successful administrative reorganizations efforts is the gradual evolution of new metaphors that guide administrative and political behavior. Changing the construction of meaning, they argue, is as fundamental to reorgan-ization as the changing patterns of decision making authority and the reallocation of resources.

With this understanding of the crucial functions of metaphors, it seems that the metaphor of interconnectedness could guide our efforts to enhance our administrative and governance capacities. It provides a point of reference, a central focus, that offers a sense of direction in dealing with the decreasing capacities for self-governance.

From Separation to Interconnectedness

American public administration unfortunately has been plagued by the notion of "separation" since its beginning. Separation has been a major conceptual focus, from the Federalists who argued for separation of powers among the branches of government and a separation of authority between the national and state governments, to Frank Goodnow (1900), who stressed the fundamental separation of politics from administration. The assumption of separation as expressed in our political theories is rooted deeply in English law and in the political philosophy of Locke and Montesquieu. It is also interesting to note that one of the distinguishing features of the "enlightenment" philosophers is their conception of man as separate from, rather than a part of, nature (McCormick 1979).

This sense of separateness and independence has become embedded in our individual value system (e.g. "frontier individualism") and has been the underlying governing principle from which most public institutions have been constructed and justified. It could be said that this value framework—the self-contained, the distinct, the separate—has become our Western legacy. This conception of separation has dominated our policy frameworks and methodologies which guide problem-solving, and has become a part of our institutionalized thought structure. Goals of independence and self-sufficiency, and the assumption of separation of existence, have guided both practical politics and administration as well as their underlying theoretical frameworks.

Governmental jurisdictions certainly have their own separate identities. Each has its own unique internal governance structure, processes and procedures that emerge from its legal, constitutional, and jurisdictional bounds. The pressing social and economic problems that are pursued by these legally, separate agencies, however, are more ambiguous, are less contained, and defy boundaries. Like an ensnarled web of tentacles or the head of a hydra (Rittle 1972), public policy issues are undeniably interconnected (Mason and Mitroff 1982). Although government agencies have legally separate jurisdictions, *they are not independent.* The notion of separation is no longer an appropriate guiding metaphor. Government jurisdictions at the national, state, and local levels are no longer autonomous, self-reliant entities, separate from each other, separate from the private sector, or separate from international issues.

Separation is a concept we have created for analytical purpose, but which now reinforces false distinctions. Data from the macro-societal level down to the most micro-level analyses of subatomic physics[4] and the human unconscious[5] now force us to replace the myth of separation and the metaphor of turbulence with the metaphor of interconnectedness.

Redefining Some Basic Concepts

If the existence of complex interconnections is as significant as it would appear, the foundational concepts underpinning administrative and political theory need to be reexamined for their accuracy and appropriateness in the new environmental context. A central concept upon which most others constellate is "power." Power may be the fundamental concept in social science; it is central in that its particular conception provides the fundamental building block for political conceptions of sovereignty and federalism, and administrative conceptions of accountability.

Shared Power

Power has been generally defined as the ability to exert influence over the actions of others. This conception has been consistent whether one utilizes a psychological framework (e.g. McClelland 1975), administrative science framework (e.g. Mowday 1978; Mechanic 1962), or sociological perspective (e.g. Perrow 1977). Etzioni stresses the point that power differs only "according to the means employed to *make the subjects comply*" (1961; 259, emphasis added). Power as traditionally defined is thus a process of imposing one's will unilaterally on others, a process of command, compliance, and domination. In administrative theory, power is commonly identified with dependence created by environmental uncertainty and resource control (e.g. Salancik and Pfeffer 1974). The common theme in these conceptions of power is one of depowering others, either coercively or non-coercively.

It is undeniable that power as traditionally defined is a function of dependence, and that power often resides in controlling dependency. Dependence commonly refers to a position of being determined or significantly influenced by external forces.

However, when the environmental context is interconnected, policy arenas crowded and shared, the web of dependencies is so widely dispersed that conventional power strategies are seldom, if ever, efficacious. The exertion of unilateral power and the use of depowering strategies in an interconnected environmental context will likely create symmetrical resistance (Lewin 1947) and little policy action.

Interconnected policy arenas are more accurately characterized by shared power and require *empowering* strategies that stimulate group movement towards a desired policy outcome. Policy formulation and implementation is multilateral and collective. Managers intending to influence a particular policy outcome must therefore recognize the existence of shared power, avoid attempts at depowering other policy actors, while developing empowering strategies. This assumes a broader conception of power, one where *power is defined as the production of intended effects,* not only unilaterally but also collectively. Power thus becomes catalytic, not commanding, facilitative rather than dominating.

Leadership

What is thus required is a new type of leadership. A leader in a context of shared power is one who can stimulate collective action towards a particular goal or vision. The historical "charismatic leader," with his or her own individual vision, may not be powerful enough to move the web of government and non-government actors in a particular policy arena. What is required in an interconnected environment is a "catalytic leader" who can facilitate the development of a collective vision. Unlike a charismatic leader who gets individuals to follow his/her vision, a catalytic leader is one who is able to stimulate the development of a critical mass of diverse policy actors, motivated by a goal or vision which they collectively create themselves.

Accountability

Conceptions of accountability typically relate back to the exercise of power by a public official. McKinney and Howard (1979) define accountability in its simplest form as

> any situation in which individuals who exercise power are expected to be constrained and in fact are reasonably constrained by external means (e.g., reversal of decisions, dismissal, and judicial review) and to a degree by internal norms (e.g., codes of ethics and professional training).

Accountability is thus interdependent with the exercise of power; traditional conceptions like McKinney and Howard's relate accountability to the constraint of power abuse by restraining individual action. Interconnected environments, however, create further external constraints on actions of public officials. More importantly, however, such environments of shared power make individual accountability for policy formulation and implementation terribly confused and virtually impossible. Accountability shifts from the individual to the group, and in its transfer, becomes so blurred that no one individual can be held accountable for creating policy.

This becomes extremely problematic in government. Traditional legislation typically makes a single agency or policy actor accountable to the legislative body. However, *everyone in a policy network is accountable, and at the same time, no one is accountable.* Therefore, the existence of shared power in an interconnected environmental context requires an expansion of the concept of accountability, from one that constrains individual action, either through external means or internal norms, to one that includes responsibility for creating action in a group or network that inhabits a particular policy arena.

The shift is one from accountable for discretionary action to accounting for results and accomplishments, or more accurately, to accounting for one's contributions to particular policy outcomes. Since no one single actor can unilaterally create specific policy outcomes in an interconnected environment, it is necessary to account for one's contributions in the multilateral or collective effort. If power is shared, accountability must also be shared. This will be difficult to operationalize in government if legislation and judicial policy making continue to identify single, accountable actors individually responsible for specific policy outcomes. New forms of accounting for one's contributions are needed, requiring perhaps the social or collective memory suggested by Ouchi (1984). A social memory is the ability to remember who contributed and who didn't. It is

> the ability to remember what group has been flexible in the past and what group has been unreasonably selfish...the social memory must also be enforced by a network of business, civic and governmental associations that have the ability to grant or withhold cooperation to those interest groups that have shown themselves deserving of assistance or punishment (p. 9).

New Organizational and Institutional Arrangements

Explorations in new arrangements required in interconnected environments have already started. A decade ago, J. Thompson noticed three factors affecting organizations of the future:

1. local problems were no longer remaining local due to the expansion of cause/effect networks;

2. the pace of change was accelerating, causing rapid dispersion and diffusion of problems and solutions; and

3. technology was becoming more knowledge-intensive rather than labor-intensive or capital-intensive.

As a result of these emerging patterns, he argued for new organizational and institutional configurations that would be more fluid, less permanent, less formal, and less local (1973, 333). He suggested that effective organizations in such an environment would need to be synthetic, temporarily organized structures. Given that the overburdened, overloaded policy systems lead to declining administrative performance, Thompson's suggestion may provide a remedy.

A second direction in exploring new institutional arrangements would include the creation of more permanent jurisdictions, but smaller and more stable in the constant web of pulling and tugging that occurs in an interconnected environment. Here, the public choice literature provides numerous examples of effective, smaller yet overlapping governmental jurisdictions. A third alternative is the delegation of service provision through contracts and agreements. Administrative linkages through contracts and formal agreements are less permanent and more flexible than the more traditional linkage mechanisms of a bureaucratic organization. There has been a considerable amount of public service contracting with recent evidence showing that more and more public sector activities can be completed through contractual arrangements without forfeiting control.

More problematic than enhancing semi-autonomous administrative capacities in interconnected environments is the development of structures for collective action—the creation of institutional arrangements that can mobilize action and resources toward the achievement of policy outcomes shared by organizations inhabiting a particular policy arena. Informal discussions and understandings provide one approach. More formal arrangements include interlocking "directorates" consisting of officials from local, regional, and state agencies sitting on a multiplicity of policy-making boards. Another strategy is direct joint ventures with other organizations, such as establishing equity partnerships with private sector enterprises to pursue economic development objectives (Kirlin and Kirlin 1982).

Institutional experiments such as these are increasingly necessary when organizations are forced to collectively, and unable to independently, impact their particular policy domain. Each strategy contains disadvantages as well as advantages which cannot be adequately covered here. New, yet unimagined, institutional forms are also likely to be conceived. The underlying theme, however, may need reiterating: that the recent crystallization of global and local interconnections now necessitates the invention of new organizational and institutional configurations—inventions fundamentally based on shared power in crowded policy arenas.

New Management Skills and Policy Frameworks

Public organizations share their environments with increasing numbers of governmental and non-governmental actors, requiring new public policy strategies and managerial skills. Managers and policy makers are having difficulties achieving the outcomes they want, and are having trouble avoiding the outcomes they do not intend.

Policy Strategies

In an environmental context of interconnectedness, public policies often have dispersed, non-local, unintended consequences. In such an environment, urban and social problems easily piggyback on one another; each problem becomes linked to every other problem, interweaving and causing unpredicted new problems. Each new public policy typically interacts with other policies, exponentially increasing the probability of unanticipated outcomes. Unintended consequences in crowded, shared environments tend to take on a life all their own, with the results not always positive.

This implies that large-scale policies can easily create more problems than they solve, generating ripple effects that unpredictably extend far into the future (temporal dimension), cross jurisdictional boundaries (spatial dimension), and interfere with other government functions and policies (functional dimension). Wildavsky notes that as large public programs are developed and implemented,

> they begin to exert strong effects on each other, increasing reciprocal relations and mutual causation; policy A affects B, B has this effect on C, and C back on A and B. An immediate effect of new large programs amid this increased interdependence is that their consequences are more numerous, varied, and indirect, and thereby more difficult to predict (1979, 64).

In fear of stimulating uncontrollable or unpalatable ripple effects, and to avoid creating actual outcomes that deviate from the intended, policy actors may narrow their sphere of action, leading inevitably to segmented and limited policy action, policy inertia, or worse yet, to policy paralysis. *A more appropriate policy strategy would be to generate a multiplicity of smaller, less grand, programs and policy initiatives,* based on some longer term goal or vision which is agreed upon collectively by the government and non-government actors who inhabit the particular policy domain.

Policy strategies must be collective, as well as smaller, in scope, since most policy issues now require intergovernmental and intersectoral participation. Such a collective strategy entails mobilizing interorganizational resources and formulating action within collectivities of governmental and non-governmental agencies. It requires a collaborative response by policy actors to pursue specific policies, based on a shared interest in certain policy outcomes (Astley and Fombrun 1983; Wamsley and Zald 1983). This, of course, requires greater skills on the part of the public manager.

Management Skills

Such an environmental context suggests a need for public managers to develop and refine skills in areas such as collaboration, networking, bargaining, and negotiation. These skills are not necessarily new, but are fundamental for developing collective strategies to cope with the interorganizational policy system. Joint ownership of solutions by policy actors, a "joint task orientation" (Agranoff and Lindsey 1983), appears critical in order to

1. mobilize the interest of various actors in policy formulation, and

2. ensure their active involvement in policy implementation.

As interdependencies in the environment increase, *there is an increase in requisite levels of coordination* (Thompson 1967) and *increased potential for conflict* (Trist 1980). Incentives for cooperation may emerge due to the shared stake in solving a particular problem (Agranoff and Lindsey 1983); however, the public manager must have the skills to further stimulate, nurture, and maintain adequate levels of cooperation outside his or her organizational boundaries.

Conclusion

The human community is moving more deeply into an interconnected, global society. What is emerging is an intergovernmental and intersectoral network existing within specific resource boundaries. The changing context is converging around the problems of ecological, political, and economic interdependencies, changing the historical nature of public policy and administration in fundamental ways at the local, federal and global levels. There is no resemblance to the environmental context which existed during the 200 years of American history. Nothing so interdependent existed during the Federalist era, nor the Wilson era prior to and immediately following World War I.

Much of our rhetoric has adapted. Political leaders, administrators, and academics have learned to talk about this new state of interdependence that now exists. Many are calling for cooperative strategies which once would have been considered a visionary ideal. Practitioners and scholars have noted that interdependence is a key feature in the changing character of the public service and the public manager in the 1980s. Public administrators increasingly recognize that they have new responsibilities which require an expanded role that includes substantial intergovernmental, intersectoral and international dimensions.

Yet it is difficult to assimilate the extraordinary implications of these new conditions. Our basic conceptions and theoretical foundations do not adequately reflect these very recent insights. The assumptions, metaphors and basic concepts that underlie political and administrative theory have not changed in response to the unfolding interdependence. Fundamental assumptions still imply the notion of separation, that one government jurisdiction is separate from every other jurisdiction, and that governmental action is separate from non-governmental action. This background assumption must now be replaced by one that can more accurately fit with the patterns of interconnections that now exist. This requires new metaphors that "guide" our investigations, new language and concepts for "mapping" the world, and a reconceptualization of the existing economic, political and administrative systems.

Today's public manager seeking to influence specific policy arenas must learn how to stimulate and manage the cooperative efforts in the intersectoral and intergovernmental environment. Autocratic, depowering leadership strategies *must now be replaced by catalytic leadership* that empowers governmental and nongovernmental policy actors and stimulates collective policy action.

The fundamental assumption for a general theory of public action is interconnectedness. As a metaphor, it may be the necessary building block from which more accurate theoretical frames of reference, concepts and policy frameworks emerge. It will force a shift of focus from managing turbulence to managing interconnectedness. The metaphor of interconnectedness provides additional clarity and conceptual leverage for analysis of such central problems as shared power and dense policy arenas. It may also provide a solid foothold for understanding the depth and scope of the transformations and complexities that Mosher (1980) suggests have now grown beyond the bounds of the most brilliant of human minds. With the metaphor of interconnectedness, we come to see things in a new way.

Footnotes

1. The term "environment" is often too ambiguous; the term "environmental context" will be utilized here instead. This conception does not describe the physically objective world in its totality, but only includes those aspects of the totality that have relevance to the field, in this instance, of public administration. It is the "life-space" of the field, borrowing from and expanding Lewin's term as he used it to describe the "life-space" of an organism.

2. For a very complete review of the history of this theoretical separation and its evolving convergencies, see Wamsley and Zald, 1985, "The Environments of Public Managers: Managing Turbulence." In Handbook of Organization Management, ed. Eddy. New York: Dekker, pp. 501-530.

3. However, some public administrators regard these new environmental constraints with relief in that they absolve responsibility for framing issues and setting specific parameters for local policy formation and implementation.

4. New evidence precipitating from physics clearly indicates the underlying web of interconnectedness at the sub-atomic levels of human existence. Contemporary physics, in general, and quantum mechanics in particular, demonstrate that all of the things in our universe are actually part of one all-encompassing organic web, and that no parts are ever really separate from this interconnected pattern or from each other. They only appear to exist independently. According to quantum mechanics, there are no "separate" parts in the universe. Parts are seen to be in immediate connection, in which their dynamic relationships depend, in an irreducible way, on the state of the whole system (and, indeed, on that of broader systems in which they are contained, extending ultimately and in principle to the entire universe). Thus, one is led to a new notion of unbroken wholeness which denies the classical idea of analyzability of the world into separately and independently existent parts. See

Zukav, An Over-view of the New Physics, New York: William Morrow, 1979, p. 315.

5. Equally profound interconnections may exist at the individual, psychological level. Huxley (Perennial Philosophy, 1960) notes that a transcendent element in the human experience is found in a large number of endurable world religious traditions, which characterized humans' essential nature as spirit, filling each individual like an underground stream filling every water well. Jung's analytical psychology implies a similar interconnectedness when he argues that there exists a "collective unconscious" that is both transpersonal and transhistorical. His findings indicate that every human being has a collective unconscious, a pool of genetically inherited symbols that function differently than the "personal unconscious" with which Freud was so concerned. Jung suggests that this common pool of unconscious information directly connects each individual in a subliminal, web-like fashion he called "unus mundus." See for example: Memories, Dreams, Reflections, New York: Random House, 1961. Willis Harman, futurist and economist at SRI in Menlo Park, California, builds on this notion and argues that humans are not merely connected with the external world through the nerve impulses in the sensory channels. "Rather, at the level of deep mind, we appear not to be separated from one another or from the earth and the universe." Quoted from "Science and Society: Implications of Research on Human Consciousness," paper presented in Fes, Morocco, May 1983, p. 10.

References

Agranoff, R. and V. Lindsay. 1983. "Intergovernmental management: perspectives from human services problem solving at the local level." *Public Administration Review* 43(3): 227-237.

Astley, G. and C. Fombrun. 1983. Collective strategy: social ecology of organizational environments. *Academy of Management Review* 8(4): 576-587.

Bailey, S. 1982. Personal letter to the Centennial Agendas Project, American Society for Public Administration.

Beam, D. 1980. "Forecasting in the future of federalism: task and challenge." In *The future of federalism in the 1980s*. Washington, D.C.: ACIR.

Bell, D. 1979. Communications technology—for better or for worse. *Harvard Business Review* 57(May-June): 20-42.

Bennis, W. 1983. "The artform of leadership." In *The Executive Mind,* edited by S. Srivastva. San Francisco: Jossey-Bass.

Black, M. 1977. More about metaphor. *Dialectica* 31:431-51.

Bryant, R. 1980. Money and monetary policy in interdependent nations. Washington, D.C.: The Brookings Institute.

Buntz, G. and B. Radin. 1983. Managing intergovernmental conflict: the case of human services. *Public Administration Review* 43(2): 403-410.

Caparaso, V.A. 1978. Dependence, dependency, and power in the global system: a structural and behavioral analysis. *International Organization* 32:13-44.

Cleveland, H. 1985. *The knowledge executive: leadership in an information society.* New York: E.P. Dutton.

Cochran, N. 1980. Society as emergent and more than rational. *Policy Sciences* 12(2): 453-67.

Drucker, P. 1980. *Managing in turbulent times.* New York: Harper and Row.

Duvall, R.D. 1978. Dependence and dependencia theory: notes toward precision of concept and argument. *International Organization* 32:51-78.

Emery, F.E. and E.L. Trist. 1965. The causal texture of organizational environments. *Human Relations* 18:21-32.

Etzioni, A. 1961. *A comparative analysis of complex organizations.* Glencoe: Free Press.

Ferguson, C.E. and J.P. Gould. 1975. *Microeconomic theory.* Homewood, IL: Irwin.

Frederickson, H. G. 1982. The recovery of civism in public administration. *Public Administration Review* 42 (6): 505.

Gardner, N. "The law of the other guy's thing." In *Cases in public administration,* edited by J. Uvegas, Jr. Boston: Holbrook Press.

Gilpin, R. 1981. *War and change in world politics.* Cambridge: Cambridge University Press.

Grodzins, M. 1966. *The American system.* Chicago: Rand McNally.

Hartle, T. 1977. The law, the courts, education and public administration. *Public Administration Review* 41(5): 595-607.

Hirschman, A. 1945. *National power and the structure of foreign trade.* Berkeley, CA: University of California Press.

Holsti, O.R., R.M. Siverson and A.L. George, eds. 1980. *Change in the international system.* Boulder, CO: Westview Press.

Horowitz, D. 1977. *The courts and social policy.* Washington, D.C.: The Brookings Institute.

Johnson, K.W., W.D. Frazier and F.Riddick, Jr. 1983. A change strategy for linking the worlds of academia and practice. *Journal of Applied Behavioral Science* 19(4): 439-460.

Keller, L. and C. Heatwole. 1976. Action research in policy analysis. *Administration and Society* 8(2): 193-200.

Keohane, R. and J.S. Nye. 1977. *Power and interdependence.* Boston: Little, Brown.

Khatchadourian, H. 1968. Metaphor. *British Journal of Aesthetics* 8:227-43.

Kirlin, J.J. 1982. *The political economy of fiscal limits.* Lexington, MA: Lexington Books.

Kirlin, J. and A. Kirlin. 1982. *Public choices—private resources.* Sacramento, CA: California Tax Foundation.

Lewin, K. 1947. "Group decision and social change." In *Readings in social psychology,* edited by T.M. Newcomb and E.L. Hartley. New York: Holt, and Co.

Lind, D. 1974. Building community wide networks. *Public Management* 56(4): 15-16.

Long, N. 1979. Government reorganization for economic development. *Journal of the American Planning Association* 45(2):190-199.

Lovell, C. 1981. Evolving local government dependency. *Public Administration Review* 41(Special Issue): 72-89.

Luke, J. 1985. "Arenas of local government negotiating and bargaining." In *Successful negotiating in local government,* edited by B. Moore. International City Management Association: Washington, D.C.

_____. 1984. New role for small cities in economic development. *Municipal Management* (Winter).

_____. 1983. "Interdependence: the environmental context of public administration in its second century as a discipline." Ph.D. dissertation, University of Southern California.

Mandel, M. 1981. "Interorganizational networks: the case of the Century Freeway." Ph.D. dissertation, University of Southern California.

Manning, B. 1977. The Congress, the executive and intermestic affairs: three proposals. *Foreign Affairs* 55(2): 306-324.

Mansback, R. and J. Vasquez. 1981. *In search of theory: A new paradigm for global politics.* New York: Columbia Press.

March, J. and J. Olson. 1983. Organizing political life: what administrative reorganization tells us about government. *The American Political Science Review* 77:281-296.

Mason, R. and I. Mitroff. 1981. *Challenging strategic planning assumptions.* New York: John Wiley and Sons.

McClelland, D. 1975. *Power: The inner experience.* New York: Irvington Publishing.

McCormick, P. 1979. The concept of self in political thought. *Canadian Journal of Political Science* 12(4): 689-726.

McGowan, R. and J. Stevens. 1983. Local government initiatives in a climate of uncertainty. *Public Administration Review* 43(2): 127-136.

McKinney, J. and L. Howard. 1979. *Public administration: Balancing power and accountability.* Oak Park, IL: Moore Publishing.

Mechanic, D. 1962. Sources of power of lower participants in complex organizations. *Administrative Science Quarterly* 7:349-364.

Mische, G. and P. Mische. 1977. *Toward a human world order.* New York: Paulist Press.

Morgan, G. 1980. Paradigms, metaphors, and puzzle solving in organization theory. *Administrative Science Quarterly* 25(4): 605-622.

Mosher, F. 1980. The changing responsibilities and tactics of the federal government. *Public Administration Review* 40(6): 546.

Mowday, R.T. 1978. The exercise of upward influence in organizations. *Administrative Science Quarterly* 23:137-156.

Neu and Sumek. 1983. Municipal governance challenges of the 1980s. *Nebraska Municipal Review* (May): 10-13.

Ouchi, W. 1984. *The M-Form society.* Reading, MA: Addison-Wesley Publishing.

Perrow, C. 1977. The bureaucratic paradox. *Organizational Dynamics* 5(4)(Spring): 3-14.

Rabinowitz, F. 1982. "The extravagant excursion," working paper for the Centennial Agendas Project. *American Society for Public Administration.*

Reed, C. 1983. "Political dynamics in the evolution of federal housing policy: the Gautreaux case, 1966-1982." Ph.D. dissertation, Brown University.

Rittel, H. 1972. "On the planning crisis: systems analysis of the 'first and second generations.'" *Bedriftsokonemen* NR8: 390-396.

Rosenau, J. 1980. *The study of global interdependence: essays on the transnationalization of world affairs.* New York: Nicholas Pub.

_____. 1971. *The Scientific Study of Foreign Policy.* New York: The Free Press.

_____. 1969. *Linkage politics.* New York: The Free Press.

Salancik, G.R., and J.R. Pfeffer. 1974. The bases and uses of power in organizational decision making. *Administrative Science Quarterly* 21:227-45.

Schon, D. 1979. "Generative metaphor: a perspective on problem setting in social policy." In *Metaphor in thought*, edited by A. Ortony. New York: Cambridge University Press.

Scott, A. 1982. *The dynamics of interdependence.* Chapel Hill: University of North Carolina Press.

Seers, D. 1981. *Dependency theory: A critical reassessment.* London: Frances Pinter, Ltd.

Selznick, P. 1957. *Leadership in administration.* Evanston, IL: Row, Peterson.

Shapiro, M. 1978. "The Supreme Court: from Warren to Burger." In *The new American political system,* edited by A. King. Washington, D.C.: American Enterprise Institute.

Smircich, L. and G. Morgan. 1982. Leadership: the management of meaning. *Journal of Applied Behavioral Science* 18(3): 257-273.

Terreberry, S. 1968. The evolution of organizational environments. *Administrative Science Quarterly* 12(March): 590-613.

Thompson, J. 1967. *Organizations in action.* New York: McGraw-Hill.

_____. 1973. Society's frontiers for organizing activities. *Public Administration Review* 33(4): 327-335.

Thurow, L. 1980. *The zero sum society: Distribution and the possibilities for economic change.* New York: Basic Books.

Trist, E. 1977. Collaboration in work settings: a personal perspective. *Journal of Applied Behavioral Science* 13(3): 268-278.

Veit, L. 1977. Troubled world economy. *Foreign Affairs* 55(2): 552-71.

Vernon, R. 1977. Storm over the multinationals: problems and prospects. *Foreign Affairs* 55(2): 498-513.

Waldo, D. 1982. "Politics and administration: a profound dysjunction." Working
    paper for the Centennial Agendas Project, American Society for Public Admin-
    istration.
Waldo, D., ed. 1971. *Public administration in a time of turbulence*. San Francisco:
    Chandler.
Wamsley, G. and M. Zald. 1983. "The Environments of public managers: managing
    turbulence." In *Handbook of organization management*, edited by W. Eddy.
    New York: Marcel Dekker.
White, M.C., M.D. Crino, and B.L. Kedia. 1984. Environmental turbulence. *Admin-
    istrative Science Quarterly* 16(1): 97-116.
Wildavsky, A. 1980. "Bare bones: putting flesh on the skeleton of American
    federalism." In *The future of federalism in the 1980s*. Washington, D.C.:
    Advisory Commission on Intergovernmental Relations.
Wildavsky, A. 1979. *Speaking truth to power—the art and craft of policy analysis*.
    Boston: Little, Brown.
Wilson, W. 1887. The study of administration. *Political Science Quarterly* 2(1).

CHAPTER 3

Current Institutional Arrangements that Create or Require Shared Power

H. Brinton Milward

Among policy intellectuals such as Theodore Lowi (1979), Hugh Heclo (1978), and Samuel Huntington (1981) there is general agreement that excessive fragmentation of power is one of the central problems of governance in the United States. For those who work for or with federal, state or local government, and this includes over one third of the workforce (Ginsburg and Vojta 1981), power sharing is a fact of life. This is why power sharing as a perspective must be integrated into policy planning and the implementation of public policy. If we do not do this, both planning and implementation studies will be little more than extended elaborations of Murphy's Law.

At the local level alone, imagine the number of actors, institutions, and programs which have an impact on the decision to revitalize part of a downtown by building a hotel and convention center. The mayor's office, city council, planning and zoning commission, neighborhood associations, trusts for historical preservation, chamber of commerce, local banks, existing businesses, downtown property owners, Urban League, college or professional sports teams, local entrepreneurs, and developers are all involved in the decision-making process. Other participants, either on an ongoing basis or with veto power at certain stages, include the state department of commerce (which issues industrial revenue bonds), the U.S. Department of Housing and Urban Development (which makes UDAG grants available), the U.S. Department of Commerce, the U.S. Representative from the Congressional district the city is in, the state's two senators, the governor, and bond rating services in New York. Major lending institutions are also involved, as is the court system of both the state and federal government. These parties either derive their power from their legal standing and thus are able to exercise some leverage over the project, or, like a neighborhood association, they ask for and are often granted standing. From this relatively uncomplicated example one is amazed that decisions are ever made and implemented.

However, decisions are made and are implemented and the fragmented system of power sharing does work, sometimes even rather well. Scholars of public policy and public organizations need to devote a major effort to understanding why powersharing sometimes works successfully and sometimes doesn't. What are the critical variables? This is the work that must be done if we are going to overcome those who argue that no government action is the preferred solution in all matters save national defense and social mores.

This paper will explore the institutional dimensions of power sharing by discussing how power sharing is necessitated by four interrelated factors: 1) institutions with overlapping authority, 2) levels of government with overlapping authority, 3) public organizations with only partial responsibility for programs they implement, and 4) instruments of public policy which cause fragmentation (grants, contracts, subsidies), and whose impact is neglected or misunderstood.

It would not be fair to academics or practitioners to write a paper consisting only of a laundry list of factors which promote power sharing and retard the aggregation of interests. Instead, this list of interactive factors needs to be seen in light of a theory of politics which makes the relationships between them understandable. The theory must also account for a large number of empirical observations regarding the effects of fragmentation and power sharing. The theory of politics that will be put forward is termed "plural elitism."

Institutional Overlap

Institutions of governance overlap in an obvious and a nonobvious manner. The obvious can be seen by anyone with a high school civics understanding of American government. We have in Morton Grodzins' (1966) words, "separated institutions sharing power." The sharing of power by Congress and the President was designed by our founding fathers to avoid the concentrated power and centralized administration they deplored in European monarchies. The same emphasis exists today. Samuel P. Huntington in *American Politics: the Promise of Disharmony* (1981) writes that Americans will not permit government to be what it would have to be for most efficient operation—to possess hierarchy, inequality, arbitrary power, secrecy, deception, and established patterns of superordination and subordination. These attributes are necessary for efficiency but antithetical to the American Ideal.

The unwieldy character of our government complicates the internal operation of agencies and programs and makes them appear or actually be inefficient, as unresolved legislative-executive conflicts are played out during the implementation process. Steps to manage the economy can cripple the effectiveness of government programs; examples are across-the-board budget cuts, personnel reductions which lay off good workers and bad, and personnel ceilings unrelated to the magnitude of the job. In another example, the U.S. Office of Surface Mining issued 800 fewer mine violations in 1980 than in 1979. OSM attributed the decrease, rightly or wrongly, not to a change in policy from Carter to Reagan, but to having been unable to replace mine inspectors who resigned during the federal hiring freeze. There are numerous other examples of different aspects of institutional power sharing. Courts stepped in to close Washington Metro subway stations because they were not accessible to the handicapped. The Surgeon General required a health warning on cigarette packages at the same time the Agriculture Department was supporting the price of tobacco. These seeming incongruities are understandable when one recognizes that a key function of democratic government is to respond to interests that are incompatible. . .which leads to incompatible policies.

There is an internal dimension to institutional power sharing as well. All organizations tend to differentiate as they grow. One example of this is what I call the "ports-of-entry" phenomenon. As Congress increased the number of committees and subcommittees from around 80 to 300 by 1973, interest groups found "ports-of-entry" tremendously increased. Furthermore, because the committees represented smaller policy domains than before, it was easier for one or a few interests to control the new committees or subcommittees. Hence there was a diminution of the committees' ability to play one interest against another or to force contending interests to work out differences before presenting new legislation for committee consideration.

The unanswered question here is whether the differentiation of society created the pressure for the increase in the number of "ports-of-entry" or whether that pressure came from internal demands within the congress. Younger congressmen may have become so frustrated with senior members who had until then (1973) largely controlled the committee structure of congress that they decided to use their collective weight to topple the congressional power structure. Whatever the cause, the result has been our "Special Interest State," where interests are so fragmented that coalition building is difficult (and even when achieved is hard to maintain for more than one vote).

The same thing occurs in the executive branch, where program proliferation has led to the development of separate, sometimes conflicting constituencies in policy domains. An example is education, which suffers from conflicts among higher, secondary, elementary, and vocational education policy constituencies. Like the increasing number of congressional ports of entry, the proliferation of programmatic constituencies makes it difficult to aggregate interests for purposes of collective choice.

The Theory of Plural Elitism
As the state grew, those seeking access to it did too. Growth has been so spectacular in the last 20 years (Walker 1983b) that our theories of interest intermediation politics haven't been able to keep up[1].

Two major theories of politics—group and elite—cannot explain what has been happening with interest groups. Elite theory with its Marxian baggage of a capitalist class and tight political control is incompatible with the increasing numbers of groups seeking to share power, from single issue groups like Right-to-Life, to social movements like the farm workers.

Group theory with its emphasis on balance was made a hash of by Lowi (1979) among others with his description of the working of the segmented politics of "interest group liberalism." Mancur Olson's 1965 withering analysis of interest group cohesion collapsed the conceptual underpinning of group theory.

A theory of politics must be able to accommodate the reality that while the system of interest intermediation is open to a growing number of interests, it is in its workings biased and varies over time in degree of openness, according to policy domain and the stage of policy process.

Andrew McFarland (1979) has attempted to create a synthesis of group and elite theory out of both those who contributed to these seemingly diverse theories and their critics. Arguing that a new view is needed, he calls this the theory of plural elitism.

> At the present the discussion of power in America is quite confused. One suspects that pluralism is very much with us [in popular discussion]. Professor Lowi writes thought-provoking essays about the cooptation of the state by status quo interest groups, but he has not set forth an alternative theory of power and the state, rigorously distinguished from the pluralists, the Marxists', and Lindblom's recently stated view of corporate dominance (McFarland 1979, 2) While astute observers have noted that "Power in America is largely a matter of cooptation of specific public policy areas by elites, serving their own private interests" (McFarland 1979, 2), no theory has been put forward to explain how and why this occurs.

While McFarland has reservations about the adequacy of the theory he offers (as do I), he feels that since it undergirds much of the current debate regarding how power is and should be shared, he sets out to list the elements in the theory. He does not, however, discuss the relationship between the elements.

McFarland has culled 13 propositions from those who have written on the problem of power sharing in America. While he points out that no writer would agree with all 13, he maintains, and I agree, that these propositions are generally consistent, and that they broadly outline a theory of how power operates and is shared in the American polity—the theory of plural elitism.

Plural Elitism Propositions

Proposition One: Organizational Costs (Olson 1965). Presuming economic, cost-benefit reasoning, widely shared interests will not be organized because it is not to the benefit of any individual to incur the time and money costs of organizing the group.

Proposition Two: The Free-Rider Problem (Olson 1965). When an interest group produces public goods (collective benefits), members lose incentive to contribute to the maintenance of the interest group, because they will receive the benefit anyway.

This is particularly true of large groups. Because of this free-rider problem, an interest group will lose influence and may cease to exist.

Proposition Three: The Few Defeat the Many (Olson 1965). The interests of a few are less prone to high organizational costs and to the free-rider problem. The organization of widespread interests, on the other hand, is susceptible to these problems. Therefore within a particular policy domain, the few tend to defeat the many because the few tend to be better organized.

Proposition Four: Symbols in Politics; the Few Defeat the Many (Edelman 1964). Widespread but unorganized publics are prone to irrational perceptions of political reality. Such publics confuse symbol with substance—that is, elites manipulate public opinion by creating political forms which give the impression that some problem is being solved, or some policy is being followed, when this is not the case. On the other hand, political groups consisting of a few corporations do not usually confuse symbol with substance. Such small groups, following rational political strategies, will frequently defeat the interests of large publics, confused by political symbols and following irrational political strategies.

Proposition Five: Restricting the Scope of Conflict (Schattschneider 1960). Manipulation of the scope of conflict is a basic political strategy. Therefore, well-organized special interests will manipulate the context of political conflict to prevent "public interests" from manifesting themselves in the conflict.

Proposition Six: The Structure of American Political Institutions (McConnell 1966). The decentralized and fragmented nature of American political institutions frequently helps the few defeat the many. Public interests are best represented by the Presidency, Supreme Court, and within general, conflictful policy debates in Washington. On the other hand, special interests tend to be more powerful in state and local politics, and within fragmented administrative policy systems, which are not subject to public control by the President or by the federal courts. Americans share an ideology of the virtue of political decentralization, but this ideology in fact helps special interests defeat public interests.

Proposition Seven: Congress Creates Unneeded Bureaucracy (Fiorina 1977). During the 1970's, members of Congress learned to increase their probability of re-election by legislating new federal bureaucracy, which created a myriad of new regulations. Members of Congress then helped their constituents with problems resulting from such regulations, which increased the popularity of incumbent members. The result was a special-interest coalition: a Washington establishment.

Proposition Eight: Ambiguous Statutes (Lowi 1979). In enacting general interest legislation, American legislators write ambiguous statutes. Such vaguely written laws provide opportunities for special interests to redirect the implementation of such laws to their own benefit.

Proposition Nine: Government Subsidies for Established Interest Groups (Lowi 1979). Beginning in the 1960's, the federal government instituted vast programs of subsidies (especially through subsidized loans) for established interest groups. This tends to freeze the political system in the status quo, retard policy innovation, and lessen the influence of newly emerging interests.

Proposition Ten: Power Structure Varies by Issue Area (Lowi 1964). While some policy areas are characterized by pluralism, other areas are characterized by elite dominance—an area-specific elite controls policy without effective political competition. In addition, class conflict may ensue if the existing distribution of property is at issue.

Proposition Eleven: Subgovernments (Cater 1964; Lowi 1979; McConnell 1966; Wamsley and Zald 1973; and many others). In American public administration, the few defeat the many through the mechanism of subgovernment. This is a coalition of interest groups, public administrators, and members of Congress serving on the relevant committees, which controls the administration of public policy for the benefit of those within the subgovernment. Such policies usually benefit established economic interests. A subgovernment will try to destroy executive agencies, operating within the same policy area but outside of the subgovernmental coalition. Such agencies, which compete with subgovernments, include a disproportionate number of those which represent general interests of the poor. The political patterns described in the other propositions are manifest in the politics of subgovernments.

Proposition Twelve: Reform Cycles (Lowi 1964; McConnell 1966; Edelman 1964; Bernstein 1955). American politics is subject to reform cycles in specific areas of policy. At times, general-interest coalitions defeat the subgovernmental coalitions and enact reform legislation in specific areas of public policy.

Later, public attention to a policy area wanes, and the subgovernment re-establishes its control.

Proposition Thirteen: Interest-Group Liberalism (Lowi 1979). Since the New Deal, an ideology, "interest-group liberalism," has been prevalent among political scientists, moderate and liberal politicians and civil servants, and intellectuals. This ideology is the phenomenological equivalent to academic pluralist theory. Interest-group liberalism implies that people know their own interests, are able to express these interests in political organizations, and are then able to gain access to policy makers. The resultant policy outcomes are seen as fair, because interest groups balance one another. It is believed that significant social change can be achieved within the present structure of group organization. However, this ideology is thrown into question by American political reality, which is primarily characterized by a lessening of the degree of democracy.

McFarland argues that taken together, these propositions constitute a general argument. The essence of this argument is that: 1) many widely shared interests cannot be effectively organized within the political process; 2) politics tends to be fragmented into decision making in various specific policy areas, which are normally controlled by special-interest coalitions; 3) there is a variety of specific processes whereby plural elitist rule is maintained; and 4) a widespread ideology conceals this truth about American politics.

The theory of plural elitism is useful in understanding the natural tendency of a political system to seek a stable equilibrium. As policy domains age, stable constellations of interests emerge to bring stability to the domain.

This is what plural elitism captures best—the system at rest. What it does not capture is the extent to which outside forces, exogenous events (the Arab Oil Embargo), structural (the President, Congress and the courts), and social movements can quickly destroy the stability of the policy domain. However well or poorly the theory of plural elitism fits a particular case or set of facts, I think it provides a good theoretical underpinning for understanding the day-to-day operation of interests in relation to government, and of the general direction of relations with little outside intervention.

Plural Elitism in Action:
The Case of the Ohio Housing Finance Agency

It is well and good to sketch the major outlines of the theory of plural elitism; it is another thing to show how it works in practice. The creation of the Ohio Housing Finance Agency provides a fine example of the open/closed nature of policy making under plural elitism.

Housing interests in Ohio in the 1960's were marked by a low degree of cohesiveness with the state government. The developers, lenders and builders were capable of looking out for their own self-interest but seemed uninterested in initiating housing proposals. They were active only in an adaptive fashion, such as trying to increase federal dollars they could get under housing and urban development subsidy programs. But, as Ohio ranked low in federal dollars received for housing, it's evident that even in federal dollar chasing, housing interests were not successful.

With the election of Democrat John J. Gilligan as governor in November, 1970, housing assumed a more prominent role in Ohio. Early in 1971, Gilligan appointed a series of task forces in areas where he felt the state should improve its performance. Housing was one such area. The Housing and Community Development Advisory Commission (HACDAC) became the most active housing group in the state. It, together with the staff of the Ohio Department of Urban Affairs (later reorganized into the Department of Economic and Community Development), was the most active supporter of an increased state role in housing (Flinn 1973).

While housing and community development are standard fare on the Democratic agenda, HACDAC was studiously nonpartisan. The commission members represented every conceivable constituency for housing in the state: banks, savings and loans,developers, and realtors. In addition, there were professors with housing expertise, representatives of local governments, and such minority groups as blacks, chicanos, the aged, and the handicapped.

The one thing the commission members had in common was an interest in housing policy at the state level. Their ideas about what should be done varied greatly. However, they represented a standard component in the development of most policy domains—the advisory committee, which is the formal link between those interested in a policy and the government. Robert Wood calls them "intervening elites" (Wood quoted in Farkas 1971, 30). He believes that through the advisory committee mechanism, intervening elites are challenging the traditional interest groups for dominant influence in setting the public agenda. Similar points are made by Walker (1983a, 1983b) and Salisbury (1984) in regard to what they refer to as "institutional interests."

Often the real expertise of an advisory committee resides in its staff. Through their knowledge and sustained work on the problem, staff can develop influence far beyond their formal powers. Policy entrepreneurs operating through professionals in the bureaucracy—the source of most committee staff—can set the agenda for groups like HACDAC, thereby determining the shape of legislation the committee may propose.

The staff of HACDAC, which came from the Department of Urban Affairs, was developing housing material even before Governor Gilligan appointed the Commission. Under the direction of chairman-designate Jim Huston, a Cleveland lawyer, the staff contracted with McKinsey and Company to prepare two reports. The first, *Overview of Ohio's Housing Problem* (Department of Urban Affairs, 1971), described the magnitude of unmet housing needs of Ohioans and addressed the question of what must be done in housing. The second, *Strategy in Formulating a State Housing Program* (Department of Urban Affairs 1971), reported that the preferred strategy for addressing housing needs was the creation of low and moderate income housing through the Housing Finance Agency (HFA).

Creating a Demand for a State Housing Agency

During early meetings of the Commission, the staff presented a 62-page report that listed the name, address and function of every conceivable interest group which might support or oppose a state housing policy. There was good reason for the staff to do this for the Commission, since there was as yet no demand from these groups for the state to have a role in housing.

In the first six months of its existence the Commission was extremely active: it held three sets of hearings, nine plenary meetings, and forty-five individual subcommittee meetings. The hearings served two purposes: 1) getting citizen input on the housing problem, and 2) giving visibility to state housing policy and perhaps encouraging local groups to view the state—not just city and federal government—as a source of housing policy.

At the conclusion of these hearings and meetings, the Commission issued a report which justified both the proposed state role and the need for a HFA. (Legislative Report Number 2: Financial and Technical Assistance Legislation February, 1972.) The report and a piece of draft legislation creating the HFA were sent to Governor Gilligan.

The committee's bill was submitted to the Ohio General Assembly with little fanfare. It gave the HFA the power to issue revenue bonds and provide technical assistance to the functions performed by the state in housing. The Housing Finance Agency would handle the former and the Department of Economic and Community Development (DECD) would handle the latter.

A similar bill was introduced in the General Assembly. These competing bills created confusion, and housing became the subject of much activity among interest groups. An internal memo dated November 21, 1972, written by the DECD staff in the Bureau of Research and Analysis, reflects what happened in the 109th General Assembly to the Commission's housing legislation.

The memo states that there was no negative reaction to an increased state role in housing. Special interests lined up, supporting and opposing various parts of the two bills but they did not object to the creation of an HFA. Labor wanted a strong prevailing wage provision in the bill which would add to the cost of construction in nonunion areas like southeastern Ohio. Lenders feared competition by the HFA if it could issue direct loans to developers. Homebuilders objected to a mandatory clause in the Commission's bill which stipulated that a certain percentage of low-income people be included in each project. Real estate interests were upset because the Commission had sponsored a landlord-tenant bill which they opposed.

The memo goes on to say:

> As for other special interest groups and citizen groups such as organized labor, Ohio Housing Coalition, fit housing groups, minority groups, consumer groups and the Municipal League, the reaction was either neutrality or uncertainty as to which bill to support because of a lack of information about different provisions in each bill, misinterpretation or disinterest.

> The major real estate and investment interests will be involved in giving their input into the bill. We anticipate a more positive reaction as a result of this involvement, particularly from those developers involved in construction of federally subsidized housing. An active educational campaign will be undertaken with other special interest groups and citizen groups to generate interest, input and support.

Mobilizing Support for Bureaucratic Demands
One important element in the theory of plural elitism is how emerging interests are coopted by an existing interest through control of the agenda setting process. Often those interests are manifested through bureaus or agencies of government. Bureau-

cratic demands can reach the public agenda in two different ways. One is the "inside access model" of agenda setting, where policy is developed by elements of the bureaucracy and those such as task force members who are closely associated with it. These insiders try to get a policy on the institutional agenda with a minimum of discussion from those who are outsiders (Cobb, Ross, and Ross 1976). While this model appears to fit the Ohio case, because the bill was complex and legislators didn't understand it, no new legislation resulted. Legislators correctly perceived that there was no ground swell of popular support for the measure, not even from likely beneficiaries in the traditional housing interest groups.

With failure of the first attempt at passage of the HFA legislation, a second model—the "mobilization model"—also developed by Cobb, Ross, and Ross (1976), seems to explain the behavior of the HACDAC. In it the public agenda is determined by "insiders," then taken to people who will hopefully support it so as to make it appear the result of popular opinion. The insiders must plan their strategy to not appear to manipulate public opinion. This is the essence of plural elitism where the agenda is set by elites, but legitimated by citizens.

The new strategy began with the Commission consulting the groups that had opposed parts of the initial bill as to what their specific objections had been and what would be acceptable to them in a new bill. In addition, the Commission and staff pushed to get Governor Gilligan's backing.

A staff memo to Gilligan aide Jack Hansen stated that to avoid duplication of bills the Commission and staff had decided to mount "an active educational campaign with other special interest groups and citizen groups to generate interest and support." This was an attempt to create a constituency for housing. Those with a direct financial interest—developers, lenders, etc.—had been consulted. The plan now was to give the bill the illusion of mass support.

In January, 1973, the chief of the Bureau of Research and Analysis outlined for the deputy director of DECD the strategy for getting the HFA legislation passed: 1) mobilize citizens, 2) mobilize HACDAC members[2], 3) create and disseminate educational materials (e.g., summary papers on housing issues and fact sheets), 4) survey legislators, 5) meet with opponents of the HFA legislation and try to win them over, 6) develop a media program, 7) gather endorsements, 8) make speeches, 9) have the Ohio Council of churches designate a "Housing Sunday" to gain visibility, and 10) hold news conferences across the state.

The day this memo was written, President Nixon declared a moratorium on federal housing subsidy programs. The moratorium which had at first seemed to doom the Ohio housing effort now was used as its major selling point. The staff and Commission argued that the states must act during the moratorium to take up some of the housing needs slack. They also said that the HFA must be operational when the new housing programs were passed by Congress.

Other states' HFA's were contacted to see what strategies had been used to pass their legislation. A memo prepared by the staff, titled "How Other States Sold Their

State Housing Finance Agency," presented strategies other state housing policy elites used to "sell" housing finance agency legislation. One aspect dealt with how to develop an appearance of mass support.

Speeches on the need for a state housing policy were prepared for Commission members and DECD officials. Press releases were sent to special interest groups, outlining what banks, savings and loan associations, mortgage bankers, cities, villages, townships, government councils, local and regional planning commissions, community action agencies, municipal housing authorities, public corporations, and, of course, developers, homebuilders, and contractors. The staff and Commission also attempted to build support among individuals by contacting low and moderate income people—the intended beneficiaries— through their unions.

In April, 1973, the Commission and staff held a Housing Finance Agency Conference. It was a carefully orchestrated affair, intended to bring together special interests in lending and homebuilding in Ohio with their counterparts from Michigan, Missouri, Massachusetts and Illinois. These states all had HFA's. The purpose was for the out-of-state lenders and developers to tell their Ohio counterparts the benefits of HFA's. This is precisely what was done. Troy Grigsby, the deputy director of DECD, charged the Ohio representatives with this mission: "Your role is to help Ohio industry understand the legislation, and particularly that the legislation will not make the state a competitor with private industry but will actually increase their business" (Minutes of the Housing Finance Agency Conference April 12, 1973). Thus ended the almost frantic effort to mobilize support for the legislation before the beginning of the 1973 General Assembly session.

While there was more support for HFA legislation than in the previous session, the issue of whether or not HFA' financial projects should pay union scale wages brought industry groups and building trades union officials into direct conflict. This dispute held up passage of the bill for another year. It put the issue squarely out of control of the housing policy community that had developed around the push for the HFA in Ohio and brought two traditional interest groups—labor (the AFL-CIO, officially the Building Trades) and industry (the Homebuilders)—to loggerheads with one another. As the "prevailing wage" was sacrosanct to the unions, compromise was difficult. Industry groups, particularly lenders, began to have second thoughts about this venture in state capitalism. The emotive and symbolic aspects of the "prevailing wage" issue to both the building trades and the homebuilders had brought a complex piece of legislation to a halt.

It was the external stimulus of the passage of the federal 1974 Community Development and Housing Act that reestablished the momentum of the bill, as the act had provisions which specifically aided HFA's. Here one sees the interrelation of state and federal legislation even where there is no direct connection. The Community Development and Housing Act made the HFA bill a viable piece of legislation again.

The provisions in the Community Development and Housing Act were favorable enough to both the unions and the building industry that they resolved their differences and supported the legislation. Much of the negotiation leading to this settlement was conducted by the staff of the Commission. Even though Governor John Gilligan was defeated for reelection there was enough support for the HFA legislation that in the interim of James Rhodes' election and inauguration, a deal was struck between the outgoing and incoming administrations to call the General Assembly back into special session to pass the HFA legislation. With all interested parties convinced there was something in the legislation for them, the General Assembly overwhelmingly passed the legislation creating an HFA in Ohio.

This example was used to see if the theory of plural elitism fits the case of the adoption of the Ohio HFA. Clearly the most general interests were difficult to organize—those in need of low and moderate income housing—and were in fact brought on board after the producers' interests had been satisfied. Housing policy was indeed fragmented and it took several years of activity by a bureaucratic elite to forge a general coalition even in this one policy area. This case also illustrates how plural-elitist rule is maintained by specific processes like agenda creation and control. Finally, all parties sought to cloak themselves in the mantle of public interest, equating support from interest groups with public interest, as interest liberalism (Lowi 1979)—which undergirds the theory of plural elitism—suggests.

At this point we will move from plural elitism and our example of it to a second concern in an institutional map of power sharing—the relationship between state power and public organizations.

Paradoxes of Power and Public Organizations

Another aspect of power sharing concerns the problem of implementation in public organizations. When we look at prevailing views of public organizations there are two major images—leviathan and joker. According to the leviathan image, the bureaucracy is like a weed—constantly encroaching on areas of activity outside its control. Gorged on red tape and mountains of files, it chokes the spontaneity out of all who come within its grasp.

The other image of the bureaucracy, the joker, is almost the opposite. This image reflects the widespread belief that there is so much fragmentation of authority that it's impossible to get the job done. Richard Elmore has referred to implementation studies as "extended elaborations on Murphy's Law."

While many reasons are cited to account for this image — multiple and overlapping goals, vaguely written laws—the focus here will be on institutional design, especially on the conflict between programs (or interorganizational networks) and agencies, including government departments. Hjern and Porter (1981) hold that to understand public organizations we must understand that there are two rationales for organizing the delivery of public services, and the conflict between them accounts for the paradoxical images that we see—joker and leviathan. The rationales are organizations and programs. Figure 1 illustrates the tension between these two. Hjern and Porter (1981) explain as follows. Organizations (agencies and departments) are the standard organizing units in the public sector. Laws are passed which give a federal agency the authority to implement a law. For example, the Food Stamp Act was given to the U.S. Department of Agriculture to administer, but it is only one of many programs administered by the USDA. The organizational rationale views agencies like USDA as consisting of parts of many programs.

From the program rationale perspective, the Food Stamp program is nested in parts of many organizations. There is the bureau in USDA which writes the regulations and funds the program. There is the office in the Department of Human Resources in every state which determines the eligibility of clients for the program. Distribution is handled by the U.S. Postal Service in some states and by private contractors in others. Food stores participate in the program, and checkers determine if the food clients bring to the checkout counter is eligible under the program. Banks then redeem the stamps for money from the food stores and return the stamps to USDA for redemption.

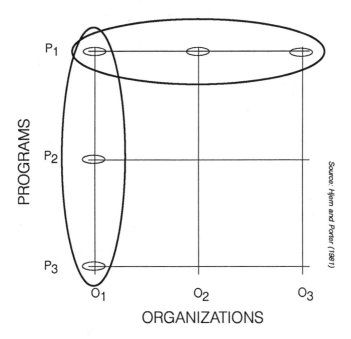

Figure 3-1   Matrix Relationships Between Organization Rationales and Program Rationales

This is the Food Stamp program as viewed from the program rationale perspective. The program viewed this way consists of pieces of organizations which are nested in one program consisting of federal, state and third party elements as well as the clients. The last public official who has contact with the program is the person or persons in the state Department of Human Resources who determines whether a client is eligible. The "program" is in many respects implemented totally by third parties. Thus the USDA and the state DHR's can do their job (funding and determining) perfectly and still be viewed as failing because of third-party fraud (a secondary market which exchanges stamps for money at a discounted rate) or misuse of the stamps by clients (finding food stores that will allow clients to exchange stamps for prohibited items like liquor).

One reason people who study the implementation of public policy do not often integrate the empirical work in organization theory and behavior into their studies is that the unit of analysis of choice in OT/OB is the organization. Implementation researchers do not see organizations as the relevant actors in their studies. This is why they emphasize individuals (fixers), coalitions, and multilevel bargaining rather than structure, technology, job satisfaction, and other concerns of OT/OB. Most of our theories of organization assume that behavior takes place within one focal organization. The reverse is the case in studying the implementation of public policy.

The organization theory literature views agencies as rulebound, rigid, and hierarchical. The public policy literature views agencies as fragmented and non-hierarchical, with much work done through informal channels. These two different images of public agencies are one major reason why there has been so little integration between the two fields. Andrew Dunshire's review of Marshall W. Meyer's *Change in Public Bureaucracies* provides a vivid example of the different images scholars in both fields bring to research on public organizations.

> Let me get one more gripe off my chest before turning to praise. Professor Meyer is not a political scientist or public administration scholar, and he is extraordinarily simple minded about actual processes in the bureaucratic setting: "But whatever the distribution of individual people and subunits within the structure of public bureaucracies are, all are bound together by relationships of super- and subordination in which conformity to rules and to wishes of superiors is expected" (p. 202). Baloney. Yet an enormous house of cards is poised on this supposed characteristic of "pervasive hierarchy" (Dunshire 1981, 147).

In the remainder of this paper I will attempt to make sense out of the paradoxes identified earlier and out of the different images of public organizations.

In an important paper which goes a long way toward resolving these paradoxes, Robert Backoff (1980), in a deceptively simple fashion, clarifies the characteristics of the dominant type of organization found in the public sector in the United States. This is the general-purpose government agency. It is equivalent to what I later term a "federative" organization. It is found at the federal, state, and local levels of government, having much in common with a conglomerate in the private sector. It has no cohesiveness of purpose among the bundle of programs it administers. It is governed by the organizational rationale.

What the Backoff paper says, in effect, look, forget about nonprofit organizations, hospitals, regulatory agencies, public authorities, etc. They only hopelessly muddle the conceptual water concerning public/private organizational differences and the nature of public organizations. According to Backoff, if we focus on the general-purpose government agency and no other public organization, look what we achieve:

1. We have captured all of the intergovernmentally linked service delivery networks.

2. We have encompassed the "federations" that "hold" the bundles of programs together.

3. We have captured roughly 80 percent of the non-defense public sector spending. We have also captured 70 percent of the public employees.

Networks and the Primacy of Programs

By focusing on the general-purpose government agency we can identify three entities which, from the point of view of why and how power sharing occurs, are vital to the question of institutional design. We will look at programs (interorganizational networks), tools (or financial incentives), and federations.

In that part of the public sector where organizations deliver services to clients, where delivery agents are separated from the funds grantor because they are at a different level of government, the program reigns supreme. The granting of funds for a program in health, welfare, transportation, energy, or housing acts as a chain, holding an enormous number of individual actors and organizations together—from the granting authority in Washington to the 50 states, to thousands of localities where the services are delivered.

When Congress makes a law and it is signed by the President, policy has been adopted which gives either existing public organizations or newly created ones the responsibility for turning the policy into programs, which will be the means by which these public organizations will deliver services to people. From the perspective of the officials in Washington, there is no one in their organization who can deliver the services. The management control system (in some cases) as well as the delivery organizations are the "property" of and responsible to the state and local governments. In the division of functions that has accompanied the growth of the "contract state" which has developed in the last 20 or so years, agencies of the federal government have become the organizations that provide money and write rules, regulations, and guidelines which govern its use in programs. These programs, largely designed in Washington, are administered by a host of semiautonomous and geographically dispersed organizations which are creatures of the state and local governments.

Aside from the fact that these program-centered delivery systems are loosely linked (Weick 1976), what makes them distinct as organizational units? First, there is not one organization involved in their administration; there are literally thousands, joined by little more than a set of financial incentives and the danger of federal takeover if the services are not provided. However, dependence is reciprocal, and so the social choice process linking these organizations is not hierarchy, but bargaining (Bish 1971; Dahl and Lindblom 1953).

Second, the grant money goes to fund programs, not just organizations. The state and local agencies which receive the grant money, on the other hand, often use the money to pay private or nonprofit organizations to help in the provision of these public services. In vocational education, for example, the Bureau of Adult and Occupational Education gives grants to state and local vocational institutes to provide training in occupational skills. These state and local institutes may then work out arrangements with private companies or nonprofit organizations, such as Goodwill Industries, to help train individuals for the world of work. If one wants to understand the complexity of public service delivery, multiply the above example first by 50 and then by several thousand. Given the number of organizations engaged in the bargaining process, the control problems in a semiautonomous interorganizational policy network are massive. However, programs to train workers are operated in every state and locality, and the people they train often find employment after their training.

How does one locate the boundaries of a community of interest? Donald Campbell (1958) has proposed "common fate" as one way to bound social aggregates like networks. Here the test is "Do objects move together?" The community of interest in regard to public decision making may well fail this test. In any given policy network there may be federal, state, local, regional and substate authorities. In addition there may be handicapped, aged, blacks, chicanos, and elderly who claim standing and who are often granted it in public policy decision making. Clearly "common fate" does not bind these diverse groups.

Some have suggested a broad functional focus like health, welfare, or education. I've rejected this approach because health or welfare are aggregated concepts. The networks I've studied (housing finance and vocational education) are organized around programs which are specifically defined in law. There is no network for welfare, housing, or health; these are abstractions. In any given area, policy is the sum of dozens of specific programs that are defined in specific terms in statutes and agency regulation. "Health policy is the sum of hospital construction, cancer research, medical school education, drug licensing, communicable disease control and dozens of other specific programs" (Fritschler and Ross 1980, 74). For these reasons I have found it useful to focus on the reward structure that surrounds the policy network.

The Reward Structure of the Policy Network

Networks are the central organizing concept in this approach, and each network has empirical referents which can be at least partially mapped. The problem with mapping is that while you know who is involved in a given program area at one time, you don't know why.

To answer the question of why a certain network exists, I start by looking at the reward structure that surrounds the policy network. At the core of every program there is a fiscal spine which flows from the federal treasury to all those who benefit directly or indirectly. Les Salamon (1981) has proposed that we reorient research on public organizations and public management away from the behavior of individuals, organizations, and institutions to the "tools" of government management.[3] A descriptive typology of tools would at a minimum include formula grants, categorical grants, regulations, loan guaranties, insurance, subsidies, and tax incentives.

> The central premise. . .is that different tools of government action have their own distinctive dynamics, their own "political economies," that affect the content of government action. This is so for much the same reasons that particular agencies and bureaus are considered to have their own personalities and styles—because each instrument carries with it a substantial amount of "baggage" in the form of its own characteristic implementing institutions, standard operating procedures, types of expertise and professional cadre, products, degree of visibility, enactment and review processes, and relationships with other societal forces (Salamon 1981, 264).

The advantage of bringing tools together with networks is to get two levels of analysis—the collective choice level and the operational level. The collective choice level is brought out in the examination of the type of tool chosen to structure a program. The tool connects the network to the social choice mechanism of the state. Thus this level of analysis will include the choice of the terms and conditions of rules that bound the play of the game. The operational level is that of the various networks. This focuses on the play of the game in relation to the rules.

The tools of public policy are the product of the processes set in motion by the theory of plural elitism. These processes then bound and shape organizational activity in the public sector and allow us to understand its rationale.

One last dimension of public organization activity is its normative structure. This is the affective dimension of policy making which Vickers (1965) terms "appreciation." The normative structure gives meaning to the action of the members of the network and the use to which the tools are put. If, for instance, the social services complex defines clients as incapable of making choices, this justifies the use of professional social workers to mediate between the client and the state by using in-kind transfer programs (food stamps) rather than cash transfers. Often what is billed as "bureaucratic pathology" may be due to the normative structure surrounding a professional or programmatic network. Officials in the former Department of Health, Education and Welfare released data which showed that the distribution of income in this country had not changed in 20 years and used this to call for more redistributive measures. In their analysis they failed to include the transfer payments to poor people that they themselves administer.[4]

Hierarchical Overlay: Federations

Earlier in this paper I advocated concentrating research on what Backoff (1980) calls "general-purpose government agencies." These include health departments, school districts, state departments of human services and those cabinet-level departments in Washington which deal with domestic policy and operate, through their bureaus, intergovernmental programs. The reason for my approach is to capture the linkage between programs and federations. I shall use the term "federation" to mean public organizations like bureaus and departments which are "general-purpose government agencies."

Studying public organizations is somewhat different from studying a single agency or firm. Many public organizations at the highest level resemble holding companies, more than the goal-seeking or profit-maximizing firms which constitute the popular notion of organizations. Large governmental departments perform a host of more or less related functions.

> Thrown together by statute or executive order they can only take on something like a federated pattern of authority. The relationships are tenuous at best between such disparate units within the United States Department of Agriculture as the Food and Nutrition Service, which administered the food stamp program, and the Cooperative State Research Service, which funds experimental stations (Wamsley and Zald 1973, 65)

These kinds of organizations are really loose federations with no cohesive purpose, representing a conglomeration of functions. We can define a federative organization as one of those larger government organizations—departments and sometimes bureaus or even offices—which are collections of unitary organizations lacking any tangible, single, overall, manifest goal with operational meaning (Simon, Smithburg, and Thompson 1950, 270). By operational meaning we refer to a causal connection between the manifest goal of the organization (picking up the garbage) and the ability of the organization to achieve that goal. It becomes obvious that the more one aggregates goals of unitary organizations the smaller chance of integrating these manifest goals in any meaningful sense at the level of the federative organization.

When Gulick (1937) developed the rationale for "holding company" cabinet-level departments, he was under no illusion that they would have a cohesive purpose. They were to be held together with budgetary, accounting, and management control devices as are multi-product conglomerates in the private sector. What he and other designers of our federal structure did not foresee was the great increase in policy activity by Congress and a succession of presidents over the last 40 years. This led to galloping differentiation and specialization at the bureau level. Bureaus now may administer clusters of programs. Each program, for those who administer it, becomes the most important goal of the agency.

The great increase in policy activity that led to increasing differentiation and specialization at the federal level also had the same effect at the state and local level, as the federal government relied on city and state, as well as private and nonprofit agencies, to actually provide the services that the federal government was paying for. With the fragmentation at the local level and with the admixture of third party nonprofit and private firms, the fundamental reality for those who administered the program was the program itself, not the level of government or the agency that had hired them to do it. As King notes:

> The term bureaucracy ". . .implies the existence or large numbers of persons arranged in ordered hierarchies and dealing with the problems of governing in a rational, highly routinized way. On this basis, the term bureaucracy as a description of the federal civil service in Washington ought. . .to be abandoned forthwith. Washington civil servants may be arranged more or less in ordered hierarchies. But they are not routine (or even nonroutine) administrators; they are, in Heclo's phase,"policy professionals." They do not administer programs themselves, but at best supervise the administration of programs by others. They are charter members of the issue networks, whose methods are anything but ordered and routinized" (King 1978, 379-380).

These issue networks exist in Washington because problems overlap or programs require clearances and also because of goals such as affirmative action or environmental regulation that necessarily encompass numerous agencies' activities. Thus parts of other agencies get involved.

Many federal programs require states, localities, nonprofit agencies, and private firms to provide the services that the agency in Washington is paying for. Each of these organizations has a set of interests in addition to the federal program they partially administer. We can conclude that the program, not the bureau, agency, or department, is the basic building block for understanding public organizations. This unit, the program, is interorganizational in nature; it is a collection of people in parts of literally thousands of agencies and firms at three or more levels of government and in the private sector as well.

In Washington these programs connect not with the head of a cabinet department, but with many people—a bureau chief, program head, chairman of one or more subcommittees of Congress, and one or more interest groups. (One interest group may be composed of officials who administer the program.)

The above elements constitute what has become known as the ubiquitous "iron triangle." The tensile strength of the triangle varies much more than popular opinion would have us believe. While the relationship posited by the iron triangle is almost always present, the strength of the relationship and the degree to which it is permeable by outside interests varies greatly. Sometimes a concerted effort is made to bring in outsiders to strengthen the claims of a given policy network, as we saw in the Ohio Housing Finance Agency example.

The "federations," on the other hand, are directly linked, through cabinet secretaries and their staffs, to the President and to other Executive-Office-of-the-President officials. Cabinet-level departments are implementors of economic management policy of the government. Administrative control processes of budgets, personnel requirements, reporting arrangements, and the like hold the programs in their departments together. This holding together in turn allows for management of the economy in regard to employment, inflation, and level of defense expenditures.

Although most policy domains are thick with programs, there are specific organizations at each level of government which attempt to hold them together. In Washington there is a Department of Education; each state in turn has a counterpart department of education; at the programmatic level, the school district serves as the comprehensive organization whose superintendent deals with the state and federal counterpart organizations. The U.S. Department of Education, The state department of Education and local school districts are all examples of "federative organizations."

Federative organizations are most important at a single level of government. They attempt to hold related programs together at that level and force what coordination there is to occur. But when viewed from the perspective of an intergovernmental service delivery system, the program is primary. The linkage between a single program at different levels of government is much stronger than the linkage among different programs at the same level of government.

The policy networks which are held in place by "federations," much as Sanford (1967) described in his "picket fence federalism" metaphor, get to the heart of one of the major differences between public and private organizations. In the public sector the basic unit of analysis is interorganizational. If we know anything about public organizations it is that they are in general more open to their environment than the typical private firm and thus less able to buffer external influences. The reason for this is not only the need for constituency support for increased budgetary allocations, but is also due to nature of the "program," which includes elements of the public, private, and nonprofit sectors.

A curious inversion has occurred. An interorganizational unit is the building block for the largest class of public organizations. This integration of the federation and the program or policy network allows us to understand and reinterpret findings that utilized a focal public organization as the unit of analysis. For example, since the late 1950's, the Advisory Commission on Intergovernmental Relations has been surveying public officials in state and cities concerning with whom they most identify themselves—their state government or their federal counterparts. Consistently, officials have answered that they identify themselves with their federal counterparts more than with the level of government which employed them (Wright 1978). This has been widely cited as an example of a growing "federalization" of the intergovernmental system.

The problem with this interpretation is that the unit of analysis is wrong. It is not "states versus fed"; rather it is intergovernmentally implemented programs versus level of government. Kaufman (1981) finds the same problem at the federal level among bureau chiefs and departmental secretaries and assistant secretaries. The problem is one of applying a unit of analysis (the level of government and by extension the federation) that does not correspond to a loosely linked, yet powerful group of functionally oriented interorganizational policy networks that have greater goal coherence and unit strength than the legislatively mandated bureaucratic edifices that house them.

Conclusion

The convention in the social sciences is to quickly state your thesis and in a "just the facts" fashion set to work testing it. The reason that this convention has been honored in the breach is that the institutional dimensions of power sharing are not neat. They cannot be reduced to three hypotheses. There are multiple and overlapping dimensions to power sharing, and what I have tried to do in this paper is to lay out complex and multiple dimensions as best I could and view them in the framework of a theory of politics—plural elitism.

In addition I have tried to show the relationship between institutional design features of the United States government and the behavioral pattern of segmented policy making that it creates. I have also tried to show how power sharing is necessitated by the tension between the organizational and program rationales that undergird public organizational behavior. And while these dimensions and their implications aren't tidy, they are vitally important for those who wish to understand the system of shared power that has evolved in the United States.

The past 20 years have been a difficult time for those who crave order and stability. We have seen conflict, uncertainty, and disorder. The implications of this are still being felt. One thing is certain—the processes of policy making and planning are far more difficult now than they have been in the past. There are two reasons. First, many more groups claim and are granted standing than in the past. Second, the decision rules by which interests are aggregated have changed and continue to change.

The argument that I have made proceeds from the premise that to be more effective policy makers in shared-power situations, we must understand what has happened. Then we must develop a theoretical underpinning that will allow us to deal more effectively with the reality of shared power.

Footnotes

1. This is being rectified as a number of scholars have recently published important works on the changing nature of interest groups. Hayes (1981), Moe (1980), Walker (1983a) (1983b), Gais, Peterson and Walker (1984), Salisbury (1984), McFarland (1979), and Milward and Francisco (1983) have all attempted to refine interest group theory in light of the changes of the last 20 years.

2. All members of the Commission were not in favor of the HFA legislation and among those who did favor it, degree of commitment varied greatly. The staff and Chairman Huston spent a major part of their efforts trying to hold the Commission solidly behind the legislation.

3. A somewhat similar approach has been proposed by Regine Herzlinger and Nancy Kane (1979). While not organizationally oriented, a major scholarly work undergirding this approach is Frederick C. Mosher (1980). This approach was first suggested by Robert A. Dahl and Charles E. Lindblom (1953) when they urged political scientists to focus on social choice techniques as a way of reorienting our theories of politics. Lindblom (1977) resurrected this earlier concern in *Politics and Markets*. The Salamon-Mosher stream of research and the Dahl and Lindblom approach come together in Eugene B. McGregor, Jr. (1981) "Administration's Many Instruments: Mining, Refining, and Applying Charles Lindblom' s Politics and Markets."

4. Likewise for two decades the U.S. Forest Service ignored the mounting evidence that certain forest fires were beneficial and should be allowed to burn themselves out. The evidence was at variance with the normative structure of the Forest Service. Hoover' s FBI in viewing most civil rights workers as communists is another example of the bias that normative structure builds into organizational and interorganizational decision making.

References

Backoff, R. 1980. "Power configurations, political processes, and strategic management in local government agencies." Paper presented at the 12th Annual Meeting of the American Institute for Decision Sciences, November, Las Vegas.

Bernstein, M. 1955. *Regulating government by independent commission.* Princeton, N.J.: Princeton University Press.

Bish, R.L. 1971. *The public economy of metropolitan areas.* Chicago: Markham.

Campbell, D.T. 1958. Common fate, similarity and other indices of the status of aggregates of persons as social entities. *Behavioral Science* 3(1): 18-20.

Cater, D. 1964. *Power in Washington. New York: Random House.*

Cobb, R.W., J.K. Ross, and M.H. Ross. 1976. Agenda building as a comparative political process. *American Political Science Review* 70(1): 126-138.

Dahl, R.A. and C.E. Lindblom. 1953. *Politics, economics and welfare.* New York: Harper & Row.

Dunshire, A. 1981. Review of Marshall W. Meyer's *Change in public bureaucracies. Journal of Public Policy* 1(1):147-148.

Edelman, M. 1964. *The symbolic uses of politics.* Urbana, Ill: University of Illinois Press.

Farkas, S. 1971. *Urban lobbying. New York: New York University Press.*

Fiorina, M. 1977. *Congress: Keystone of the Washington establishment.* New Haven: Yale University Press.

Flinn, T.A. 1973. "State governments and housing." In *National housing policy study papers.* U.S. Department Of Housing and Urban Development.

Fritschler, A. Lee and B.H. Ross. 1980. *Business regulation and government decision making.* Cambridge Mass: Winthrop.

Gais, T.L., M.A. Peterson and J.L. Walker. 1984. Interest groups, iron triangles and representative institutions in American national government. *British Journal of Political Science,* forthcoming.

Ginzburg, E. and G. Vojta. 1981. The service sector of the U.S. economy. *Scientific American* 244:48-55.

Grodzins, M. 1966. *The American system.* Chicago: Rand McNally.

Gulick, L. 1937. "Notes on the theory of organization." *Papers on the science of administration* edited by L. Gulick and L. Urwick. New York: Institute of Public Administration, 3-45.

Hayes, M.T. 1981. *Lobbyists and legislators.* New Brunswick: Rutgers University Press.

Heclo, H. 1978. "Issue networks and the executive branch." In *The new American political system*, edited by A. King, 87-124. Washington, D.C.: American Enterprise Institute.

Herzlinger, R. and N. Kane. 1979. *A managerial analysis of federal income redistribution mechanisms: The government as factory, insurance company and bank.* Cambridge, Mass: Ballinger.

Hjern, B. and D. Porter. 1981. "Implementation structures: a new unit of administrative analysis." Paper presented at the International Conference on the Analysis of Intergovernmental and Interorganizational Arrangements in Public Administration, Indiana University, Bloomington, Indiana, May 11-14.

Huntington, S.P. 1981. *American politics: The promise of disharmony.* Cambridge, MA: The Belknap Press of Harvard University Press.

Kaufman, H. 1981. *The administrative behavior of federal bureau chiefs.* Washington, D.C.: The Brookings Institution.

King, A. 1978. "The American polity in the late 1970's: building coalitions in the sand." In *The new American political system*, edited by A. King, 371-395. Washington, D.C.: American Enterprise Institute.

Lindblom, C.E. 1977. *Politics and markets.* New York:Basic Books.

Lowi, T.J. 1964. "American business, public policy, case studies and political theory." In *World Politics* 16.

_____. 1979. *The end of liberalism*, Second Edition. New York: W.W. Norton.

McConnell, G. 1966. *Private power and American democracy*. New York: Knopf.

McFarland, A.S. 1979. "Recent social movements and theories of Power in America." Paper presented at the American Political Science Association Meeting, Washington, August 31-September 3.

McGregor, E.B, Jr. 1981. Administration's many instruments. *Administration and Society* 13(3): 347-375.

Milward, H.B. and R.A. Francisco. 1983. Subsystem politics and corporatism in the United States. *Policy and Politics* 11(3): 273-293.

Moe, T.M. 1980. *The organization of interests*. Chicago: University of Chicago Press.

Mosher, F.C. 1980. The changing responsibilities and tactics of the federal government. *Public Administration Review* 40(6): 541-548.

Ohio Department of Economic and Community Development. 1973. Minutes of the Housing Finance Agency Conference, April 12.

_____. 1973. Internal Memo "How states sold their state housing finance agency." February 23.

_____. 1973. Memo from Bill Hale, Chief of Bureau of Research and Analysis, to Troy Grisgby, Deputy Director DECD. January 23.

_____. 1973. Memo to Jack Hansen. January 6.

_____. Internal Memo. November 21, 1972.

_____. 1972. Legislative Report Number 2: Financial and Technical Assistance and Legislation. February.

Ohio Department of Urban Affairs. 1971. Overview of Ohio's Housing Problem. August.

_____. 1971. Strategy in Formulating A State Housing Program. August.

Olson, M. Jr. 1965. *The logic of collective action*. Cambridge: Harvard University Press.

Salamon, L.M. 1981. Rethinking public management: third party government and the changing forms of government action. *Public Policy* 20(3): 255-275.

Salisbury, R.H. 1984. "Interest representation: the dominance of institutions." *American Political Science Review* 78(1): 64-76.

Sanford, T. 1967. *Storm over the states*. New York: McGraw Hill.

Schattschneider, E.E. 1960. *The semisovereign people*. New York: Holt, Reinhart and Winston.

Simon, H.D., D.W. Smithburg, and V. Thompson. 1950. *Public Administration*. New York: Alfred A. Knopf.

Vickers, G. 1965. *The art of judgment*, London: Methuen.

Walker, J.L. 1983a. "The mobilization of political interests." Paper presented at the American Political Science Association Meeting, Chicago, September 1-4.

_____. 1983b. The origins and maintenance of interest groups in america. *The American Political Science Review* 77(2): 390-406.

Wamsley, G.L. and M.N. Zald. 1973. *The political economy of public organizations.* Lexington, Mass: Lexington Books.

Weick, K.E. 1976. Educational organizations as loosely coupled systems. *Administrative Science Quarterly* 32(2): 1-19.

Wright, D.S. 1978. *Understanding intergovernmental relations.* North Scituate, Mass: Duxbury.

CHAPTER 4

Policy Coordination and Interorganizational Relations:

Some Guidelines for Sharing Power[1]

David A. Whetten and Barry Bozeman

Introduction

Fragmentation is an omnipresent characteristic of American policy making; it is as common in one level of government as another, in one branch as another, in one policy domain as another. As Gawthrop (1971, 39) notes, "public policy decisions... reflect the basic characteristics of the administrative structures in which they are formed—they are disjointed fragmentary agreements upheld tenuously by temporary coalitions." Partly as a result of fragmentation, policy making in the United States is generally an exercise in the sharing of power (Lindblom 1968).

In large measure fragmentation is an outgrowth of the U.S. Constitution and the legal context of American policy making. The constitutional principle of separation of powers among the three branches has far-reaching effects, especially on the "fourth branch," the public bureaucracy. Public agencies are directed by executive superiors, dependent on legislators for their resources, and subject to the rules, interpretations and injunctions of the judiciary. The constitutional principle of federalism serves to further fragment political authority in the United States (Rearan 1972). The U.S. Constitution specifies and limits the prerogatives of state and federal government with the result that "lines of control are blurred, organizational patterns are diverse, and in general unity is absent" (Woll 1977, 64).

The Constitution is not, of course, the only source of fragmentation in public policy making, and, furthermore, problems in the coordination and sharing of political power are not restricted to interactions among government agencies. Relations between public and private sector organizations are often crucial determinants of policy effectiveness.

In a fragmented policy system little can be achieved by solitary actors and, thus, virtually every major policy initiative becomes a "joint venture." The purpose of this paper is to suggest some guidelines for enhancing policy coordination among policy actors sharing power. The guidelines presented here are chiefly derived from organization theory, particularly interorganization theory, and they are broad in scope.

Before reviewing the interorganizational relations literature and distilling guidelines for policy coordination, we discuss below some of the more common barriers to policy coordination for various categories of policy making interdependence.

Barriers to Policy Coordination

Many of the barriers to policy coordination are best understood in the context of the particular policies and actors in question. Our focus here, however, is on policy coordination barriers which are, at least in some respects, generic problems. The barriers we discuss here are not restricted to any particular policy domain or combination of policy actors. These barriers are pervasive and can be viewed as fundamental problems in policy coordination.

Resource Barriers

Large, complex organizations, in both the public and private sectors, have similar underlying motives for resource acquisition. Typically, organizations seek to preserve autonomy in the use of resources, maintain control of their deployment, and increase the likelihood of sustained, stable growth (Bozeman and Straussman 1983).

To the extent that shared power is perceived as reinforcing these objectives, resource processes are unlikely to prove a major impediment to policy coordination. However, the sharing of power is rarely inconsequential in respect to organizations' resource goals, and since sharing is likely to have uneven consequences for organizations, resource disputes of various types comprise a major class of policy coordination barriers.

1. **Competition for budget allocations and other funding sources.** The political dynamics of budgetary processes are by now well understood (viz., Wildavsky 1964). Budgetary processes are often conflictual (Gist 1982), and sometimes adversarial. According to Niskanen (1979, 173), "competition among bureaus is the natural condition of a bureaucracy." While there is reason to believe that policy actors' competition for budget shares may have some salubrious effects (Niskanen 1971; Downs 1967), there is ample evidence that budgetary struggles can impede policy coordination efforts. Organizations which are partners in policy delivery, but competitors for budget allocations, have strong disincentives for policy coordination and, in particular, are prone to withhold information from one another (Rossi and Gilmartin 1981).

2. **Resistance to negative growth coordination.** The "natural" competitiveness of policy actors is accentuated during periods of decline (Bozeman and Slusher 1978). Policy coordination is difficult to achieve under conditions of zero or negative

growth and particularly when the policy to be coordinated is itself concerned with the means of managing decline (Whetten 1980; Bozeman and Straussman 1982) or termination (Behn 1978; Bardach 1976; Brewer 1978). Policy coordination problems in such circumstances can be explained in part by straightforward self-interest, but it is also likely that the coordination of policy cutbacks is intrinsically more complicated because of the "paradox of irreducible wholes" (Levine 1979), which suggests that the web of interdependencies that develops among public programs introduces complexities not present when the programs are created.

3. Pluralism in the budgetary processes. The budgetary processes of the federal and state governments are themselves uncoordinated and fragmented. There are multiple actors playing distinctive roles (Fenno 1966; Davis and Ripley 1967; Kamlet and Mowery 1980) and they often find themselves at loggerheads. Perhaps the most compelling case of fragmentation is in the U.S. Congress, which has yet to find an effective means of dealing with backdoor spending and various off-budget expenditures (Schick 1980). The pluralism of the budgetary process serves as a barrier to policy coordination in two major respects. At the policy formulation stage, pluralism increases the likelihood of built-in contradictions in policy because so many different actors in the budget process will succeed in putting their stamp on budget outcomes. Budgetary pluralism can also undermine accountability and policy control because policy actors are aware that any of several potential budget patrons can be cultivated and, thus, policy actors are not completely dependent on the good will of a single benefactor. The latter principle can also be extended to private sector policy actors who have many sources for government contracts.

4. Diversion of resources for side-payments. We assume, with Downs (1977, 89), that "every official acts at least partly in his own self-interest, and some officials are motivated solely by their own self-interest." Since the self-interest of officials is not always at odds with the objectives of policies this does not necessarily pose a problem. However, there is some theoretical reason to believe that side-payments (Cyert and March 1963, 29) play an especially large role in public programs and that the self-interest of public officials is typically less congruent with organizational interests than is the case with business firms. According to property rights theorists in economics, the most important distinction between private and government organizations lies in the in ability to transfer the rights of ownership in government organizations (Alchian 1973; Alchian and Demsetz 1972; DeAlessio 1981). Since there are no shares of government stock, the individual cannot alter his "portfolio" of investments in government programs and cannot exchange ownership rights. In private firms, entrepreneurs and wealth-sharing managers exert pressure for the combination of economic input that maximizes productivity. In government, managerial activity centers around diverse rationales (Shelton 1967; Clarkson 1980), particularly side-payments related to political power, budget expansion, and increments in personnel. Davies (1981, 115) observes that "lacking binding market constraints...a public manager will have greater opportunity to increase his well-being at the expense of owner's (i.e., taxpayer's) wealth because it is relatively less costly to do so." If the property rights hypothesis is valid, and there is some empirical evidence which is supportive (Clarkson 1972; Davies 1977; Meyer 1975), the implications for breakdowns in policy coordination are serious.

Mission Barriers
One reason for the failure of policy coordination is that the missions of policy actors are not in accord. Organizations may be brought together (either by mandate or by mistake) for concerted action in pursuit of a given objective even though their missions are not compatible. However, almost inevitably, such incompatibility serves to frustrate any common purpose.

   1. Conflicting or ambiguous missions. Studies of policy implementation often point to unclear or conflicting goals and missions as a major impediment to policy effectiveness (Bardach 1977; Murphy 1971; Smith 1973). Ambiguity can be explained in part by the need to defer specificity in order to mobilize the political support of diverse groups (Lerner and Wanat 1983). Even when it is possible to resolve ambiguity, the resolution sometimes only underscores the incompatibility of interests of policy actors.

   2. Differences in public/private missions. Public and private organizations frequently find points of common interest, and a sense of shared mission often serves as a catalyst for public-private partnerships. However, there is usually a point at which public and private missions begin to diverge and that point begins where the joint effort is no longer in the economic self-interest of the firm. Policies which rely heavily on the goodwill of private sector policy actors (rather than their desire for tax incentives, favorable publicity, or direct profits) are usually ill fated. Private firms, like public agencies, can often be induced to serve the public interest, but not when the public interest is at odds with the firm's private interest. In public-private partnerships, policy coordination often breaks down when differences in mission are ignored. As Bower (1977, 132) points out, there are important differences in the purpose of the public and private sectors: "What does purpose mean in the public sector? As in the private sector, the administration motive is self-interest; but the stated organizational motive is not....Though it may motivate administrative success, self-interest is venal."

   3. Differences in public/private interdependence. Related to the above point, is the fact that the nature of interdependence of public agencies is often fundamentally different than that of private agencies (Bozeman 1981). The major difference is the competitive basis of economic activity versus the political authority basis of government activity (Lindblom 1977). We can illustrate this point with reference to Vincent and Elinor Ostrom's (1965) public industry concept. Just as private firms (say, the Zenith Corporation) may be thought of as a part of a larger industry (say, the electronics industry), public agencies may be thought of as part of a broader public industry. In the case of the public agency, its mission and goals are (at least theoretically) subservient to those of the public industry. For example, it is not acceptable for the U.S. Patent Office to attain its self-interest goals (e.g., increased budgets, operational efficiencies) if it is clear that in doing so it is inhibiting the broader public industry goal of increasing the rate, effectiveness and utilization of invention. By contrast, Zenith Corporation does not necessarily violate the public interest in pursuing its self-interest goals at the expense of the electronics industry. Indeed, in a competitive market the success of Zenith might be at the expense of less efficient firms and, thus, a virtue from the standpoint of market theory.

Political Barriers

A great many of the barriers to policy coordination could be aptly termed "political," but the usage here is more narrow and intended to focus on the electoral and partisan aspects of political. There are three political struggles which are especially likely to influence attempts to coordinate policy: clashes of political leadership, conflict between political executives and career bureaucrats, and partisanship in the evaluation of programs.

   1. Diverse political leadership/allegiance. Even in those instances where there is no true two-party competition, the American political system is fractionated by rivalry and party factions (Casstevens and Press 1969). Public policies often provide the battle ground upon which partisan combat transpires. Sometimes the struggle is between a statehouse controlled by one party and a federal executive controlled by another, sometimes it is between state legislatures with different political allegiances. Partisan political differences may revolve around parties, party factions, or individual political leaders. But whatever the source of such political conflict, there is usually some potential for the breakdown of cooperation and, ultimately, policy coordination. Generally, power is shared more easily when there is common political alliance and shared leadership (Warwick 1975; Wilson 1973).

   2. Political executive/bureaucracy cleavages. There are two very different stereotypes of the public manager and each has some validity. There is the "invisible bureaucrat" buried deep in the bowels of bureaucracy and making seemingly anonymous decisions. But there is also the "life in a goldfish bowl" stereotype which envisions the public manager as constantly under the watchful eye of the media, constituents, and political superiors. The first stereotype often fits the lower-and mid-level career bureaucrat whereas the latter is a suitable description of the political executives (Blumenthal 1979; Rumsfeld 1979; Dunlop 1980). Cleavages between political executives and career bureaucrats are partly responsible for some of the more infamous breakdowns in policy coordination (e.g., Allison 1971; Heclo and Salamon 1981). In assessing the qualities most needed by political executives and senior-level bureaucrats Kaufman (1981) places patience and self control near the top; the ability of career bureaucrats (whether motivated by sense of mission or by venality) to thwart centralized policy leadership is one reason those two qualities are necessary.

One reason for the power of career bureaucrats is that they can play a waiting game. Political executives' tenure is relatively brief and the turnover among political executives can serve as a barrier to policy coordination. Since the average tenure of political executives is only about two years (Stanley et al. 1967), there is often a temptation to "wait for a better deal" or simply outlast the political executive. There is less incentive to share power when the other player will soon be out of the game. When the brief tenure of political executives is considered in connection with the brevity of the "issue attention cycle" (Downs 1972), one sees that opportunities to frustrate policy coordination are usually available.

3. **Evaluation politics.** Even summative evaluation (Scriven 1967) can affect policy coordination. If there is a perception that evaluation will be used to achieve partisan advantage, policy actors may view policy coordination as a noose tightening around their necks (Glaser and Taylor 1973). This is especially likely to be the case in those instances where evaluations are easily manipulated and highly visible (Banner et al. 1975).

Legal Barriers

One of the chief legal/constitutional barriers to policy coordination has been discussed above—the fragmentation resulting from federalism and separation of powers. Constitutional barriers are not viewed as directly manipulable (though some steps can be taken to reduce the potential for inhibiting political coordination).

1. **Legal constraints on coordinated policy actions.** Policies involving public-private partnerships are often limited by legal constraints imposed on one or another partner. One way to reduce the impact of such constraints is to create institutions, such as government-sponsored enterprises or government corporations which are quasi-public (Walsh 1980). In the past decade there has been a significant proliferation of such hybrid organizations (Finney 1978). At the same time, there has been an accompanying trend which has been referred to as "sector blurring": public organizations are increasingly using techniques and approaches developed in the private sector, and private organizations are increasingly penetrated by government (Bozeman 1984). Sometimes, however, specific legal constraints serve as barriers to policy coordination among quasi-public policy actors (Congressional Budget Office 1984; U.S. General Accounting Office 1989). Further, Smith (1983) argues that sector blurring and the breakdown of the traditional roles of public and private sector have created confusion and disarray. Rather than promoting shared power and responsibility, the trend has instead caused avoidance of responsibility for public problems.

2. **Constitutionally based fragmentation.** This barrier to policy coordination is best viewed as a constant or as a cardinal rule. The question then becomes "is it possible to exploit the advantages of legal fragmentation while minimizing the cost incurred in uncoordinated policy making and implementation?" As mentioned previously, constitutionally based fragmentation introduces healthy elements of

pluralism and competition, as well as checks and balances. But these are not benefits valued without limit.

Constituency Barriers

Some of the more important barriers to policy coordination revolve around constituencies—their development, uses, disparate interests, and parochial influences. The pluralism of U.S. policy-making processes magnifies the importance of constituencies by providing multiple access and diverse opportunities for influence or obstruction.

1. Constituency conflict. There are several varieties of constituency conflict which can impede policy coordination. "Internal constituency conflict" occurs when a single policy actor is seeking to serve two or more incompatible constituencies. This is especially likely to occur when an agency's (or other policy actor's) basis of support is built on a fragile coalition of interests, none of which is ascendant, (Sabatier and Mazmanian 1979). The effort to simultaneously serve contradictory interests fragments the directions of policy and impedes coordination. In such cases the likely outcome is a compromise based on the relative strengths of the competing interests. In some cases such equitable solutions serve political effectiveness, but rarely do they serve policy coordination.

In the case of "constituency based inter-organizational conflict," two or more policy actors with different and incompatible constituencies are at odds with one another. Typically such policy actors are very poor candidates for sharing power' but, nevertheless, the vagaries of public policy sometimes result in the linkage of natural rivals. In such cases policy coordination is virtually unachievable unless there is a substantial disparity in the resources or dependencies of the policy actors.

2. Bureaucratic imperialism. One type of constituency conflict is sufficiently different and important to require separate treatment. "Competition for constituency" is common among policy actors with similar jurisdiction and responsibility and often leads to bureaucratic imperialism (Holden 1966). Policy actors' conflicts over jurisdiction have served as the grist for many classic political science studies (Maass 1951; Wengert 1955) but have generally had disastrous effects on policy coordination. As Rourke (1969) notes, bureaucratic imperialism has sometimes had damaging effects on the "victorious" agencies as well, at least in those instances where the missions of the agencies were undermined or where the expansion led to the linking of constituencies with inimical interests.

3. Cooptation. As Huntington's (1952) study illustrates, agencies' relations with interest groups sometimes evolve from regulation to protection. This is especially likely when the agency is dependent on the interest group for political support (Selznick 1949; Jacob 1972). In the most extreme case, the policy actor becomes an institutionalized advocate for the dominant interest group and a predictable opponent of any policy that runs counter to the interest of the group to which it is critically linked. This cooptation can serve as a serious barrier to policy coordination when the sharing of power requires a more balanced view of the parties affected (Sosin 1981).

Bureaucratic Barriers

A number of barriers to policy coordination are grouped together here; their point of commonality is that they are rooted in one or another dysfunctional form of bureaucratic behavior. Bureaucratic barriers are not restricted to any one type of policy actor. They can plague legislators, even the judiciary, just as well as executive agencies. Nor are they sole province of the public sector.

1. **Bureaupathology.** Bureaucracy is a persistent and enduring social invention and, according to some observers (Goodsell 1983; Waldo 1980), a vital element of civilization. It entails a number of characteristics (such as neutral competence, reliance on records, and routinization of activity) which are cornerstones of modern governance. But taken to extremes, the very qualities of bureaucracy which are responsible for its efficiency and rationality can result in "bureaupathological" behavior. Thompson (1964, 152) notes that "(w)ithin bureaucracy we often find excessive aloofness, ritualistic attachment to routines and procedures and resistance to change," in effect, exaggerations of the characteristic qualities of bureaucracy. A number of explanations have been provided for such bureaupathological symptoms as excessive red tape, hoarding of authority, and overly rigid adherence to rules. But whether the explanation lies in goal ambiguity (Buchanan 1974), perceptions of reward (Rainey 1983) or individuals' insecurity (Thompson 1964) bureaupathological behavior is often a threat to policy coordination.

2. **Goal Displacement.** We have already suggested that the objectives of public policy may be set aside in pursuit of self-interest (see the discussion of side-payments), but goals may be displaced as a result of organizational drift (Lodahl and Mitchell 1980). This may pose no problem if the movement is in the direction of valued but not yet formalized objectives. Another reason for goal displacement is that actors often find it much easier to agree on means than ends (Lindblom 1959) and, thus, the ends—the policy outputs—are displaced in favor of policy inputs. Goals may be displaced because they are perceived as too difficult or too damaging to the organization. Thus, social services programs ignore the neediest clients, the ones that are abjectly poor or severely handicapped, in favor of clients which are less needy and more likely to provide the "successes" needed for future funding increments (Anderson and Ball 1978).

3. **Separation of knowledge and authority.** Often the knowledge required for effective policy coordination is possessed by individuals in the lower echelons of the authority hierarchy. If this knowledge is not tapped in the design and execution of policies, they are more likely to fail and are more difficult to coordinate. Kogod and Caufield (1982, 983) suggest that this problem may be especially acute in the public sector; "In the public sector, because of specialization and policy interests rather than managerial or operating interests, decisions tend to rise several levels above where the data are..." The rapid turnover of political executives often serves to exacerbate the problem.

4. Dysfunctional communications systems. Patently, effective communication is an indispensable requirement for policy coordination. Among some of the better known crises that might have been averted with more effective communication systems are the Cuban missile crisis, the Watergate scandal, the attack on Pearl Harbor, and the swine flu vaccination fiasco. The policy implementation literature is strewn with evidence of the damage that can be wrought by ineffective communication systems (Bardach 1977; Mazmanian and Nienaber 1979; Rosenthal 1982). Nor does the reliance on computerized management information systems necessarily lead to greater communications effectiveness (Dery 1981).

The barriers to policy coordination are summarized in Figure 1.

MODERATING VARIABLE	AS A BASIS OF INTERDEPENDENCE	AS A BARRIER TO POLICY COORDINATION
RESOURCES	Link between service and funding agent	Competition for budget allocations and other funding sources
		Diversion of resources for side-payments
		Resistance to negative growth coordination
		Pluralism in budgetary processes
MISSION	Joint purpose and compatible objectives	Differences in public/private missions
		Differences in public/private interdependence
		Conflicting or ambiguous missions
POLITICAL	Partisan ties and shared political leadership	Diverse political leadership/allegiance
		Political executive/bureaucracy cleavages
		Evaluation politics
LEGAL	Mandated interdependence	Legal constraints on coordinated policy actions
		Consitutionally-based fragmentation
CONSTITUENT	Common clients for goods or services	Bureaucratic imperialism
		Co-optation
		Constituency conflict
BUREAUCRATIC	Bureaucratic routines, centralized administrative apparatus	Bureaupathology
		Goal displacement
		Separation of knowledge and authority
		Dysfunctional communication systems

Figure 4-1   Summary of Policy Coordination Barriers

Interorganization Theory and Policy Coordination

In seeking guidelines for policy coordination under conditions of shared power, the growing literature on interorganizational relations stands out as a source of knowledge that is underutilized by students of public management. For our purposes interorganizational relations theory has much to recommend it: it is not keyed to any single context of shared power, it is not the private preserve of a single discipline or theoretical perspective, and, most important, it addresses many of the factors affecting policy coordination.

Forms of Interorganizational Relations

Research on organizational relations has focused on several forms, or types of interaction. Since an understanding of this technology is essential for a discussion of coordination options, we will briefly examine four of these forms: dyadic linkages, organization sets, action sets, and networks. [2]

The simplest form of interaction is dyadic. A dyadic linkage is formed when two organizations find it mutually beneficial to collaborate in accomplishing a common goal. For example, joint ventures are often created to share the risk of innovation. This may involve two universities sharing the expense of installing a new research computer or two oil companies forming a partnership to explore a remote section of the earth for natural resources. Dyadic linkages tend to grow out of interpersonal associations between organizational representatives. Once established, joint ventures tend to be project specific in focus and duration.

The less formal model of dyadic interaction entails simple coordination of various aspects of two organizations' production activities. For example, people processing organizations (Hazenfeld 1972) often developed interorganizational agreements to improve the quality of service provided to a common client pool.

A related form of interorganizational interaction has been labeled an organizational set by Evan (1972). This refers to the total sum of interorganizational linkages established by an organization. An organization set is constituted around a focal organization. Hence, it is not a true network because although the dyadic linkage between the local and interacting organizations are examined, the relations between the interacting organizations are ignored.

The research on organization sets has focused primarily on two issues: 1. What are the factors that affect the size and composition of the set (e.g., Whetten and Aldrich 1979)? 2. How does the focal organization cope with the conflicting expectations of other set numbers (e.g., Whetten 1978; Evan 1966; Elesh 1973)?

The third form of interorganizational relations is called an action set. Action sets are essentially purposive networks. That is, they are coalitions of organizations working together to accomplish a specific purpose. The concept of "action set" refers to an interacting group of organizations, whereas the concept of organization set is explicitly centered on a single focal organization. However, it is possible for an action set to be centered around a single organization, as in the case of a price leader in an oligopoly, or the largest university in a state higher education system.

Organizational federations represent a specific form of action sets. Stern's (1979, 1981) research on the National Collegiate Athletic Association has provided useful insights into the development and operation of one of the largest federations in our country. Stern's research points out the difficulty of a federation simultaneously serving both as coordinator and regulator.

The final form of interorganizational relations is a network. A network consists of all interactions between organizations in a population, regardless of how the population is organized into dyads, organization sets, or action sets. There are two types of interorganizational networks: attribute and transaction. Attribute networks consist of organizations that possess common characteristics, such as resource requirements, or outputs. Transactions networks focus on the exchange relationships that link different organizations (Fombrun 1982).

To date more research has been conducted on the determinants of network structure than of network evolution. However, a network characteristic that has been examined in both contexts is "loose coupling." Systems theorists such as Granovetter (1973), Glassman (1973), and Simon (1969) have posited that systems evolve in such a way that critical functions are performed in subsystems which consist of densely coupled linkages between internal elements. However, these subsystems are in turn only loosely joined to each other by means of linking pin relationships between few representatives. It is argued that systems arrayed in this manner possess maximum adaptive potential since changes can be made in one subsystem without seriously disrupting the performance of other subsystems.

Interorganizational Coordination

Although a great deal of the interorganizational relations research has been descriptive, a large segment of it has been explicitly prescriptive in that it has sought ways to improve interorganizational coordination. We will review this material by organizing it into four categories: Structural forms of coordination, antecedents of coordination, a model for improving coordination, and unintended side effects of coordination.[3] Since most of this literature has focused on relations between local public service delivery organizations, it is particularly appropriate for our purposes·

Structural Forms of Coordination

The phenomena covered under the concept "coordination" is extremely broad. It ranges from simple ad hoc agreements between two organizations to participation in formally organized coordinating councils. Most of the literature on coordination focuses on a limited part of this spectrum, namely two or more organizations coming together periodically to plan future activities or to work on joint projects. The more ad hoc side of this continuum often is conceptualized as interorganizational cooperation.

The wide range of coordinating structures is best described by Warren (1974), Thompson (1967), and Lindblom (1965). Although the range of coordinating structures is very large, we have chosen to collapse these structures into three types, following Clark(1965). These three categories vary in terms of intensity, form of social power, formalization, and scope of the coordination activity.

1. Mutual Adjustment. The mutual adjustment structure typifies the type of coordination that occurs in a competitive market. Consequently, the focus in mutual adjustment situations is on the participating agencies or on their clients (Haas & Drabek 1973; Lehman 1975; Warren 1967). There are few if any shared goals toward which the units work. When common goals do emerge, these are apt to be only temporary. Coordination tends to focus on specific cases rather than on the development of a comprehensive delivery system.

The rules used in this strategy are developed ad hoc in the process of interaction. They are likely to grow out of interpersonal rather than organizational concerns. Consequently, the violation of rules and norms is not regarded as severely as in other coordinating strategies. This strategy can be characterized as providing for the narrowest range of benefits and also as involving the fewest costs.

2. Corporate. As its name implies, in the corporate structure coordination occurs under the umbrella of an overarching formal authority structure. Units being coordinated are members of an encompassing organization or system. Examples are departments of a state government, or campuses in a state-wide higher education system (Warren 1967; Lehman 1975; Lindblom 1965).

In a corporate system, the objective of each unit is to achieve the interagency system's goals. Activities are divided among specialized units, and each performs in accordance with a central plan. In the corporate structure, the basis of control resides in the legitimacy of collective decisions. This means that interagency decisions are accepted and become part of the program repertoire of the member organizations.

In the corporate structure, there is a strong central administration that establishes system-wide policies and monitors their implementation by member organizations. Control is achieved through the use of regulations that constrain the actions of member units, or through the distribution of conventional sanctions, such as funds, manpower, and promotion.

3. Alliance. Intermediate between the corporate and mutual adjustment structures are strategies containing elements of both; they represent efforts to coordinate autonomous organizations without the authority of a formal hierarchy (Clark 1965; Warren 1967; Lindblom 1965). This intermediate category is very wide and includes a range of strategies, e.g., federations, councils and coalitions.

There are two major variations in the distribution of power within this immediate strategy. One involves the formation of a central staff employed to develop programs and administer day-to-day operations as responsibilities are delegated by the member agencies. For example, to increase coordination between federation members the central staff assumes the role of mediator, or broker, between the member agencies to facilitate agreements and resource transfers. The second variation is represented by a coalition, or council. Coalitions, unlike federations, typically do not create a central administrative unit. Here the authority system is more informal and the power is lodged in each member agency. Within the alliance structure, both the system and the member units exercise power.

Guidelines for Enhancing Policy Coordination

Problems of policy coordination are best understood with reference to particular events and particular problem sets. But one must balance the advantages of specificity against those of generalizability. The balance here is toward the latter and our broad guidelines should be viewed as problem-solving heuristics rather than "solutions." Figure 2 summarizes the guidelines, identifies studies which support the respective guidelines, and identifies policy coordination problems which the guidelines address.

POLICY COORDINATION GUIDELINES	STUDIES RELEVANT TO PRESCRIPTION	COORDINATION BARRIER ADDRESSED
1. Identify needs for policy coordination, promote a positive attitude, emphasize instrumental value of coordination	Akinbode and Clark, 1976; Davidson, 1975; Van de Ven, 1976; Whetten and Aldrich, 1979; Whetten, 1977; Becke, 1970.	Resistance to negative growth coordination
		Bureaucratic imperialism
2. Identify a wide array of potential policy partners and seek to link partners who are compatible	Boje and Whetten, 1981; Galaskiewicz and Shatin, 1981; Ried, 1969; Schermerhorn, 1975; Paulson, 1968; Rogers and Glick, 1973	Bureaucratic imperialism
		Constituency conflict
		Diverse political leadership/allegiance
		Conflicting missions
		Differences in public/private missions
		Differences in public/private interdependence
3. Private support for formal and informal policy coordination systems	Whetten and Aldrich, 1979; Aiken and Hage, 1968; Form and Noscow, 1958; Leifer and Delbecq, 1981	Bureaupathology
		Separation of knowledge and authority
		Dysfunctional communication systems
		Differences in public/private missions
4. Anticipate and reduce the negative side-effects of policy coordination: (1) enhance adaptability, (2) reduce barriers to innovation, (3) institutionalize service competition, redundancy	Warren, et al., 1974; Schmidt and Kochan, 1977; Hall, et al., 1977; Whetten and Leung, 1979; Provan, 1982; Whetten and Aldrich, 1979	Differences in public/private interdependence
		Evaluation politics
		Goal displacement
5. Recognize limits and set reasonable goals: (1) identify constitutional and legal constraints, (2) assess resources especially budget resources, and reciprocal effects of resources and policy coordination, (3) identify legitimate differences of self-interest, (4) avoid overadvocacy	Whetten, 1977; Davidson, 1976; Whetten and Aldrich, 1979; Aiken and Hage, 1968; Benson, 1975; Hall, et al., 1977	Competition for budget allocations and other funds
		Resistance of negative growth coordination
		Pluralism in budgetary processes
		Differences in public/private missions
		Evaluation politics

Figure 4-2   Summary of Policy Coordination Guidelines

Guideline No. 1: Identify internal needs for policy coordination and emphasize the value of interorganizational collaboration.

A positive attitude towards coordination can stem from a number of different sources. For example, Whetten (1978) found that staff members with a strong professional background who place a high value on meeting client needs tended to encourage coordination activities. Also, Becker (1970) found that staff members with a cosmopolitan ethos were willing to take greater risks with staff members from other organizations. A staff member's natural inclination to value coordination can be reinforced by organizational norms and rewards. For example, Schermerhorn

(1975) and Akinbode and Clark (1975) found that organizations that encouraged group-centered client treatment fostered greater interorganizational coordination. In state and federal service delivery systems, the attitude of top level administrators towards collaboration between local organizations is reflected in organizational policies and rewards.

Akinbode and Clark (1976) and Davidson (1976) found that a necessary prerequisite for this felt need is the recognition of partial interdependence. When organizations share the same client pool, the same resource base, or provide the same type of services, the need for coordination becomes apparent. Van De Ven (1976) has argued that there is an optimal level of interdependence for fostering coordination. If organizations share too little in common then they have little incentive to collaborate. On the other hand, if they share too much, they perceive one another as strong competitors, and they refuse to work together. Whetten and Aldrich (1979) found that an organization is likely to perceive interdependence with a large number of other members of its population if it has broad goals, provides diverse services, and serves a wide range of clients.

In promoting a positive attitude and emphasizing the instrumentality of policy coordination, it is often possible to discourage bureaucratic imperialism and in-fighting and sometimes to reduce the resistance to the most unpopular form of coordination negative growth coordination. By underscoring the interdependence of policy actors and rendering attention to client services and program coordination, the competition among public organizations is reduced as the organizations become less inward-looking.

Guideline No. 2: Once the need for coordination becomes salient, identify a wide array of potential policy partners and seek linkage with those who are most compatible.

Unless linkages are mandated, coordination among policy actors will not occur without some awareness of complementary needs. This generally occurs in one of three ways. First, through informal contacts between staff members. These might occur while attending professional training meetings, community-based voluntary association meetings, or in smaller communities between neighbors who work in related organizations. Also, friendships formed while working in previous jobs have been shown to be particularly salient communication channels (Boje and Whetten 1981; Galaskiewicz and Shatin 1981). Second, coincidental interactions between staff members from different organizations due to geographical proximity. Reid (1969) and Schermerhorn (1975) report that coordination is more likely to occur between adjacent organizations for this reason. Third, formal communications sent from one organization to another conveying information about resource availability, client needs, and service opportunities. Klonglan and associates (1976) found that newsletters, bulletins, letters, and program announcements were effective tools for stimulating interest in coordination.

Assessing the costs of coordination is a salient aspect of this step. Potential coordination partners are screened to reduce the costs of coordination which increase as a function of differences among the collaborating organizations. Hence, organizations are sought that have roughly equal status (Paulson 1966), share a common definition of the problems to be addressed (Rogers and Glick 1973), have an encompassing professional ideology (Benson 1975), do not present a threat to respective domain claims (Hall et al. 1977), and do have compatible organizational structures and procedures (Form and Noscow 1958).

A number of policy coordination barriers can be ameliorated by surveying a broad array of potential policy partners and linking with those who are compatible. Almost by definition, the problem of conflicting missions is reduced since mission agreement is perhaps the most fundamental type of compatibility. Relatedly, differences between public sector and private sector policy actors can be reduced by careful screening. Especially in those cases where there are external inducements (e.g., government funding or tax incentives) for public-private joint programming, there is some danger that linkages will be forged without sufficient thought to asymmetrical interests of policy actors from the respective sectors. Any systematic attempt to rate potential partners as to compatibility is likely to mitigate the disruptive effects of public/private differences in mission and interdependence.

It is important for potential partners to consider not only compatibility of mission but also compatibility of political leadership. This is not to say that policy actors should only seek partners among those who have vowed allegiance to the same political leaders, parties, and interests. In many instances it is not possible to ensure political unity; in a few instances, it is not even desirable. Linkage to policy actors with divergent political interests can expand the base of political demands and supports, often at relatively little costs. If policy actors differ in their political interests and allegiance, it is important to construct linkages which are minimally based on "distancing factors" while emphasizing points of compatibility.

Guideline No. 3: Once a joint venture has been initiated, provide adequate support for formal and informal policy coordination systems.

Policy coordination often breaks down because one or both of the partners are incapable of maintaining the relationship. This could result from a resource cutback, a small staff becoming overloaded with administrative responsibilities, staff inefficiency or ineptitude, inadequate internal and interorganizational communication channels, or a lack of flexibility in organizational policies for dealing with exceptions (Whetten and Aldrich 1979; Aiken and Hage 1968).

Policy coordination requires nurturing and support. Adequate resources and staff, especially professional staff, are critical needs which must be supported. Communications channels, both formal and informal, must be in place and should reflect "need to know" rather than just the formal authority hierarchy. Moreover, there is a need to support both formal and informal elements of the policy coordination system.

Even when formal linkages among policy actors are mandated by legislation there is room for informal coordination mechanisms such as those entailed in mutual adjustment (Haas and Drabek 1973) and alliance (Clark 1965; Warren 1967). In mutual adjustment, common purposes may be short-lived and actors will move in and out of dyadic relations as the occasion demands. Such mutual adjustment processes are as important to policy actors as to market-based actors in that they permit some coordination while entailing few costs. To the extent that there are ad hoc and pragmatic elements to policy coordination and implementation, mutual adjustment can be an effective tool for realizing short-range objectives. Boundary-spanning activity (Leifer and Delbecq 1978; Tushman and Scanlan 1981) is likely to be especially valuable in promoting informal ties and facilitating mutual agreement.

Alliance strategies are already prominent as responses to the rigidity of policy mandates. Informal councils, coalitions and advisory groups are usually responses to perceived policy coordination problems. However, alliances can be planned at the outset of policy implementation and, with some care, can exist alongside the formal policy coordination structure. Just as the "informal organization" can compensate for errors and biases of an ossified formal organization structure, alliance structures can complement formal policy coordination mechanisms.

The provision of support and informal policy coordination systems has an effect on virtually all the major barriers to policy coordination but is especially relevant to four. Dysfunctional communications channels are often remedied by emphasizing informal system supports (e.g., boundary-spanning). In part, this is because a disregard for informal communication is a common source of dysfunctional communication. Similarly, the separation of knowledge and authority is often addressed by a dual focus on formal and informal supports. When informal supports are not in place, policy coordination proceeds largely through formal mechanisms. Since relevant knowledge and expertise is as often vested in staff and middle managers or in those in positions near the top of the hierarchy, informal supports which enhance the role of such actors are especially important.

A welding of formal and informal supports can also reduce the likelihood of certain bureaupathological behaviors. If one assumes that Thompson (1964) is correct in assuming that bureaupathology is largely determined by uncertainty and insecurity, provision of informal and formal system supports should prove an effective antidote.

Guideline No. 4: Anticipate and reduce the negative side-effects of policy coordination.

(1) Interdependence and shared power may reduce adaptability.
When the dyadic linkage between two organizations forged by a joint program is placed in the larger context of an encompassing action set, one of the natural consequences is an increased interconnectedness among all members of a network. Hence, the more joint programs established in a network the more richly joined it becomes. As we mentioned earlier, one of the characteristics of a richly joined

network is that a change in one organization creates turbulence throughout the network since the interconnected organizations are forced to adapt. Because each organization in the network must be responsive to slightly different environmental contingencies and at the same time maintain linkages with other members of the network, the result is a low degree of network stability.

This negative side effect of coordination is minimized under the following conditions: 1. Network members all interface with essentially the same (or at least compatible) environmental conditions. 2. The network's environment consists of homogeneous elements that do not change frequently. 3. There is a central authority structure in the network that can be used to coordinate internal change and reconcile conflicts between members. Unfortunately, these conditions are difficult to obtain in most service delivery systems.

(2) Joint programming may reduce innovation.

Conventional wisdom posits that "striking two unlike substances together produces a spark." In the context of program development this suggests that a program is most likely to be innovative if it is designed by representatives from a diverse group of organizations.

While this is an intuitively appealing proposition, it does not hold in practice for two reasons. First, the more diverse the background and orientation of joint program planners, the more difficult the planning process becomes. Following the logic of the proposition above, an innovative joint project would result from the cross fertilization of ideas from the most diverse representatives of the participating organizations. However, establishing a common language, set of working assumptions, and a high degree of trust between highly dissimilar people is very difficult. Consequently, as the joint program planning process advances, frustrations created by communication difficulties mount and pressures from superiors to reach a decision increase. As a result there is a natural tendency for participants to search for safe solutions that also turn out to be rather mundane.

The second reason why joint ventures often turn out to be less innovative than programs sponsored by single organizations is that they are subject to intense political bargaining. Either, or both, of the participating organizations is likely to have a "hidden agenda" for establishing the joint venture. As a result, the new program becomes a pawn in the larger chess game being played by the participating organizations. The consequence of the resulting bargaining and compromising is often a "watered down" program that is inferior to what both organizations were capable of producing on their own. This is especially likely to occur when participating organizations enter the planning process with unequal power, since the wishes of a dominant actor typically prevail in a bargaining situation.

(3) Extensive coordination may reduce the quality of services.

Warren, Bergunder, and Rose (1974) have argued that one of the negative side effects of extensive coordination among members of a service delivery system is that it works to reinforce the status quo by hindering entrance of new organizations, technologies, and ideologies. In their study of the "war on poverty" programs these researchers observed that while members of this action set frequently criticized one another and disagreed on points of program administration, they all subscribed to an underlying ideology that the problems of the poor could best be addressed by utilizing the technologies administered by members of the current human services system. Hence, these organizations typically responded to criticisms of ineffective service delivery by proposing that the problems could best be remedied by increasing coordination among existing organizations. As a result, innovative propositions grounded in a private sector model of competition (such as issuing a social services credit card to clients for purchasing services from the organization of their choice) were strongly opposed by the existing organizations.

The anticipation of negative side-effects has direct consequences for policy actors' ability to deal with and minimize those side-effects. But there are also indirect consequences for the policy coordination barriers outlined here. Evaluation politics becomes less a threat to policy coordination because evaluation parties are not surprised to find that the policy coordination which may have been difficult to achieve is not without its costs. Likewise goal displacement is somewhat less likely because policy actors are encouraged to view policy coordination as a cost-benefit proposition which will require some front-end agreement about the diverse objectives to be obtained.

(4) The maintenance of interorganizational relations represents a substantial cost to the exchange partners.

The organizational costs associated with initiating and maintaining interorganizational coordination linkages have received relatively little attention in literature. These include increased expenditures for boundary-spanning personnel, reduced internal decision making autonomy, and increased conflict. As one would expect, the perceived cost associated with maintaining a given linkage has been shown to vary according to the perceived instrumental value of the linkage. Seeking to optimize the cost/benefit ratio of their interorganizational linkages, organizations tend to avoid interacting with organizations of marginal utility (Schmidt and Kochan 1977); reduce the intensity of their interactions with mandated linkages perceived as liabilities (Hall et al. 1977); Whetten and Leung 1979), and enlarge and diversify their organization sets to reduce dependence on any particular linkage (Provan 1982; Whetten and Aldrich 1979).

There is, however, a limit to an organization's ability to mold its network of interorganizational linkages to its advantage. It may find itself forced to honor contracts for services that are no longer useful, or feel obligated to interact with external interest groups or participate in federations and associations with no direct payoffs in order to maintain a desirable status or image.

Since interorganizational linkages represent both assets and liabilities, it is important that policy makers avoid the trap of assuming that all exchange relationships are equally advantageous to both partners, or that interorganizational linkages in general represent a cost-free opportunity for the focal organizations.

Guideline No. 5: Recognize limits and set reasonable goals.

Policy success is to some degree a matter of perception. A great many well known "failures" seem, at least in retrospect, attributable to rash claims made on behalf of relatively modest policy initiatives. Claims about eradicating poverty with a program initially funded at less that $1 billion are worse than rash (Levitan 1969). Often public managers snip the already short wick of their candle by making impossible claims about their programs. This tendency is understandable when we consider that political superiors must be convinced that new programs are worthwhile. It is easy to fall into the "overadvocacy trap" (Campbell 1969). But when initial expectations are set at such a high-level, policies have little chance to succeed. Policy coordination often gives way to attempts to shift the blame as promises begin to fall short.

Policy coordination is not costless and every effort should be made to determine the net effects of policy coordination on policy actors' resource base. There is often a recognition of the intraorganizational administrative costs associated with a program, but it is more difficult to calculate the costs of policy coordination, especially when a large number of policy actors are involved. If private sector policy actors are parties to the coordination effort, the calculation of policy coordination costs becomes even more crucial. There should be no surprises which lead the private sector partner to pull out of the policy agreement as policy coordination costs are revealed.

The setting of reasonable goals for policy coordination not only alters expectation about policy coordination success but can go beyond perception to positively affect behavior. Competition for budget shares and other funds can be reduced if there is a realistic initial recognition of differences in self-interest. A valid assessment of both the direct and indirect costs of partnerships can often stave off the disappointment that can result after resources have been invested only to find subsequently that there is no legal provision for the enabling mechanism required for policy coordination. Also, private sector actors should know at the beginning just what the "total bill" is likely to be for any given policy initiative. It is in the interest of all parties to make sure that the firm never reaches the point where benefits and sunk costs are insufficient to balance the drain on resources required for continued participation in the incomplete policy venture.

Summary and Conclusion

Fragmentation of policy responsibilities is an integral component of our democratic society. Pluralism checks the natural tendency towards centralization of power, but it also creates frustration and conflict among actors as they struggle to perform their mandated responsibilities under the structures of shared power. There are several specific barriers to effective coordination under these conditions. These include, competition for scarce resources, conflicting or ambiguous mission statements, conflicting political allegiances, legal restrictions on certain forms of collaboration, competing constituency demands, and internal bureaucratic pathologies.

Research on interorganizational relations represents a germane body of knowledge for this problem. To begin with, it provides a lexicon for describing various forms of interorganizational linkages: dyadic, organization sets, action sets, and networks. These multiple forms demonstrate the scope of the coordination process which varies from negotiating an agreement among two actors, to grappling with the complex interdependencies between multiple parties. This literature also sensitizes us to the differences among various structural forms of collaboration: mutual adjustment, which occurs on an ad hoc basis; corporate, which occurs under the umbrella of an overarching authority structure; and alliance, which includes federations, councils, and coalitions.

However, for our purposes the principal utility of the research on interorganizational coordination is that it suggests several guidelines for overcoming the various obstacles to effective policy coordination discussed in this paper. These guidelines focus attention on the importance of identifying the needs for policy coordination that will appeal to the self-interest of participating parties, assessing the compatibility of potential linkage partners, providing adequate internal organizational support for the coordination process, anticipating and neutralizing the potential negative consequences of coordination, and recognizing the practical limits of coordination and setting reasonable goals and expectations.

Footnotes

1. Some of the material presented here appeared in David A. Whetten, "Interorganizational Relations," in Jay Lorsch (ed.), *Handbook of Organization Behavior*, Prentice-Hall, 1984.

2. See Aldrich and Whetten (1981) for a more elaborate discussion of these forms.

3. For a more extensive review of the interorganizational coordination literature see Rogers and Whetten (1982). This section has drawn heavily from that work.

References

Aiken, M. and J. Hage. 1968. Organizational interdependence and intra-organizational structure. *American Sociological Review* 33:912-990.

Akinbode, I.A. and R.C. Clark. 1976. A framework for analyzing interorganizational relationships. *Human Relations* 29:101-114.

Alchian, A.A. 1973. The property rights paradigm. *Journal of Economic History*. 39:16-27.

Alchian, A. and H. Demsetz. 1972. Production, information costs, and economic organizations. *American Economic Review* 62:777-795.

Allison, G.T. 1971. *Essence of decision*. Boston: Little, Brown and Company.

Anderson and S. Ball. 1978. *The profession and practice of program evaluation.* San Francisco: Jossey-Bass.

Banner, D., S. Doctors and A. Gordon. 1975. *The politics of social program evaluation.* Cambridge, Mass: Ballinger Publishing.

Bardach, E. 1977. *The implementation game.* Cambridge, Mass: M.I.T. Press.

Becker, M.H. 1970. Factors affecting diffusion of innovations among health professionals. *American Journal of Public Health,* 60(February): 294-304.

Behn, R. 1978. Closing a government facility. *Public Administration Review* 38:992-338.

Benson, J.K. 1975. The interorganizational network as a political economy. *Administrative Science Quarterly* 20: 229-249.

Boje, D.M. and D.A. Whetten. 1981. Effects of strategies and contextual constraints on centrality and attributions of influence in interorganizational networks. *Administrative Science Quarterly* 26:378-395.

Blumenthal, M. 1979. Candid reflections of a businessman in Washington. *Fortune,* January 29.

Bower, J. 1977. Effective public management. *Harvard Business Review* 55:131-140.

Bozeman, B. 1984. "Dimensions of 'publicness'." In *New directions in public administration,* edited by B. Bozeman and J. Straussman. Monterey, Calif.: Brooks-Cole Publishing.

_____. 1981. Organization design in the public bureaucracy. *American Review of Public Administration* 15:107-118.

Bozeman, B. and J. Straussman. 1983. "Publicness' and resource management strategies." In *Organization theory and public policy,* edited by R.H. Hall and R.E. Quinn, 75-92. Beverly Hills, CA: Sage Publishing.

_____. 1982. Shrinking budgets and the shrinkage of budget theory. *Public Administration Review* 42:509-515.

Brewer, G. 1978. Termination: hard choices, harder questions. *Public Administration Review* 38:938-943.

Campbell, D.T. 1969. Reforms as experiments. *American Psychologist* 24:409-429.

Casstevens, T.W. and C.O. Press. 1963. The context of democratic competition in American state politics. *American Journal of Sociology* 68:536-543.

Clark, B.R. 1965. Interorganizational patterns in education. *Administrative Science Quarterly* 10:224-23f.

Clarkson, K.W. 1980. "Managerial behavior in nonproprietary organizations." In *The economics of nonproprietary organizations,* edited by K.W. Clarkson and D.L. Martin, a supplement to *Research in Law and Economics* 1.

Clarkson, K.W. 1972. Some implications of property rights in hospital management. *Journal of Law and Economics* 15:963-384.

Congressional Budget Office. 1984. *Federal Support of U.S. Business.* Washington, D.C.: U.S.G.P.O.

Coser, L., 1956. *The functions of social conflict*. New York: Free Press.

Cyert, R. and J. March. 1963. *A behavioral theory of the firm*. Englewood Cliffs, N.J.: Prentice-Hall.

Davidson, S.M. 1976. Planning and coordination of social service in multi-organizational centers. *Social Service Review* 50:117-137.

Davies, D.G. 1981. Property rights and economic behavior in private and government enterprises. *Research in law and economics* 3:111-142.

Davies, D.G. 1977. Property rights and economic efficiency. *Journal of Law and Economics* 20:229-226.

Davies, J. and R. Ripley. 1967. The bureau of the budget and executive branch agencies: Notes on their interaction. *Journal of Politics* 29:749-769.

DeAlessi, L. 1980. The economics of property rights: a review of the evidence. *Research in Law and Economics* 2:1-47.

DeLeon, P. 1978. Public policy terminations: an end and a beginning. *Policy Analysis* 5:248-263.

Downs, A. 1972. Up and down with ecology: the issue attention cycle. *The Public Interest* 28:98-50.

Elesh, D. 1973. Organization sets and the structure of competition for new members. *Sociology of Education* 46:371-395.

Evan, W. 1972. "An organization set model of interorganizational relations." In *Interorganizational decision making*, edited by M. Tuite, R. Chisholm, and M. Radnor. Chicago: Aldine.

Evan, W. 1966. "The organization set." In *Approaches to organizational design*, edited by James Thompson. Pittsburgh: University of Pittsburgh Press.

Fenno, R. 1966. *The power of the purse*. Boston: Little, Brown and Company.

Fombrun, C.J. 1982. Strategies for network research in organizations. *The Academy of Management Review* 7:280-291.

Form, W.H. and S. Noscow. 1958. *Community in disaster*. New York: Harper and Row.

Galaskiewicz, J. and D. Shatin. 1981. Leadership and networking among neighborhood human service organizations. *Administrative Science Quarterly* 26: 434-448.

Gawthrop, L.C. 1971. *Administrative politics and social change*. New York: St. Martin's Press.

Glaser, E. and S. Taylor. 1973. Factors influencing the success of applied research. *American Psychologist* 28:140-146.

Glassman, R. 1979. Persistence and loose coupling. *Behavior Science* 18:89-98.

Gist, J. 1982. Stability' and "competition" in budgetary theory. *American Political Science Review* 76:859-882.

Granovetter, M. 1973. The strength of weak ties. *American Journal of Sociology* 78:1360-1380.

Haas, J.E. and T.E. Drabek. 1973. *Complex organizations: a sociological perspective.* New York: Macmillan.

Hall, R.H., J.P. Clark, P. Giordano, P.V. Johnson, and M. Van Roekel. 1977. Patterns of interorganizational relationships. *Administrative Science Quarterly* 22: 457-474.

Hasenfeld, Y. 1972. People processing organizations: an exchange approach. *American Sociological Review* 97:256-263.

Heclo, H. and L.M. Salamon (eds.). 1981. *The illusion of presidential government.* Boulder, Colo: Westview Press.

Holden, M. 1966. Imperialism in bureaucracy. *American Political Science Review* 60:943-951.

Huntington, S.P. 1952. The marasmus of the I.C.C. *Yale Law Journal* 61:467-509.

Kamlet, M. and D. Mowery. 1980. The budgetary base in federal resource allocation. *American Journal of Political Science* 24:804-821.

Kaufman, H. 1981. *The administrative behavior of federal bureau chiefs.* Washington, D.C.: The Brookings Institution.

Klonglan, G.E., R.D. Warren, J.M. Winkelpleck, and S.K. Paulason. 1976. Interorganizational measurement in social services sector: differences by hierarchical level. Administrative Science Quarterly 21:675-687.

Kogod, R.P. and S.C. Caulfield. 1982. Beyond corporate responsibility: toward a fundamental redefinition of the roles of the public and private sectors. National Journal 22:981-985.

Jacob, H. 1972. Contact with governmental agencies. *American Journal of Political Science* 16:123-146.

Landau, M. 1969. Redundancy, rationality, and the problem of duplication and overlap. *Public Administration Review* 99:946-358.

Lehman, E.W. 1975. *Health care: explorations in interorganizational relations.* Beverly Hills, Calif.: Sage.

Leifer, R. and A. Delbecq. 1978. Organizational/ environmental interchange: a model of boundary spanning activity. *Academy of Management Review* 3:40-50.

Lerner, A. and J. Wanat. 1983. Fuzziness and bureaucracy. *Public Administration Review* 43:500-509.

Levine, C. 1979. Move on cutback management. *Public Administration Review* 99:179-189.

Levitan, S. 1969. *The great society's poor law.* Washington, D.C.: The Brookings Institution.

Lindblom, C.E. 1965. *The intelligence of democracy.* New York, New York: The Free Press.

_____. 1977. *Politics and markets.* New York: Basic Books.

_____. 1968. *The policy-making process.* Englewood Cliffs, NJ: Prentice-Hall.

_____. 1959. The science of muddling through. *Public Administration Review* 19:78-88.

Lodahl, T. and S. Mitchell. 1980. "Drift in the development of innovative organizations." In *The organizational life cycle* by J. Kimberly, R. Miles and Associates. San Francisco: Jossey-Bass.

Maass, A.A. 1951. *Muddy waters.* Cambridge, Mass.: Harvard University Press.

Neustadt, R.E. 1960. *Presidential power.* New York: Wiley.

Niskanen, W.A. 1971. *Bureaucracy and representative government.* Chicago: Aldine Atherton.

_____. 1979. "Competition among government bureaus." In *Making bureaucracies work*, edited by C.H. Weiss, 167-1704. Beverly Hills, Calif.: Sage.

Ostrom, V. and E. Ostrom. 1965. A behavioral approach to the study of intergovernmental relations. *The Annals* 359:137-146.

Paulson, S.K. 1976. A theory and comparative analysis of interorganizational dyads. *Rural Sociology* 41:311- 329.

Provan, K.G. 1982. Interorganizational linkages and influence over decision making. *The Academy of Management Journal* 25:443-451.

Rainey, H.G. 1983. Public agencies and private firms: incentive structures, goals and individual roles. *Administration and Society* 15:207-242.

Reagan, M. 1972. *The new federalism.* New York: Oxford University Press.

Rossi, R. and K.J. Gilmartin. 1981. Information exchange among public agencies in three California counties. *Knowledge* 2:413-436.

Rourke, F.E. 1969. *Bureaucracy, politics and public policy.* Boston: Little, Brown and Company.

Rumsfeld, D. 1979. A politician-turned executive surveys both worlds. *Fortune*, Sept. 10.

Rogers, D.L. and E. Glick. 1973. "Planning for interagency cooperation in rural development," In *Card Report* by U.S. Center for Agricultural and Rural Development. Ames, Iowa: Iowa State University.

Sabatier, P. and D. Mazmanian. 1979. The conditions of effective implementation. *Policy Analysis* 5:481-504.

Schermerhorn, J.R. Jr. 1975. Determinants of inter-organizational cooperation. *Academy of Management Journal* 18(December): 846-856.

Schick, A. 1980. *Congress and money.* Washington, D.C.: The Urban Institute.

Schmidt, S.M. and T.A. Kochan. 1977. Interorganizational relationships: patterns and motivations. *Administrative Science Quarterly* 22:220-294.

Scriven, M. 1967. "The methodology of evaluation." In *Perspective of curriculum evaluation*, edited by R.W. Tyler, R.M. Gagne and M. Scriven. Chicago: Rand McNally.

Selznick, P. 1949. *TVA and the grass roots.* Berkeley, Calif.: University of California Press.

Shelton, J. 1967. Allocative efficiency vs. x-efficiency. *American Economic Review* 57:1252-1258.

Smith, B.L.R. 1983. Changing public-private sector relations. *The Annals* 446:149-164.

Smith, T.B. 1979. The policy implementation process. *Policy Sciences* 4:197-198.

Sosin, M. 1981. Organizational maintenance, sensitivity to clients, and vulnerability. *Sociological Quarterly* 22:347-358.

Straussman, J. 1981. More bang for fewer bucks? or how local governments can rediscover the potentials (and pitfalls) of the market. *Public Administration Review* 41:150-158.

Thompson, J.D. 1967. *Organizations in action.* New York: McGraw-Hill.

Thompson, U. 1964. *Modern organizations.* New York: Alfred Knopf.

Tushman, M. and T.J. Scanlan. 1981. Boundary spanning individuals: their role in information transfer and their antecedents. *Academy of Management Journal* 24:289-305.

U.S. General Accounting Office. 1983. *The federal role in fostering university-industry cooperation.* Washington, D.C.: U.S.G.P.O.

Van de Ven, A.H. 1976. On the nature, formation and maintenance of relations among organizations. *Academy of Management Review* 4:24-36.

Waldo, D. 1980. *The enterprise of public administration.* Novato, Calif.: Chandler and Sharp.

Warren, R.L. 1967. The interorganizational field as a focus of investigation. *Administrative Science Quarterly* 12:396-419.

Warren, R., A. Bergunder, and S. Rose. 1974. *The structure of urban reform.* Lexington, Mass.: Heath.

Warwick, D.P. *A theory of public bureaucracy.* Cambridge, Mass.: Harvard University Press.

Wengert, N. 1955. *Natural Resources and the Political Struggle.* Garden City, N.Y.: Doubleday.

Whetten, D.A. and H. Aldrich. 1979. Organization set size and diversity: links between people processing organizations and their environments. *Administration and Society* 11:251-282.

Whetten, D.A. and T.K. Leung. 1979. The instrumental value of interorganizational relations: antecedents and con- sequences of linkage formation. *Academy of Management Journal* 22:925-944.

Whetten, D.A. 1978. Coping with incompatible expectations: an integrated model of role conflict. *Administrative Science Quarterly* 23:254-271.

Whetten, D.A. 1980. Organization decline: a neglected topic in organizational science. *Academy of Management Review* 5:577-588.

Wilson, J.Q. 1973. *Political organizations.* New York: Basic Books.

Wildavsky, A.B. 1964. *The politics of the budgetary process.* Boston: Little, Brown and Company.

Woll, P. 1977. *American bureaucracy.* Second Edition. New York: W.W. Norton and Company.

Wright, D.S. 1982. New federalism: recent varieties of an older species. *American Review of Public Administration* 16:56-76.

CHAPTER 5

Towards a Synergistic Model of Power[1]

Nancy C. Roberts

We live in a challenging world. Our resources are limited and our world is complex. No one person or group possesses the necessary resources, information, or know-how to go it alone. We need one another to get things done, to survive. This need for others, however, creates an imperative in our world that is annoyingly difficult to realize. Interdependence with others demands at least some level of coordination, negotiation, and cooperation. Unfortunately, many obstacles make this coordination and cooperation difficult to achieve.

We jealously guard and defend our resources and turf; we define our power as the ability to get what we want despite someone else's resistance; and we assume that power comes from winning out over others rather than working with them. While we may need one another, cooperation is not that easy to accomplish in this competitive world. Our initial response is to avoid the dependencies and inter-dependencies lest they diminish our autonomy and control. Although we may grudgingly admit that our world often requires collaboration and collective response to its challenges and dilemmas, our initial preference is to try to protect our power and to avoid, if at all possible, the need to share it.

I have been asked to prepare a paper to summarize what the literature has to say on the topic of "shared power." As I understand the concept, shared power describes a situation in which no one person, group, organization, institution nor society has complete control. Instead, multiple actors share resources and re-sponsibility for planning and decision making. Interdependent ventures are required because no one actor has the requisite resources to accomplish the desired ends.

Work on shared power, directly or indirectly, can be found in a variety of literatures. Although the term may not be used explicitly, its meaning is implied in writings on participation, bargaining and negotiation, and conflict.[2] Direct reference can be found in certain professional fields such as education, intergovernmental relations, and health care [3]. These references to shared power are understandable given the interdependent nature of the teaching, health care, and political professions.

A literature review spanning this diversity would be an enormous task. A more manageable assignment, for our purposes here, is to select key themes that undergird most of the work on shared power, whatever the field, or whatever the area of professional application. These themes emerge from an analysis of the power literature which has sought to conceptualize the nature, form, usage and consequences of power. Part one of this review will summarize these themes, attempting to show how and why they are important to understand for the construction of a shared power perspective.

Part two of the paper will take these themes and weave them together to form an integrated model of shared power, or as I refer to it, the collective perspective on power. The creation of such a model is important in order to eventually derive propositions and submit them to empirical verification. Later in part two, the collective (shared power) perspective is juxtaposed with the traditonal model of power, which I refer to as the distributive or "zero-sum" perspective. In a final section of part two, these two perspectives are combined to create a synergistic power model that has both collective and distributive components.

The synergistic model is examined in part three. Its analysis begins with the question, Under what conditions will each type (collective or distributive power) be used? Results from game theory suggest some interesting answers that need to be confirmed in organizational settings.

Shared Power Themes in the Literature

Debates in the power literature have centered on the key questions about the nature of power. Is power an active force or is it a potential force? Does power only apply to intended actions or does it include acts unintended by the actors? Is power being exerted when two parties are equal in strength, or must there be an imbalance of resources between the two before power is wielded? Should analysis of power be conducted from the powerholder's point of view, or should it also include the view of those over whom power is exercised? Is power a "positive" or "negative" force in promoting social life? That is, is power achieved by exerting dominance over others or is power attained by joining forces with others? What forms can power take? Are there different types of power exercised? And finally, how are the concepts of authority, influence, and control related to power and in what ways are they distinctive? [4]

How all these questions are answered has implications for the development of a shared power perspective. However, three questions in particular put the issue of shared power into bold relief. The review in part one will focus on these three. To what extent is power a "positive" or a "negative" force in society? What are the different means to power? Can power exist when there is a balance of resources between the parties, or must there be asymmetry in resources before power exists?

Power as a "Positive" and "Negative" Force in Society
The question of whether or not power is a negative or positive force in society is one that many writers have dealt with implicitly in their work. The heart of the question is concerned with the ends of power, or the ultimate goals to be pursued. For example, Machiavelli (1952) focused on the techiques that successful princes needed to use against their rivals and subordinates; he maintained that manipulative and coercive practices were often required to protect the security of the state. The implication was that, although power had its elements of "force and fraud" (negative force), power was being exercised for the collective good of the state (positive force).

Hobbes (1946) also understood this duality of power, although he had a different view on what constituted its positive and negative aspects. He argued that stable relations among men only could come into being when men agreed to submit to a power in the form of the state. The coercive power (negative force) of the state over the citizenry ultimately would permit people to achieve their diverse individual ends. Thus, while power had its coercive properties, it had its positive elements for the individual who was now able to pursue his particular goals free from the tyranny of lawlessness and disorder, the natural state of man (positive force).

Recent analysis of this question was touched off in the early 1960's with the confrontation in sociology between Talcott Parsons and C. Wright Mills. The debate began with the publication of Mills' *The Power Elite* (1956). Mills developed the thesis that a coincidence of economic, military, and political power, in the post World War II years, had created a power elite in the United States that strategically controlled American society. The group made decisions at the expense of other subordinate groups to perpetuate its power. Power was exercised over others as the power elite sought to impose its will, protect its interests, and retain its control (negative force).

Parsons (1969) criticized this view and labeled it the "zero-sum" conceptualization of power. Assuming Mills' definition, power would have to have finite limits. If one party wanted to expand its power, it could only do so by reducing the power of the other, hence the name zero-sum.

Instead, Parsons presented an alternative conceptualization of power. He saw it associated with consensus, authority, and the pursuit of collective goals (positive force). For him, power began with value consensus that bound together the group in the pursuit of some collectively defined ends. It eventually came to be legitimated as authority when the collective will became institutionalized. Power, therefore, became a property of the entire system, a resource that made possible the attainment of collective goals to which a commitment had been made.

Parson's view represents what I refer to as collective or shared power. By joining forces, people can accomplish what they as individuals could not achieve. They have the "power to" or the "capacity to" accomplish their goals. They also have a "power with" others not a "power over" others. Power begins with consensus, not from resistance or conflict. In contrast to zero-sum power, the Parsonian view could be described as "variable-sum". It does not rely on a finite amount of power. The assumption is that power can grow as the collective goals are successfully achieved. All are empowered who participate in the system.[5]

Mills, on the other hand, saw power in distributive terms. With not enough of it to go around, it must be contested and reallocated from losers to winners in a battle for control. If one party wanted to increase its power, by necessity, it had to reduce someone else's. Power in this sense is power over others.

This distinction between distributive and collective power is a modern-day example of how power continues to be viewed as a negative and positive force. Reconciliation between these two perspectives is still elusive, although there has been a definite preference in the literature to define power as power over others. In fact, some theorists eliminate the collective perspective from a definition of power altogether (Lukes 1974). To study power usually has been to study distributive power.

Despite these disagreements on whether power is a positive or negative force, there is one point of agreement between the two views. Both assume that the attainment of goals is important to establish power. Distributive power focuses on how the goals between the parties differ, and how one party is able to accomplish its goals despite the resistance of the other. Collective or shared power begins with the assumption that the goals of both parties are similar, and that the consensus achieved increases the likelihood that collective goals will be realized.

What are the Means to Power?

Questions about the means to power concentrate on the ways power is exercised. They are questions of process rather than questions of outcomes. They describe *how* something is accomplished rather than *what* is accomplished. As with collective and distributive types, there is a debate over what constitutes an appropriate definition of means.

The outline of this debate was suggested in the previous section. Power over others implies an element of coercion while power with implies consensus. Things are more complicated than this, however, since various strategies, tactics, methods and styles have been introduced as alternative paths to power. For example, over 370 strategies have been documented in the power literature alone (Roberts 1983).

Classification of these strategies, tactics and methods are numerous, but when these classifications are compared with behavioral or perceptual reports, the data do not fit the conceptual schemes. Attempts to impose some order through empirical work have not achieved the desired consistency either (Roberts 1983). In fact, the results from both the empirical and conceptual work suggest that the debate on what constitutes power processes will continue for a while. Much of this confusion is, in part, due to the multiple definitions of power in the literature. If power is defined to exclude various processes—such as consensus—from consideration, it follows that consensus would not appear in any subsequent analysis.

At the risk of adding further confusion to this literature, I submit that we take a comprehensive rather than exclusive perspective on power processes. That is, the list of power means or processes should be expanded to include the total set of possible means that are consistent with the various definitions of power. Because power is often defined "as the ability to get what you want against resistance," then the processes should include such means as force and coercion. Because power is also defined as "the capacity to effect an outcome," then the processes should also include means such as consensus and cooperation. Ultimately then, the means used depend on the two parties and how they choose to exercise their power.

With an expanded set of means, the goal would be to find a dimension on which they all could be compared and contrasted. The one dimension that suggests itself and cuts across all power processes is the dimension of control, or the level of mutuality between two parties. Unilateral control anchors one end of the continuum and reflects the situation when there is no mutuality — one party dominating the other. Multilateral control anchors the other end of the continuum and reflects the case in which control is shared between the parties. The following examples illustrate how some means to power can be positioned on this control continuum.

Charisma is an example of multilateral control because the relationship between the leader and the followers requires an attraction to the leader and a voluntary association with him or her. The leader does not compel followership, s/he attracts it. Leadership is sustained with the consent and willingness of the led, in much the way Gandhi led South Asians in their pursuit of independence from Britain. Control is shared despite the fact that one party "leads" and the other "follows."

The recognition of charisma, as a means to power with multilateral control, does not deny the possibility of using charisma for the purpose of eventually establishing unilateral control. Hitler or Jim Jones come to mind in this regard. Charisma may begin with a voluntary association among people; it may not stay that way over time. If a structure of power is created to guarantee the perpetuation of charisma, or to coerce the nonbelievers into joining the followers, then in order to characterize the means to power, we would have to change our description from charisma to force.

Consensus is another example of multilateral control, but it differs from charisma in that it implies greater sharing. Consensus, by definition, requires mutual problem solving and decision making so that the needs and desires of all parties are taken into account in getting an outcome. No one person or group is viewed as more powerful or more in control than another.

This typology of means would also place manipulation toward the unilateral end of the continuum. One party exerts its will without the other being aware of its intent. Thus control is exercised in a unilateral way, although it is less overt and obvious than coercion and force, two means which would anchor the unilateral control end of the continuum.

Bargaining and negotiating strategies also should be included on this control continuum. They would occupy a place in the midrange between the two anchors. The reasoning is straightforward. Bargaining and negotiating tactics have two different orientations depending on how the parties involved in the interactions approach their association. One orientation calls for "win-win" strategies in which both parties mutually benefit from their transactions. The second calls for a "win-lose" strategy in which one party gains at the expense of the other.[6] This same distinction is also made in the conflict resolution, conflict management literature.[7] Thus, depending on how they are used, bargaining and negotiating strategies can move to either unilateral or multilateral control ends of the spectrum.

Figure 1 illustrates how this continuum of control can be designed.

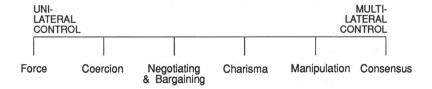

Figure 5-1   Continuum of Control for Power Means

The exact location of each means to power remains tentative until empirical work can specify where each belongs in relation to the others. Temporarily, force, coercion, and manipulation should be placed toward the unilateral control end of the continuum. Charisma and consensus should be located toward the multilateral control end. Bargaining and negotiating should cluster around the midpoint to indicate the potential for either type of control, depending on the orientation of the parties to one another.

From this analysis of various means to power it can be seen that shared power has much in common with various multilateral means to power. Shared power calls for mutual decision making and planning, and requires collaboration and cooperation among the parties. Means to power are collective and mutually supportive. References to the multilateral means to power, then, are references to shared power.

Asymmetry or Balance in Power Relations

A third question in the power literature, relevant to shared power, focuses on the nature of a power relationship. Must there be an asymmetry between social actors or can power exist when there is a balance between the two parties? Three answers to this question have been formulated in the literature, only one of which allows for a shared power interpretation.

The first response posits that power only exists when there is an imbalance in the relationship. One party gets what it wants because it has more resources to get its way and impose its will on the second party. Therefore, the idea of a "balance of power," or shared power, is logically contradictory from this point of view. For example, Blau (1964) writes that "interdependence and mutual influence of equal strength indicate a lack of power" (p. 118). This type of power has been referred to as "integral power" (Wrong, 1979), and it represents the predominant view in the literature.

A second response to the question looks at multiple transactions between two parties. While an imbalance may exist in one simple act-response sequence, over time, this imbalance may be equalized as the parties alternate control. For example, the power of actor A in relation to arena x is balanced by the power that actor B possesses over arena y. There is a division of scopes between the two parties; one dominates in a particular situation, while the other dominates in a different one. Thus, the employer sets the conditions of work and the employee contributes the expertise. Both have power, but in different spheres at different points in the interaction sequence. This type of power has been referred to as "countervailing power" (Galbraith, 1983) or "intercursive power" (Wrong, 1979). It is built on the assumptions of integral power, but it extends the analysis of power beyond one act-response sequence to multiple act-response sequences.

The third response to the question allows for a balanced relationship among the parties. The balance derives from a pooling of each parties' resources for the purpose of some mutual goal. One party contributes the expertise, another money, still another time or labor, or whatever is needed to produce the desired outcome in which all have an interest. They acknowledge their interdependence and realize that to accomplish the task, all must contribute. While the resources are different, they are equally valued, and the contributions of the parties are viewed as balanced.

This type of power has been described as "pooled resource power" (Swingle, 1976). The assumption is that resources need not be guarded nor defended, but rather they can be combined and shared since no one party has the necessary resources for goal accomplishment. A good example of pooled resource power is the Chrysler corporation's recent recovery from financial ruin. Labor, management, government, and financial institutions all contributed their resources and worked together to bring about Chrysler's turnaround.

Of the three responses in the literature to the question of balance or asymmetry in power relationships, only one allows room for the concept of shared power. Integral power eliminates shared power by definition. Intercursive power allows for shared power only if the power of one party is countervailed by the power of the other party. The concept of shared resource is the only one broad enough to encompass the concept of shared power as it was orginally defined. Shared power requires mutual planning and decision making, and interdependence is assumed. Also implicit in its definition is the idea that no one party has the requisite resources to affect the desired outcomes. Hence, shared power and pooled resource power are similar in concept and definition.

Summary

Three questions from the literature on power provide the base on which to analyze shared power: Is power a positive or negative force in society? What are the means to power? And, are power relations asymmetrical in nature or can they be balanced between or among the parties?

Answers to these questions suggest that the ends of power can be collective as well as distributive; the means to power can range from consensual to coercive; and the resources or bases of power can be integral, countervailing or pooled. Each aspect of power, its ends, its means, and its bases contains an element of shared power. What is missing from this analysis, however, is a view of shared power that integrates the various components into a complete model. The creation of a model of shared power becomes the challenge and goal of the next section.

Models of Shared Power

The three components of power identified in the previous section are combined to form a model of shared power (Figure 2).

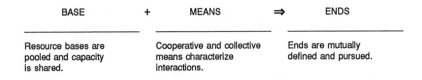

BASE	+	MEANS	⇒	ENDS
Resource bases are pooled and capacity is shared.		Cooperative and collective means characterize interactions.		Ends are mutually defined and pursued.

Figure 5-2   Model of "Shared Power"

The base or source of power represents the resources on which power is ultimately built. Resources can be personal or structural in nature: money, information, expertise, personal attractiveness, contacts, membership in a select group—whatever is valued and seen as a possible source that can be utilized to get a preferred outcome. A resource base, then, represents a capacity or a potential that can be activated. It is the potential for power rather than the actual exercise of power. A person who has money but does not spend it in some transaction, is not exercising power. In this case, money only represents a potential to buy something, it does not guarantee its purchase. That can depend on a number of other factors such as the seller's willingness to part with the item, or other potential buyers in the market. In the case of shared power, the resource base is pooled so that the potential or capacity for power is shared among all the participants in the power transaction.

The means of shared power in the model are collective and cooperative. Two examples introduced in the previous section were consensus and charisma. In both cases, multilateral control is exercised by the parties in the interaction. One party does not dominate or have power over the other.

And finally, the shared power model includes the pursuit of ends that have been collectively defined. The goals have been identified for the group and by the group. The creation of a job corps program by various community organizations, governmental agencies, and private enterprises, for the purpose of training the unemployed, is one such example of ends collectively defined and pursued.

When all these components of shared power are combined, the definition of shared power can be stated as the utilization of pooled resources in the collective pursuit of ends mutually defined. This model of power is very different when compared to those typically presented in the literature.

The definition of power as the ability to get what one wants against resistance serves as an example.[8] This definition and those similar to it imply that resources are expected to be scarce and guarded, certainly not shared or pooled. As a result, the means will be competitive and coercive in order to protect one's individual interests and goals.

Power, then, is typically viewed as either a collective experience that all who participate enjoy, or it is seen as the expression of individual will independent of others' concerns.

This "either-or" view of power did not emanate only from those who saw power in zero-sum terms. In their attempts to compensate for what they saw as an overemphasis on distributive power, the consensus theorists argued for the elimination of the distributive perspective. From Hannah Arendt (1970) we read:

> Power and violence are opposites; where the one rules absolutely, the other is absent. Violence appears where power is in jeopardy, but left to its own course it ends in power's disappearance (p.56).

Thus, as distributive power focuses on power over others, shared power envisions power as working with others. Each defines power in ways to exclude the other. Unfortunately this division leaves us with a literature that is confused and difficult to understand. In their attempts to be precise, theorists have written a literature that excludes alternative perspectives and competes for the definitive conceptualization of power.

The challenge to those working in the area of power is ultimately to develop models that integrate these two competing views. The theorists of the past were helpful in delimiting the various perspectives on power, but the theorists of the future must work to integrate them. Both views are essential to describe the reality of power in all of its complexity. For example, consensus may explain how a group is formed and maintains itself internally, but coercion may best describe how that group survives in competition with other groups over time. Both perspectives on power are helpful, but each examines a different level of analysis and a different point in the history of the group. The issues raised in the debate between Mills and Parsons illustrate the point.

Parsons is concerned with power as a property of the entire system. Power represents the ability of a society to attain the goals to which a commitment has been made. Mills, on the other hand, sees power as the ability of individuals or groups to impose their will on others in order to establish their preferred system. At the societal level, there is power because the society maintains itself in the pursuit of collective goals. At the individual and group level, there is power because one group is able to prevail and change the terms of their association. Both of these perspectives on power are useful, depending on the level of analysis and what stage of the relationship between the parties one is examining. While Parsons describes how a system maintains itself, Mills describes how the sub-parts of the system push to change and redefine the system. Both see the explanatory value of power, but they use it in different ways.

If the goal of an integrated model of power is to be realistically pursued, then two steps need to be taken. First, power should be defined in such a way so as to include both the distributive and collective perpsectives. And secondly, a model of power should be developed to specify the conditions under which collective or distributive power will be used. These are the tasks of the next section on synergistic power.

Synergistic Power

Synergy is defined as the combined effect of two or more parts, the sum of which is greater than the individual components. Synergistic power combines both distributive and collective power into one model and specifies the conditions under which each type is manifested.

The synergistic model of power needs to be based on a definition of power that is broad enough to encompass its diverse sub-parts. Bertrand Russell's definition (1938) is useful for this purpose: power is "the production of intended effects" (p. 35) in an interaction with at least two parties. From a distributive perspective, the intended effects can be particularistic; they can be pursued with force, coercion, or manipulation to protect the limited scarce resources. From a collective perspective, the production of intended effects allows for two or more parties to cooperate, pool their resources and seek mutual goals. The definition is inclusive in scope, without bias toward one type or the other.

The model of power that follows from this definition is presented in Figure 3. The upper half of the model presents the distributive type of power: resource bases that are protected and guarded, means that are coercive or manipulative, and ends that are independently defined and pursued. The lower half of the model represents the collective or shared power type: resources pooled and shared, means consensual and charismatic, ends mutually defined and pursued. Thus, the model represents a comparison between the two types of power.

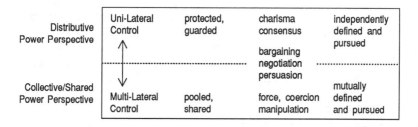

Distributive Power Perspective	Uni-Lateral Control ↑	protected, guarded	charisma consensus bargaining negotiation persuasion	independently defined and pursued
Collective/Shared Power Perspective	↓ Multi-Lateral Control	pooled, shared	force, coercion manipulation	mutually defined and pursued

Figure 5-3   Synergistic Model of Power

The vertical dimension that links the two types of power was introduced in an earlier discussion on the means to power. Recall that these means to power were found to lie on a continuum of control which ranged from shared control by both parties to uni-lateral control by one party (Figure 1). This same dimension of control also separates the resource bases and the ends of power. Resources can be protected and guarded, or pooled and shared. The ends of power can be independently or mutually defined. The dotted line in the middle suggests that making a distinction between the two types of power may be difficult in some cases. As previously noted, negotiation can be distributive or collective, depending on the skills, beliefs, and actions of the parties.

The horizontal axis describes a temporal process, a chain of events by which resources are converted into outcomes or ends through interactions between two or more parties. The temporal process shown in Figure 3 only indicates one base-means-ends sequence. As has been discussed in the case of intercursive power, many base-means-ends sequences are possible. Figure Four represents the logic of multiple sequences.

Starting at time 1, the sequence begins with the collection of resources which will be activated by some means in the pursuit of specific, predetermined ends. (Recall that power is defined as the production of some intended effect.) Successful accomplishment of predetermined ends in time 1 leads to a greater capacity or resource base at time 2. For example, if one party has been successful in achieving its ends, it may add to its base of power by winning a reputation for getting things done, or gaining some expertise from the experience. Thus, the results from time 1 are combined with previous resources, and both provide the potential that can be utilized in future transactions. This cycle continues through time *n*.

The illustration of a resource base growing over time in Figure 4 does not mean that all transactions will result in greater resources in the future. Resources diminish if the outcome of a power transaction is not successful. Suppose a party fails to win a vote in the city council. The failure to produce its intended effects not only demonstrates a lack of power, but during the transaction, resources are expended which are difficult to recoup. And furthermore, the failure has the potential of diminishing the party's reputation for getting results. Therefore, only successful accomplishment of ends represents power. The alternative scenario describes a lack of power, and a reduction of the party's resources on which it can rely in future interactions.

Figure 4 demonstrates what a successful chain of resource base-means-end sequences looks like over time. As the first sequence ends with the production of intended effects, the base in time 2 increases in capacity or potential. The increased potential in time 2 does not guarantee an increase in power in time 2, however. Power only can be realized when a capacity through an interaction with another party produces an intended effect. Therefore, the arrow goes from ends in time 1 to resource base in time 2, illustrating that a party's resource base increases but not necessarily its power.

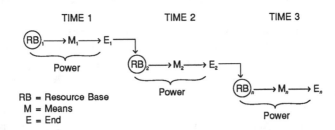

Figure 5-4   Temporal Model of Power

The example of presidential power illustrates why this distinction is an important one (Neustadt, 1960). Presidents complain of a "lack of power" despite the tremendous resources they command. While they have a large resource base, they are not guaranteed that every base-means-end sequence will lead to power. Vietnam was a case in point. Some resources were not utilized (tactical nuclear weapons) and certain ends were not pursued (total victory). The Presidents who struggled with Vietnam understood that their power had limits; not all of their resource bases could be deployed and not all their ends could be achieved. They had an enormous potential for power but it did not produce the intended effects, a win in Vietnam. Hence, they experienced a "power deficit" or a "power gap," a difference between their potential and their actual achievements.

Advantages of the Synergistic Model of Power. In relation to previous models of power, this one has several major advantages. First, the model distinguishes between the bases of power and the means to power. A distinction between the two has not always been made, and this lack of clarity has produced enormous confusion in the literature.[9] The position taken here is that *how* something is accomplished is conceptually different from the resource base on which it is built.

Another advantage of the model is that the definition of power separates the means from the ends. The production of intended effects does not specify whether the means are collective or distributive. This is an important point. The choice of means is left up to the participants in a power transaction; it is not forced upon them by definition. Thus, *what* is done is seen as qualitatively different from *how* it is done. One group may use very coercive means in an intergroup competitive battle, and yet at the same time, it may employ cooperative intragroup tactics to pursue its collective goals. Its intra-group relations can be characterized as collective power, while its inter-group relations can be described in distributive power terms. Other definitions of power do not allow for this flexibility.

It is also good to point out at this time how important it is to be precise with our terms. The use of phrases "balance of power," "exercise of power," "shared power," and "increased power" are not accurate technically. We protect, exchange, or pool resources, but we do not "balance power." We choose alternative means to activate resources, but we do not "exercise power." We pursue independent or mutually held goals, but we do not "share power". Power is the production of intended effects; it assumes a sequence of activity from the accumulation of resources, the exercise of means, and the achievement of ends. And although it is the sucessful completion of this temporal sequence, it can never be seen directly. To establish power with certainty we would have to estimate what would have happened without the "exercise" of power, to guess what the intentions of the actors in the power transaction were, and to calculate the effect of the actor's actions on the probability that what was desired would be likely to occur (Pfeffer 1981, 4). Thus, power is a very ephemeral concept; it should not be concretized to the point that we lose the essence of its meaning. In our need to operationalize and measure concepts, we should not violate the integrity of the reality that we seek to understand.

Conditions of Synergistic Power
The conditions under which the means to power—coercion, force, manipulation, bargaining, consensus or cooperation are used have been explored in laboratory and field settings for a number of years. Both situational variables—such as resources controlled, the extent of one's legitimacy, organizational structure—and individual variables—such as sex, age, personality orientation—have been examined for their effects on behavior (Roberts 1983).

A recent work by Robert Axelrod, *The Evolution of Cooperation* (1984), continues in this same tradition. He seeks to understand under what conditons the two types of power in the synergistic model will exist. He explores the conditions under which *cooperation* is chosen and maintained between two parties, as opposed to the responses of cheating or *competition*. He uses the Prisoners' Dilemma Game to delimit the conditions under which these behaviors occur.

What is unique and provocative about Axelrod's work, is that he constructs a theory of cooperation from the results of computer simulations. He then tests the theory against the reality of historical example, such as trench warfare in WWI, and the evolution of cooperation in biological systems. He moves well beyond the confines of the laboratory to a complex and interdependent world to test his propositions about cooperation and competition, a transition that is difficult to make.

Axelrod's work is also important because it demonstrates a way to test the components of the synergistic model of power. While he only concentrates on the means to power, his approach also could be used to test the other components. Because of its implications, it is worth some time to review it in depth.

The scenario for the Prisoners' Dilemma is that two accomplices to a crime are arrested and questioned separately. They have two choices. Either they can defect (compete) with the other by confessing to the crime and hoping for a lighter sentence, or they both can cooperate and refuse to confess, and the district attorney can only convict them on a minor charge. However, if both confess, their confessions are not as valuable. No matter what the other prisoner does, defection (competition) always yields a higher payoff than cooperation.

The point of the game is that it pays to defect if you think the other player will cooperate. It is also better to defect if you think the other player will defect. The problem is that the same logic holds for the other player as well. Therefore, both players should defect no matter what the other one does. It pays for each player acting individually to defect. The result is that both will defect, and in the final analysis, each will only be rewarded with 1 point, much less than the three points both would have received if they had cooperated. Thus the players, acting out what is rational choice for each of them, will end up with worse outcomes for both of them than is possible with mutual cooperation. Hence, their dilemma.

Two players playing this game once will choose to defect and each will therefore get less than what they could have gotten if they had cooperated. Even if the game is played a finite number of times, the results will remain the same. The game with a finite end always unravels back to mutual defection.

The same results do not occur given other conditions. In particular, mutual cooperation is chosen during the computer simulated prisioners' dilemma with: 1) greater frequency and durability of the interactions between the two players; 2) greater importance placed on the players' future relative to their present; 3) reciprocity of behavior between the two players; 4) greater long-term than short-term incentives for individual gain; 5) recognition between the two players, and the ability to remember and know the relevant features of their interactions; and, 6) the use of a strategy that had both players cooperating on the first move and thereafter doing whatever the other player did on the last move.

These conditions were embedded in the assumptions of a computer program called "Tit-for-Tat." This program proved superior to all of the other programs submitted; it produced the highest score for the players every time the game was run, with one exception when it came in second.

Extrapolating from these results we would predict that shared power will tend to occur when the following conditions exist: there is opportunity for frequent and durable interactions between the parties; the parties put more emphasis on their futures than on their pasts; they observe reciprocity in their interactions; they have greater incentives to maintain a long-term commitment than short-term gains for themselves; they are able to recognize each other and remember (and know) relevant features about each other and their interactions; and they begin their interactions with cooperation and continue to treat each other as they have been treated in the immediate past transaction.

Distributive power, on the other hand, will be more likely to occur under a different set of conditions: little contact between the parties; more emphasis on the present than on the future; greater incentive for short-term gain than long-term interest; inability to recognize the other party and remember relevant features about the other; little or no observance of reciprocity; and few experiments with cooperation.

There is some difficulty in taking the theory of cooperation which was developed in a two-person game and applying it to n-person games. For example, we know from previous research that n-person cases of prisoners' dilemma are qualitatively different from the two-person case in three ways: the harm caused by the competition is diffused over many players rather than focused on just one; behavior may be anonymous in the n-person game; and, each player does not have total reinforcement control over all players since the payoffs are determined by the overall effect of what many players are doing (Axelrod 1984, 221, note 3).

Despite these limitations, the research framework and methodology, especially the use of computer simulations to model the "behavioral" choices, provide a sophisticated tool to answer the question: Under which conditions will shared power and distributive power be utilized? Simulations also could be developed to analyse when resources would be pooled and ends collectively pursued. This promises to be a fruitful line and method of inquiry.

Conclusion

Three questions have been addressed in this examination of shared power. What is shared power and what are its components? How does shared power differ from other types of power? And, under what conditions does shared power exist? The synergistic model of power provides answers to these questions by juxtaposing two types of power — shared power and distributive power.

Shared power is the utilization of pooled resources in the collective pursuit of mutually defined goals. It is composed of three parts: 1) a pooled resource base and

2) cooperative means by which the resources are activated to 3) pursue ends that are collectively defined. Shared power tends to occur under "Tit-for- Tat" conditions as simulated in Axelrod's prisoners' dilemma game.

Distributive power, in comparison, is the utilization of separate resources in the competitive pursuit of goals unilaterally defined. It too is composed of three parts, but the resources are guarded in competition with other parties in order to protect self-interests. It is most likely to occur with the reversal of "Tit-for-Tat" conditions.

While these questions about these two types of power formed the basis of this analysis, there are others that must be addressed if we are to increase our understanding of shared power. The following questions illustrate some of the issues that need to be examined in the future, although they, by no means, are exhaustive.

What happens when a party or system using shared power meets with another party or system using shared power? What occurs when both or all use distributive power? An even more complicated question is, what results when one party or system uses distributive power and the other party uses shared power? What are the consequences for situations that consist of both kinds of power? Will people or groups using shared power be at a disadvantage against distributive power? The questions become even more complicated when multiple sequences of power transactions are considered. Is there an evolutionary process by which certain types of power will prevail?

Axelrod (1984) suggests that there is indeed an evolutionary process in his analysis of cooperation. "The machinery for the evolution of cooperation contains a ratchet," he writes (p.177). He demonstrates, using computer simulations, that the overall level of cooperation, once begun in a system, will go up, not down. That is, despite the presence of distributive power, under certain conditions, cooperation or shared power will prevail. And furthermore, the necessary and sufficient conditions under which cooperation begins, is sustained, and grows in a system, are minimal. His analysis suggests that the long-term trends will be toward shared power — providing that we can survive the learning experiences in the confrontations between shared power and distributive power. Failure of cooperation results in loss of points in the computer game, and the opportunity to try again and learn from previous moves. Failure of shared power in one transaction in the real world may end the opportunity to play "the game" altogether (e.g. the present nuclear weapon crisis). With the stakes and the outcomes so qualitatively different, we may not have the luxury to learn from past mistakes. And it remains to be demonstrated that shared power can be sustained and even grow in a world far more complex than computer simulations.

This first set of questions suggests that there is a coexistence between shared and distributive power, although we may expect to find a reduction of distributive power over time. Another set of questions has to do with the optimal mix between shared power and distributive power. Is shared power always the appropriate and optimal form of power to be employed? Are there certain conditions under which distributive power should be utilized? For example, collusion, monopolies, and "group-think," constitute shared power as we have defined it. There are some who would argue that these forms of shared power are problematic and destructive; they need to be tempered with some form of distributive power that a government or neutral third parties could provide. Consequently, we must ask questions about the ratio of shared power to distributive power, and what the appropriate mix might be under various conditions. Beyond that we need to ask what mechanisms and interventions should govern the mix of distributive and collective power, and with what constraints? Interventions to restructure the conditions and context are a possibility, but each has its own drawbacks and problems so that some combination may be necessary to consider (Axelrod 1984).

Ultimately, the last set of questions leads us to ask, as the title of this paper implies, is there a third type of power that exists as a combination of both shared and distributive power? Can the synergy between the two create another type that we have yet to identify and understand? All of the issues that we have considered here, suggest that this is a question of fundamental importance.

Footnotes

[1] My special thanks and appreciation to Professor Raymond Bradley for his very helpful and thoughtful critique of this chapter.

[2] The concept of shared power is implied in the participation and cooperation literatures, e.g. Mulder (1971), Schermerhorn (1975), Strauss (1963), and Whyte (1983); in the conflict literature, e.g. Filley (1975) and Thomas (1976); and in the bargaining and negotiation literature e.g. Bachrach and Lawler (1981), Thomas (1976).

[3] References to shared power can be found in education e.g. Chesler (1970), Estes (1971), Fahey (1971); intergovernmental relations e.g. Fisher (1981), Griffith (1976), and Goldwater (1979); and health care e.g. Paulson et al. (1980).

[4] Three books that are especially helpful in providing an overview of the power literature are Olsen (1970), Lukes (1974), and Wrong (1979).

[5] The collective perspective on power can be found in Arendt (1970), Craig and Craig (1974), Hartsock (1974), Parsons (1969), and Swingle (1976).

[6] See Bacharach and Lawler (1981) and Rubin and Brown (1975).

[7] See Deutsch (1973), Filley (1975), Thomas (1976), and Walton (1969).

[8] The distributive perspective on power predominates in the literature. Typical examples are in Blau (1964), Emerson (1962), Dahl (1957), and Weber (1947).

[9] The French and Raven typology (1959) does not distinguish between the resources one has and the means that one employs. For example, if one has legitimate power (resource base), then one has a legitimate style. There is no attempt to describe the behavioral patterns that distinguish the means from the base of power.

120   SHARED POWER

References

Aram, J. and W. Stratton. 1974. The development of interagency cooperation. *Social Service Review* 48:412-421.

Arendt, H. 1970. *On violence*. London: The Penguin Press.

Axelrod, R. 1984. *The evolution of cooperation*. New York: Basic Books.

Bachrach, R. and M. Baratz. 1962. Two faces of power. *American Political Science Review* 56:947-952.

Bachrach, S.B. and E.J. Lawler. 1981. *Bargaining, power, tactics, and outcomes*. San Francisco: Jossey-Bass.

Blau, P.M. 1964. *Exchange and power in social life*. New York: John Wiley & Sons.

Chesler, M.A. 1970. Shared power and student decision making. *Educational Leadership* 28(1): 9-14.

Craig, J.H. and M. Craig. 1974. *Synergic power: Beyond domination and permissiveness*. Berkeley, CA: Proactive Press.

Dahl, R.A. 1957. The concept of power. *Behavioral Science* 2: 201-215.

Deutsch, M. 1973. *The resolution of conflict: Constructive and destructive processes*. New Haven: Yale University Press.

Emerson, R.M. 1962. Power-dependence relations. *American Sociological Review* 27:31-41.

Estes, N. 1971. The concept of shared power. *NASSP Bulletin* May: 69-75.

Fahey, J.J. 1971. "Shared power in decision-making in schools: Conceptualization and implementation." Unpublished dissertation, University of Michigan.

Filley, A.C. 1975. *Interpersonal conflict resolution*. Glenview, IL: Scott, Foresman.

Fisher, L. 1981. *The politics of shared power - congress and the executive*. Washington, D.C: Congressional Quarterly Press.

French, J.R.P. and B.H. Raven. 1959. "The bases of social power." In *Studies in social power*, edited by D. Cartwright, 150-167. Ann Arbor, MI: Institute for Social Research, University of Michigan.

Galbraith, J.K. 1983. *The anatomy of power*. Boston: Houghton Mifflin.

Goldwater, B.M. 1976. Treaty terminination is a shared power. *Policy Review* 8:115 -124. New York: New York University Press.

Griffith, E.S. 1976. *The American presidency: The dilemmas of shared power & divided government*. New York: New York University Press.

Hartsock, N. 1974. Political change: Two perspectives on power. *Quest* 1(1): 10-25.

Hobbes, R. 1946. *Leviathan*. Oxford: Blackwell's Political Texts.

Lukes, S. 1974. *Power: A radical view*. London: The Macmillan Press.

McClelland, D. 1979. The two faces of power. In *Organizational Psychology* edited by D.A. Kolb, I.M. Rubin, & J.M. McIntyre. Englewood Cliffs, N.J.: Prentice-Hall.

Machiavelli, N. 1952. *The prince*. New York: Mentor Books.

Metcalfe, L. 1981. Designing precarious partnerships. In *Handbook of organizational design*, edited by P.C. Nystrom and W.H. Starbuck, 503-530. New York: Oxford University Press.

Mills, C.W. 1956. *The power elite*. New York: Oxford University Press.

Mulder, M. 1971. Power equalization through participation? *Administrative Science Quarterly* 16:31-40.

Neustadt, E. 1960. *Presidential power*. New York: John Wiley & Sons.

Olsen, M.E. (Ed.) 1970. *Power in societies*. London: The Macmillan Company.

Parsons, T. 1969. *Politics and social structure*. New York: The Free Press.

Paulsen, S.K, G.E. Konglan, and D.L. Rogers. 1980. A model for the cooperative relationships among health related organizations. *Management International Review* 2(2): 96-107.

Pfeffer, J. 1981. *Power in organizations*. New York: Pitman.

Roberts. N. 1983. "Organizational power styles: Their determinants and consequences." Unpublished dissertation, Stanford University.

Rubin, J.Z. and B.R. Brown. 1975. *The social psychology of bargaining and negotiation*. New York: Academic Press.

Russell, B. 1938. *Power*. London: George Allen and Unwin.

Schermerhorn, J. R. 1975. Determinants of interorganizational cooperation. *Academy of Management Journal* 18(4): 846-856.

Stinchcombe, A.L. 1968. *Constructing social theories*. New York: Harcourt, Brace & World, Inc.

Strauss, G. 1963. Some notes on power-equalization. In *The social science of organizations*, edited by H.H. Leavitt, 41-84. Englewood Cliffs, NJ: Prentice-Hall.

Swingle, P.G. 1976. *The management of power*. Hillsdale, NJ: Lawrence Erlbaum Associate.

_____. 1970. *The structure of conflict*. New York: Academic Press.

Thomas, K. 1976. Conflict and conflict management. In *Handbook of industrial and organizational psychology*, edited by M. Dunnette, 889-935. Chicago: Rand McNally.

Walton, R.E. 1969. *Interpersonal peacemaking: Confrontations and third-party consultation*. Reading, MA: Addison-Wesley Publishing Co., Inc.

Weber, M. 1947. *The theory of social and economic organization*. New York: Free Press.

Whyte, W F. 1983. Worker participation: International and historical perspectives. *Journal of Applied Behavioral Science* 19(3): 395-407.

Wrong, D.H. 1979. *Power: Its forms, bases and uses*. New York: Harper & Row.

CHAPTER 6

Urban Planning
in Shared Power Settings

Richard S. Bolan, Ph.D.

Urban planning, in its theory and in its practice, has had a difficult time dealing with power. The pursuit of a planning model that offers an idealization of rational logic—that stresses an optimum fit between desirable ends and efficient means—simply has not stood the test of application in the real world of complex social dynamics. The rational planner has historically been extremely uncomfortable in the face of political power.

The purpose of this paper is to explore underlying reasons for this discomfort, and to suggest ways it might be overcome. The primary thesis is that urban planning has been operating under a limited and truncated view of rationality. The urban planner's idea of rationality is narrowly conceived and, consequently, fails to account for the multidimensional nature of rationalization processes. The nature of this broader view will be explored based on recent scholarship concerning Max Weber's views of rationality, particularly as these bear on the modernization processes of Western society. This expanded sense of rationality will then be examined for its implications in a world that is increasingly differentiated in a way that makes power more widely shared between and among large-scale social systems.

Urban planners today encounter communities where the tradition of pluralism continues and, indeed, seems to be expanding. The private, public and voluntary sectors of urban economic and social service activity are increasingly interconnected, with each having a share of political power but with no one of the three over-whelmingly dominant. This is not to suggest that power is equitably or equally distributed, or even appropriately wielded; only that one is less and less likely to find any single interest in the urban community so powerful that its aims are never thwarted, resisted or modified by the aims of another interest.

Shared power is not a new characteristic of American urban areas. In the 1950's Norton Long spoke of the urban community as an "ecology of games" (Long 1958), and in the 1960's Roland Warren described the varying structures of "the interorganizational field" (Warren 1967). Both of these visions depicted a highly diffused configuration of power distribution in American communities. In recent times, however, we have begun to see a growing disciplined and systematic effort to study the interactions of a group of interrelated organizational entities (Gamm 1981; Whetten 1981; Negandhi 1980). What has emerged from these efforts is an image of complex networks of exchange, information, support and competition. Increasingly, urban planning processes are conceived, developed, and carried out within these networks. Indeed, the planning network itself has become more differentiated and specialized. Under these circumstances a naive means-ends model of rationality is inadequate as a functioning or practical generalization of contemporary urban planning efforts.

Government at every level in the United States shares power with a wide variety of other economic and social institutions, many of which have become very powerful as political entities as well as dominating economic or social arenas. Contemporary patterns of shared power are also marked by a very high level of technological, organizational and administrative sophistication. They spread across urban areas and span state and regional boundaries. Differentiation and specialization of *labor* may have been the hallmark of the Industrial Revolution. The post- industrial world, in contrast, seems to be characterized by differentiation and specialization of *organizations*. The ways in which we as a society cooperate and coordinate our mutual labors have become more complex and interrelated, with a resulting increasing diffusion of power.

My interpretation of the word "power" is very close to that of Giddens. He asserts (1979, 91) that power is not a description of a state of affairs but, rather, a capability or, as he puts it, a "transformative capacity." Such capacity begins with individual egos and energies and becomes translated into collective power through reproduced interactive social practices that enhance command over resources. The dynamics of such processes will be discussed subsequently. For the moment, however, I envision no permanent, homogeneous "power structures"—power resides in the will and energy of human beings mutually interacting. In this sense, power is a social phenomenon that is constantly subject to renegotiation in some degree, no matter how small. Such a view of power clearly includes the notion that both individual and collective aims may be resisted by other individuals and collectivities. Each one of us has capabilities and energies, both as individuals and as members of organizations, but these are never absolute. They are always situated in circumstances of participation in an interactional social world where all the other actors have capabilities and energies. This is important to keep in mind, since I will later note that the rational model of urban planning tacitly assumes the absence of an interactive social world and, hence, a near unchecked power of the planner.

From this, one would logically assume that power is inherently shared. Some individuals and organizations may be perceived as more powerful than others, but this arises through social negotiations and agreements—not by some divine right or natural law.

This paper, then, seeks to broaden understanding of the full scope of rationalization processes implicit in urban planning under conditions of shared power. First, I will show the varied dimensionality of rationalization processes as has been elucidated in recent scholarship. From this, I sketch a model embracing three distinct forms of rationalization. On the basis of this model, I then seek to analyze how these forms of rationalization are socially manifest in organizational and interorganizational settings, including the notion that forms of rationalization provide a foundation for differentiation and specialization in the division of labor in such settings. From this, I argue that urban planning cannot be based merely on instrumental rationality as has been its tradition. Rather I suggest a more inclusive concern for all aspects of rationality; particularly taking into account that planning is practiced in complex, multi-organizational social settings under conditions of shared power.

A Multifaceted View of Rationality

Max Weber's interest in rationalization is the beginning point of my analysis. This has been the subject of recent scholarly inquiry, and I will try to build on this in suggesting an approach to understanding rational processes in a complex interorganizational field. I draw upon two recent works that explicitly analyze Weber's ideas about rationality: the first is an essay by Stephen Kalberg (1980), the second a recent work of Jurgen Habermas (1984).

Weber's primary question was: Why did capitalism and industrialization occur only in the Occidental societies of Europe and America (Weber 1958, 25)? He felt the Marxian view that capitalism emerged from the conditions of economic production was inadequate and he sought more fundamental clues in religion, law and other social institutions. In doing so he focused on rationalization processes. While Weber never systematically articulated the concept, Kalberg and Habermas have attempted to piece together the various senses in which Weber applied the term "rational." Emerging from their work is a concept of rationality that contains, in Kalberg's terms, "multivalent embodiments."

Kalberg's Analysis of Weberian Rationality

Kalberg suggests that Weber identified four distinct types of rationality (Kalberg 1980, 1151-1159): two of which focus on the practical interests of securing the needs and wants of life while the other two are focused on value and meaning springing from the problems of human association. These four can be described as follows:

1. *Practical rationality* pertains to the thought processes associated with the pursuit of pragmatic and egoistic interests. It is the means by which individuals take account of the world as it exists and calculate the most expedient means of dealing with it.

2. *Theoretical rationality* is the process in which humans seek mastery over the world through the attribution of causality developed by increasingly precise abstract concepts. While we generally associate this with science and philosophy, Kalberg points out that Weber also saw this as a critical element in theological reason.

3. *Substantive rationality* is a form of rationalization that embodies not a purely means-ends calculation but rather the development of patterns of action based on value postulates or clusters of values.

As Weber states:

> Something is not of itself "irrational," but rather becomes so when examined from a specific "rational" *standpoint*. Every religious person is "irrational" for every irreligious person, and every hedonist likewise views every ascetic way of life as "irrational," even if, measured in terms of *its* ultimate values, a "rationalization" has taken place. (Quoted in Kalberg 1980, 1156.)

Thus, in Weber's terms, differing life styles or life worlds defend their own values as rational and label others irrational. If I stand and salute the American flag, that is seen by fellow Americans as rational, but a resident of Nepal might perceive my action as rather odd, or irrational. Weber also argues that there is, thus, no absolute standard for substantive rationality.

4. *Formal rationality* relates to those thought processes which attempt to codify practical rationality with reference to a substantively rationalized world view of value. The result is formal laws, rules, regulations, and formally structured patterns of domination and administration.

Kalberg notes that all four types are manifest in rationalizing at all levels of collective processes. Thus, the reference points for the mental processes associated with rationalization include: interests, abstractions about the world, values, world views, laws and regulations. Purely means-ends calculations are but a single manifestation of these multiple processes.

The Habermas View of Weber

Habermas (1984, Ch. 2) views the Weberian concept of rationality in progressive, developmental terms. Rationality, in the first instance, emerges from experience. It is thus rooted in practical rationality. It begins with "techniques" for dealing with the world, ways of doing things honed by experience. Thus, there are techniques of building, techniques of prayer, techniques of making love, techniques of making war, and so forth. In time, alternative techniques to meet the same purpose are devised, so that techniques thereafter are qualified by introduction of varied prospects of success where subjectively purposeful-rational schemes are contrasted with traditional, customary action.

Further articulation of rationalization occurs not only when alternative means are more or less rational, but ends can be deliberately chosen as well. Habermas terms this the "rationality of choice" or the process of choosing ends to be sought in accord with values. He then argues, in somewhat different fashion than Kalberg, that the Weberian notion of formal rationality is the combination of the instrumental rationality that specifies technique and the rationality of choice that specifies ends. Thus, formal rationality, in Habermas' view is embedded in substantive rationality. This latter form of rationality is the evaluation of value postulates or clusters or systems of value that underlie the preferences expressed in the "rationality of choice." As Habermas puts it, "the *way* in which an actor grounds his preferences is for Weber an aspect under which an action can be viewed as rationalizable."

Even though the views of Kalberg and Habermas are different, two basic aspects of rationality are evident from this discussion. First, rationality takes place at many levels and, second, the various levels are correlative. Practical rationality, theoretical rationality, and formal rationality all presuppose and derive from substantive rationality, as Weber defines this.[1] However, while granting the interaction between these levels, I will argue below that we do indeed create social roles and social structures that differentiate and foster specialization of rationalization processes. As a prelude to this, however, it is important to come to grips with the term "rationality" itself and its verb form, "to rationalize."

Standard dictionary definitions beg the question. To rationalize is to reason, to calculate, to cause something to seem reasonable. Interestingly, the term "rationalization" has also developed a negative, deceptive connotation—to provide plausible but untrue reasons. ("He 'rationalized' that the failure of his team to win the game was due to incompetent officiating.") Each of these definitions, of course, begs the question: What is reason, or what are the characteristics of being reasonable? To reason properly, or to be reasonable invoke standards or norms and thereby implicate a value stance.

The giving of reasons for an action, either before or after the fact, is essentially a linguistic action. Thus, Habermas argues that being rational is primarily embedded in what he terms "communicative competence." Indeed, Weber originally conceived of rationality as the formal organization of symbol systems, originally emerging from primitive systems of religious belief. The view of Schlucter, quoted by Habermas, seems especially relevant to our concerns here:

(R)ationalism means...systematizing of meaning complexes, intellectually working through and consciously sublimating the "aims of meaning."

It is a consequence of the "inner compulsion" of civilized beings not only to grasp the world but also to take a position on it; it is thus metaphysical-*ethical* rationalism in the broadest sense. (Quoted in Habermas 1984, 176.)

Rationalization, in these terms, is a *willful* action which takes a stance through the medium of the primary human symbolization system, language.

Habermas argues that Weber's focus of rationality—orientation toward explaining or "giving reasons for" different forms of social action—is not wholly adequate and the effort to be rational is, more correctly, the effort of mutual participants in communicative interaction seeking to reach an understanding that fundamentally provides a framework of agreement for mutual coordination of plans and actions. Thus, for Habermas, rationality is less a reason for behavior than it is a basis for the establishment of interpersonal relations.

Thus, rationality is something more than the ability of individuals to "utter well grounded factual beliefs and to act efficiently" (ibid., 15). Habermas suggests that it involves a four-fold array of *validity claims*: 1) the truth of propositions, 2) the rightness of norms of action implied by propositions, 3) the adequacy of standards of value, and 4) the sincerity or truthfulness of the speaker. Thus, the concept of rationality extends beyond the standard rules of logical inference and suggests a broad array of legitimating forms of argument.

Habermas further distinguishes between communicative action and strategic action. Communicative action, he suggests, is oriented toward achieving *understanding*, while strategic action is oriented toward achieving *success*. Strategic action does not give rise to validity claims, as just described, but rather to claims of power. In his view, strategic action is rooted in rationalization processes which are technical and practical and which tend to presuppose the normative background of prior communicative action on which they rest. A medical protocol, for example, is strategically rational in that its outcome results in a cured patient. However, its *fundamental* rationality is not solely its technical efficacy but also implicated is the rationality of the terms, conditions and agreements under which medicine is practiced in a given community. Similarly, that the capitalist makes a profit depends not only on the rationality of the strategic moves that he makes but also on the rationalization of the social system that legitimates making a profit.

Toward a Social Rationality

I am uncomfortable with the distinction between communicative action and strategic action, and would agree more with Watzlawick et al. (1969): just as a speech act implies validity claims so does it also imply performative or quasi-performative dimensions, and hence, implicates *relational* claims — i.e. implicit claims concerning the speaker's *relation* to the listener. Such claims are not confined to strategic action but are embedded in communicative action as well. Thus, the normative rationalization of validity claims is intertwined with the normative rationalization of claims to power. Indeed, Habermas' validity claims of rightness and legitimacy presuppose a prior sense of social obligation and privilege and, hence, a tacit understanding of power.

Giddens (1979, ch. 2) also stresses the primary grounding of rationalization processes in language. He begins by analyzing the work of Derrida, who argues that speech and language (the signifier and the signified) are not separable and that they are "two sides of one and the same production." From this, Derrida claims that all signification, or all human processes of creating meaning, imply constant processes of mutation, by the play of identities, differences and distinctions in our descriptions of the world and in the positions we take in the world.

We have an image of a process of linguistic genetic mutation such as suggested by Piaget (Los 1981, 73). The interaction of speech and language becomes recursively implicated in the production and reproduction of social practices. These linguistically grounded processes of "the structuring of structure" can be conceived as processes of rationalization. Rationalization is itself a linguistic performance; simultaneously a description, an explanation and a justification; rooted in the play between what Giddens calls "a virtual world of differences." Rationalization is thus a process of differentiation that is recursively dynamic.

Seen in this way, rationalization is a form of social practice—a mode of social action. Rationalization is deeply embedded in social structures (i.e., the division of labor, the configuration of institutions; themselves the products of reified, reproduced social action). Yet rationalization has an impact on social structures involving the transformational capacities cited above. Rationalization in these broader perspectives, then, extends far beyond mere logical calculation. The canons of logical reasoning are themselves the products of rationalized social action in this view.

From this discussion, we more clearly see the limits of the urban planner's traditional model of rationality. Its stress on the efficacy of calculated action is an ego-centered Cartesian model, presupposing no resistance, or at best a benign indifference, on the part of other social actors. It is a view that presumes a homogeneous and highly stable normative backdrop for action. The planner's rationality is a technical or practical model rather than a substantive, social model. It is rooted in transforming the physical world, particularly under assumptions of individual autonomy. However, when the concern is the transformation of the social world, such a model is incomplete and lacking. Thus, planning needs to seek a communicative, multivalent *social* rationality in the sense that Kalberg, Habermas and Giddens suggest; a rationality that takes account of the production and reproduction of social action in its broadest sense.

From these varying perspectives of rationality, Figure 1 offers a conceptual framework from which a new model of planning rationality might be derived. Figure 1 is an effort to consolidate the foregoing argument. The diagram depicts the interplay of language and speech embedded in a situational context of social institutions (or reified, or "frozen" social practices). Speech acts are manifested in three forms. From Habermas, there is communicative action oriented toward reaching understanding in the sense of reaching agreement on meaning, value, and the rules of human association. Additionally, strategic action is indicated—action oriented toward success in the sense of reaching mastery over both the physical and social world.

There is added a third category of social action. Characterizing an action purely as either seeking understanding or seeking mastery only works in relatively small, undifferentiated social structures. Understanding or mastery can be

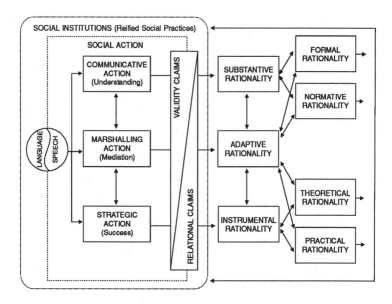

Figure 6-1   A Franework of Social Rationality

viewed, in effect, as two ends of a continuum. Social action in general, and certainly that in elaborated interorganizational networks and large-scale social systems, would more commonly entail combinations of these two motivations. In this sense, I suggest a distinct form of social action that is oriented toward *mediating* between communicative action and strategic action. On Figure 1, this is identified as *marshalling action*. This term suggests action, in the context of an interactive, intersubjective social framework that is oriented toward *mobilizing* cooperative and coordinative effort. Marshalling action seeks *both* understanding *and* success. Its focus is action oriented toward bringing together multiple, socially based—as distinct from individually based—actions.

In concurrently seeking both understanding and success, marshalling action acknowledges potential contradictory facets of these two motivations; hence, the vision of marshalling action as mediational in character. Its motivation is "resolution" of these contradictory facets.

Each of the three forms of social action is subject to public scrutiny pertaining to their respective validity claims in the manner suggested by Habermas. Each, as well, is simultaneously subject to scrutiny of their relational claims, or what Habermas terms claims of power. Each draws on the intersubjective exchange of meaning concerning the obligations and privileges associated with reaching understanding. They are claims of one actor on the values, understandings, and actions of one or more other actors. Thus, every social action is subject to simultaneous scrutiny from the viewpoints of both validity and power.

This can be illustrated by an example of technological change: the introduction of, say, a CAT scanner into a hospital. This is no simple change in hardware. While introducing a new level of technical sophistication, it simultaneously triggers a new social configuration of the hospital as a community of workers. In the first instance, it affects the division of labor by requiring new activities embodying new skills. These, in turn, generate the need for new understandings of privilege and obligation (e.g., power and authority) because of the need for new patterns of coordinating old and new activities within the hospital. Hence, the new machine does not merely serve the strategic, instrumental aims of better patient care; it also challenges the substantive nature of the previous level of communicative understanding. Whoever undertakes to introduce this innovation simultaneously has to address the motivations of both strategic action and communicative action. Since the two are not necessarily complementary and may indeed be contradictory, there is need to mediate between them in an effort to reach resolution as to how both might be simultaneously pursued. The hospital example also illustrates the pluralistic character of such mediation—the need for widespread acceptance of new patterns of coordination and cooperation deriving from the required new behaviors and relationships.[2]

Using Weber's terminology, the different forms of rationalization of social actions either planned or already performed are depicted in Figure 1. Substantive rationality flows primarily from communicative action and embodies both normative rationality (or the rationalization of values) and formal rationality expressed in laws, rules, and regulations. These, in turn, act back and affect social institutions and practices—either in reifying or reproducing them, or in modifying or altering them.

Similarly, instrumental rationality flows primarily from strategic action and manifests itself in both practical or technical rationality and in Weber's theoretical rationality. These similarly feed back to existing social practices.

A form of rationality also flows from marshalling action, which I label adaptive rationality. It is that form of explanation or justification that expressly mediates between substantive rationality and instrumental rationality, while articulating justifications for both. It is, moreover, an explicitly *social* rationality.

Differentiation and Specialization in Rationalization Processes

This broader view of rationalization has been discussed at an abstract level. To more fully understand its implications, it is important to think of these processes in the context of the shared power of complex social systems. When we do this, we find that the broader, Weberian view has been differentiated to a marked degree so that there is evidence of institutionalized specialization in rationalization. Not only do rationalization processes yield a division of labor of instrumental tasks; they also generate a division of labor in substantive or normative tasks—and a still further division of labor among the different processes of rationalization. Social action is recursive; since rationalization is the process of endowing social action with meaning, it is thereby integral to social action. Hence, rationalization is equally recursive and the act of rationalization itself is rationalized.

Rationalization and Organization
These processes can be seen in examining both a single organization and the field of interorganizational relations. The combination of these two offer a portrayal of what might be termed the field of rationalization. When combined together, a picture of the framework for developing a new sense of a rational model for planning is further shaped.

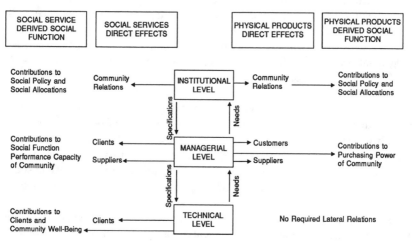

See: Parsons, *Structure and Process in Modern Societies*, Chapter II.

Figure 6-2   *Sub-system Hierarchy and System-wide Relations at Each Level*
                (Formal Organizations)

   Figure 1 portrayed rationalization processes in general. Figure 2 is an effort to depict the nature of rationalization in the social practices of those individuals bound together in a single collectivity. Figure 2 is adapted from a discussion by Parsons (1960) concerning the patterns of functional relations that are differentiated within a formally organized collectivity. This differentiation into specialized functional roles evolves as the collectivity strives to relate to its environment. Figure 2 is a familiar portrayal and reflects the traditional hierarchy of organizational design (see:

Van de Ven, Emmett, and Koenig 1980, 31-32). At the bottom of the hierarchy is a technical level where the actual work of production is performed. Above this is a managerial level which coordinates the activities and sets the specifications for the technical level and mediates between the technical level and the outside world, in terms of resource mobilization and effective disposition of the organization's output. At the top is the institutional or fiduciary level which mediates between the managerial level and higher-order, system-wide interests and values. This hierarchical pattern is common to both private and public activities in the United States. Manufacturers and social service agencies alike exhibit these three levels.[3]

Within this tri-level hierarchy, Parsons suggests a reciprocal relationship in which specifications are passed downwards and demands for "needs" are passed upwards. Specifications at the top (board of directors, stockholders, etc.) are necessarily general and become more specific in working downwards from managers to production workers (or service providers). The overall configuration rests heavily on a centralized, articulated authority structure. It is the dominant Western institutional pattern of mobilizing motivation, sentiment and resources designed to yield coordinated, goal-directed activities.

Parsons further argues that each level relates to the larger social environment principally in a lateral fashion. Communications outside the organization at the technical level are confined to external counterparts at the same level. Those at the managerial level are similarly restricted. At the top, those in fiduciary roles relate primarily to those at a similar level in external lateral relations. This will be further explored below in discussing interorganizational relations.

Figure 2 also portrays the functional social action dimensions of the tri-level hierarchy. Their respective "functions" illustrate the "rationalization of rationalization." Persons acting at each level "give reasons for" their tasks and activities of their respective level. For example, in a hospital: 1) physicians, nurses, technicians, etc., "rationalize" the activities involved in patient care (the instrumental rationality of the hospital); 2) hospital administrators rationalize patterns of coordination and oversight, introduction of new technology, expansion of services, procurement of resources and patients, maintenance of buildings and grounds (the adaptive rationality of the hospital vis-a-vis its environment); and 3) the members of the hospital's board of directors "rationalize" the legitimacy and social role of the hospital—they "give reasons for" the very existence of the hospital (the substantive rationality in terms of the hospital's *public trust* in its community). The hierarchical levels of bureaucratic order are thus designed in a manner that separates out distinct forms of rationality in keeping with distinct forms of social practice.[4]

Figure 2 also distinguishes between the production of goods versus the production of services. Parsons argues that what is important in this distinction is that for those organizations producing a physical product, lateral relations are greatly diminished (and more effectively controlled) since there are no required lateral relations between those functioning at the technical level and the outside world.[5]

Instrumental rationality is a necessary but insufficient condition for explaining organizational structure. Traditional organization theory argues that the technology of an organization plays a major role in shaping both its internal social practices and its external relations. Contemporary views suggest things are more complex than this. Meyer and Rowan state the case graphically:

> ...the formal structures of many organizations in postindustrial society dramatically reflect the myths of their institutional environments instead of the demands of their work activities (Meyer and Rowan 1977, 341).

Similarly, Milner notes: "Different historical and cultural backgrounds can produce significantly different patterns for organizing what is, technically speaking, the same activity" (Milner 1980, 82).

Environmental demands on the organization involve both the original array of formal agreements and a continuing process of emergent legitimation and trust throughout the life of the organization. There is ongoing interplay between the codified canons of formal rationality and the continual evolution of new agreements and new understandings through the dynamics of normative rationality. Meyer and Rowan elaborate:

> In modern societies, the elements of rationalized formal structure are deeply ingrained in, and reflect, widespread understandings of social reality. Many of the positions, policies, programs, and procedures of modern organizations are enforced by public opinion, by the views of important constituents, by knowledge legitimated through the educational system, by social prestige, by the laws, and by the definitions of negligence and prudence used by the courts. Such elements of formal structure are manifestations of powerful institutional rules which function as highly rationalized myths that are binding on particular organizations (Ibid., 343).

Organizations come into being through a substantively rationalized framework of understandings and agreements, within which is worked out the technical, practical demands as shaped by these understandings and agreements. As Benson notes, part of an organization's ideology is its way of rationalizing its technology (Benson 1975, 237). The distinction is clearly discernible. The ideology, or "culture" of General Motors is different than that of Ford which, in turn, is different than Chrysler—and all three are vastly different than the ideology or culture of auto manufacturers in Japan or Sweden. At the same time, there is constant interplay between substantive and technical rationality. Each organization, in effect, is engaged in the creation, control and manipulation of complex systems of symbolization that permeate both internal and external relations.

Substantive rationality becomes differentiated within each level of the organization in the course of its recursive reproduction. Thus, understandings relating to individual activities and relationships become specialized according to the level of institutionalized social practices in which they take place. The formal norms of individuals at the technical level are embedded in the normative specifications set at the managerial level; similarly, those of the managerial level are embedded in the larger normative framework of the fiduciary level.

This does not suggest that normative structures cannot develop internally within a single level. Both informal and formal norms occur within a given level as has generally been observed in the so-called "Hawthorne effect." One should also not make the mistake of viewing substantive rationality as purely constraining; the understandings as expressed in norms, conventions, practices, etc. are primarily oriented toward creating the conditions for *enabling* action.

This structure of a single organization is, itself, a normative rationalization. Weber, of course, argues that it represents one of the significant elements in the development of modern Occidental society. The important point, however, is that it is the result of multiple processes of *social* rationalization. It is never merely instrumental rationality.

Finally, these levels of rationalization also address the relationships between claims to validity and claims to power. As the history of the organizational literature suggests, these claims are continually in tension. In this context, however, the tension can be seen to be more than merely a struggle between expertise and authority. It is a struggle that crosses all levels of relations within an organization.

Rationalization and Interorganizational Relations

Turning to interorganizational relations, there has been increasing study of how organizations interact with other organizations. The general result portrays a picture of modern urban life in the United States characterized by a multiplicity of separate but interdependent organizations. Local government is one institution within this configuration functioning to integrate this diversity but it is, by no means, the only one—modern urban society is marked by a host of federations, associations, coalitions, networks and leagues reflecting the multiple ways in which individual organizations link together.

I suggest an expansion of the usual theoretical orientation of interdependency, particularly the notion of resources exchange (Gamm 1981). Levine and White (1961) argued that interdependencies arise because of scarcity, so that no single organization commands the full array of resources necessary to fulfill its goals. Giddens, however, argues that social structures arise from the genesis of recursive social practices that yield not only the means of dealing with resources but also with *rules* (agreements, trusts, contracts, sanctions, legitimating processes). The development of interorganizational relations is consequently more than mere exchange. It is exchange within a substantively rationalized arena — a rationally organized *normative* field for exchange.

Patterns of interaction in an interorganizational field—as with those of a single organization—are explained more fundamentally by embracing the full range of processes of social rationalization. The character of these processes, moreover, becomes more complex in the interorganizational field than in a single organization. Three basic characteristics mark this enhanced complexity.

1. The interorganizational field in the American culture possesses no central decision-making authority. This, itself, is a manifestation of substantive rationalization, characteristic of a widely shared world view strongly influenced by the preeminence of market concepts—a view that, in part, contributes to the conditions for widely shared power. Authority patterns are always contingent and never firmly fixed. Claims to power are continually being scrutinized and renegotiated. This fact does not mean the field actually is a pure market, guided only by a "hidden hand." A variety of configurations of differential sharing of power are characteristic of interorganizational fields in the U.S. (see: Warren 1967; Lehman 1975). In fact, Milner (1980) notes an interesting paradox: some interorganizational fields are considered "private" where purely market forces are expected to rule (particularly economic production); yet these fields often show evidence of high levels of interorganizational coordination particularly, as Milner points out, in oligopolistic conditions. Other interorganizational fields are considered "public" or "non-profit" (e.g., social welfare services) where central coordination is deemed to be ideal but, in actuality, is absent. Competition and struggles for dominance are commonplace in the social services network.

2. With neither a pure market model nor a pure central bureaucratic model holding sway, the next point of complexity lies in the fact that many relationships in the interorganizational field are particularistic and take place within informal or tacitly accepted patterns of dominance or inequality. Milner's study of health care providers in a local urban community is illustrative here. In a neighborhood with three general hospitals and diverse other public and private health care providers (nursing homes, clinics, etc.), both formal and informal patterns of interaction served to sustain images of both status and quality of care. Issues around expansion of services, allocation and referral of patients, appointments of staff physicians all take place in the context of what Milner terms "symbiotic inequality." This field of interdependence is characterized by the simultaneous existence of: a) particularistic linkages based on personal relationships and ad hoc problem solving; b) informal structures of quasi-authority; and c) "highly imperfect quasi-markets" (Milner 1980, 78). The highest status hospital dominates the field, yet is highly dependent on even the lowest status hospital—indeed to the extent where the high status hospital acted (rationally) to prevent the imminent bankruptcy of the low status hospital (ibid., 46).

3. Given the lack of central authority and the particularistic nature of inter-organizational relations, each individual organization retains some measure of autonomy. As with individuals, however, no organization enjoys total autonomy or unrestricted freedom of action. Every organization seeks to realize its goals and, in the process, attempts to express and impose its values. Thus, organizations can be said to have *contingent* autonomy. Given this, the potential for conflict is inherent.

Consequently, a third key characteristic of interorganizational relations is what one author describes as mixed patterns of "partial autonomy" and "partial conflict" (Gamm 1981, 26).

Benson (1975) argues that there is a "political economy" to interorganizational networks and that power relations among the organizations of any given network will largely be a reflection of the power relations of the larger society. He identifies what he terms four elements of the "superstructure of sentiments and interactions" of a given interorganizational network. What is important in these elements is that they, too, bear close resemblance to Weber's multivalent notion of rationality. Benson argues there is 1) a domain consensus, 2) an ideological consensus, 3) a climate of basically positive evaluation among the parties to the interaction, and 4) an agreed upon pattern of work coordination within the network (Benson 1975).

The relation of these four elements to our schema of rationality is evident. The domain consensus refers to agreement among the parties in the network regarding the appropriate role and sphere of activities of each of the participants, as well as the agreed upon scope of activities of the network as a whole. (See also: Warren, Rose and Bergunder 1974.) The ideological consensus reflects agreement about the nature of the tasks confronting the network and the appropriate approaches to those tasks. The evaluatory consensus reflects the historical experience of a flow of net reciprocal satisfactions in mutual goal attainment which contribute to rationalizing the maintenance of the other areas of agreement. The coordinative consensus reflects agreements that rationalize the detailed divisions of labor among the participating organizations.

The processes by which these four agreements are reached are based in linguistic acts pertaining to the creation and maintenance of social action. The result is a differentiated field of agreements concerning activities, jurisdictions, shared tasks, shared resources and shared values. Warren (1974) refers to this as the prevalent "thought structure" of the field of interaction. As Zeitz puts it, the network is the product of "the creative acts of intentional subjects." These acts are in some measure constrained "by structures that are the residues of previous actions" (Zeitz 1980, 73-74). In short, to create a domain consensus, an ideological consensus, a coordinative consensus, and a satisfaction consensus as Benson uses these terms, requires the full array of rationalization processes depicted in Figure 1.

Figure 3 portrays a simple space-time interorganizational field, wherein the lateral relations of the individual organization specified in Figure 2 are shown in relation to their targets—i.e., other organizations. Figure 3 expresses the interorganizational manifestations of the specialized forms of rationality of Figure 2 extended to a multi-organizational field. The pattern of differentiation that takes place in a single organization is reproduced in the interorganizational field.

Vertical communication between levels is difficult across the interorganizational field stemming from the formal, controlled nature of vertical communication within individual organizations. For example, an invitation for interaction between

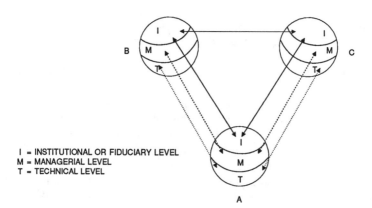

I = INSTITUTIONAL OR FIDUCIARY LEVEL
M = MANAGERIAL LEVEL
T = TECHNICAL LEVEL

Figure 6-3   *Differentiated Channels of Rationalized Interaction in the*
                Interorganizational Field

Organization A and Organization B originating at the technical level at A is not likely to be communicated directly from the technical people at A to those at the institutional level of B. Norms and protocols of the rationalized field of interaction would tend to discourage such an overture. The invitation, then, would be extended from a person at the technical level at A to a technical level counterpart at B. If this invitation and its response are fully within the substantive climate of both organizations, nothing further may be needed. For example, two social workers in two separate agencies may initiate communication leading to a particularistic agreement to refer clients, share information, and so forth. However, if such an invitation seriously modifies domain consensus, resource allocation, or broader patterns of coordination, the invitation received at the technical level at B must be relayed vertically and internally to the managerial and institutional levels at B before being acted on. Moreover, further elaboration at these higher levels becomes necessary with higher level counterparts at A. Thus, vertical interactions across organizational structures is not a general characteristic of the interorganizational field.

It is interesting to explore the reasons for this. My hypothesis again returns to the linguistic sources of social action. I would propose, with Wittgenstein, that the specialized rationalizations of each level, together with their associated activities (or "forms of life" to use Wittgenstein's term) comprise different "language games." Each level has characteristic vocabularies, expressions, meanings, and symbols that are bound together with the activities, interests and intentions of that level. The intertwining of language and activity into distinct "forms of life" creates different systems of symbolization and, thus, different forms of self-definition.

Such "forms of life" extend beyond organizational or work life. They interact with broader social class distinctions of the larger society, as Benson noted. The institutional, managerial and technical levels of many organizations reflect the upper-, middle-, and working-class distinctions of society at large. Thus, leisure and recreational associations and networks will often be extensions of the different "forms of life" shaped in the interorganizational work environment.

Empirical evidence of these patterns is available. Van de Ven, Walker and Liston (1979) examined the interactions of health and welfare organizations in a southwestern locale and found their communications tended to cluster into three groups: 1) a resource transactions cluster, 2) a planning and coordination cluster, and 3) a direct service cluster. Looking at the characteristics of these three, we find the first marked by formal contracts, written communications, close monitoring—all evidences of transactions within a framework of formal rationality. The third cluster clearly relates to the demands of instrumental-technical rationality. The second cluster is marked by face-to-face meetings of actors at the managerial level, some of which were formal but most of which were informal. These attributes clearly indicate flexibility and openness—activities involving adaptive search behavior for innovative approaches to marshalling resources, coordinating tasks, and striking new agreements.

Examining interagency coordination among organizations serving the mentally retarded in five cities, Aiken et al., found that:

> ...resources are best coordinated at the institutional level, programs at the organization level, clients at the individual case worker level, and information at all three levels (Aiken et al. 1975, 16).

Their findings suggest the same point as above: communications in interorganizational networks do tend to stay within different levels which generally reflect the patterns outlined on Figures 2 and 3.

Another recent study of intergovernmental networks in six widely different cities offers further evidence of the specialization of rationalization processes. This study, by Agranoff and Lindsay (1983), examined conditions of successful intergovernmental management. Their findings suggested the need for identifying a similar three-part division of interactional rationalization.

Urban Planning, Rationality and Shared Power

On various occasions, government has tried to mandate coordination among a group of organizations whose collaboration would be assumed necessary for a given public policy program (Raelin 1982). But these efforts have generally not proven successful.

Herein lies the problem for urban planning. The traditional concept of the comprehensive plan assumes that someone, in some fashion, can mandate that participants in the various community interorganizational networks collaborate around a specific policy of community betterment. The tradition assumes that decision units are monolithic entities (such as "the city," "the health system," and so forth). But this analysis would suggest that such a view is overly simplistic on three counts: first, the failure to take into account the diffused distribution of power in the urban community; second, the failure to grasp the particularistic, idiographic nature of interorganizational relationships; and third, a lack of understanding of the full breadth of rationalization processes in these networks and how such processes are recursively and historically produced, reproduced and differentiated.

From the foregoing argument, the outline of a more comprehensive view of rationality can be seen. The accumulating complexity of the social world yields settings for public planning in which power is increasingly shared and, hence, increasingly diffuse. As the interorganizational field expands in its complexity and in the resultant broadening base of power sharing, rational planning of public policy requires an understanding of what it means to be rational in new and more fully elaborated ways.

There has been a growing body of literature in urban planning critical of the so-called "rational model" and suggesting that alternative conceptions of what it means to plan be devised. Counter critics have argued that those who would drop the rational model offer nothing in its place, leaving urban planners with only confusion concerning their methods and their skills. What is suggested here is neither radical abandonment nor conservative defense of the rational planning model. Rather, the need is for an expansion of the model—an expansion based on a more fundamental and inclusive view of what it means to be rational.

Figure 1 sketched the beginning contours of such an enlarged view of rationality. Figure 4 derives from this a beginning typology of differing characteristics associated with the various elements of a broader view. Figure 4 attempts to articulate not merely an instrumental rationality nor a substantive rationality, but rather a *social* rationality that emerges from primordial communicative relations in the social world. It is a rationality that is *dialectical* in character. It first springs from a Cartesian, ego-centered calculating process where to be rational is defined in terms of a single agent, totally autonomous, seeking mastery over the physical world. This is countered by an orientation stemming from the ideas of obligation in Rousseau's *Social Contract* in which individual needs, and the capacity to meet those needs, are inextricably bound up with those of a social community. Rational action, in this counterview, is embedded in a network of social expectations and social values.

The synthetic "moment" of rationality emerges from an adaptive approach to social action that mediates between autonomous instrumental rationality and communal normative rationality and seeks mechanisms for social collaboration that further both understanding and mastery. Thus, we can envision a *gestalt* of rational action where all three elements are dynamically intertwined. The pursuit of any given form of rationality cannot succeed without taking into account the other forms.

Figure 4 sketches out the primary features of this dialectical view. In the left hand column are shown key characterizing elements that form the presuppositions, approaches and orientations of each of the three types of rationality. These range

SKETCH OF A COMPREHENSIVE MODEL OF RATIONALITY

CHARACTERIZING ELEMENT	INSTRUMENTAL RATIONALITY (Practical-Theoretical)	ADAPTIVE RATIONALITY (Mediating)	SUBSTANTIVE RATIONALITY (Normative-Formal)
MODEL OF "MAN"	Descartes: Solitary Thinking Ego	Dialectical Ego	Rousseau: Socially Obligated Ego
ATTITUDE OF CONSCIOUSNESS	Ego-focused Intentionality Cognitive Objectivating	Ego-Alter Struggle	Alter-focused Intentionality Interactive Conformative
WORLD VIEW	Naturalistic Objective World	Combined Objective Intersubjective World	Socially Intersubjective World
ETHICAL BASE	Utilitarian Calculus of Optimization	Socially Contingent Optimization	Social Interactive Contingent Freedom Partial Autonomy Legal-Regulative
ATTITUDE TOWARD POWER	Individualistic Absolute Freedom Total Autonomy	Social Interactive Open to Development and Change	Social Interactive Contingent Freedom Partial Autonomy Legal-Regulative
COMMUNICATIVE ORIENTATION	Success in achieving individually formulated goals	Success based on understanding in achieving socially formulated goals	Understanding Social formulation of rules of association
VALIDITY CLAIMS	Effectiveness	Mutually shared Effectiveness within agreed upon legitimacy	Truthfulness-Sincerity Rightfulness- Legitimacy
METHOD OF EVALUATING CLAIMS	Objective, quantitative calculation	Pluralistic bargaining	Axiomatic application of principle and/or precedent
TYPE OF KNOWLEDGE DOMINANT	Technically and strategically useful	Knowledge of particularistic arrangements of shared power in moral-legal context in face of technical needs	Moral-Practical Knowledge Legal Representations Aesthetic Knowledge
THEMES OF SPEECH ACTS	Speaker's Intentions Descriptions Predictions	Eliciting needs	Intentions
TONE OF SPEECH ACTS	Imperative	Negotiative	Regulative

Adapted From: J. Habermas (1984). *The Theory of Communicative Action, Reason and the Rationalization of Society,* Volume One. Boston: Beacon Press.
J. Habermas (1979). *Communication and the Evolution of Society.* Boston: Beacon Press.

Figure 6-4

from the presupposed "model of man" to the ethical and communicative stances that each model implies. Included are the claims of each, the approach to evaluating claims, the kinds of knowledge that dominate each, and the characteristic themes and tones of speech that comprise the "language game" of each.

The mediating, or synthesizing character of adaptive rationality is highlighted in the center column of Figure 4. The dialectical "model of man" recognizes a continual struggle between the individual and the world of social obligation; between the demands of the objective world and those of the intersubjective world; between effectiveness and legitimacy. The mediating role of adaptive rationality features an openness to development and change in both the material world and the social world. The dialectical character emerges from the recognition that the understandings and rules of human association are not fixed for all time but need to be continually renegotiated to take account of a dynamic and changing social or collective consciousness.

Hence, the planning and management of large-scale social systems for delivering goods and services requires the synthetic elements of adaptive rationality. Planning in settings of shared power requires the integration and synthesis of instrumental and substantive rationality in a way that recognizes the dynamic processes of change occurring within each and is sensitive to the contradictory and often conflictual intermixing of each.

Planning focused purely on instrumental rationality is one-dimensional in the sense that Marcuse noted in the 1960's; it is technocratic and obscures the value dilemmas inherent in planning processes. For example, it is insufficient for hospital planners to "rationalize" the installation of a CAT-scanner solely on the grounds of its superiority or efficiency in patient care—the planning of such a move also has to account for and "rationalize" what the innovation implies for the hospital as an organizational entity and for the hospital as an integral part of a larger community. Similarly, it is not enough for urban transportation planners to justify a new highway on the grounds of its capacity to carry traffic. They also need to account for the highway's likely impact on the larger community in broader terms—e.g., its associational and affective networks, its "forms of life" and their symbolic expression in a spatial-temporal framework.

On the other hand, planning that focuses purely on substantive rationality can easily fail to take acccount of resource limitations or technical feasibility. Moreover, concentration on formal rationality can give planning its perhaps unjustified image of being coercive or even inherently totalitarian. At best, concentration on formal rationality casts the planner in the role of rule-maker or regulator—as a wielder of the police power rather than a progressive problem-solver.

Thus, the need to develop a synthetic model of adaptive rationality is vital for planning in settings of shared power. The synthetic, adaptive model incorporates both instrumental and substantive rationality but adds the dimensions of creating new meanings and new thrusts of achievement through a communicative process that concentrates on understanding the existential interstices of shared power and their potential for creation and mobilization of social and political as well as material resources.

This dialectical model of rationality for planning requires a communicative skill that can successfully integrate validity claims and claims for power in a manner that evokes the mobilization of collective social action. It suggests not only the calculation of means and ends within cost accounting frameworks but also the identification and balancing of claims of legitimacy, morality and social power. It involves not only the mobilization of resources but also the mobilization of sentiment. It ordains seeking to reveal the distribution of good and harm in any policy. The dialectical model embraced by adaptive rationality, in sum, requires concurrently a technical, political and moral imagination in the service of creating new forms of social practice which can be responsive to new expression of needs.

This has implications for planning on the level of methodology, procedural theory and, most fundamentally, at the level of language—i.e., how urban planning is talked about and thought about.

Stating this in practical terms, urban planners need to strive for approaches which expand their perceptive acuity in dealing with shared power in urban communities and how that power is mobilized. Traditionally, the urban planner in a new community has set out to "know" the community through exploring its physical geography: its streets, neighborhoods and districts. In my suggested broader vision of rational planning, "knowing" the community would also include systematically exploring its social and political environment. This implies not only the traditional views (such as neighborhood segregation and stratification) but also the more critical, phenomenological view of the niches, nooks and crannies of associational understandings, agreements and interactions, both formal and informal, together with their underlying patterns of privilege and obligation (see: Forester 1984). Following from arguments of Argyris and Schon (1978) about barriers to organizational learning, a planner's explorations would inlcude how interorganizational networks "learn" and what forms of both formal and tacit norms help to shape and influence the manner in which community problems are identified and taken up. How are sentiments mobilized? How are resources mobilized? How are actions coordinated? How are these different mobilization processes explained or justified (rationalized)? What languages, or language "games," are employed and under what circumstances? In sum, where traditionally planners have sought to "know" their community *objectively*, my thesis in this paper argues that planners need to "know" their community *intersubjectively*.[6]

The particularistic, idiographic features of this social terrain are important aspects to explore, especially the accommodations which lay down the division of labor in community rationalizing processes. Who is looked to in a given interorganizational network for instrumental analysis or judgment? Who specializes in normative judgment? What status and respect do such persons command? What language do they offer in justifying a position? What implicit or hidden rationalizations are involved? Who focuses on the integration and social control of the network in collectivistic terms? What is the linguistic style of these communications? Most significantly, who plays the mediational, adaptational role? Who effectively operates to balance private and public interests? Who is capable of mediating across networks? What words and symbols seem to be effective in this?

Answers to these questions can point to both individuals and organizations, to visible leaders and to seemingly monolithic institutions. They provide an awareness and insight of situational context that help to shape the kinds of designs that might be posed to solve problems and the kinds of processes that might most effectively manage change processes.

Perhaps the greatest danger in increasingly complex configurations of shared power lies in the potential for rigidified social institutions that work to resist change or inadvertently produce unwanted results. It is in seeking to overcome this problem that the traditional truncated view of rationality most fails us. Instrumental rationality simply (and erroneously) takes goals and values for granted and, as a result, aids in freezing in bureaucratic rigidity.

The real promise for coping with increasing organizational and system differentiation, and thus increasingly shared power, lies in the further development of this dialectical model of rationality that recognizes and fully takes account of the *gestalt* qualities of the intermixture of instrumental and normative forms of reason. The potential for dealing with this lies in the recognition of the linguistic, communicative base of all rationalization processes. Herein, I believe, lies the source for a more effective rational planning model.

Footnotes

1. Readers familiar with the theoretical literature of urban planning should be alert to an important difference in Weber's use of the word "substantive." Theorists in urban planning distinguish between "substantive theory" and "procedural theory" (Faludi 1978, 162). For them, procedural theory is theory about the subjects doing planning; substantive theory is theory about the objects being planned (a theory of city growth, a theory of economic development, etc.). In such a context, procedural theory tends toward being normative (what a planner *should* do); substantive theory tends toward being descriptive. Weber's terminology is more in accord with traditional definitions, particularly the philosophical sense of the word "substance" referring to that reality which underlies or is anterior to outward manifestation and change (see: *Webster's New Collegiate Dictionary. G. and C. Merriam Company* 1980. p. 1153). Thus, substantive rationality, as used in this essay is viewed as prior to and giving shape to all other forms of rationality.

2. Indeed *resistance* to new technology has been a frequent experience. Strategic advantages of an innovation can often be predicted with reasonable accuracy, but its impact on agreements and relationships is more difficult to evaluate. One illustration lies in the many organizations that long delayed the introduction of

computer technology. Also see Schon's discussion of what he calls "dynamic conservatism" (1971, Chapter 2), in which he relates the difficulties encountered in the late 19th century trying to persuade the U.S. Navy to install gun sights on shipboard cannons.

3. Historically, capitalist production emerged from the dual differentiation of owners and workers into a three-level differentiation as technology and tasks increased in complexity (Warsh 1984). Coordinative tasks became further differentiated (as illustrated in the CAT-scanner example) creating the "managerial class" (Burnham 1941).

4. Warren, Rose and Bergunder (1975) noted these same levels of rationalization and, indeed, described them directly as such. These authors portray the "technical rationale" of an organization as that which asserts that the organization possesses the knowledge, skill, and programs that should be operable in its domain. Next noted is an "administrative rationale" which is described as the ability of the organization to mediate between the environment, the technological tasks and the tasks of essential maintenance. Finally, they speak of the "institutional rationale" which, they assert, pertains to the organization's "right to exist"—its legitimacy (Warren et al. 1974, 56-58).

5. In making this claim, Parsons apparently overlooked the service and repair functions performed by manufacturers of physical products. He seemed to assume that once a product is sold it is consumed and disposed of with no further contact between manufacturer and customer. In the contemporary consumer market this is clearly not always the case.

6. A number of techniques for developing such knowledge are becoming available. Noteworthy among the more sophisticated of these are the recent studies of Galaskiewicz (1979) and Boje and Whetten (1981). While the elaborate research these studies represent is not feasible in every planning situation, they do offer perspectives that can alert planners to particular features of the dynamics of interorganizational relations that are of central concern in the planning process. Of more immediate practicality for planning practice, perhaps, would be the inclusion of more specific training in qualitative research as part of the education of professional urban planners with particular emphasis on linguistic and symbolic interactions that shape and influence planning episodes (Forester 1980, 1982). Tools of research that would offer guidance in the analysis of linguistic acts include: 1)examination of the structure of argument such as the work of the logician Toulmin (1958) or the application of Toulmin's ideas to policy analysis by Dunn (1981); and 2) the techniques of content analysis (Krippendorf 1980). An excellent illustration of research that strongly hints at some of the overall themes of my argument is found in Allison's 1971 study of the Cuban Missile Crisis. For recent texts in qualitative research see: Bogdan and Taylor 1975; and Bogdan and Biklen 1982.

References

Agranoff, R. and V.A. Lindsay. 1983. Intergovernmental management: perspectives from human service problem solving at the local level. *Public Administration Review* 43(3): 227-37.

Aiken, M., R. Dewar, N. DiTomaso, J. Hage, and G. Zeitz. 1975. *Coordinating human services.* San Francisco: Jossey-Bass.

Allison, G.T. 1971. *Essence of decision: Explaining the Cuban missile crisis.* Boston: Little, Brown and Company.

Argyris, C. and D. Schon. 1978. *Organizational learning.* Reading, Mass.: Addison-Wesley Press.

Benson, J.K. 1975. The interorganizational network as a political economy. *Administrative Science Quarterly* 20:229-249.

Bogdan, R.C. and S. Taylor. 1975. *Introduction to qualitative method.* New York: John Wiley and Sons.

Bogdan, R.C. and S.K. Biklen. 1982. *Qualitative research for education: An introduction to theory and methods.* Boston: Allyn and Bacon, Inc.

Boje, D.M. and D.A. Whetten. 1981. Effects of organizational strategies and constraints on centrality and attributions of influence in interorganizational networks. *Administrative Science Quarterly* 26:(3): 378-95.

Burnham, J. 1941. *The managerial revolution.* Bloomington, Ind.: Indiana University Press.

Dunn, W.N. 1981. *Public policy analysis: An introduction.* Englewood Cliffs, N.J.: Prentice-Hall, Inc.

Faludi, A. 1978. *Essays on planning theory and education.* Oxford: Pergamon Press.

Forester, J. 1980. Critical theory and planning practice. *Journal Of The American Planning Association* 46(3): 275-86.

Forester, J. 1982. Planning in the face of power. *Journal of the American Planning Association* 48(1): 67-80.

Forester, J. 1984. Bounded rationality and the politics of muddling through. *Public Administration Review* 44:23-31.

Galaskiewicz, J. 1979. *Exchange networks and community politics.* Beverly Hills, Calif.: Sage Publications.

Gamm, L. 1981. An introduction to research in interorganizational relations (IOR). *Journal of Voluntary Action Research* 10(3-4): 18-28.

Giddens, A. 1979. *Central problems in social theory: action, structure and contradiction in social analysis.* Berkeley, Calif.: University of California Press.

Habermas, J. 1984. *The theory of communicative action: Reason and the rationalization of society,* Vol. One. Translated by T. McCarthy. Boston: Beacon Press.

Kalberg, S. 1980. Max Weber's types of rationality: cornerstones for the analysis of rationalization processes in history. *American Journal of Sociology* 85(5): 1145-1179.

Krippendorf, K. 1980. *Content analysis: An introduction to its methodology.* Beverly Hills, Calif.: Sage Publications.

Lehman, E.W. 1975. *Coordinating health care: Explorations in interorganizational relations.* Beverly Hills, Calif.: Sage Publications.

Levine, S. and P.E. White. 1961. Exchange as a conceptual framework for the study of interorganizational relationships. *Administrative Science Quarterly* 5:583-601.

Long, N.E. 1958. The local community as an ecology of games. *American Journal of Sociology* 64(3): 251-61.

Los, M. 1981. "Some reflections on epistemology, design and planning theory." In *Urbanization and Urban Planning in Capitalist Society,* edited by M. Dear and A.J. Scott. London: Methuen.

Meyer, J.W. and B. Rowan. 1977. Institutionalized organizations: formal structure as myth and ceremony. *American Journal of Sociology* 83(2): 340-363.

Milner, M., Jr. 1980. *Unequal care: A case study of interorganizational relations in health care.* New York: Columbia University Press.

Parsons, T. 1960. *Structure and process in modern societies.* New York: The Free Press.

Raelin, J.A. 1982. A policy output model of interorganizational relations. *Organizational Studies* 3:243-267.

Schon, D. 1971. *Beyond the stable state.* New York: Random House.

Toulmin, S. 1958. *The uses of argument.* Cambridge: Cambridge University Press.

Van de Ven, A.H., G. Walker and J. Liston. 1979. Coordination patterns within an interorganizational network. *Human Relations* 32(1): 19-36.

Van de Ven, A.H., D.C. Emmett, and Richard Koenig, Jr. 1980. "Frameworks for interorganizational analysis." In *Interorganization Theory,* edited by A.R. Neghandi. Kent, Ohio: Kent State University Press.

Warren, R.L. 1967. The interorganizational field as a focus for investigation. *Administrative Science Quarterly,* 12:396-419.

Warren, R.L., S. Rose, and A. Bergunder. 1974. *The structure of urban reform; community decision organizations in stability and change.* Lexington, MA: D.C. Heath and Co.

Warsh, D. 1984. *The idea of economic complexity.* New York: The Viking Press.

Watzlavick, P., J.H. Beavin and D. Jackson. 1967. *Pragmatics of human communication.* New York: W. W. Norton and Co.

Weber, M. 1958. *The protestant ethic and the spirit of capitalism,* translated by T. Parsons. New York: Charles Scribner's Sons.

Whetten, D.A. 1981. Interorganizational relations: a review of the field. *Journal of Higher Education* 52(1): 1-28.

Zeitz, G. 1980. Interorganizational Dialectics. *Administrative Science Quarterly* 25(1): 72-88.

CHAPTER 7

Power-sharing and System Change: The Case of Public Education

Ted Kolderie

In much of the basic discussion about power sharing there is implied (or can reasonably be inferred) an authoritarian or political model of decision making: It used to be that somebody would simply tell somebody else what to do; today that is no longer possible; now, and preferably, all those affected will decide together what they will do.

This implication is visible, for example, in the description of the contemporary situation as one in which there is "nobody in charge"; the implication being that traditionally somebody *was* "in charge." So there emerges, for anyone accustomed to thinking in the traditional terms, the question which Harlan Cleveland, the former dean of the Hubert H. Humphrey Institute of Public Affairs, continues so usefully to raise: "How do we get everybody in on the act and still get some action?" ... "the act" being the participative process of discussion, deliberation and decision.

The Two Processes of Decision Making

In approaching the power-sharing concept it will be useful to begin by examining this traditional model of authoritarian political decision making in which somebody is somehow chosen to decide for others.

In a real sense power is always shared. Even in nominally "authoritarian" situations, as Chester Barnard (1938) pointed out so effectively, an order is not executed simply by being given: It remains within the power of the person who receives the command to decide whether or not to comply. And because, therefore, authority resides in the person *to whom* the order is given there is — as Barnard went on explain — a strong case for the efforts at consultation, education and persuasion that will so far as possible induce cooperation and consent. The driving force for the power-sharing idea is often, realistically, the effort to reduce the influence of the powerful and to increase the influence of the powerless. But the intellectual rationale is this argument that participative decisions will be more effective and better decisions. And there is, in truth, a broad recognition today among experienced practitioners of the fact that "You don't plan the future; you *negotiate* it."

There remains however the question that Cleveland raises about the practical results and the difficulty of this participative model of political decision making. It arises especially in those cases where the enterprise is faced with problems (or opportunities) that require a long-range vision to make some strategic decision and to take some decisive action that will change in fundamental ways what it is and what it does.

The fear is clearly that—especially in these situations requiring major system change—a broader sharing of the decision-making responsibility will increase the influence of the individual and "particular" interests, which lack a vision of and a strong sense of responsibility for the success of the enterprise as a whole; with the result that the sharing will simply paralyze the effort to make any decisions at all. The effort required to educate this broader constituency, and to persuade its members to take a long-term view of their interests, may simply be too great; so that an effective decision out of a broad and participative process is as a practical matter unachievable. Or, the practical techniques for such an educative and participative process may simply not yet be available.

So it is important to ask whether there might be some *non*-political process of decision making, broadly participative, which might avoid the problems that arise in trying to make the *political* process fully participative.

Such a nonpolitical process has been described by Charles Lindblom (1965) as "the process of mutual adjustment". Lindblom saw this as a mechanism or process in which the various affected parties, each in its own interest, make a number of independent decisions, sequentially or simultaneously. It is, as Lindblom points out, the mechanism most widely in use, at the very small scale and at the scale of the largest operating systems (think, for example, about the world energy system or the world food system) to secure the necessary *coordination* of action. And, because the introduction of new technology and new practices are not subject to a process of political control, "mutual adjustment" is likely to be a superior process for introducing *innovation* into a system.

And this is important. Quite simply:

1. If some major changes are needed and the processes of discussion, debate and political voting are not producing the kind of action required, then perhaps the answer is to move away from these (as Lindblom called them) processes of central decision making.

2. If the necessary decisions are not appearing and the necessary change is not occurring, either, in the participatory situation in which there is "nobody in charge," then perhaps the strategy should be precisely to move away from political decision-making entirely; and toward that process of mutual adjustment, in which action proceeds through a set of independent decisions taken by the individual parties.

The choice between these two models of decision-making—between these two approaches to change—is now a topic of intense debate, in the strategic discussion about how to deal with the problems of the public sector in general and how to deal with the problems of public education in particular.

There is a powerful assumption that public action should work through the processes of collective discussion, debate and voting. Clearly, this process is associated with many of the major policy decisions and with many of the most important public actions of the past century.

These were in large part, however, decisions and actions either to curb abuses by nongovernmental institutions or to create new governmental institutions or programs where none had existed before. Now the situation has changed. It is within these governmental institutions and programs that many of the current problems have arisen; and the question now is whether the process of central, political decision making will be effective in restructuring and revitalizing those institutions which it has itself created.

There is a powerful and appealing argument that this process of political decision making does remain the appropriate approach even now that the problems are so largely within the public sector. And that it can be made effective.

But there is also, on the other side, a strong argument that institutions do not reform themselves from within. The power of existing interests in the contemporary legislative process, and the short-term considerations imposed on electoral politics especially by the electronic media, make the argument for a political reform of the *public* sector simply unrealistic. The rule has become: "Thou shalt do no direct harm" (Schultze 1976). And how is major change to occur without "doing harm"? Without unsettling in some major way the dominant interests; upsetting established routines and threatening incomes and power positions?

What is essential, it is argued, is find some way to permit innovations to be tried and changes to occur, protected from the defensive forces which dominate the political institutions and processes at the moment.

Public Education and the Limitations of Shared Power
All this comes to focus especially in the problem of public education, in which the governance has been so entirely the processes of political decision making.

Education is conceived of as a governmental function. It is "provided" publicly: that is, mandated by governmental action and paid for with tax funds. There is a deep feeling in many people that education is fundamentally an activity of the community; something which, through the public schools, we do for (or to) the kids.

Education is also "produced" governmentally. Except in a few isolated cases and in a few remote corners of New England it is taken for granted that a school board will set up, own and operate its own schools. The board functions in a dual role: a buyer of instructional services, buying from itself; a seller of instructional services, selling to itself.

Education is independent of general government, especially in the Middle West. It has its own governing structure, its own financing sources and formula, its own committees in the legislature, its own facilities and personnel; even its own election day.

Education is organized in the classic public-administrative model. Within a school district there is a board; and a chief officer who is to "superintend" the instruction in the schools of the district. Like the fire service, schooling is physically decentralized but organizationally centralized: budgeting, personnel, purchasing, transportation, etc. are responsibilities of the central office. People in district offices frequently talk not about their "schools" but about their "buildings." Within the school there is a principal. The instruction is organized into departments. Over time the trends have been toward fewer and larger districts, and toward greater centralization. Schools are real places, but have no legal existence and usually little autonomy.

Students are usually assigned to a school. Generally, the school a child will attend is determined by the place the family lives. You are "in," and therefore attend the schools of, a particular school district. Traditionally, you were also "in" a particular attendance area and therefore went to the school which it served. If you did not want to go to this public school you had to go to a private school. This was not impossible; but it was expensive. The taxes paid by a family can be used only in a public school.

Teachers are employees of the district. They do not work for themselves, or for an independent organization. It is a fairly conventional labor/management model. Teachers must be licensed. They receive a salary. In many states in recent years they have become unionized and have won the right to strike.

It does not seem right to describe public education as a system in which there is "nobody in charge." It *is* clearly a system in which nobody is *entirely* in charge. Several different parties are, each, partly in charge. Certain of them would like to be more fully in charge.

There is an intense concern about "control": Each party fights for it; each believes some other party has it; no one will admit to having it. Legislatures and state departments of education often describe the real power as residing in the local districts. School boards frequently feel dominated by the superintendent. Superintendents are very conscious of the power of the union. Principals talk about the central office. Teachers see their authority in the classroom increasingly being eroded by directives from "the bureaucracy." Parents often point simply to the power of "the system."

It is a system in which the major elements are tightly locked together, with little freedom of movement. The legislature is locked into the local public school district as the mechanism through which it discharges its constitutional responsibility to provide an education for the children of the state. Districts in turn (superintendents and boards) are locked into a particular set of schools: those which the district itself owns and runs. Teachers are increasingly locked into the district in which they have been employed; the longevity-based compensation system and the shrinking market for new teachers make mobility difficult. Families are locked in by the system of districts and attendance areas, by the barrier represented by the additional cost of nonpublic-school tuition and by the disinclination of public schools and public school districts to compete with each other for the enrollment of children from other districts.

Frustration levels are high, especially on the part of those individuals—board members, superintendents, principals or teachers—who are personally committed to improvements in teaching and learning and who are struggling to make changes.

"Adversary" is the word frequently used to describe the state of relations within this system, especially where (as in Minnesota) there has been a transition fully into the private-sector model of collective bargaining in labor relations.

Much of the responsibility for this is often laid at the door of the teacher unions and of the master contract which contains teachers' uniform salary scale and the terms and conditions of their employment by the district. Probably too much.

Certainly, the provisions of the contract are among the factors which inhibit change and restrict the freedom of action of principals, of superintendents and of school boards. But those administrators and those boards certainly bear an equal share of responsibility for the situation that has developed.

In Minnesota, for example, (except in the three largest cities) state law has not *mandated* seniority as the governing principle for the reductions-in-force made necessary by the recent decline in enrollment. State law simply says that seniority will be the test unless the district negotiates some other arrangement with its teachers. Few have done so.

The results have been appalling: The maximum *number* of teachers lost, for any given dollar reduction in state aids (as a $36,000 reduction in revenue requires, for example, the termination of two junior teachers each earning $18,000 rather than one senior teacher earning twice as much); minority teachers disproportionately reduced, since they were disproportionately represented among the most-recent hires; more teachers teaching outside their principal field of knowledge, given the provisions for "bumping"; and a rising average age of teaching staffs, foreshadowing a major crisis in the size and quality of the teacher cadre in the 1990s.

All these consequences were perfectly predictable, from an understanding of a) the enrollment declines, b) the demographics of the teaching staff, c) the operation of the state-aid system and d) the rules of the seniority system. Given the existing system it was mainly a management responsibility to avoid this catastrophe. And virtually nothing was done.

The real responsibility for the resistance to change, however, lies even deeper—in the powerful underlying pressures for uniformity in the system.

This is a system in which users are given only quite limited options about the service they receive and about the institutions from which they receive it. Public education is deeply hostile to the principle of user-choice. In Albert Hirschman's terms (1971) it is governed mainly by "voice"; scarcely at all by "exit." And in this (largely "assignment") system, differences among schools therefore become a stimulus for comment, questions and controversy, since these differences are created (or are not created, producing dissatisfaction among other users) by the action or inaction of central political authority.

School boards and school superintendents can tolerate only so much controversy in their meetings and in their lives. Understandably, they try to reduce the level of it. Reducing differences is one effective way to do this. And powerful arguments can be summoned in its defense: law (the constitution mandates a "general and uniform" system of public schools); economics (economies of scale vs. the costs of diversity); politics (the ease with which uniformity can be represented as equity).

Over the years, in this system so largely governed by the political institutions of "voice" and in which no single party can dominate the decision making, proposals have been made from time to time to alter the process in ways that will strengthen the role of one party or another, hopefully in the interests of the enterprise as a whole. Some are power-sharing ideas.

Currently, the proposal most prominently discussed for re-balancing the power relationships is probably the proposal for site-based management; that is, for delegating certain responsibilities and certain authority to the individual school; increasing its powers relative to the present power of central administration. (This would seem in concept to represent more a separation than a sharing of power between the district and the school. That is, more a sorting out of decision-making responsibility between the two parties than an increase in their joint responsibility for a single decision.) At the school site the concept currently most popular calls for a sharing of decision making among the so-called "stakeholders," through the mechanism of a school-site council. Site-management is strongly advocated by John Goodlad (1984) and others who are convinced that the improvement of education must follow a *school*-improvement strategy; since it is in schools, after all, not in districts, that teaching and learning actually go on.

Mixed Results
Where such experiments have been tried the results have often been positive. When a school is given control over its budget, for example, and allowed to keep (for other uses in that school) what it does not spend, incentives and opportunities are created which can serve the interests both of greater economy and of improved instruction. In some schools in Florida, for example, there have been reports (Pierce 1981) of significant reductions in energy use, as teachers and as students made real efforts to turn off the lights and air conditioning when leaving the classroom, thereby saving money which they could spend for other activities. Where a school principal is aggressive and where a superintendent is sympathetic and where the board is at least

neutral, this kind of arrangement can frequently be tried and will frequently have some success.

Too often, however, the idea brings out some of the most authoritarian tendencies at the central district level.

When the story about the schools in Florida was told at a meeting sponsored by the Minnesota School Boards Association in 1981, for example, a prominent member of the association accosted the speaker afterward and said, "I'd never have handled it like that. I'd have sent them a directive to turn off the lights and to turn off the air conditioning. And if they didn't do it, I'd fire them."

And when the former chief executive of a major Minnesota company appeared before a statewide meeting of the Minnesota Association of School Administrators in 1983, explaining patiently why—in the interests of the enterprise—he had reorganized that company in such a way as to devolve much more broadly many of the decisions previously centralized in the chairman's office, he was met by essentially a single response: "If we let other people make the decisions some of those decisions will be wrong; and how can we permit that?"

Too often the site-management arrangement lasts only so long as the term of the superintendent who encouraged or permitted it. And too often it results not in the delegation of real authority over budget, curriculum, personnel or teaching methodology but only in the creation of a school-site council: one more voice, discussing the problems and making suggestions, but unable to act on its own.

There are other efforts to increase the influence of parties presently not listened to. There are proposals for "quality circles" of teachers (perhaps an echo of the teachers councils that existed until suppressed, as in Chicago, by the superintendents in the 1920s). In Minnesota there are the PER committees—the participatory mechanisms set up during the 1970s in response to the pressures for greater accountability, which are now responsible (variously, at the school or the district level) for planning, evaluating and reporting on curriculum and performance. There are proposals to revive the PTA. There are hearings for the public on the district budget for the coming year; even as the district moves away from the public referendum and toward legislative action as the major source of revenue decisions.

All these efforts, however, are subject to the fundamental observation that "voice" is weak where "exit" is absent (Hirschman 1971). The question is always what motivation exists for any institution to listen to its internal critics—users or employees or subordinate administrators.

What is that motivation in the case of education, structured as it is around mandatory school attendance, the assignment of pupils to schools and the political appropriation of revenues to districts based on costs? What consequences will it suffer if it fails to listen, and to act? Will its students leave? Will its revenues fall?

Public Education and a Strategy of Mutual Adjustment

The alternative approach is to think about the situation of shared power in public education not in terms of the traditional model of political decision making but rather in terms of the model of mutual adjustment (Lindblom 1965). This would lay aside—as an approach to the problem of the "gridlock" in public education—the strategy of trying to increase the opportunities for debate and discussion and influence within a political and bureaucratic structure. It would substitute for this a strategy of increasing the opportunity for the parties involved to break out of that relationship. Opportunities, that is, for districts, schools, teachers and families to disengage themselves to some significant degree from the present arrangement set by law and to assume new relationships based on voluntary decision.

This effort to think through . . . and hopefully to design and demonstrate . . . this new approach is the principal business of a Minnesota nonprofit formed in 1981, known as Public School Incentives. It began with the remark by a public high-school principal, "I would really like to have a contract relationship with my school district"; and with an interest on the part of several persons concerned with the future of the public schools to think through the implications of that remark.

There was a problem, in the initial discussions. Some of the people, and especially some with business firms and private foundations, were puzzled by the talk about the central office and the obstacles it puts in the way of the constructive things the principals would like to do. Puzzled, because the exposure of persons in the private sector had been so largely to the superintendent's talk about the difficulties he faces in getting his programs implemented by the schools and teachers who work for him.

Fairly quickly, however, it proved possible to secure some modest financing for an effort to support the effort by principals interested in developing what was then being referred to as "a de-regulated public school." The idea was to identify such principals, and to provide them with the kind of encouragement, legal service, technical advice and occasionally political support they might need in their efforts to secure an exemption from the rules and regulations normally controlling school operations.

At about the same time a major local private foundation, the Northwest Area Foundation, became interested in school-site management; and invited schools interested in that idea to apply by March 1982 for a first round of grants with which to plan such a decentralized arrangement. The principals working with PSI did so. Most were awarded the $10,000 planning grants. Most applied in March 1983 for the implementation grants. Site-management experiments are, as a result, under way in Robbinsdale, Hopkins, St. Louis Park and Rosemount, within the metropolitan area.

With this first effort successfully under way, PSI began thinking about other ideas that might be prepared for demonstration; some of which were already under discussion or in design elsewhere within the local area. In the summer of 1983, with encouragement and support from The McKnight Foundation, the project was refinanced and reorganized as a kind of "design shop" for ideas and proposals for change and improvement in the public schools. Byron Schneider, formerly principal of Southwest High School in Minneapolis and currently state director of Minnesota 4-H, became chairman. Betty Jo Zander, formerly a teacher, principal and associate superintendent in the Minneapolis system, became coordinator.

In the late spring of 1983, of course, the first in the series of national reports about public education had begun to stimulate a broad and vigorous discussion within Minnesota about the condition of the schools and about improvements that might be needed.

This was intensified in Minnesota by the introduction into the Minnesota Legislature of a bill for a modified voucher system for the schools. Based on an earlier report by the Citizens League, a local and private policy-studies group, the bill was authored by state Rep. John Brandl, a Minneapolis DFLer, a Minneapolis resident and a professor of public affairs in the Hubert H. Humphrey Institute of Public Affairs at the University of Minnesota.

By early 1984 the question of school improvement was active in a wide variety of study and action groups, public and private: the new Legislative Commission on Public Education; the Department of Education; the Minnesota Business Partnership; the College of Education and the Center for Urban and Regional Affairs at the University; the Spring Hill (conference) Center; in addition to the work being done in individual foundations, business firms and independent school districts.

PSI continued, however, to play a somewhat different role: not doing research studies, on the one hand; not running the demonstrations, on the other. It continued to focus on that intermediate function of "design": identifying promising ideas for change and improvement in the schools; finding people who would think through the practicalities and the details of how these might be made to work; and looking for schools and districts willing to give them a try.

One such idea was the "choice," or voucher, idea embodied in Brandl's bill. This idea was also being encouraged by a former teacher and assistant principal in the St. Paul school system, Joe Nathan, whose book *Free to Teach* (1983) had been published just as the wave of interest in school improvement had begun to rise and who had made a considerable impact both locally and nationally. At the McKnight Foundation's suggestion, Nathan also became a part of the group working through PSI.

Brandl's bill raised questions about the redistribution of power in public education in a way that had considerable political impact. It proposed a family-choice system open on the "seller" side to nonpublic as well as to public schools, but open on the "buyer" side only to families of $15,000 annual income and below. It was, in other words, aimed straight at the group of the poor and minority children who had been doing least well, and whose parents were least able personally and financially to help with the child's education at home and least influential politically in getting the help needed at school. In effect it offered the "exit" option which this disadvantaged community did not have, as a strategy for getting the system to listen to its members' "voice" in a way it had not been willing to do before.

Any such introduction of the principle of family choice into the educational system, converting a compulsory relationship into a voluntary relationship, would introduce a new opportunity for change, and potentially therefore for improvement, into the public school system. The "options," or open-enrollment, programs offered in recent years within particular school districts do not really have this effect. There are two reasons why they do not.

1. They are usually introduced as a result of a decision by the board and central administration. The number, location and length-of-life of the alternative schools is, in other words, centrally controlled rather than being determined by the *school* itself. This means that:

2. The traditional schools are likely to be protected from the impact of a pattern of family choice favorable to one of its own schools and unfavorable to another. A large number of applications for enrollment in the alternative school is, in other words, likely to play out into a waiting list for that school rather than into the closure of less popular schools from which parents want to withdraw their children. At the extreme, successful schools that make the district's other schools look bad may be actively discouraged (as, by their relocation or by the transfer of the principal responsible for its success) or even closed.

The impact of the alternative, innovative schools would obviously be much more effective in system-change in a situation where the choices of families could be made from among a broader offering of schools, freer than are those controlled by a single district to respond by varying their program offerings.

This could conceivably be accomplished by a choice system working on the seller side between and among *public* schools, assuming the districts were willing really to differentiate their programs (curriculum and/or pedagogy) and were free to compete with each other for enrollments. To date most have not been (and continue to support a Minnesota law prohibiting districts from competing for enrollments).

There is, however, another way around this limited ability of the public school districts to provide an adequately diverse array of program offerings, responsive to the diverse needs and desires of students. Other governmental entities besides the traditional local public school districts can own and run "public" schools. Teachers' colleges have, in the past; other public institutions of higher education could as well. Or, the state itself could establish and operate one or more schools, competitive with the schools of the local public districts. Some state-run schools are now appearing (as in North Carolina). They tend to be specialized for a particular type of student (the deaf, the gifted) or by curriculum (the arts, the sciences). But they could equally be general comprehensive secondary schools.

Failing the establishment of new schools, there is an option in law, far too little understood, for parents to enroll their children in the schools of an adjoining public school district, paying the tuition themselves. Districts are reluctant to compete openly for students. But if families will take the initiative, a good many districts, especially in a period of declining enrollment, will accept those willing to pay the fee. The Minnesota tuition tax-deduction law, upheld by the U.S. Supreme Court in *Mueller vs. Allen*, had the unusual feature of permitting a deduction for tuition paid to public as well as to private schools.

The movement of families among districts, and the incentives this movement would create particularly among school districts to reshape and to improve their programs, would create an opportunity for "mutual adjustment" which could open the way to much of the change in public education which has been so difficult to secure while districts, schools, parents and teachers have been locked into the traditional arrangements. This opportunity would be further increased by including the nonpublic schools—with their wider variety of teaching styles, their lower cost structures and their greater freedom to innovate—in any program of family choice in education.

Proposals for programs of choice do, however, arouse strong opposition. The local, neighborhood school is of course gone in many areas, with the transportation programs created either by consolidation or by the need to achieve a racial balance in the schools of a district. Still, the specifically "public" character of the schools is seen to be fundamentally eroded by the idea of family choice . . . certainly where the choice program is open to the nonpublic schools and even where it is not, if the receiving schools are able (as "magnet" schools sometimes are) to be selective among applicants for admission.

Some other approach to the disengagement sought in the system—some other effort to "get everybody in on the act, and still get some action"—would therefore be helpful.

One such alternative approach would be to focus the effort on the seller side; altering the relationship first between the teachers and the school or school district.

In effect, the choice or voucher programs work their principal change on the buyer side; substituting for the decisions of the school board and administration the decisions of individual families about who shall go to school where, and with whom. The definition of "school" is seldom if ever changed, even in voucher plans that include the nonpublic schools; since these tend to organize themselves much on the model of the public school. The teacher remains an employee, assigned to a course and to a classroom, supervised and directed by an administrator.

The alternative would concentrate on creating opportunities for "mutual adjustment" initially for teachers. Almost alone among professionals teachers have no private-practice option. Architects, doctors, accountants, engineers, lawyers, journalists, consultants, researchers, planners—all have a choice between working in and for an organization, on salary, and working independently for themselves or with others in a single-specialty or multi-specialty professional group for a fee. Some in fact do one; some do the other. And some move, over time, from one form of professional practice to the other. The teacher, however, is locked in: The policy of financing education by funding public school districts ensures that no other significant market for teaching develops. So teachers have been limited to the bureaucratic form of organization offered by those public districts, with their traditional employment arrangement and their severely limited opportunities for professional advancement and personal reward.

Preliminary discussions by Public School Incentives have indicated a genuine interest on the part of teachers in the idea of some form of teacher partnership through which a self-selected group could develop curriculum and/or offer instructional services to a variety of public districts. Typically, teachers have never thought about this possibility, having accepted the traditional employment relationship as given. But they perceive immediately its implications for their desire to grow professionally.

Such a partnership could be organized around the design and delivery of instructional services for a course, for a department (say, foreign language or natural science) or for an entire school. It would be responsible internally for selecting its pedagogy and for assigning, evaluating and compensating its personnel: These would no longer be functions of the central district administration. Between the partnership and the district (or the administration of a school, in a site-managed district) there would be a conventional fee-for-service contract relationship. Teachers would gain in professional autonomy; and by virtue of the transfer of administrative responsibilities to the partnership, the buyer (board and administration) would be enabled and required to concentrate on learning objectives and student outcomes—presumably their primary responsibility. Indeed, in a situation where a multi-specialty partnership took responsibility for an entire school, it would be large enough for one of its functions to be the selection of the administration of that school.

It has been fascinating to raise, in extended and confidential conversations with public-school teachers (some of them active members of teacher unions) the question of how the school—its administration and its pedagogy—would change, were the school under school-site management to be defined not as the principal and not as the site council but as the group of teachers; and were that group of teachers then to be "capitated"—given, in advance, the entire sum of money which the district would spend on the school's program during the coming year, given the authority to decide for themselves how that money would be spent, and held accountable for results.

Quickly, they reformulate the essential question: "What could we do to improve teaching and learning, that would require us to spend a minimum of the money we can otherwise keep as ours?" The same list of responses tends to emerge from the various conversations. *Community people*: There are many persons who have much to offer who would contribute time to the instructional program, at minimum charge. *Peer teaching*: Kids are often very effective in helping other kids with their learning, either at the same grade level or between grades; and frequently find this a useful and rewarding learning experience themselves. *Parents*: There would be enormous rewards from getting parents involved as partners in the learning enterprise at the home end. *Independent study*: Students, where able, motivating themselves and directing their own learning. *Technology*: There would be a positive incentive for the professional teachers to move to computer-based instruction where that would be more effective or less costly. *Administration*: Not the traditional principal, expected unrealistically to be both instructional leader and administrative manager; but a dual leadership consisting of a business manager and (as in a hospital) a chief of the professional staff.

What emerges, in short, is something very much like the program of school improvement that comes through most of the studies and reports as the ideal, but which has heretofore seemed unattainable within the traditional model of the teacher-employee in the "factory," even with the efforts at teacher (and parent) participation being added to it.

This approach—which is essentially one of sharing power increasingly with teachers by increasing their autonomy and their opportunities for movement in the system—has not so far been tried. It would be interesting to see it further explored, and tested.

The Implications for Planning

In the late spring of 1983 Charles Lindblom visited the University of Minnesota, as a speaker in the series of colloquia organized jointly by the Humphrey Institute and the School of Management.

At the end of his lecture about the two models of coordination and decision making a listener suggested that the model of mutual adjustment seemed to lack any sense of collective purpose and left no scope for policy or for planning and management.

Not at all, Lindblom replied: Planning for coordinated action is by no means confined to planning for the "mechanisms of central authority." It must also be applied to the mechanisms of mutual adjustment, each of which consists of a set of rules for action which must also be designed, and periodically redesigned. This will involve and require the most careful efforts at policy-analysis and planning; and certainly a concept of management at the level of the system as a whole.

It will also, of course, shift the focus from the producer side to the buyer side of the public-service market.

In education this means that public planning at the state and district levels will be concerned mainly with the structuring of the incentives and opportunities within the system.

It will be concerned with what is to be bought and how that is to be paid for, with the ways in which families select schools and schools select students, and with the scope those actually in the schools then have to decide how to use money, time, facilities, equipment and people to accomplish the learning outcomes sought by public policy and by private aspirations.

Simply put: The way to escape from the shared-power gridlock that presently exists in public education, and to "get more people in on the action," is to create more action. More opportunity, that is, for independent decisions by families and by districts and by schools and by teachers—and by all in combination—about the method of learning that is best for particular students and groups of students. In a word, to move from an essentially political to a nonpolitical definition of power sharing.

How to accomplish the reallocation of roles and the re-division of power that are involved remains a question. A sharing of power is not created only when a broader set of groups and interests comes to be represented and involved in the making of a decision through the process of discussion and debate. It may also be created when powers previously held by one group (previously superior) come—in one way or another—to be delegated to or devolved onto some other group (previously subordinate) so that decision-making responsibility is shared by being separated, and divided between the parties.

There would seem to be four such ways this separation could occur in education. 1) The present holder of the dominant power may elect to relinquish some or all of it, voluntarily. 2) A party presently lacking power may decide to increase its own power by increasing its activity or level of skill in the debate about what is taught and about the way the schools are organized and run. 3) A third and independent entity may decide to reapportion the balance of power between or among the various parties involved; either on its own initiative or at the request of one involved party seeking to have its own influence increased or that of the dominant party reduced (as, for example, teacher groups going to the state legislature seeking a law requiring school boards to enter into collective bargaining). 4) Some outside force may intervene in such a way as to alter the distribution of power among the parties involved; perhaps unsought and even unanticipated by any of them. It is possible, for example, that the cutting-edge electronic technology—the computer integrated with the laser/video-disk—represents such an intervention in the educational system, altering the balance of power between learner and teacher and perhaps between family and school in something like the way that the communications satellite radically altered the relationship between broadcast networks and cable operators in the television industry.

All these efforts are visible in the current education policy debate in 1984. But they are different than they have been in the past.

The involvement of elected figures from outside the education profession (most conspicuously, the governors in the South) and the involvement of leaders from the business community are altering significantly the balance of power in the debate, and enlarging the possibility for a different outcome than in past debates. So, too, is the growth of the new technology and of the efforts by business firms to make it available directly to students and to families outside the framework of the traditional institution of school.

Much will depend on the strategy followed by these new and influential intervenors in the debate: In particular, on the decision they make between the political and the nonpolitical path to the reallocation of power which will provide the opportunities for change that will open the way to the improvement of education.

References

Barnard, C.I. 1938. *The functions of the executive.* Cambridge, MA: Harvard University Press.

Goodlad, J.I. 1984. *A place called school.* New York: McGraw Hill.

Hirschman, A.O. 1971. *Exit, voice and loyalty.* Cambridge, MA: Harvard University Press.

Lindblom, C.E. 1965. *The intelligence of democracy.* New York: The Free Press.

Nathan, J. 1983. *Free to teach.* St. Paul, MN: The Pilgrim Press.

Pierce, L. 1981. Talk to a seminar on school-site management sponsored by the Northwest Area Foundation, September 7.

Schultze, C.L. 1976. *The public use of the private interest.* Washington, D.C.: Brookings Institution.

CHAPTER 8

Schooling and Shared Power: Educating for Democracy

George H. Wood

Democracy, as a scheme of shared power, necessitates particular forms of schooling. The establishment of both formal and informal schooling arrangements in all societies is seen as fundamental to the enculturation or socialization of the culture's young. Thus, in a democracy, the task before the school is to educate the young in ways which encourage or enable them to embrace democratic social practices. Education in a democracy thus becomes a form of social empowerment, in which the young gain the tools needed to effectively share democratic power. This chapter is an attempt to explore what such education for empowerment means in our twentieth century democracy.

The social role of schooling in America's post-industrial capitalist democracy should be seen within the implicit contradiction between the promise and reality of American education. The promise is that children of our society will be educated in ways that will aid their development as literate, thoughtful, and perhaps even compassionate democratic citizens. The reality is schooling which emphasizes the routine, rewards rule-governed behavior, and values conformity over independence, reflecting our limited conception of democracy. This contradiction stems from the inconsistencies inherent in attempting to achieve a system of political equality (democracy) within the confines of a system of economic and resultant cultural, social, and political inequality (capitalism). The question before us is how educators might work within this reality in order to achieve schooling's promise through establishing a definite social role for schools consistent with the ideals of democracy.

The current contradictory nature of schooling's promise and reality is best seen as the most recent expression of the quintessential educational paradox. Since Plato's great dialogues, philosophers and educators have grappled with the notion that while state supported schools are, on one hand, expected to serve the state, such actions may not be possible if educators take seriously their obligation to meet the needs of a culture's children. Within our own context this paradox has been illuminated by the revisionist historians who argue that if the school is beholden to the industrial demands of the economy for docile, obedient, and low-paid laborers, it cannot possibly function to enhance the creative and liberational powers of the lower class children expected to fill those positions (Bowles and Gintis, 1976; Feinberg, 1975; Katz, 1968; Spring, 1972). Thus, when contemplating the school's role, how it functions as an institution concerned with the evolution of the culture within which it is located, educators seemingly need to choose between the demands of the capitalist state and the needs of children. This paradoxical nature of public schooling is easily cast aside by a culture which is either able to meet the physical and spiritual needs of its population or eliminate through legal or quasi-legal means (e.g. censorship, declarations of martial law, etc.) the dissent of those who are expected to go without. However, during times of cultural stress the educational enterprise becomes the battleground for the hearts and minds of future generations.

This paradox becomes even more central to the educational enterprise in a democracy. On one hand, the state strives to obtain legitimacy and stability for the existing order. On the other hand, it embraces a creed that stipulates the right of citizens to alter any existing social arrangement. Children are caught in the middle of this ideological tug of war through the educational process. On one hand, schooling is to make children fit the system; on the other, it is to help children remake the system to fit them. Even this paradox can be overcome by a democratic culture if that culture provides for an equal, just, and plentiful social order. When that existing order begins to deny the basic material and social goods to certain of its members, schooling is forced into deciding between the social order or the interests of each of its members.

George S. Counts (1932) epitomized this paradox when, over a half a century ago, he challenged the educational community to consider whether or not the schools dare build a new social order. His attempt to put into practice Marx's dictum, "The philosophers have only interpreted the world in various ways; the point is to change it" (Marx 1976), was a response to the social dislocations of the Depression. Called into question was the very nature of the state, democratic rule, and its relationship to capitalism. Counts observed capitalism in its apparent death throes; glut accompanied by scarcity, hunger with plenty, insecurity with mastery over the physical environment. All accompanied by

> ...an ideal of rugged individualism, evolved in a simple pioneering and agrarian order at a time when free land existed in abundance, used to justify a system which exploits pitilessly and without thought of the morrow the natural and human resources of the nation and the world (Counts 1932).

Count's challenge to educators, his attempt at forcing them to recognize the paradoxical nature of the schooling enterprise, was destined to be a mere footnote in educational history. Capitalism, despite the dire predictions by its opponents, was able to survive in the albeit altered form of the welfare state. World War II provided the social glue needed to set aside the demands of women, minorities, and the poor in the name of national defense and an artificially stimulated economy. Educators, either unable to generate the will to grapple with Counts' stark claims or unwilling to believe that capitalism and democracy were at best odd bedfellows, devoted themselves to "life adjustment" methods and materials working to fit children to the existing social order (deLone 1979).

Counts would recognize the current social context immediately. The world economy seems locked into a glut/scarcity cycle that befuddles all current economic wisdom. The geopolitical arena seems to follow a course which defies rationality— today the Middle East, the Falkland Islands, and Chad; tomorrow the possibility of the unthinkable. Our civic institutions seem stripped of all legitimacy, a legacy of public lying and deception that seems summarized by the term Watergate and a string of subsequent-gates. Psychological disorders abound in our culture, in which children are expected to be merely small adults and adults behave like children (Elkind 1981; Lasch 1979). Additionally, public participation in governance declines, factories close, and membership in civic, political or labor organizations follows a downward trend. In the face of this, no one seems to believe that recovery is possible and we seem to lack the civic courage, talent, or will called upon in the 1930s and 1940s to resolve capitalism's latest heart attack. Once again the irrationality of economic accumulation and concentration in a society which supposedly places a premium on political equality has become apparent. Educators are forced to face the paradox of their calling in deciding upon a social role for the schools.

My argument is that there can be a definite, purposeful, and democratic social role for schools, or more precisely the educators within them. During the current period of cultural crisis and disarray, educators have the opportunity to exert some of the leadership necessary for a social rebirth. This will only be possible, however, if they can capture for themselves a vision of democracy and social life that celebrates rather than condemns the right of all individuals to self-governance. In so doing, they would be forced to side with children and the promise of education as opposed to the state and schooling's current reality. This is an attempt to locate legitimate grounds for educators to claim such a role, focused in the political empowerment of individuals, and begin the discussion on what this implies for educational practice. To do this, it is first necessary to ask what is meant by democracy as a form of shared power. Second, the current social role played by schooling within the nexus of the state, our limited current conception of democracy, and the recent rising crescendo of criticism of public schooling must be examined. Third, the form of a pedagogy which fulfills the promise of schooling in a democracy must be explored. Finally, the limitations of such a proposal and the hope it bears for a better world can be discussed.

Democracy: Protectionist or Participatory?

Establishing what we mean when we talk about democracy is essential to locating a democratic role for schooling. What does it mean to invoke democracy as an organizing principle for social life? What forms of power sharing are invoked by democratic norms? Leaving aside the question of institutional structures, can we establish the theoretical and normative parameters within which democratic sharing is to occur?

Democracy is a term frequently invoked as both an organizing principle for our collective social lives and as rational for public education. Yet often absent from discussions relying upon democracy is a definition of the concept itself. It is seemingly assumed that the way our social and political structures currently function suffices as an operational definition of democracy. What such assumptions miss is the fact that competing versions of democracy exist, each with its own normative framework within which to judge the democratic or anti-democratic nature of social institutions. The two major versions of democratic theory are the classical, or participatory, and contemporary, or protectionist. Before moving to a discussion of schooling for democracy the nature of democratic theory will be outlined and an attempt to claim one as a legitimate basis for civic education will be made.

Contemporary democratic theory has come forth in an attempt to eliminate the felt instability of classical democratic theory. According to Pateman (1970) recent democratic theory has at its heart two crucial concerns: First, that classical theory, which rested heavily upon public participation in the governing process, is obsolete due to the inability of the populace to participate politically. Second, the fear of totalitarianism based upon the belief that mass participation in political affairs would predicate a collapse into instability. These arguments draw heavily from the experience of the Weimar Republic in which it is claimed that increased political participation by low socioeconomic status groups supposedly not possessing a democratic attitude brought about a collapse into totalitarianism. How is this argument translated into democratic theory for the modern world?

Primarily, contemporary democratic theory has rested upon the tenets of empirical science. Schumpeter (1943) first argued that classical democratic theory rested upon empirically unrealistic grounds which ignored the undemocratic attitudes among the populace. Given such an attitudinal problem, fundamentally a desire to absolve oneself of decision-making responsibility in favor of the decisions of a "leader," Schumpeter proposed that democracy could best function as a competition between decision makers for public support. Thus, classical theory was abandoned for a theory based upon popular selection of elite decision makers (who seem to mirror members of the economically elite classes) as opposed to direct decision making itself.

Continuing the transformation from participatory to protective democratic theory Bereleson (1952), in agreement with Schumpeter, argued that not only were the masses willing to abdicate decision-making responsibilities, but were generally politically apathetic. Citizens took little or no interest in decisions which did not directly influence them. Thus, nonparticipation takes on a positive dimension as it prevents those with limited interest and expertise from creating undue stress on the system. Through limiting demands and thus conflict, the stability of the democratic system is preserved. In fact, those very elements which have the least democratic attitudes, lower socioeconomic status groups, participate less than anyone else as they have less at stake (generating more apathy) than other segments of the populace.

Dahl (1956) completed the transition of democratic theory from participatory to protectionist. His argument was that the most important or distinguishing element of a democratic system is the election process through which non-elites choose governing elites. These representatives of the public then set and act upon a general agenda through which all major public decisions are made. The role of the public is to verify that their political elites are protecting self- or group-interests. In this way democracy is best seen as a protectionist scheme, devoted to the selection of elites who protect the rather stable interests of the electorate. The role of the citizenry in this model is the making of leadership choices, not decisions themselves, in order to protect their perceived interests.

Not only are citizens removed from direct decision making in protectionist theory, the range of what are considered political issues is severely limited. Those issues which deal with the structure of the capitalist order, private ownership of capital, distribution of income and wealth, plant relocation, etc., are deemed not be part of political debate. Rather, the interests to be protected must operate within the existing economic structures. Again, the dual concerns of stability and efficiency dominate contemporary theory. The assumption is that excessive debate over the very nature of the economic system would not only threaten the system's stability but would additionally hamper the efficient economic machine.

The argument can be made that contemporary democratic theory is an accurate description of the current American political context. Indeed, those who gain the least from the current economic and social order are the least likely to vote. The social system is thus guaranteed relative stability as issues of concern to nonvoters, which frequently might involve an alteration of existing economic structures, are not addressed. Additionally, the role of citizens in Western democracies is largely limited to attendance at the ballot box. Direct action on social issues—such as picketing, protesting, and democratic take-overs—is widely discouraged as counter-productive or only symbolic. Finally, while voters may pick political leaders, they are mute when it comes to the selection of economic decision makers.

Most recently, such an analysis of democracy has been put forth by one of America's leading conservatives, George Will. Will argues that nonvoting is a virtue, indicating general satisfaction with the ways things are and preventing the intrusion into the electoral process by those with a nondemocratic attitude. Recent attempts to increase voter turnout are wrong headed and can only lead to the experience of the Weimar Republic. The best democracy seems to be the least democracy as Will states:

> In two presidential ballotings in Germany in 1932, 86.2 and 83.5 percent of the electorate voted. In 1933, 88.8 percent voted in the Assembly election swept by the Nazis. Were the 1932 turnouts a sign of the health of the Weimar Republic? The turnout reflected the unhealthy stakes of politics then: elections determined which mobs ruled the streets and who went to concentration camps.

> The fundamental human right is to good government. The fundamental problem of democracy is to get people to consent to that, not just to swell the flood of ballots. In democracy, legitimacy derives from consent, but nonvoting is often a form of passive consent. It often is an expression not of alienation but contentment...the stakes of our elections, as they affect the day-to-day life of the average American, are agreeably low (Will, 1983, p. 96).

Unfortunately, the contemporary democratic theories in practice say little, if anything, about power sharing. Rather, power is a commodity shared only in the most restricted sense. Groups of elites monopolize political power, and, simultaneously, economic and social power, such that any power sharing which occurs is in and among a relatively closed group. We can only assume, therefore, that power sharing in any genuine sense, is not an element of contemporary democratic theory.

Later it will be argued that public schooling in the United States educates within this protectionist framework. This would be fine were there no alternatives. However, protectionist democracy is only one way of perceiving our collective democratic heritage. What follows is an attempt to recapture an alternative version of democracy to be used as an organizing principle for public education.

It is argued above that current democratic theory and practice are locked within a protectionist rationality. That rationality favors limiting participation in the governing process to the elite and narrowing the scope of those issues deemed worthy of the political process. The social toll of our protectionist theory is becoming all too clear. Millions of the culturally disenfranchised recognize that they are not wanted nor needed by the political system and abandon it. Elections have become merely fundraising contests and politics seem to be mainly an attempt to bring out the darker side (the racist, sexist, fearful, selfish side) of the electorate's protectionist nature.

An alternative understanding of democracy, which embraces power sharing, is the classical, participatory framework upon which the dream of American democracy rests. Pateman (1970) demonstrates such a framework's rationale found in Rousseau's *The Social Contract*: 1) Participatory systems are self-sustaining because the very qualities required of citizens if such a system is to work are those that participation itself fosters; 2) Participation increases one's "ownership" over decisions thus making public decisions more easily acceptable by individuals; and 3) Participation has an integrative function—helping individuals establish the feeling that they belong. These premises were further developed by John Stewart Mill (1963,

1965) and G.D.H. Cole (1920). Mill argued that the primary consideration in judging a society or government to be good was the effect that system had upon individuals. Rather than concern himself with efficiency, as contemporary theorists seem to do, Mill argued that participatory democracy fostered within individuals the psychological attributes needed in self-governance. In addition, Mill and Cole argued that these characteristics are best developed at the local level. Through such local participation, citizens come to their own decisions on an immediate level and develop those skills and attitudes necessary for self-governance at the national level.

What particularly are the attributes needed for self-governance? Mill argued that an active character would emerge from participation and Cole suggested that a nonservile character would be generated. That is, individuals should have the confidence that they indeed are fit to govern themselves. The term often utilized to describe such a state is known as a sense of political efficacy—i.e., as Campbell et al. (1954) have pointed out, the belief that individual political action does have an impact on decision making and thus it is worthwhile to perform one's civic duties. Empirical evidence suggests that participation does enhance feelings of political efficacy. Studies by Almond and Verba (1945), Carnoy and Shearer (1980), and those cited by Wirth (1983), point out that participatory models in local governments, workplaces, and associations do lead to higher levels of participation in national politics. In all of these studies, local participation in self-governance increased a sense of control over the immediate political environment and a concurrent desire to participate in controlling the national political agenda.

Let us be clear about what is meant in these theories and studies by the term participation. Three conditions must exist: first, the participants must be in the position of decision maker rather than decision influencer; second, all participants must be in possession of, or have access to, the requisite information on which decisions can be reached; and third, full participation requires equal power on the part of participants to determine the outcome of decisions. When individuals experience participation in this sense at a local level, the research suggests that they will gain a greater sense of political efficacy in the national arena (Boyte 1980).

This implies that contrary to claims made by contemporary protectionist theorists, democracy best functions as a lived process of participation, a process in which citizens do not merely choose between elites but actually transform themselves through debate and contestation over public issues. This was the original vision of democracy upon which the foundations of our political practice were laid (more on this below). Additionally, as has been pointed out in Wirth's review of workplace democracy, it is a vision of democracy which continues to be relevant as it humanizes shared social spheres, empowers democratic citizens, and leads to more effective and efficient decision making. Most certainly, ongoing debate over how such participation is to be facilitated in our evolving society is necessary (Barley 1984; Cohen and Rogers 1983; Jenowits 1983). The point here is that participatory theory holds us closer to a democratic society than does protectionist theory.

Educators need to realize that the social role they play depends upon the conception of democracy, participatory or protective, they choose; a choice between two polar opposites. On one hand rests a conception of democracy within which the participation of the minority elite is crucial and the nonparticipation of the ordinary man is necessary to maintain the system's stability. On the other hand democracy is conceived as encompassing the broadest participation of the people working to develop political efficacy and a sense of belonging in order to further extend and enhance more participation.

The question is which form of democracy facilitates shared power? It seems reasonable to argue that if shared power is to have any substance it is only to be found with the framework of participatory democracy. Conversely, there seems to be little or no room within protectionist democracy for the sharing of political, economic, or social power. Thus, if shared power is valued, and the evidence about the effects of such shared power cited above seem to justify such a valuing, it would seem that participatory democracy should stand as the normative framework for our social order. Given such a preference, what does this mean for the the process of public schooling?

Schooling for a Corporate Order

Before turning to questions of what schools should do to foster participatory democracy, one must address the current social role of schooling. However, an attempt to segregate the social role schools play from any other role, be it academic or vocational, is to ignore what we have come to see as the deeper meaning of school curriculum, organization, and methodology. Since Jackson's (1968) pioneering look at life inside classrooms, an extensive number of theoretical and empirical studies have emerged to illuminate school's social role through the covert messages of the hidden curriculum. While the history and relative merits of such discourse have been extensively discussed (Apple 1983; Giroux 1983a, 1983b), it is worth reexamining what this material reveals, and often conceals, about the social role currently played by schools. To do this, the most significant findings from hidden curriculum work will be discussed and citizenship education, a deliberate attempt at establishing a social role for schools, will be examined within the hidden curriculum paradigm. How these understandings of the hidden curriculum reflect protectionist democracy will then be considered. Finally, the way in which this rationality dominates current reform efforts will be explored and used as a stepping stone to exploring an alternative social role for schools—empowering children to act as citizens in a shared-power democracy.

The Hidden Curriculum

Not always hidden, the covert messages of schooling penetrate the social role of the entire educational enterprise. Moving beyond earlier discoveries of random instances of domination, intimidation, or indoctrination, work on the hidden curriculum has matured to linking the structures of schooling to the structures of society. These theories suggest that the state/child paradox has currently been resolved in favor of the state. Schools, according to these theorists, reproduce the necessary human capital to maintain existing social relations. At the same time, they work to limit —even to prevent—the raising of questions or the launching of challenges against the prevailing order by those who would most benefit by a change.

What has inquiry into the hidden curriculum revealed about the social role of the schools? First, it seems clear that traditionally the schools have operated to support and legitimate the dominant culture, social, and economic order. This is not a remarkable finding. What makes it important are the aspects of the social order that seem most clearly reflected by schools. In a state which pays frequent lip service to political equality, at a minimum equality of social opportunity, the schools instead reinforce political, cultural, social, and economic inequality (Anyon 1981; Oakes 1985; Sieber 1982; Rist 1970). One of the most crucial current roles of public schooling seems to be the reproduction of an unequal social order.

What messages do schools convey to students in order to perpetuate social inequality? This query leads us to the second lesson one can take from exploring the hidden curriculum: schools teach a limited, very limited, vision of democracy. By removing economics from politics; imposing only particular cultural configurations as being appropriate; limiting students—and teacher—participation in school decision making; glorifying a hierarchical, rule-governed administrative organization; and removing from the curriculum any mention of citizen action or resistance— schools limit our vision of democracy to an occasional trip to the ballot box. Gone is the active participant; enter the passive consumer. Through adopting this protectionist, as opposed to participatory, sense of democracy, schools often play a social role characterized again as supporting the existing social order—even when doing so is not in the best interest of students.

The third function of the hidden curriculum is to generate a positivistic, pseudoscientific notion of teaching and learning. Curriculum reflects only "truths" handed down from authorities in the field. Knowledge is reified and human agency is removed from considerations of how one "knows." Students are given a steady stream of objective facts, instead of being encouraged to see knowledge as a contested terrain. Teaching as well ceases to be a creative activity, but is instead a cookbook process based upon "scientific" methods. As Apple (1982) has pointed out, the curriculum has become "teacher-proofed" and thus reflects a world where all the important issues are resolved (Goodlad 1983; Sirotnik 1983). Creative thought, critical inquiry, reflective thinking all seem unnecessary in a society in which the problems are merely technical. The social role of the school seems best described as working to depoliticize questions of value, social policy, and cultural goals by substituting a faith in science and technology. These twin cures for all of our ills are not subject to citizen control, but are best placed in the hands of experts removed from the political sphere. Again, schools function to support the dominant, unequal social order by limiting the democratic sphere to choices between competing elites, not between competing social visions.

Finally, through the hidden curriculum we see the ways in which schooling elevates particular culture forms at the expense of others. While the school claims to be merely presenting a previously agreed upon and generally resolved cultural heritage it is, in fact, doing cultural violence to the diverse traditions children bring to school. By reflecting the supposed norm, which operates within the larger framework of political and social power, the cultural traditions borne by children which vary from this norm—including traditions of political resistance, economic conflict, and social creativity—are seen as only deviant and best rejected. This process is easily seen in the work of social linguists who link language forms to social power (Bernstein, 1977). More important, the notion of cultural capital—those meanings, symbols, and objects that legitimate particular forms of social action (or inaction)—helps us understand the role schools play as a cultural moderator. Moderating the struggle between oppressed and dominant cultures, schools lead students to see the dominant culture as the norm and any of their own lived cultures that vary from that norm as deviant. Thus, they reject their own heritage and take a second-class position in culture imposed upon them.

It seems clear that for the moment, schools have resolved the state/child paradox in favor of the state. Only by ignoring the unequal outcomes of schooling as demanded by the culture at large can educators continue to play the school role currently employed. This is not to argue that educators have, in fact, literally abandoned their charges to serve the needs of the state. Rather, by serving the state they seem to believe that they are meeting the needs of students in the best possible manner.

Schools, operating as quasi-reproductive institutions, work to produce students "safe" for protective democracy. Endorsing a system of limited democracy, giving the impression that all "real" knowledge is objective and thus best used by impartial technocrats to solve public problems, and legitimizing a culture that comfortably functions in such a limited democracy, schools are encouraging passive citizenship. This is even more clear in looking at what currently passes for "civic education"—the most direct attempt by schools to shape our democratic relationships.

Civic Education
In what is currently referred to as civic education, the current social role of schools presents itself most clearly. Civic education has generally come under the banners of either citizenship transmission or social science. In both models, knowledge is assumed to be value free and democracy a concept limited to only a few public spheres. With the former, the idea is that students will learn, through reading or simulation, the appropriate role of a citizen. Such a role is best demonstrated by Remy's *Handbook of Citizen Competencies* (1980), in which the emphasis seems to be upon making citizens safe for democracy. This is done by endorsing only political

tools and citizen activities which fit within the current democratic rationality such as voting, letter writing, interest group formation and the like. In addition, lower socioeconomic status groups explicitly feared by contemporary democratic theorists for their destablizing impact upon the system are seldom, if ever, addressed.

This reflection of contemporary theory in the citizenship transmission model is evident in the explicit content of citizenship education programs. Witness the emphasis upon choosing leadership elites wisely and holding them responsible. Seldom, if ever, do such programs focus on the actual making of decisions—the focus is on the once-removed step of choosing the decision makers. Secondly, the social studies content in general is filled with examples only of great men and/or women making decisions—never of common people banding together to change their lives and circumstances through direct decision making. Third, the Western democratic system itself is seemingly removed from scrutiny. Once it passes muster in comparison to Soviet totalitarianism (not to be confused with South African authoritarianism) the protectionist democracy of the West is fully embraced. Nary a word is mentioned in the curriculum of the potential contradictions between capitalism and democracy, the need of the system for nonparticipation, or the limits on decision making.

The social science model, while it goes beyond the notions of citizenship transmission by seeking to make students active and creative thinkers, recycles the very assumptions of citizenship transmission it seeks to redress. This is because normative terrain in which varying notions of right and wrong are put forth is outside of objective scientific discourse. Instead, students face a cookbook approach in which only certain types of knowledge are legitimate and solutions to problematic situations are judged on their technical rather than humane merits.

How is it that civic education, stemming from a genuine desire on the part of educators to help students be democratic citizens, turns out to serve such a limited conception of democracy? Again we come face to face with the paradoxical nature of education's social role: In attempting to serve students, the overriding logic of the state directs educators to work at fitting students to the preexisting roles for them in the cultural, political, and economic matrix of the post-industrial capitalism. Of course, to adopt such roles may, on the surface, make a great deal of sense. But in the long run, the roles and actions endorsed and embraced limit and perhaps destroy the abilities, hopes, potentialities, and dreams students have for a better world. Thus, civic education works to reproduce the established social order through limiting the sphere of democratic operations and refusing to develop the skills needed by the democratic citizens to examine critically claims to objective truth, to challenge the opinions of experts, and to utilize their own histories in both questioning the dominant order and building a new one.

Any suggestion that such models are soon to be repudiated by schools is belied by recent government-sponsored reports on the future role of the schools. Take for example the report of the National Commission on Excellence in Education (NCEE).

The commission claims that "our educational foundations are presently being eroded by a rising tide of mediocrity threatening our very future as a nation and a people" (1983, 5). To combat this feared flood, a program of "New Basics" is recommended. The ways in which this program of "New Basics" would merely extend the current social role of schooling as described above is most clearly seen in the recommendation dealing with science and social studies:

> 3. The teaching of science in high schools should provide graduates with an introduction to: (a) the concepts, laws, and processes of the physical and biological sciences; (b) the methods of scientific inquiry and reasoning; (c) the application of scientific knowledge to everyday life; and (d) the social and environmental implications of scientific and technological development. Science courses must be revised and updated for both the college-bound and those not intending to go to college. An example of such work is the American Society's "Chemistry in the Community" program.

> 4. The teaching of social studies in high school should be designed to: (a) enable students to fix their places and possibilities within the larger social and cultural structure; (b) understand the broad sweep of both ancient and contemporary ideas that have shaped our world; (c) understand the fundamentals of how our economic system works and how our political system functions; and (d) grasp the difference between free and repressive societies. An understanding of each of these areas is requisite to the informed and committed exercise of citizenship in our free society.

The ways in which such proposals operate are quite clear. First, they would only operate to reinforce the dominant society by linking politics with the economy (recommendations 4a and 4c) and setting up our society as "free" and thus superior to all others (recommendation 4d). In addition, the very content of such curricular programs would be dictated by those who have the greatest stake in containing democratic inquiry so as to leave their own actions beyond control (i.e. the American Chemical Society).

Second, the notion of democracy would be limited to current conceptions of protectionist democracy. Stressing the present system's "long standing" nature (recommendation 4b), its ability to provide everyone a "place" (recommendation 4a), and its comparatively positive nature (recommendation 4d), conveys the message that there is no need for expansion of change, struggle, even revolution as democratic tools.

Third, the very conception of knowledge here is locked within the positivistic notion of objective facts. The solution to social problems rests within the correct, objective application of science (recommendations 3a and 3b). The scientific knowledge to be used is, of course, objective, rational, and true, conforming with a positivist notion of science (recommendations 3a and 3b). Nothing is said here which would lead us to believe that knowledge is at best problematic, and that the positivist notion of science itself is not generally accepted (Feyerabend 1978; Kuhn 1970). Rather, truth exists in a vacuum, to be merely passed on and absorbed.

Fourth, the recommendations seem to occur in a cultural vacuum in which only one cultural tradition of knowing (recommendation 3b) and of social organization (recommendation 4b) is acceptable. These recommendations are silent on the existence of oppositional culture. In fact, the very idea that students come with divergent cultural backgrounds is totally lost throughout the monolithic structure proposed for schools. The report's recommendations suggest that the school is an educational arena in which students are evaluated solely on their ability to reproduce precisely the knowledge, values, and cultural symbols of the dominant culture.

Yet the recent spate of such reports may prove advantageous to educators desiring to relocate the role of public schooling within the best intentions of democratic empowerment. Public interest in public education is increasing. A primary concern among many parents is the seeming inability of public schooling to give their offspring the benefits so often claimed—simply stated, a better life. Educators might seize the moment, work with parent groups to help locate this failure within the relationship of schooling and the dominant social order, and present the alternative of educating for participatory democracy. Such a relationship should be informed by Johnson's argument:

> Being actively educative is not just a question of "carrying a policy to the public" or destroying myths about public education. It involves learning too. It involves really listening to popular experiences of formal education. It involves research, centering around particular struggles and local issues. It involves making links with other local agencies— researchers, community activities, black groups, women's groups—not to take them over, but learn from their experiences and practices (1981 p. 27).

In doing so, educators might be able to better come to the defense of the public education, fending off attacks that only insist on more of the same and taking the offensive in arguing that schools do have a definite social purpose—a service defined by the imperative to create a literate, democratic and active citizenry. That is, schools have the social purpose of empowering citizens to be self-governing and active in shaping welfare.

Educating for Democratic Participation

If schools and educators are to recognize their potential to serve students, liberating them as it were from protectionist democracy, they must themselves display and instill in students a sense of civic courage. As put by Giroux, civic courage means helping students gain the willingness to act as if they were living in a democratic society. At its core, this form of education is political, and its goal is a "genuine democratic society, one that is responsive to the needs of all and not just of a privileged few" (1983, 201). Or, as Connell et al., have put it:

Education has fundamental connections with the idea of human emancipation, though it is constantly in danger of being captured for other interests. In a society disfigured by class exploitation, sexual and racial oppression, and in chronic danger of war and environmental destruction, the only education worth the name is one that forms people capable of taking part in their own liberation. The business of the school is not propaganda. It is equipping people with the knowledge and skills in a disordered world. In the most basic sense, the process of education and the process of liberation are the same. They are aspects of the painful growth of human species' collective wisdom and self-control. At the beginning of the 1980s it is plain that the forces opposed to that growth here and on the world scale are not only powerful but have become increasingly militant. In such circumstances, education becomes a risky enterprise. Teachers too have to decide whose side they are on (1982, 75).

The primary function of such a pedagogy would be the empowerment of citizens. How might we educate the young so as to facilitate their active participation in self-governance? What elements of school curriculum could enable students to function as democratic citizens? How could schools better operate as institutions of power sharing, creating the values, attitudes, and skills necessary if such power sharing is to be a reality? What follows is informed by the understanding that schools always operate within an existing social reality, but that men and women can alter reality to mirror what they favor as possibility.

Pedagogy for Democratic Participation
It is important to note at the outset that what is suggested here is not a full-blown and predetermined curriculum. To suggest such would only be one more step in the devaluing of teaching and would encourage the debasing of teaching into mere cookbook practice. What is suggested are parameters that educators concerned with democratic empowerment can use as referents. In what follows, the case will be made that teachers can assist in developing participatory democracy by employing an academic program consisting of critical literacy, diverse cultural heritages, exemplars of the democratic spirit (or civic courage), and a system of democratic values. What this means for the direct public role of teachers will also be explored.

A pedagogy of critical literacy must begin with what parents have long understood—the necessity of basic academic skills. The transformative power of the basic academic skills was proposed by no less a radical democrat than Antonio Gramsci (1971). He recognized that to create a potential counter-ideology embracing widespread democratic participation, citizens must be able to manipulate communicative and analytic symbols in ways that enable them to challenge the dominant elite (Entwistle 1979). It is not possible for students to comprehend a new world view, to critically analyze their place in society, to resist in a positive way the demands of a fundamentally unequal social system without having obtained basic academic skills. This is not to argue for the totality of the basics, overwhelming every other facet of the curriculum, or for a rote memory approach that merely forces students to accept, predigested, the rudiments of workbooks, dittos, and drills. Rather, it suggests that basic literacy skills—understood as the comprehension, not merely memorization, of the way in which language, numbers, and logic function—be the basis for any social role of the schools.

Such an understanding would move beyond mere literacy to critical literacy if schooling in the basics could be informed by the work of Paul Freire (1970). Working with impoverished Brazilian peasants, Freire drew directly from their experience to teach academic skills. Rejecting a banking approach to education used by most programs for basic literacy, he felt that information could not be deposited in students' heads for withdrawal later but should be drawn out of their daily lives. Of course, the dominant reality of their lives was their economic, political, social, and cultural oppression. It was by concretizing these experiences through the written word that peasants not only learned how to read but how to oppose the structures enslaving them. This is critical literacy, students gaining a critical consciousness of the world about them while obtaining basic literacy skills.

A similar program of critical literacy needs to be undertaken for students in this country. Kohl suggests an approach similar to Freire's:

> Perhaps the most important thing we can do at present is point out. . .and expose our students to the biases of texts in all subjects as well as in the structure, management, and financing of schools . . . The system itself is an object worth studying with our pupils. Let them find out what it is, how it works, who serves it, and whom it serves. Let them research and find out for themselves, and let us as teachers and educators find out for ourselves, since often we are ignorant as our students (1980, p. 62).

Beyond the school, students can use the conditions of their daily existence in the search for critical literacy. Uncovering the ways in which select social and economic areas are removed from democratic decision making, students can name, thus potentially oppose, limits on democracy. A simple example from Appalachia can illuminate this. While rich in natural resources, the Appalachian region continues to be one of the poorest in the country. One of the main tools used to exploit the region is known as a broad-form deed, clauses of which entitle those holding title to minerals to remove them in any way they see fit—including strip-mining. Further, many of these mineral rights deeds grossly undervalue the raw materials to be removed. Using these deeds as a basic element of the curriculum one can teach reading (vocabulary), math, law, economics, etc. and at the same time open up ways in which these documents deprive the people of the region of their rich birthright. Additionally, exploring how these documents are able to survive legal challenges and do not become a part of political discourse not only teaches subject matter but raises questions about the legitimacy of the entire political system. Thus, students become critically literate—not only able to read and do math, but able to penetrate the very structures which oppress them. This is the first step towards a pedagogy for democratic participation.

If students are to develop the civic courage that makes it possible for them to act democratically it is necessary that they understand their own histories. When students become aware of the worth of their own histories they can come to value their own perceptions and insights. They will not have to rely upon the history of the dominant culture to validate their experiences and truths. Rather, they can look to themselves as useful members of a cultural tradition that empowers them to speak with their own voices. This has indeed been the experience of minorities in this country as they have worked to recover a sense of their own worth within an understanding of their value to the culture at large. Teachers need to incorporate such an historical perspective within the curriculum for all children so that this sense of self-worth will permeate their social actions.

Such work, which celebrates the contributions of working people, women, and minorities, to our general cultural pool would provide students with their own "cultural capital." A concept that illuminates the way in which one's stock of cultural understandings empowers one to action, cultural capital has traditionally been used to understand how students stockpile the symbols, meanings, understandings and language of the dominant culture. Here it is being argued that students could stockpile an alternative "bundle" of cultural capital. These symbols etc. would be taken from the "peoples' histories" of groups and individuals who have strived and are striving to expand the meaning of democracy. Already existing curricular materials which focus on the struggles of American men and women to expand the terrain of freedom and to improve the quality of their lives could be employed to demonstrate to students actions taken by those in situations analogous to theirs. (Cluster 1979; Cooney and Michalowski 1979; Zinn 1980). Such material could operate to change the current way students are led to view social history as linear, conflict free, dominated by white males, and occurring almost without human agency. This alternative stock of cultural capital could indeed encourage and empower students to speak with their own voices as they link their own reality to struggles for a possible alternative future.

It is not enough to merely arm students with the intellectual tools and cultural understandings of them to transform rejection into resistance and action. Educators concerned with participatory democracy must go one step further and arm students with the understanding that there are other ways to organize social life. Allowing students to continue to think that current social arrangements are merely "natural," causes the critical moment of moving from critique to change to be lost. Rather, students merely become distrustful, angry, and cynical. Part of this is due to the unfounded supposition, laced throughout the curriculum, that change always occurs in an orderly and linear fashion. Students are deceived into believing that they can alter existing social arrangements by merely voting in preferred ways. What this misses are the powerful forces lined up behind the status quo, ready to defend current arrangements against any frontal attack. In presenting alternatives to students, teachers should honestly face the fact that change only occurs with struggle and sacrifice, and hope that they can act accordingly.

But act in the name of what? Currently the curriculum offers no alternatives to our accepted order. As Kohl suggests, teachers should be prepared to present to students, both through example (more on this below) and study, alternatives to the existing order:

> The most important educational thing we can do is have our students understand that socialism, communism, anarchism, and other noncapitalist forms of organizing human life are serious, and must be thought about; and that people have a right to choose the social systems they believe will meet their needs and the needs of their communities. Young people also ought to be given an opportunity to know that people fight for such abstractions as justice and for such concretions as the eliminations of poverty and oppression (1980, 64).

Additionally, Dreier (1980) suggests that students be exposed to attempts in the Third World to transform a harsh reality into a humane society as examples of what people, through cooperative action, can accomplish. Making the connection between the Third World and our technological society can be enhanced by exploring examples of similar social alternatives in this culture. Such examples range from the publicly owned and operated plants and utilities in the United States providing products and services at significantly lower costs with more efficiency than similar private owned utilities, to such large scale projects as Canadian socialized health systems, England's nonprofit housing system, and Sweden's mass transit system. Coupling these sets of examples together provides alternatives to the existing order, illuminates the possibilities of genuine power sharing, and demonstrates the means by which such alternatives arise and take their places in a transformed state.

Beyond the analysis of systems, lies the analysis of values that are conducive to civic courage. Butts (1982) has proposed a schemata of civic values that are conducive to a democracy including justice, freedom, equality, diversity, authority, privacy, participation, due process, personal obligation for the public good, and international human rights. Indeed, these values do form the nucleus of the democratic society. But it is not enough to merely teach students to embrace such values. Rather, they should first be linked to democracy and then students should attempt to see how such values are treated in the culture. Through the examination of their own lives and those of others they should directly face the powerful forces lined up against justice, freedom, equality, and the rest. In contrast to this, students should be given examples of lives lived in pursuit of these goals by peoples of both sexes, all colors, and any creed. Thus, they will be given not only the tools for transformation, but the alternatives available, values to strive for, and the courage to undertake such a role—that of living and behaving democratically in an undemocratic society.

At this point, it is important to note that students confronted with such a curriculum might reject participatory democracy. They might take a cynical route claiming that given current limits on political power sharing, citizen participation makes little if any difference. Responding to such a claim requires teachers to draw upon both historical and current reality. The recent history of the Vietnam era demonstrates graphically how citizen action altered public policy (Gitlin 1983). The current nuclear freeze campaign, while not yet successful, has not only affected the Administration's arms policy but has made nuclear armaments a key issue in recent elections. Citizen action has forced power sharing and had dramatic effects across the nation. Cynicism is factually unsound and teachers are obligated to point this out to their students.

Alternatively, students may argue that the populace is indeed incapable of sharing power democratically, necessitating the adoption of a less democratic but more efficient political system (e.g., fascism). The obligation of the teacher is again to confront students with the historical and current reality of such claims. Would they be willing to live in Hitler's Germany or Mussolini's Italy? At what cost did these cultures achieve their so-called efficiency—and at what were they efficient? How does the claim of efficiency made for more authoritarian systems square with current social practice? What does one do with evidence that in many cases greater participation leads to greater efficiency (Wirth 1984)? Finally, can those systems which blatantly override the rights of the individual be in any way remotely compatible with the credo and founding documents of our republic? Raising these issues potentially deepens students' understanding of democracy as shared power and offers them a realistic choice of alternatives.

Many proposals for the schools' social role fail to recognize that teachers teach by example. If the school is to act for a democratic transformation, teachers will have to behave consistently with shared-power goals both inside and outside of their classrooms. In their classrooms they will have to avoid belittling students and devaluing their cultures and celebrate with them the wealth of their diversity. They will have to be willing themselves to look deep into the structures of oppression, see how they inform their own practice, and search for alternative classroom practices consistent with democratic values. Taking seriously the democratic values listed above, can teachers treat children in ways that demonstrate those same values? Taking, for example, the value of equality, can teachers overcome the class-biased ways in which the children are treated and curriculum is parcelled out? With the value of participation, can teachers allow students a meaningful role in the making of classroom decisions? Can they share power within the classroom and school? Similar questions can be raised about all the values mentioned. Only when teachers can replicate these values in the classroom, will students take them seriously.

Outside of the classroom, teachers need to demonstrate both a genuine concern for children and the civic courage they are attempting to instill in students. If they are sincere about adopting a social role for schools which takes the side of children and the possibilities of education, they need to have the civic courage to act for children now. Currently, teacher unions are primarily interested in teachers' working conditions, and professional associations are most interested in establishing the legitimacy of and furthering a subject area. These are certainly important goals. Yet one is hard pressed to find teachers actively working through their organizations for the welfare of children. Campaigns against child abuse and for adequate child nutrition, housing, and health care are more often carried on outside of the educational community than within it. Such campaigns would certainly call into question the dominant social reality and be challenged by those with political power. Educators, by taking on such struggles, would demonstrate both to students and parents the very civic courage they are attempting to instill.

Through this combination of pedagogy and action, educators can work to turn student resistance into action for a shared-power, participatory democracy. This would be the most valuable role in this democracy schools could play. By working with the possibilities of education, teachers could build this definitive, justifiable social role while simultaneously attending to the academic role the public expects of schools. It is only when schools, and educators within them, can capture this role of democratic empowerment that they can justify their claim to being the social agency primarily concerned with children. Otherwise, they need to admit that their main allegiance is to the state and that their social role is to reproduce the unequal social order that hides itself behind the guise of democracy.

Conclusion

Like Counts, I am not naively optimistic that the schools, and educators within them, can be relied upon to take the social role suggested herein. Nor should this be taken as an argument that schools alone will alter existing social, political, and economic relationships. We have too often relied solely upon children to restore a world order damaged by adults. However, schools will certainly be an essential part of any attempt to develop and instill the civic courage needed to reclaim our democratic heritage. Thus, what has been been proposed here is that educators can play a distinct and vital role with respect to shared power by developing in children the tools, skills, and attitudes necessary to live democratically. Further, it has been argued that teachers as citizens have a valuable role in directly altering the current social order, working for a society in which justice and democracy have real meaning.

I am struck by two limitations of the preceding argument. First, do teachers currently in the field or preparing to enter the field have the potential to take on the role described herein? There are times when my answer to this question is an unequivocal no—when I witness teachers demeaning children, belittling parents, avoiding political and social action and, in general, teaching their subject rather than teaching children. And yet, I do believe that most teachers enter teaching because they are concerned about children and the lives they will lead. This concern gets lost in the technocratic rationality of teacher preparation, the mundane duties forced on teachers, and a lack of professional rewards and esteem (for instance the teacher-proofing of the curriculum). Teachers are not inherently better than any other occupation group when it comes to reacting to the reality of the workplace. Thus, their often destructive actions must be seen within the reality of their jobs and education.

As a beginning step towards changing this reality I believe it is necessary to take seriously recommendations of Goodlad (1983) and others with regard to the conditions of teaching. Teachers should be released from all extraneous duty, empowered to deal directly with curriculum, be given more time for research and development (perhaps through expanding contracts to eleven months), and be paid a reasonable wage. Further, teachers should be entitled to a career ladder which rewards good teaching. Finally, teachers who are unfit for duty should be removed from classrooms through evaluation by either more adequately trained and screened administrators or committees of administrators, teachers, and parents. If we seriously expect teachers to play a vital social role, it is necessary that the structure of the job allow them to play that role. Not all teachers will respond to such a change in conditions in the ways suggested. But when these changes are coupled with the changes suggested for teacher education above, there is reason to hope that many teachers will respond by taking the side of children over the state.

State funding of education raises the second limitation. Is it true, as has been suggested by many writers (Arons 1982; Illich 1970; Spring 1980) that schools can do nothing but serve the needs of the state as long as it pays the bills? Earlier it was argued that, internally, schools do not work in lockstep with the demands of capitalism as suggested by reproductive theorists. Here I want to suggest that much of the criticism of state domination misses the great degree of potential local automony schools have. Local school authorities, or school boards, have jealously guarded their authority to hire staff, set curriculum, and manage the local schools. Only in a few states has this authority been overridden, and even such mandates as competency testing have been left to local authority. This is not to deny that school boards often abandon their authority to school administrators or are controlled by the most conservative elements in a community. It does mean that educators must take seriously the political potential of school boards and work to populate them with individuals who will join the struggle for a new social order.

Even given these limitations and the schools' history of dashed promises, it is imperative that educators strive to claim a social role for schools that speaks to the best of our potential. Today the world is a fearful place for children. Not only is real life terrifying—wars, crime and domestic violence all too common—but fantasy, as represented by the cultural regulator television, is itself a frightening world full of guns, gratuitous violence, and useless consumption. Even more unnerving is the feeling that nothing is to be done in the face of this ruthless world.

But ultimately, the promise of democracy is that people can and should control their own destiny. It has been my argument that the only justifiable role for schools in our democracy is to equip students with the tools necessary to do this. This means possessing skills to critically analyze the ways in which present structures prevent our taking control of our collective destinies. Further, it means equipping students with the knowledge that they and their cultures are important. Finally it means instilling the values necessary in a participatory democracy and the civic courage necessary to act upon those values. It is only when educators see, and act, upon these proposals that schools justifiably lay claim to their urgent, unique, and crucial social role: preparing children to act democratically in an undemocratic society. When educators so act they will ultimately have to side with children against the state, an act demanding civic courage of them as well.

References

Almond, G.A. and S. Verba. 1945. *The civic culture.* Boston: Little, Brown, and Co.

Anyon, J. 1981. Social class and civic culture. *Curriculum Inquiry* 11, (Spring): 3-42.

Apple, M. 1982. *Cultural and economic reproduction in education.* London: Routledge and Kegan Paul.

Arons, S. 1982. *Compelling belief: The culture of American schooling.* New York: McGraw-Hill.

Barber, B. 1984. *Strong democracy: Participatory politics for a new age.* Berkeley, CA: University of California Press.

Berelson, B.R. 1952. Democratic theory and public opinion. *Public Opinion Quarterly* 16 (Summer): 313-330.

Bernstein, B. 1977. *Class, codes, and control: Towards a theory of advocational transmission.* London: Routledge and Kegan Paul.

Bowles, S. and H. Gintis. 1976. Schooling in capitalist America. New York: Basic Books.

Boyte, H. 1980. *The backyard revolution.* Philadelphia: Temple University Press.

Butts, R.F. 1982. The revival of civic learning requires a prescribed curriculum. *Liberal Education* Winter: 377-401.

Campbell, A., G. Gurin, and W. Miller. 1954. *The voter decides.* Chicago: Row and Peterson.

Carnoy, M. and D. Shearer. 1980. *Workplace democracy.* White Plains, N.Y.: M.E. Sharpe.

Clustor, D. 1979. *They should have served that cup of coffee.* Boston: South End Press.

Cohen, J. and J. Rogers. 1983. *On democracy: Toward a transformation of American society.* New York: Penguin Books.

Cole, G.D.H. 1920. *Social theory.* London: Methuen.

Connell, R.W., D.J. Ashenden, S. Kessler, and G.W. Dowsett. 1982. *Making the difference.* Sydney: George Allen and Unwin.

Cooney, R. and Michaelowski, H. 1977. *The power of the people.* Culver City, CA: Peace Press.

Counts, G.S. 1932. *Dare the school build a new social order?* New York: John Wiley.

Dahl, R.A. 1956. *Preface to democratic theory.* Chicago: University of Chicago Press.

deLone, R. 1979. *Small futures.* New York: Harcourt Brace Janovich.

Drier, P. 1980. Socialism and cynicism. *Socialist Review* 53 (September-October): 105-131.

Elkind, D. 1981. *The hurried child.* Reading, MA: Addison-Wesley.

Entwistle, H. 1979. *Antonio Gramsci: Conservative schooling for radical politics.* London: Routledge and Kegan Paul.

Feinberg, W. 1975. *Reason and rhetoric: The intellectual foundations of twentieth century liberal educational policy.* New York: Wiley.

Feyerabend, P. 1978. *Science in a free society.* London: New Left Books.

Freire, P. 1970. *Pedagogy of the oppressed,* translated by M.B. Ramos. New York: The Seabury Press.

Giroux, H.1983a. Theories of reproduction and resistance in the new sociology of education: A critical analysis. *Harvard Educational Review* 53 (Summer): 257-293.

Giroux, H. 1983b. *Theory and resistance in education: A pedagogy for the opposition.* South Hadley, MA: Bergin and Garvey.

Giroux, H. 1981. *Ideology, culture, and the process of schooling.* Philadelphia: Temple University Press.

Gitlin, T. 1983. Seizing history. *Mother Jones* (November): 32-38, 48.

Goodlad, J.I. 1983. *A place called school.* New York: McGraw-Hall.

Gramsci, A. 1971. *The prison notebooks,* translated by Q. Hoare and G.N. Smith. New York: International Publishers.

Herbers, J. 1983. Grass-roots groups go national. *The New York Times Magazine* 4 (September): 12-15.

Illich, I. 1970. *Deschooling society.* Cuernavaca, Mexico: CIDOC.

Jackson, P.W. 1968. *Life in classrooms.* New York: Holt, Rinehart and Winston.

Janowitz, M. 1983. *The reconstruction of patriotism: Education for civic consciousness.* Chicago: University of Chicago Press.

Johnson, R. 1981. Socialism and popular education. *Socialism and Education* 8 (Winter).

Katz, M. 1968. *The irony of early school reform.* Cambridge, MA: Harvard University Press.

Kohl, H. 1980. Can the school build a new social order? *Journal of Education* 162 (Summer): 57-66.

Kuhn, T. 1970. *The structure of scientific revolutions.* Chicago: University of Chicago Press.

Lasch, C. 1979. *The culture of narcissism.* New York: W.W. Norton and Company.

Marx, K. 1976. *Collected works,* Vol. V. New York: International Publishers.

Mill, J.S. 1965. *Collected works.* Toronto: University of Toronto Press.

Mill, J.S. 1963. *Essays on politics and culture.* New York.

National Commission on Excellence in Education. 1983. *A nation at risk*. Washington, D.C.: U.S. Department of Education.

Oakes, J. 1985. *Keeping track: How schools structure in equality*. New Haven, CT: Yale University Press.

Pateman, C. 1970. *Participation and democratic theory*. Cambridge: Cambridge University Press.

Remy, R.C. 1980. *Handbook of citizen competencies*. Washington, D.C.: Association for Supervision and Curriculum Development.

Rist, R.C. 1970. Student social class and teacher expectations: The self-fulfilling prophecy in ghetto education. *Harvard Educational Review* 40 (Spring): 416-451.

Schumpeter, J.A. 1943. *Capitalism, socialism, and democracy*. London: George Allen and Urwin.

Sieber, T. 1981. The politics of middle-class success in an inner city school. *Journal of Education* 164 (Fall): 30-47.

Sirotnik, K. 1983. What you see is what you get: Consistency, persistency, and mediocrity in classrooms. *Harvard Educational Review* 53 (January): 16-31.

Spring, J. 1980. *Educating the worker-citizen*. New York: Longman.

Will, G. 1983. In defense of nonvoting. *Newsweek*, 10 October: 96.

Wirth, A. 1983. *Productive work — in industries and schools: Becoming persons again*. New York: University Press of America.

Zinn, H. 1980. *A people's history of the United States*. New York: Harper and Row.

CHAPTER 9

Downtown Shopping Malls and the New Public-Private Strategy[1]

Bernard J. Frieden and Lynne B. Sagalyn

The rebuilding of American cities since World War II has been a mixed public-private enterprise. Government agencies have taken the lead in planning and starting renewal projects, while development companies have been responsible for building and managing them. Beginning in 1949, the federal urban renewal program separated the public and private sectors in a way that minimized opportunities for city favoritism or for collusion at the expense of the federal government. This separation also reflected a sense of the relative strengths of each party. City governments, using their power of eminent domain, were far better equipped to assemble land for redevelopment than were private firms; and through their access to federal loans and grants the cities were better able to raise the necessary start-up funds. Developers, for their part, were better equipped than the cities to assess the demand for new buildings and to design their projects accordingly, to attract long-term investors, market the newly built space, and handle the entrepreneurial risks of the entire process.

Despite this underlying logic, relations between cities and developers were troublesome. Operating under federal rules that excluded developers from the early stages of planning, cities had to figure out in advance what projects would be feasible for the private sector to build. After the land was assembled and cleared, many renewal agencies were unable to find a developer willing to buy it, or willing to build the type of project they had planned for it. After years of costly and complicated planning, followed by politically controversial land acquisition and relocation of the prior occupants, these cities had nothing to show for their efforts but fields of rubble.

The large number of sites that remained vacant were an embarrassment to mayors and federal officials alike. In addition to the rubble problem, many cities simply abandoned their projects before they ever reached the clearance stage, while others had to change their plans once they discovered what developers were prepared to build (Kaplan 1966, 247; Abrams 1965, 99). By 1968, a White House commission asked to review the urban renewal program identified as its prime weakness "the unconscionable amount of time consumed in the process" (US NCUR 1968, 165).

The Implementation Problem

The delays and frustrations of urban renewal were characteristic of a broader group of community development programs undertaken in the 1960s and early 1970s. Even though federal aid flowed freely at that time, the cities had enormous problems trying to complete the projects they started.

One program, "New Towns In-Town," offered surplus federal land at low prices, plus other federal assistance, for large developments that would include some housing for the poor. The land was not only cheap, but it came in large tracts and it was unoccupied, so that cities could bypass the usual delays, costs, and protests of relocation and clearance. Even so, four years after the program began, three of the seven participating cities had abandoned their projects and the others were stalled indefinitely as a result of local controversies or development problems (Derthick 1972).

In late 1965, top officials of the federal Economic Development Administration began to put together an ambitious public works program to create jobs for unemployed workers in Oakland, California. Their program included construction of an airport hangar, marine terminal, industrial park, and access roads; and they expected to attract private businesses that would provide work for more than 2,000 of the hard-core unemployed, most of them members of minority groups.

The fanfare surrounding this effort attracted the attention of Jeffrey Pressman and Aaron Wildavsky at the University of California in Berkeley, who decided to study the results. They found widespread support for the program among Oakland's decision makers, particularly at the outset. Nevertheless, the obstacles were numerous and progress turned out to be painfully slow. Five years later, the aircraft hangar, which was supposed to provide more than half the promised jobs, was still not built, and the industrial park had created only 30 jobs instead of an anticipated 420.

Pressman and Wildavsky attributed Oakland's problems mostly to the extreme complexity of decision making and to use of the wrong incentives with the private sector. Their pioneering book established implementation as an important field of study and stimulated other investigations of how well government programs worked once they went into operation (1973). At the same time, the federal government became increasingly aware of managerial difficulties at the local level and tried several different ways of improving the capacity of cities to handle complicated programs. Yet implementation problems continued to blunt federal initiatives in community development. In the model cities program—a large-scale effort to improve living conditions in low-income neighborhoods—even after five years of operations the cities were able to spend only 54 percent of the funds the Department of Housing and Urban Development made available to them (Frieden and Kaplan 1977, 229).

Since the early 1970s, the federal government has terminated the urban renewal program and cut back the flow of federal aid to local governments. Still, many cities have succeeded in breaking the development deadlock and resolving some of the main problems of implementation, particularly those resulting from poor public-private relationships. The most striking demonstration of city progress in managing complicated public-private projects is the wave of new retail centers built in downtown areas across the country.

The new retail projects are important to the cities for several reasons. First, most of them are big, typically providing space for more than one hundred stores with the potential to generate substantial sales and property tax revenues. The successful ones are focal points of downtown activity, drawing crowds of ten to twenty million visitors a year—as do regional shopping malls in the suburbs. Further, they mark a break with the long-term movement of retailing away from downtown. During the suburban boom that began in the late 1940s, retail trade was one of the early central-city functions that began to shrink. Department stores as well as other retailers followed their middle-class customers to the the new shopping malls. City retail sales at first declined relative to the suburbs, and then began to decline in real dollars.

Many cities tried to reverse the trend by converting downtown shopping streets into landscaped pedestrian malls, but only a few of these were notable successes. The 1960s produced a handful of new retail projects in the cities, such as Rochester's Midtown Plaza and San Francisco's Ghirardelli Square, but most analysts of urban affairs continued to anticipate a bleak future for central cities in general and especially for downtown shopping.

Yet the development of more than one hundred downtown retail centers since 1970 suggests that a growing number of cities are finding ways to compete effectively against the suburbs for a share of retail sales. By 1983, one of every four new shopping centers in the United States was a downtown project (ULI 1983, B-1 to B-3; WSJ 1983). The downtown centers follow several different retailing strategies. Some, such as Plaza Pasadena, are regional shopping malls offering a wide variety of goods aimed at the middle of the market. Others, such as Boston's Faneuil Hall Marketplace, are specialty malls that draw people by offering unusual foods and a festive atmosphere. Still others, such as Town Square in St. Paul, are mixed-use projects that combine stores with hotels, offices, convention centers, or other activities. Some are intended to appeal especially to tourists, conventioneers, and business visitors, while others have a shopping mix geared to nearby residents and in-town workers.

The earlier decline of downtown retailing was rooted in a major shift of population and jobs from the cities to the suburbs. These underlying trends have not changed: in fact, the central cities lost people and jobs at an accelerated rate during the 1970s. Nor has there been a reversal of the long-term trend in retail sales. While sales continued to expand strongly in the suburbs, the central business districts of major cities recorded even greater losses in real dollars in the 1970s than they had in the 1960s (US HUD 1980a, chaps. 1 and 3).

What has changed is that for the first time in thirty years, central cities have found ways to gain a competitive edge on their surrounding suburbs for certain kinds of development. This turnaround resulted in part from limited changes in the central-city economy and in the make-up of city neighborhoods. But it resulted much more from changes in public policy than it did from changes in real estate markets.

Federal urban policy played a two-fold part, by pressing the cities to take greater responsibility for managing their own economic development while also offering them some help to do it. Suburban governments tightened their control of growth and enacted regulations that were both cumbersome and costly. But while the suburbs were having their "quiet revolution in land use control" (Bosselman and Callies 1972) a series of central cities were staging a quiet revolution in development management. Public officials decided that they wanted downtown shopping malls and took steps to find developers willing to build them. The steps they took moved away from the usual adversary relationship between the city as regulator and the developer as a business firm applying for permits, and from the carefully circum-scribed public-private relationships that had been mandated in the urban renewal program.

The result of these efforts was a new style of joint action for cities and developers that worked effectively for downtown retail centers. Because we believe the new relationships are an important advance in the management of city-building, we have studied the development of six retail projects in detail and have analyzed many others on the basis of available data and brief interviews [2]. This chapter focuses on why and how the retail centers were built, how the new public-private relations differ—for better or worse—from earlier approaches, and what effects this recent experience is likely to have on cities in the future.

Motivating the Cities: Pressures and Opportunities

Among the leading contributors to the new approach were federal actions during the 1970s, which gave the cities good reasons to take more responsibility for their own economic future, at a time when downtown development opportunities were begin-ning to improve.

The basic pressure motivating mayors to search for new strategies was a growing reluctance in Washington to continue funding annual increases in federal aid to cities. Public and media attention to urban problems reached a peak in the late 1960s. Soon afterward, the environmental crisis and then the energy crisis pushed urban problems out of the limelight. Yet the fiscal problems of the older cities grew worse in the 1970s. Hard pressed to keep costs down, raise additional taxes, or increase bonded debt, several cities reached the brink of default and bankruptcy, most notably New York, Boston, Cleveland, and Philadelphia. Many cities cut municipal services but continued to bear high tax burdens (US HUD 1980a, 6-8 to 6-9, 6-17).

Despite this ominous turn, the political alignment that had supported earlier federal aid programs lost much of its strength and both the news media and the Congress grew increasingly indifferent to the pleas of the mayors. By 1978, *Harper's, Newsweek,* and the *New York Times Magazine* were declaring an end to the urban crisis (Allman 1978; Fleetwood 1979; Newsweek 1979). A restless public and elected officials trying to bring the federal budget under control were inclined to agree for different reasons. The federal-aid budget for states and local governments peaked in real dollars in 1978, midway in the Carter Administration, and declined further in the Reagan Administration (US ACIR 1983, 66-67). The message to cities was clear: with less outside aid, they would have to do more to help themselves.

Federal Urban Policy

The federal government made it easier for cities to commit funds for downtown development by relaxing its earlier controls on the uses of federal aid. Of nine major community development programs in 1970, only urban renewal and historic preservation grants could be tapped easily for downtown revitalization. Several other programs were intended for residential areas, and the one that received greatest attention—the model cities program—had to be used to improve low-income and minority neighborhoods. In 1974 Congress merged these nine separate programs into a single community development block grant that cities could use flexibly to meet their own priorities, with a minimum of federal review and supervision. The cities lost no time in changing their pattern of spending on development projects.

Under the earlier system, eighteen percent of the Department of Housing and Urban Development's community development aid budget went into poverty neighborhoods through the model cities program. In just the first year of block grants, cities cut their spending in low-income areas by more than one-third. The bulk of expenditures under the model cities program was for such public services as education, health, and job training. The block grant program set limits on local spending for service activities and required cities to use most of their aid for construction projects. Under the new arrangements, hardware expenditures, public works, and downtown development were soon back in fashion; and poor people and minorities were soon out of fashion (Frieden and Kaplan 1977, chap. 11).

Further, in 1977 Congress enacted the urban development action grant program ("UDAG") to fund local construction projects that stimulate private investment to create jobs and improve the tax base. By the second year of operations, three-fourths of the federal funds went for central city projects, and close to sixty percent of the central-city funds were for commercial developments (US HUD 1980b).

Other federal actions also had the effect of promoting downtown revitalization. Historically, federal tax laws greatly favored investment in new structures over investment in preservation and improvement of old ones. As of 1970, accelerated depreciation was available to firms and individuals that invested in new commercial and industrial buildings, but not to those that bought or rehabilitated existing buildings. Beginning in the mid-1970s, a series of revisions introduced special tax incentives for investors who improved older and historic buildings and in 1981 equalized the depreciation benefits for new and existing buildings (Peterson 1980; Gensheimer 1982).

New federal measures also made home financing more readily available in city neighborhoods. Regulations and laws of the mid-1970s directed against "redlining" required fuller disclosure of mortgage finance patterns and broadened the lending powers of thrift institutions in urban areas, thus helping homeowners to renovate older houses. The Department of Housing and Urban Development and the Federal Home Loan Bank Board set up an urban reinvestment task force in 1974 to fund neighborhood housing service programs offering below-market loans and help with home renovation. These programs, later administered by the Neighborhood Reinvestment Corporation, helped stabilize and improve many old neighborhoods and in so doing provided a middle-income market for downtown shopping malls.

Gentrification
An important but misunderstood change of the 1970s was the movement of relatively well-off people into old houses in what had been low-income city neighborhoods. This trend resulted in part from the continued departure of earlier residents who left behind many interesting older houses at prices that compared favorably with rapidly inflating suburban housing costs. Couples who liked in-town conveniences discovered that by pooling two incomes and having few children or none at all, they could afford to renovate brownstones and still have money left for a suitable lifestyle. At the same time, an expansion of downtown office districts created some fresh demand for walk-to-work housing. Changes in the national economy generated increases in office and professional service jobs in many cities in the 1970s. Denver more than doubled its office space in the 1970s, while Atlanta, Detroit, Newark, Pittsburgh, and Seattle were among the cities that had increases of more then 50 percent (Black 1980).

For a series of loosely related reasons, enough newcomers invested in the older houses to make a visible difference in selected neighborhoods. These changes caught the eye of journalists and other trend-watchers who concluded that the urban crisis was on the way out.

Yet this new commitment to in-town living remained a very limited movement —limited by the number of city-loving families able to put together an income package of $50,000 or more, by the number of neighborhoods with the right combination of charm and access, and by the fact that house prices in popular locations soon climbed out of reach of all but a few people. In a survey of the thirty largest cities, Phillip Clay found some upgrading in almost all of them, but he also found that declining neighborhoods greatly outnumbered those enjoying a revival. And contrary to popular impression, he and other researchers found no sign of the long-awaited back-to-the-city movement from suburbia: most of the renovators turned out to be families moving from one city residence to another (1979; James 1980).

Still, the gentrification trend was a positive one for the cities. Housing renovation dovetailed with both retail growth and with the expansion of downtown office districts. It raised the prospect that all three activities might be mutually supportive in encouraging people who worked in the expanding service and professional occupations to live and to shop in the central city.

Taken together, these and other changes in the central cities created the basis for fresh attempts to reinvigorate downtown areas. The need for stimulating economic development was clearer than ever, and the prospects for success seemed to be improving. For the first time in many years, the cities actually had a competitive edge over the suburbs in some ways. An unexpected shift in public taste was partly responsible for this turn of events. The 1970s were a time when many Americans rediscovered the past and found they enjoyed it. Nostalgia was in and it was marketable. (A scrap dealer who handled salvage from the New York City transit system advertised old subway handstraps mounted on wood with the slogan, "Hang on to a piece of the past.") If the latest fashion called for renovating a Victorian townhouse rather than living in a contemporary deck model, the central cities had a corner on that market. And if tourism and convention visits were emerging as important economic activities, then the old buildings of central cities had acquired new value as charming reminders of bygone days.

Options for Developers
City initiatives triggered recent retail construction downtown, but city actions alone do not explain why developers were responsive. A combination of circumstances made downtown sites more attractive in the 1970s than they had been earlier. First, changes in family life were creating new marketing opportunities. The same changes that encouraged young people to live in the city—late marriage, shared incomes, few children—enabled them to indulge their taste for entertainment, restaurants, boutiques, and specialty retail items for the home.

Second, the increasing number of workers in central-city offices were potential customers who would shop for clothes, fashion accessories, books, and other small items in stores near their jobs. As a result, retailers considering a new or expanded downtown location were not totally dependent on bringing the suburbanites back to the city. In addition, the growing public interest in old buildings and historic places also prompted developers to recognize the special value of sites in port and warehouse districts and other long-neglected settings.

Meanwhile, retail development opportunities in the suburbs were no longer as promising as they had been. A network of regional shopping centers was already well established in the suburbs of most major cities, and finding good sites for more malls was getting harder all the time (Sternlieb and Hughes 1981, 3). Compounding the search for sites was a rapid buildup of suburban growth regulations during the early 1970s. Prompted in part by the environmental movement and in part by local opposition to further growth, suburbs across the country were putting into place a network of new and demanding review and permit requirements for proposed developments of all kinds (Frieden 1979, chap. 11). These had the effect of stretching out the development process and making it more costly, while also giving opponents of shopping centers easy and repeated chances to block them. Further, the mood of local citizens and their representatives was turning increasingly hostile to development, particularly in areas that had experienced high growth in the recent past.

On top of local regulatory snags, the newly created federal Environmental Protection Agency posed an even more direct threat to suburban mall development. In an effort to prevent automobile emissions from lowering air quality in places that already met pollution standards, it drew up plans to restrict the construction of major new parking facilities in the outer suburbs.

A further consideration in the suburbs was the high cost of building the infrastructure necessary for regional shopping centers—water mains, sewer connectors, and road improvements. In the past, suburban governments had been willing to pay for some of these costs or to use local bond issues to finance them. By the early 1970s, the suburbs were increasingly transferring these costs to the developer (Frieden 1980). City sites, in contrast, were more likely to have the infrastructure in place and, to the extent they did not, the cities were more willing to use tax-exempt financing to pay for it. Developers looking at mounting construction costs and rising interest rates began to think carefully about the benefits of tax-exempt municipal bond financing not only for streets and utilities but also for the parking garages they would need.

Department stores, considered the indispensable "anchor tenants" that would draw customers to large shopping malls, were generally committed to suburbia for their new branches. But as retail trade had become increasingly competitive, some department store chains recognized that specialization to serve a particular segment of the market could be an effective strategy. A few department store executives, at least, were willing to consider locating a new store downtown as a way of capturing a share of the market that the outlying malls had bypassed (Bluestone et al. 1981, 32-34).

New Development Policies

In the 1970s the cities began moving away from the social agenda of the 1960s and returning to earlier concerns with revitalizing the central business district. The earlier political upheavals around urban renewal efforts had taught them to avoid clearance projects that pushed out large numbers of people, and they looked for smaller-scale projects, new public financing tools, new funding sources, and negotiated risk-sharing relationships with private developers. As these development initiatives progressed, several features of earlier city development practice began to reassert themselves: an involvement of downtown business interests in setting the redevelopment agenda; a preference for construction projects rather than public services; a predominance of commercial, governmental, and industrial projects over housing; an emphasis on projects that interested the broad middle class rather than the poor; a search for projects likely to stimulate additional development; and a strategy of creating conditions to attract private enterprise into ventures that served the city's purposes.

These redevelopment efforts built on several legacies of the urban renewal experience, literally as well as programmatically. First, many recent downtown projects filled in long-vacant parcels cleared through urban renewal; others made use of buildings that were rehabilitated with renewal funds. Both types of projects commonly benefited from outlays for site acquisition and preparation that were financed earlier at lower rates and by large federal subsidies. Second, city officials had inherited both tested procedures and experienced staff from the urban renewal program.

The earlier urban renewal strategy focused on removing two key obstacles blocking private redevelopment: the difficulty of assembling construction sites out of parcels held by many separate owners, and the high cost of urban land. The more recent strategy expanded the public role well beyond site assembly and land subsidy, to include risk sharing and help with financing some of the private components of the project.

The new approach gave high priority to establishing market acceptance of a project as early as possible and nailing down commitments from developers and investors before the city made major outlays of its own. By the mid-1970s, the federal government also shifted its stance. Federal regulations for the new urban development action grants (UDAGs) called for legally binding commitments from private participants in advance. Program rules gave local governments discretion over how to use federal funds to attract private investment, but the private dollars had to be "live," ready to commit; hence the term "action grant."

As in urban renewal, public sector money continued to be an important ingredient in recent downtown retail projects. Boston's Faneuil Hall Marketplace, for example, involved public outlays of $12 million and private development costs of $32 million. In others, government paid for half or more of total development costs, spending some $35 million for Milwaukee's Grand Avenue project and $52 million for Seattle's Pike Place Market. In a sample of 32 projects for which information was available, the public share ranged from as little as three percent to as much as 81 percent, with a median of 30 percent. In the early projects, such as Faneuil Hall and Pike Place, federal grants supplied most of the public funds, but in more recent ones local financing either complemented or substituted for federal sources.

City Roles

City governments have been heavily involved in numerous ways, innovative and often entrepreneurial, to bring major retail activity back downtown. Some limited their activities to traditional roles of planning, grantsmanship, site assembly with a write-down of land costs, and provision of supporting utility and street improvements, sometimes adding public financing of parking structures to the package. Others did more to increase the financial feasibility for private development by leasing the land and buildings, making loan commitments, and sharing operating as well as capital costs. Many helped work out regulatory problems, improved the administration of city functions, or created a special public development organization to assist the project. A few even became developers and owners of retail property.

The strategies and incentives used by individual cities reflected differences in a wide range of local circumstances: prevailing beliefs about the role of government in private development, traditions among business elites, community activism and attitudes toward growth, physical and economic constraints affecting redevelopment opportunities downtown, local resources for investment and public financing, and the commitment of political leadership to rebuilding downtown.

Political Protection

One way city officials helped these projects was by insulating them from political pressures. Local governments almost always face pressure to spread available funds throughout the community and not to concentrate them on a few large projects. In many cities, strong mayoral leadership and commitment were necessary to safeguard downtown retail projects against other claims on local and federal resources. Mayors Kevin White in Boston, Pete Wilson in San Diego, George Latimer in St. Paul, and Wes Uhlman in Seattle were all closely identified with the rebuilding of downtown areas and made use of their considerable political leverage to get projects built.

Regardless of the strength and commitment of the mayor, city officials who wanted to promote downtown development had to search for politically feasible ways to justify concentrating funds in a single project. One strategy was to make use of a defined project area as the only place eligible for the funds in question. Applying for federal UDAG assistance, for example, tied the city to spending the funds on a specified project and allowed no diversion to other places. Similarly, setting up a carefully drawn tax district as a redevelopment area limited the possible spread of project funds.

Even where there is solid public support for starting a major downtown project, the political climate may change while the project is in midstream. Developing a large retail center is a complex process subject to many unanticipated events that may jeopardize the initial deal. One way to buffer the project is to negotiate a detailed formal agreement that can serve as a long-term commitment. In California, a standardized disposition and development agreement outlines: specific provisions for disposition of the site; developer conditions for going ahead with the project; construction obligations of the redevelopment agency and developer; and a schedule for developer and public agency performance.

San Diego's experience with the Horton Plaza retail center illustrates the flow of events that can threaten a project. Development planning for Horton Plaza went through three mayoral elections, three economic recessions, nine design plans, four changes in anchor tenants, two lawsuits, enactment of the tax-cutting Proposition 13, and a change in ownership of the development company. Despite the problems created by unforeseen events, the disposition and development agreement—renegotiated several times—committed all the participants to actions and interrelated obligations that were difficult for political interest groups to upset.

In recent projects, public officials usually coped with the political objections while private developers stayed in the background. A clear example of this coping behavior took place in Pasadena. The Pasadena Redevelopment Authority planned to finance public parking garages for the Plaza Pasadena shopping mall through lease revenue bonds. In California, a bond issue of this type can be blocked by a referendum. Within three weeks after opponents collected enough signatures on petitions to get a referendum on the ballot, city officials repealed the ordinance authorizing the lease agreement between the city and the redevelopment authority, and the authority switched its financing to tax allocation bonds which were not subject to referendum.

Cities also assisted retail projects by limiting or restricting competition for a few years until the new shopping development was well established. In California, public revenue bond finance legislation required cities to avoid sponsoring competitive projects (Horler 1982, 31). Elsewhere, cities acted without a legal requirement in order to protect their own interest in a new shopping mall. In St. Paul, city officials used their influence with the metropolitan planning agency for the Minneapolis-St.Paul area to block a suburban shopping mall that threatened to compete with their Town Square project.

Financial Incentives

Cities commonly provided supporting facilities for new shopping malls: utility relocations and replacements, street improvements, connecting walkways above street level ("skywalks"), and parking facilities. Some built parks or other public open spaces to increase the attractiveness of a project. For Town Square in St. Paul, the concept of a public space evolved from urban landscape improvements in a covered "galleria" over an existing street to a more elaborate interior park on the top level of the mall structure. In the final form, the park and the walkways leading to it—which also served as paths between the storefronts in the mall—cost the city $8.5 million or nearly forty percent more than the original plan.

Cities used their skill to write persuasive proposals and their political contacts to get outside grants. They found federal aid in many places, particularly in the urban renewal, UDAG, urban mass transportation, economic development, and historic preservation programs. And they were creative in the ways they used it. In Philadelphia, for example, an urban mass transportation grant financed direct access between a renovated subway station and the first anchor department store, meeting one of the store's basic conditions for participating in the mall. City staff also brokered contributions from business interests, historic preservation groups, and private foundations. In St. Paul, downtown businesses contributed $400,000 or nearly a quarter of the city's direct costs for project planning and management; and in Milwaukee forty-six business firms formed a limited-profit redevelopment corporation that invested $16 million, which was more than one-fifth of the total development cost of the Grand Avenue project.

Another way some cities helped with project financing was by assuming a long-term share of project risks through lease agreements with the developer. Leasing the land, building, or garage structure offers the developer certain advantages over ownership. It lowers the required front-end investment, reduces the costs to be financed privately, and can increase the equity return after federal taxes. Leasing potentially offers the city two main advantages: the ability to control the site through continual ownership, and a share in future profits through rental income and appreciation of the property value. Leasing may also be the only way to develop the property when the city is actively searching for buyers but no firm bidders come around, or when the developer is unwilling to take on the risks of a complex development.

Philadelphia is a case in point. In 1973, when the city found a developer for The Gallery, the center was to be one of the first contemporary malls in an older, deteriorating downtown area. In this high-risk environment, the city's plan called for a complex mall design offering several points of access into adjacent department stores, public transit stations, and parking garages, plus provision for truck service and coordination of the construction with substantial street and transit improvements. Moreover, the decision-making process involved three public authorities, two anchor stores, two federal agencies, local lenders, and the developer. To secure the developer's commitment to operate the mall, the city agreed to an unconventional solution in which it would act as developer, general contractor, and owner of the mall shell. It would then lease the shell, with improvements to be completed by the developer, for 99 years at a fixed rental.

Cities have increasingly financed development by using their tax-exempt borrowing powers to issue tax increment or lease revenue bonds. Cities with statutory powers to form tax increment districts have had a distinct advantage. Tax increment financing allocates to the city or redevelopment agency all property taxes resulting from increased assessments generated within a project area, including tax increases that would otherwise go to county government and school districts. Targeting a revenue stream, whether pledged to service debt or as agency revenues to be used for further development activities, gives cities a way to finance development projects outside of annual budgetary appropriations, and makes it possible for a project to "pay for itself." Used extensively in California, even after Proposition 13 limited the property tax rate to one percent of assessed valuation, tax increment financing substituted public investment for private funds that would otherwise cover certain development costs.

When cities shared the risks of developing retail centers, sometimes they acted like investors and shared future profits as well. Profit sharing by cities took different forms—participation in a share of gross revenues, net cash flows, or rents collected from retail tenants—but it was distinct from arrangements in which project revenues were pledged to repay tax-exempt bonds, or loans from UDAG or community development block grant funds. As an investor in the project, a city earned a return in addition to what it would receive in its role as tax collector or public lender. In San Diego, for example, the redevelopment agency was to receive 31 percent of all parking revenue from a garage owned and financed by the developer, and ten percent of rents paid by Horton Plaza mall tenants in excess of their minimum base rents. In Philadelphia, the city receives ten percent of the Rouse Company's share of the annual net cash flow from Gallery II. City profit sharing in retail developments is very new, appearing mainly in projects completed in the 1980s. But as the cities have become increasingly entrepreneurial a growing number have found ways of getting their investments back through income as well as through tax collections.

Creating New Development Organizations
Cities also established new organizations to manage redevelopment activities. In Seattle, an unusual mandate to preserve a farmers' produce market led to the creation of two new agencies. A voter initiative set up the Historical Commission as a regulatory and policy-making body to oversee the preservation of the Pike Place market. This commission interpreted its mandate to include holding rents below market levels, giving preference in tenant selection to merchants who sold their own produce and to small untried businesses rather than national chain stores, and following design guidelines intended to maintain the colorful but somewhat battered character of a well-used public market. As the commission's director put it, "We want graffiti—we want vagrants." Acting on the reasonable assumption that no profit-seeking developer would be able to live with these restrictions, the city established a public Preservation and Development Authority to renovate the buildings and manage the market, subject to the policies and review procedures of the Historical Commission.

In San Diego, the city created a public, nonprofit corporation, the Centre City Development Corporation (CCDC), to plan, implement, and manage the redevelopment of 300 acres in the downtown core. Separate from city government and its redevelopment agency, CCDC has acted as a broker under contract in negotiations with property owners, businesses, and developers. For Horton Plaza, CCDC acquired the property, relocated tenants, cleared the land, and contracted for public improvements and facilities. In its role of streamlining the redevelopment process, CCDC arranged for public financing, conducted urban design reviews, and served as liaison between city government and interest groups in the community.

There is thus a tremendous contrast between the recent development policies of central cities and of suburbs. Suburban governments have increasingly required developers to build infrastructure improvements and to pay a series of fees and charges, and have entangled their projects in layers of reviews and permit requirements. A few cities—most notably San Francisco—have also followed this pattern, but many more have been sharing the costs and risks of downtown retail projects, protecting them from political pressures, and easing them through administrative and regulatory requirements instead of regulating growth in an adversary style.

The Public-Private Relationship
In addition to providing many forms of aid for the downtown projects, the cities have also changed their way of dealing with the developers. In the urban renewal program, cities following federal rules maintained an arm's length relationship with developers. City officials would define the project and carry out several years of operations to acquire the land, relocate the people and business firms from the area, and clear the site for redevelopment. They would invite proposals or organize a competition to select a developer. Then city staff would negotiate an agreement with the developer specifying what was to be built, how the responsibilities were to be divided between the city and the developer, how the costs were to be shared, and what the schedule was to be for performance and payments. The city would then transfer the property to the developer and monitor the results. If the developer was unable to carry out the project on schedule, the city could—and sometimes did—take back the land and offer it to another company. Once the parties reached an agreement, their relationship was essentially a contractual one.

From Contractual Relations to Shared Decisions
With the termination of the urban renewal program, cities were able to work out their own ways of managing redevelopment. Most continued to make use of urban renewal precedents, while changing those procedures that were unnecessarily troublesome or time consuming. Soon several cities that had downtown retail projects found new ways of working cooperatively with the developers. First, they broke down the former barrier between public planning and private implementation by involving developers in the early stages of project planning. These cities then negotiated agreements with the developers covering the same points as the earlier urban renewal agreements. But once an initial agreement was made, the relationship changed from what it had been under urban renewal. As new problems emerged, the developer and the city consulted on what to do, and from time to time they renegotiated their earlier agreement to fit changed circumstances. Both sides operated with an understanding that when major issues had to be resolved the decisions would be made jointly.

Large retail projects are vulnerable to changes in interest rates, consumer demand, construction costs, department store expansion plans, and many other factors that are likely to shift several times during the typical development period of five to eight years. When these changes threatened the viability of a project, the city and the developer usually found some solution by reconsidering the division of public and private responsibilities, the cost-sharing arrangement, or the schedule.

A year-long renegotiation was necessary in San Diego to rescue the Horton Plaza project from a crisis that emerged when plans were already well advanced. In 1980, a combination of rising interest rates and the tax-rate limitation mandated by California's Proposition 13 made it impossible for the city to keep its commitment to finance the parking garage through the sale of lease revenue bonds. The city and the developer eventually resolved the problem by making three significant changes in their earlier agreement. First, the developer agreed to take responsibility for financing and building the garage, thereby cutting the public share of project costs by 40 percent, or $22.3 million. In turn, the city reduced the sale price of the land, and the developer then agreed to give the city additional benefits from the project's future cash flow.

Joint Development
In some cities, the relationship went beyond a sharing of decisions to include joint public-private development. In these cases, the city developed key elements of the project, such as interior public spaces or the mall shell itself. For these elements, the city's role varied from responsibility for design and financing to actual ownership and ongoing management. In St. Paul's Town Square project, the city designed, owns, and manages a public park on the third floor and contributes to management costs for pedestrian ways throughout the entire retail area.

Academic analysts of implementation problems in the early 1970s pointed to complexity of decision making as the main reason for delays and failure, and urged simpler projects as the solution. Downtown retail projects did not get simpler, however. Some must be among the most complex ever done. Milwaukee's Grand Avenue, for example, consists of six historic buildings connected by a series of skywalks and shopping arcades and served by two new and two old parking garages. The maze of property interests and legal agreements is so intricate that a large insurance company spent more than two years working on the title insurance for the center. According to the underwriter in charge, "I have been involved in the business 35 years and I have never seen a title this involved and probably never will again" (*The Guarantor* 1982, 4).

These projects did not survive the problems of implementation because of their simplicity. They survived because:

1) cities and developers worked together to establish project feasibility in the early stages;

2) both parties were willing to consult and revise agreements when circumstances changed;

3) both became increasingly committed to having a project as they got in deeper and deeper; and

4) both showed great flexibility and ingenuity in coming up with solutions to unexpected problems.

One of the effects of this sustained interaction was that each side became more knowledgeable about the other and made decisions that reflected this new awareness. City negotiators had to learn about development economics and finance, and they tempered their regulatory policies in the light of what they learned. Developers, on the other hand, learned to operate in the fishbowl of local politics, and they adjusted their plans and their negotiating positions to cope with political realities.

Assessing the Results

The spread of downtown shopping malls is evidence that city governments are capable of generating major new development when economic circumstances provide even a limited and uncertain opening. If the cities had sat back to wait for development firms to recognize the investment opportunity and come forward with construction plans, they would still be waiting. Public action was required, but it had to be something more than the traditional approach. If city officials had organized typical urban renewal projects, they would now be trying to explain to angry voters why, after much trouble and expense, they had not yet found a developer for the rubble-filled site they were holding downtown.

The cities have found a better way than either relying on the invisible hand of the real estate market to revitalize downtown or planning an urban renewal project to do the job. What they have done is to restructure traditional relationships between the public and private sectors to make development more of a joint venture than ever before. The results are not all in, but the record so far is promising. The time needed to complete a project is shorter than it was under earlier arrangements. A few, such as Detroit's Renaissance Center and Atlanta's Omni Center, have failed economically, but most of the projects are attracting large numbers of people downtown and returning tax revenues to the cities.

Whether the downtown retail projects live up to all the cities' expectations for them will not be known for some time. Cities have promoted retail malls for several different reasons. Most often, local officials talk in terms of economic development when they describe the ripple effects they expect the retail centers to generate. Yet many also regard them as public amenities, much like an attractive park or zoo. Still others see them as necessary components of a campaign to create a new image for their city, as symbols of a healthy downtown and a well-managed community. To others, they are a way of restoring some of the traditions that make city life enjoyable and interesting: street activity both day and night, shopping, food markets, and open air celebrations. These traditional elements take on special importance as the cities are trying to replace their traditional functions of manufacturing and shipping with new functions of service and entertainment.

Regardless of the mix of purposes behind the construction of these projects, several cities can supply evidence of their economic ripple effects. Even before the new retail centers were completed in St. Paul and Pasadena, city officials made use of the project commitments to persuade other firms to develop office buildings nearby. In the case of Pasadena, both downtown office development and the commercial renovation of historic buildings accelerated greatly after the opening of Plaza Pasadena. In San Diego, housing and hotel developments have been linked directly to the plans for the Horton Plaza retail center. Even in Seattle, where Pike Place Market was renovated not for economic development reasons but because the voters wanted to save a popular farmers' market, the success of this project has attracted a ring of apartment, office, and commercial complexes around it, representing new investment on the order of $230 million. Further, the shopping malls themselves typically generate one thousand or more permanent retail and service jobs.

Yet the retail projects are too new for their effects to be demonstrated convincingly—particularly those effects that result from their value as symbols of investor confidence and community well-being. While there is evidence of ripple effects in a number of cities, it is hard to judge how many of the ripples were created by the retail centers and how many by other downtown projects built at about the same time. As for the direct employment in the retail stores, there is a question of how many of the jobs are net additions to the local economy and how many are substitutes for other retail jobs that are being lost.

In short, the early evidence suggests that downtown retail centers are helpful for economic development; but it is not yet clear how helpful they are, or how the benefits compare with the substantial public costs. At the same time, it is clear that they do not have the negative impacts of many earlier urban renewal projects. City governments have learned to avoid projects that threaten residential neighborhoods, and most of the current ones are either in downtown business districts, in port and warehouse areas, in areas specializing in pornography and "adult entertainment," or in similarly marginal locations. As a result, these developments have been built without significant damage to low-income neighborhoods or the supply of housing.

The Development Process

While the effects of the downtown retail centers will emerge only slowly, the unusual development process that gave rise to them can be assessed on the basis of experience so far. Many of the strengths of this process have already been suggested, and more will be noted later in this paper. But there are also problems to report.

For the city, learning to work with private developers in close, ongoing relationships is not trouble-free. The work of hammering out a complex development agreement that can run as long as 150 pages takes place behind closed doors. Since the city is sharing cost and risks, the final terms of the agreement become public information. But the details that are needed to understand the issues seldom come to light, and even with the best will in the world it is hard to imagine a way of keeping the public informed of the choices that must be made. Usually the issues are too complicated to lend themselves to a vote or a referendum; but once the agreement has been negotiated, elected officials are in the position of either rubber-stamping it or looking like enemies of progress.

City officials could become vulnerable to accusations that the public-private relationship is little more than a giveaway of public funds. The substantial transfers of city money that characterize these projects serve mainly to narrow the gap between development costs downtown and those in comparable suburban malls. Yet there are legitimate grounds for concern about giveaways. The risks of downtown projects are great enough to make developers ask for plenty of financial help, and city officials unfamiliar with development may indeed agree to give excessive aid for projects they are anxious to have.

So far the cities have gone only part way toward creating staffs that are capable of analyzing the economics and finances of large private developments. The most typical safeguard has been city use of expert consultants who know enough about real estate to probe the claims of developers critically and to come up with their own estimates of what is needed. In the long run, a more reliable safeguard would be to have specialized city staff capable of keeping an eye on the proceedings and advising elected officials on the major issues that arise.

The problems of these joint relationships are not all one-sided. Developers are also put in roles that are new, involve additional risks, and require practical accommodation to the political situation. On major decisions, they have a public partner who has to be consulted, which means that they are not free to decide and act alone. They have to share information that they used to consider confidential. They may get locked into a public sector schedule and lose the freedom to time their moves, including even the ability to arrange their long-term financing whenever they consider interest rates most favorable.

From the point of view of public agencies involved in regulating city development, the new relationships with the private sector are potentially troublesome in other ways. They break with the long-established tradition that calls for uniform rules and procedures for everyone who does business with a city. The new style is one of negotiating special arrangements to suit each project and each developer. Administrators have more discretion than before, but they are losing the protection of established rules. Because the city is increasingly both a financial partner and a regulator of development projects, administrators may come under great political pressure to compromise their regulatory standards for the sake of financial returns to the city. Or, when they agree to special arrangements for a project, they may become vulnerable to charges of favoritism. In short, the new relationships are likely to politicize decisions that used to be easier to handle in an equitable way.

The first response of many administrators, however, has been to welcome the opportunity to operate in a more free-wheeling style. Those administrators who negotiate development projects appear to attract many professional rewards, including recognition, high prestige, and high salary. Even the bureaucracies value entrepreneurial skills. Meanwhile, some of the nation's leading professional associations for city officials, including the International City Management Association, have been praising the new entrepreneurship in city government and helping to spread knowledge of how the entrepreneurs go about their work (Moore 1983).

Balancing Public and Private Control

The new public-private relationships do not remove conflicts between cities and developers, but they do provide reasonable ways to resolve them—ways that often improve the quality of the development projects. Cities and developers share common interests in getting projects done, but at times each bargains hard for advantages at the expense of the other. Yet cities need the developers to put together the projects and make them work; and developers need the cities because of their legal authority and their many forms of assistance. City governments face a special problem in maintaining enough control to satisfy important public purposes while leaving the developer enough control to make the project a commercial success.

An ongoing relationship tends to prevent arbitrary action by either side. When the cities managed urban renewal projects in a more contractual style, the requirements they set were often arbitrary because they kept a great distance from the developers and understood very little of their perspective. City staffs then were strong on design, physical planning, and administration, but they were weak on real estate analysis. In the newer relationship, the cities are less likely to act in ignorance or to try imposing unrealistic regulations. At the same time, developers have learned to come up with proposals that meet both their economic needs and the city's political needs. In this setting, conflicts are usually resolved through negotiation rather than through threats or one-sided decisions.

By having a seat at the bargaining table, cities are able to advocate their own interests in a project, and these interests often challenge developers to depart from conventional solutions. In Pasadena, the city insisted on several design features that complicated life for the developer but in the end made striking improvements in the Plaza Pasadena shopping mall. The Pasadena Redevelopment Authority made a special point of requiring some stores to face the street, in contrast to the usual suburban layout where all stores face an interior mall and the street frontage consists of blank walls and parking lots. The authority also insisted on having a public passageway through the mall structure to link the public library and city hall on one side with the civic auditorium on the other. Both requirements were troublesome. The public space requirement put the development company in conflict with one of its department store tenants over the location of an entrance to underground parking, and required special security arrangements for hours when the passageway was open after the mall shops were closed.

Yet the street-front stores enhanced the exterior appearance of the building, and the requirement for a public space passing through the mall led to a widely acclaimed design solution in which a series of monumental arches and huge glass panels enclosed the passageway, and panoramic murals decorated the arches. Taken together, these special city requirements made Plaza Pasadena into a structure that differed from suburban shopping centers in ways that helped integrate it successfully with its surrounding downtown. As in other cases, the city was able to shape the project according to its conception of public needs without forcing the developer into an untenable position.

Will the Public-Private Strategy Spead?

A question that remains is whether the new public-private relationship was simply a temporary expedient brought on by the special circumstances of the 1970s, or part of a learning process likely to continue in the future. With the threat of municipal defaults and bankruptcy in the air during the early 1970s, the cities were understandably willing to experiment with new ways of managing development despite the political and financial risks involved. Many cities still have serious fiscal problems, but with the mood of desperation gone, city administrators may want to return to more traditional ways of handling development.

Our interviews indicate that city officials (as well as developers) who have made use of the new public-private management style see many advantages to it, and they are unlikely to give it up without compelling reasons—such as the emergence of scandals from these relationships. City staff members who have had personal experience with public-private developments are still a very small minority of their profession, and the details of the process are still not well known. Yet there is widespread interest in the entrepreneurial style of public administration, and by now similar methods have been applied to a number of other developments besides the downtown retail centers.

One type of project that combines public and private elements is the mixed-income housing development in which public funds are used to provide some apartments at below-market rents. Local examples have been numerous, and federal housing legislation in 1984 includes a new program for mixed-income housing linking city governments with developers (Kurtz 1983).

A joint development strategy has also been proposed for public parks that contain commercial facilities. Recently announced plans for Bryant Park in New York, for example, involve a public-private combination in which the private sector will provide a restaurant, food kiosks, and security force (Carmody 1983).

In Pittsburgh, a development group including the U.S. Steel Corporation, the city, and two public authorities, is building an office tower and shopping center combined with the main downtown subway terminal. In Toledo, the city has worked with two large corporations to build an office complex together with a new riverfront park, parking garage, boulevard and downtown street improvements (US HUD 1982, 63). And in Los Angeles, Washington, D.C., and several other cities, transportation agencies have made extensive use of joint development methods to promote the construction of private buildings on public land next to transit stations (Padron 1984).

There are also development situations where the public-private combination is either unnecessary or inappropriate. Many types of development—such as downtown office buildings—can be done privately with no special need for public assistance. Using public resources to share costs or risks for development of this kind would be wasteful. At the other extreme are projects that are unlikely to offer attractive profit opportunities without a level of public assistance that would be politically unacceptable. This category would include many facilities serving primarily low-income populations.

But between these extremes are many situations where a mix of public and private elements is appropriate to serve a public purpose. The notion of public-private partnerships has become very fashionable, so much so that the partnership image has taken on a suspiciously promotional ring. Because the idea is politically attractive, and because the shortage of public funds makes it practical to bring in private resources, city officials are likely to keep searching for ways to apply it.

The public-private process for downtown retail projects has four key elements that are broadly applicable to other settings:

1) assembling a mix of local and private resources to
complement available federal funds;

2) establishing political and economic feasibility during early stages of project planning;

3) utilizing ongoing negotiations rather than arm's length regulation of the private sector, with a continuing role for the city in decisions throughout the development process; and

4) trading public sector sharing of front-end risks for participation in future benefits.

Downtown retailing has been a good proving ground for these strategies, but many cities are likely to turn their attention next to other types of projects in other parts of the community. When they want to develop job centers outside downtown, their recent strategies for dealing with the private sector should provide useful precedents. When they want to rebuild residential neighborhoods, some of the same methods may prove applicable to small commercial centers, recreational facilities, and housing renovation. Conceivably the same negotiation style that worked well with commercial firms will work with neighborhood organizations that want a role in local development. If public-private developments continue to spread as they have in the past few years, and if the cities can make their new managerial methods work for a broader development agenda, then the process that built the downtown shopping malls could turn out to be even more important than the mall themselves.

Footnotes
1. We are indebted to a number of organizations whose support made this research possible: the Office of Policy Development and Research of the U.S. Department of Housing and Urban Development, the M.I.T. Center for Real Estate Development, and the M.I.T.-Harvard Joint Center for Urban Studies. We have made use of a group of case studies of retail development prepared with the support of the Ernest W. and Jean E. Hahn Foundation and the M.I.T. Department of Urban Studies and Planning.

We are also indebted to many colleagues for advice and critical comments, especially Robert Einsweiler, Robert Fogelson, Marshall Kaplan, Martin Levin, Gary Marx, Francine Rabinowitz, Deborah Stone, and Raymond Vernon.

2. The six projects studied in detail through interviews and reviews of city and developer files are: Faneuil Hall Marketplace, Boston; Plaza Pasadena, Pasadena; Town Square, St. Paul; Horton Plaza, San Diego; University Town Centre, San Diego; and Pike Place Market, Seattle. Our research assistants who prepared the case studies were Christi Baxter (Town Square and University Town Centre), Nancy Fox (Pike Place Market), and Jacques Gordon (Faneuil Hall Marketplace and Horton Plaza).

References
Abrams, C. 1965. *The city is the frontier*. New York: Harper and Row.
Allman, T.D. 1978. The urban crisis leaves town. *Harper's* 257(December): 41-56.
Barabba, V. 1980. The demographic future of the cities of America. In *Cities and Firms*, edited by H.J. Bryce, 3-45. Lexington, Mass.: Lexington Books.
Bardach, E. 1977. *The implementation game*. Cambridge, Mass.: M.I.T. Press.
Black, J.T. 1980. "The changing economic role of central cities and suburbs." In *The prospective city*, edited by A.P. Solomon, 80-123. Cambridge, Mass.: M.I.T. Press.
Bluestone, B., P. Hanna, S. Kuhn, and L. Moore. 1981. *The retail revolution*. Boston: Auburn House.
Bosselman, F.P., and D. Callies. 1972. *The quiet revolution in land use control*. Prepared for the Council on Environmental Quality. Washington, D.C.: Government Printing Office.
Carmody, D. 1983. Vast rebuilding of Bryant Park planned. *New York Times* December 1: A1.
Clay, P. 1979. *Neighborhood renewal*. Lexington, Mass.: D.C. Heath Lexington Books.
Derthick, M. 1972. *New towns in-town*. Washington, D.C.: The Urban Institute.
Fleetwood, B. 1979. The new elite and an urban renaissance. *New York Times Magazine* January 14: 16-33.
Frieden, B.F. 1979. *The environmental protection hustle*. Cambridge, Mass.: M.I.T. Press.

Frieden, B.J. 1980. Allocating the public service costs of new housing. *Urban Land* 39 (January): 12-16.

Frieden, B.J., and M. Kaplan. 1977. *The politics of neglect.* Cambridge, Mass.: M.I.T. Press.

Gensheimer, C.F. 1982. Rehabilitation tax credits: a real estate tax shelter of the 1980s. *Journal of Real Estate Taxation* 9 (Summer): 299-318.

Horler, V.L. 1982. *Guide to public debt financing in California.* San Francisco: Rauscher Pierce Refsnes, Inc.

James, F.J. 1980. "The revitalization of older urban housing and neighborhoods." In *The prospective city*, edited by A.P. Solomon, 130-60. Cambridge, Mass.: M.I.T. Press.

Kaplan, H. 1966. "Urban renewal in Newark." In *Urban renewal: The record and the controversy*, edited by J. Wilson, 233-58. Cambridge, Mass.: M.I.T. Press.

Kurtz, H. 1983. New grants designed to push for housing for the poor. *Boston Globe* December 11: A4.

Moore, B.H., ed. 1983. *The entrepreneur in local government.* Washington, D.C.: International City Management Association.

Newsweek. 1979. A city revival? 93 (January 15): 28-35.

Padron, M. 1984. Build here: transit's rallying cry. *Planning* 50 (June): 6-10.

Peterson, G.E. 1980. "Federal tax policy and the shaping of urban development". In *The prospective city*, edited by A.P. Solomon, 399-425. Cambridge, Mass.: M.I.T. Press.

Pressman. J., and A.B. Wildavsky. 1973. *Implementation.* Berkeley and Los Angeles: University of California Press.

Sternlieb, G., and J.W. Hughes. 1981. *Shopping centers U.S.A.* New Brunswick, N.J.: Rutgers Center for Urban Policy Research.

The Guarantor. 1982. Milwaukee's Grand Avenue. November-December: 2-5.

Urban Land Institute. 1983. *Revitalizing downtown retailing: Trends and opportunities.* Washington, D.C.: U.S. Department of Housing and Urban Development, Office of Community Planning and Development.

U.S. Advisory Commission on Intergovernmental Relations. 1983. *Significant features of fiscal federalism: 1981-82 edition.* Washington, D.C.: Government Printing Office.

U.S. Department of Housing and Urban Development. 1980a. *The president's urban policy report.* Washington, D.C.: Government Printing Office.

U.S. Department of Housing and Urban Development. 1980b. *Urban Development Action Grant Program: Second Annual Report.* Washington, D.C.: Department of Housing and Urban Development.

U.S. Department of Housing and Urban Development. 1982. *The President's national urban policy report: 1982.* Washington, D.C.: Department of Housing and Urban Development.

U.S. President, National Commission on Urban Problems. 1968. *Report: Building the American city.* Washington, D.C. Government Printing Office.

Wall Street Journal. 1983. Downtown shopping areas again drawing customers. May 2.

CHAPTER 10

Sharing Power Among Organizations: Coordination Models to Link Theory and Practice

Ernest Alexander

Introduction: Interorganizational Coordination

Complex social problems demand "interdependent delivery systems" to achieve social goals or policies which are "too big for one organization to handle" (Hage 1975:211; Van de Ven, Emmet and Koenig 1975:26-27). A vast set of activities falls within this definition: it includes general policy areas such as economic stabilization or a new "industrial policy"; policies and programs addressed to the needs of specific clients or groups such as the elderly or handicapped; comprehensive spatially defined policies, programs and projects, such as regional development or "enterprise zones"; and functional sectors like intermodal transportation, water pollution abatement, and health delivery systems.

For any organization, these or similar activities imply a degree of interdependence with the other members of the "implementation set," "action set," or "interorganizational field" (Hjern and Porter 1981; Aldrich and Whetten 1981) that requires it to share power, and to concert its decisions and activities with other organizations. Such a process may be called interorganizational coordination (IOC) (Rogers and Whetten 1982).

Mulford and Rogers have analyzed the different meanings proposed for IOC over the years, and conclude that coordination can be viewed as a structure of specified relationships among the organizational participants, or as a process of joint decision making among them (1982:16-17). The aspect of deliberate intervention to change prior organizational interactions is inferred when IOC is defined as:

> ...a means of directing the operation of units so that their joint behavior attains a specific goal with higher probability and at lower costs (and with) a common expectation of reward (Kochen and Deutsch 1980:126).

In fact, "coordination means getting what you do not have," by influencing or compelling participating organizations to act in a desired manner (Dunshire 1978:16-17).

Preceding study of IOC provides a good deal of information on how organizations undertake IOC, but though some of the consequences of different approaches to IOC have been identified (Rogers and Mulford 1982), much of this research is taxonomical. Some hypotheses have been advanced and tested, such as the need for compatibility and consensus for successful IOC (Braito et al. 1972; Hall et al. 1977; Gillespie and Mileti 1979), but on the whole theory and research offer little to answer the question that is raised in practice: how can we coordinate organizations more effectively?[1]

Despite the familiarity and importance of the notion (of coordination) in policymaking and administration, we lack a clear formulation of the range of possible formats... the development of criteria of evaluation in choosing one format over another, and an identification of the factors which condition the objectives, procedure, and results of policy coordination in different settings (Brickman 1979:73).

This "range of possible formats" is explored below; here they will be called coordination models.

Coordination Models

The coordination model is needed to link theory with practice, if we are to develop "a theory of confederative organization" (Clark 1965:233). This question has also been addressed in the context of single organizations; Mintzberg (1973:161-168) called such organizational responses to the problem of coordination "liaison devices." An early study of IOC in human services used the term "mechanisms of coordination" (Litwak and Meyer 1966:39-42).

Table 1 shows how coordination models provide the missing link between the linkages—at the lowest level of abstraction and at the micro-scale of activity—and the strategies—at the highest level of abstraction—which have been the subjects of previous research. Coordination models, operating, as they do, between organizations, occupy the intermediate range of this continuum.

Linkages are the smallest unit of coordination related activity, and its most concrete manifestation. They include informal linkages such as telephone contacts, including another organization in a distribution list for mailings, informal adhoc meetings, etc. More formal linkages include joint membership of boards, review and signoff by one organization of another's budget proposals, contracts and agreements between organizations setting the terms for mutually beneficial activities, and regulations or legislation mandating one agency to control another's behavior. These micro-units of coordination activity are the basic components of the other higher level models.

At the next, or meso-level of activity, informal linkages, for example, are composed of some of the micro-elements suggested above, while formal models, such as the coordinating unit, may work through some of the formal micro-linkages, such as joint budgeting, contracts, or regulatory mandates. These meso models may themselves be components of larger, macro-level coordination models which characterize the interactions of an entire action set of organizations or an implementation network. A non-administered program such as the U.S. New Communities program was actually implemented through a coordinating unit created within HUD to run the program, while HUD, this time as a lead agency, attempted to coordinate other federal bureaus involved in the model cities program through several interorganizational groups, and administered the program at the local level through a specially formed coordinating unit.

TABLE 10-1: COORDINATION MODELS

(MICRO: Linkages)	MESO-MODELS	MACRO-MODELS	(META: Strategies/Fields)
Informal Linkages	A. Informal Linkages	("Action-Set" "Implementation Network")	Mutual Adjustment/"Feudal" Network Laterally Linked Fields
Formal Linkages:	B. Interorganizational Group	E. Non-Administered Program	Alliance/Federation Coordinated Network "Mediated" Fields
—joint membership —joint planning	C. Coordinator	F. Lead Organization	Corporate Hierarchy "Guided" Fields
—plan review approval —joint budgeting —budget review/ signoff —colocation —contract/agreement —mandated: regulation/statute	D. Coordinating Unit	G. Single Organization	

Finally, at the highest level of abstraction are the meta-strategies identified by researchers to characterize the coordination related behavior or structure of interorganizational fields or systems. Such strategies include the laterally linked field made up of a "feudal" network only employing informal linkages to produce coordination by mutual adjustment, and more formal structures ranging from coordinated networks (such as interorganizational alliances or federations, e.g. a Chamber of Commerce, or a hospital consortium) in "mediated" fields to "empires" or "corporate hierarchies" in "guided" fields. These, again, deploy macromodels to coordinate their participating units: the holding company which forms a single organization to encompass its affiliates, the hospital consortium which is coordinated by the major teaching hospital as a lead organization, or the federation of businesses which establishes a coordinating unit to run its activities, and coordinate those aspects of its members' behavior which are of mutual interest.

A good deal of discussion has been devoted elsewhere[2] to linkages and strategies, so there is no need to elaborate on them any more here. Below, the coordination models proposed at the meso- and macro-scales are presented in more detail.

Informal Linkages
Concerted decision making, including partisan mutual adjustment, may be effected through informal interorganizational linkages alone. They also frequently (perhaps even always) supplement other formal coordination models, in the expression of the ubiquitous intermeshing of formal and informal organizational networks (Katz and Kahn, 1966:80-81), and are one of the most widespread forms of interaction.[3]
    Informal interorganizational linkages cover a range of interactions, from contacts through telephone calls, meetings or correspondence, to adhoc issue-related meetings between representatives of affected organizations. Such meetings, if routinized over a period of time, may span the gap between this model and the next: an interagency working group.
    As a supplement to other forms of coordination, informal linkages may be found in any type of interorganizational system. But as the sole channel for concerting decisions in an interorganizational network, informal linkages are clearly limited to the lowest level of coordination. A higher degree of objective interdependence and sharper awareness of mutual interest and concerns will elicit more formalized coordinative models.

Interorganizational Group
The lowest level of coordination in any institutionalized form is the interorganizational group. Such a group may have different names: interagency task force, working group, coordinating committee, steering committee, standing committee, etc. Interorganizational groups may come into existence through the routinization over time of adhoc meetings or working groups, and in response to the need to address ongoing problems arising out of perceived or actual interdependencies. They can and do undertake the whole gamut of coordination tasks, from the lowest to the highest levels.
    The Interministerial Committee on Social Policy in Israel is an example of such an interorganizational group while another is Britain's PESC (Public Expenditure Survey Committee) (Heclo and Wildavsky 1974). Brinkman (1979) also offers examples of interorganizational groups for R & D policy coordination. Interorganizational groups at intermediate levels of organization and government are legion, ranging from area health services committees and regional planning commissions, while at the lowest level they are equally frequent—from the interagency steering committee entrusted with monitoring a particular research project to the community organizations' task force set up to establish a joint program rehabilitation service and ensure its funding.
    In its "pure" form, the interorganizational group consists of people who are totally identified with their organizational affiliations, and has only an uncertain prospect of continuing in existence over a longer period of time. It has no identifiable "place" or budget, and has no staff of its own. Any services it needs are provided by the member organizations of the system. Few interorganizational groups are so

"pure"; most occupy intermediate points on the continuum of autonomy (Lehman 1975:83-95), where the higher part of the spectrum is occupied by coordinating units (see below).

The limitations of the interorganizational group as a coordinating model are aptly stated by Derthick (1974:197-202), based on her analysis of interagency Federal Regional Councils. Such bodies are reluctant to invoke the authority which calls them into existence, but nothing less would enable them to fulfil their tasks: mediating disputes between powerful line agencies, facilitating relations with central government and achieving operational coordination.

Coordinator
An individual can be appointed whose only (or major) function is to coordinate the activities of an interorganizational system with respect to a given area, issue, problem, or program.[4] This model is often used in combination with other forms of coordina- tion. An example is the federal member of interstate regional commissions in the U.S. who was given the special task of coordinating between the region and the federal bureaucracy. Given the federal agencies' resistance to any invasion of their domains, and the commissioner's lack of authority, his failure was a foregone conclusion (Derthick 1974:65-72, 195-197).

The independent coordinator as the sole instrument for concerting inter-organizational decision making, unattached to any coordinating unit, and unsupported by any other coordination model, is rare, I suspect. One case is Israel's development of its Galilee region, where public agency actions are supposed to be coordinated by an official appointed by the Minister of Commerce, Industry and Tourism whose title is: Coordinator of Government Activities in the Galilee.[5]

Coordinating Unit
The coordinating unit is formed for the sole (or major) purpose of coordinating decisions and their implementation in the relevant interorganizational system. The coordinating unit is distinguished from the interorganizational group by its greater autonomy: it will generally have its own organizational identity, enjoy "ecological autonomy" in the form of a distinct location and its own offices, will have a budget for its operations, and will be staffed with its own personnel. However, in contrast to the "single organization" model (described below) the coordinating unit does not directly have any "line" functions, or implement any of the tasks it is charged with coordinating.

The restriction of this unit's functions to coordination does not necessarily mean that it is powerless. An example of a coordinating unit which has often been, and still is, very powerful in its relevant environment—the U.S. federal bureaucracy—is the U.S. Office of Management and Budget (OMB). At the opposite end of the power spectrum, perhaps, are the numerous planning agencies, national, state, regional and local, which have the ostensible task of coordinating public development, regulatory, and investment decisions and their implementation, but which in fact have hardly any impact.[6]

Coordinating units exist in many interorganizational systems, but they are not always labelled as coordinating units. For example, a prevalent form of coordinating unit in the private sector, for concerting the activities of all the organizations involved in the execution of a construction or manufacturing project, is the principal contractor.[7]

In the public sector, coordination is often (perhaps usually) effected through fiscal policy and planning; accordingly coordinating units are to be found in these areas. In the U.S., an example would be the OMB; similar coordinating units are to be found in most countries, and at every level of government. Planning-type coordinating units may be found as "staff" agencies attached to a government's or organization's chief executive, or as local government planning commissions, regional and areawide planning agencies, in fields as diverse as transportation, land use, environment pollution, welfare and health services.

We should be careful to distinguish between a coordinating unit's autonomy and its power. For example, the coordinating unit will always be more autonomous than the interorganizational group, but there are some of the latter that are more powerful than many coordinating units. Britain's PESC is probably nearly as powerful in its system (though it is "only" an interorganizational group) as the American OMB is in its environment, though the latter is a fully autonomous coordinating unit. And it is certainly much more powerful than other autonomous planning agencies are in their interorganizational systems, for example, Australia's National Urban and Regional Development Agency, or the Israel Interior Ministry's Planning Bureau.[8]

Non-Administered Programs

The simplest macro-scale coordination model, on the face of it, is the non-administered program. In this model, the decisions of the units making up the relevant interorganizational system are concerted by invoking an appropriate set of stimuli— which can be incentives, sanctions, or both (Levine 1972).

Non-administered programs involve some adjustment of the pre-existing system of market incentives and, even at a minimum, require some apparatus for their monitoring and supervision. The self-administered part of the U.S. income tax system, a classic non-administered program, is actually managed by a substantial bureaucracy. In the U.S., the non-administered program has been the darling of economists and political scientists. In fact, it is the model for federal intervention in many fields. Most categorical grant programs, for example, were designed on the assumption that the prospect of funding for a particular activity or purpose would bias decisions by firms, organizations, or local governments in a desired direction.

However, experience has shown that the "pure" case of the non-administered program is rarely found, and that it has to be supplemented by other administrative apparatus, including, often, other coordinative models, to ensure that its conception is matched by its execution (Williams 1975:541-542). Responses to preferred resources, for example, have to be formalized as proposals, which require administrative review. Program implementation has to be ensured by drafting and administering a complex set of regulations, which can be quite a coordination problem in itself (Rabinowitz, Pressman and Rein 1976).

The success of this model demands the adequate deployment of power by the organization which sets up the system of non-administered concerted decision making. In other words, the organization implementing such a program must have, and be prepared to use, either its authority in the form of the effective threat of sanctions in case of non-compliance (as is the case, in fact, in the U.S. income tax system), or appropriate resources which will provide an incentive for organizations to adjust their decisions in the desired direction, or both.[9]

Lead Organization

Another macro-scale coordination model is the lead organization. This term is taken from the American expression "lead agency," which has been used for this type of coordination in the public sector. It refers to the arrangement where one organization in an interorganizational system is charged with, or assumes, the responsibility for coordinating the activities of all the relevant organizations in the network.

The lead organization's special status vis a vis the other organizations in the field may be the result of the issue or problem being more in its domain than in the others', or of its superior power, or both. Beside its coordination tasks, the lead organization also has functional responsibilities—otherwise it would be a coordinating unit. However, a significant proportion of the implementation activity is the responsibility of other organizations in the network. If this were not the case, and most of the relevant functions were performed by the coordinating organization itself, we would be confronted with a different model, the "single organization" described next.

In the private sector this coordination model is widespread. For example, it is a variant of the coordinating unit model in the construction industry or in product development and production, which was illustrated above. In the building industry, for example, a major construction firm will be the prime contractor, with functional responsibility for casting the building's foundations and erecting its frame. The same firm, however, will also be responsible for coordinating the activities of numerous subcontractors. In similar fashion, Litton Industries coordinates the production of the U.S. navy's destroyers in its shipyards, and aerospace contractors such as Lockheed or McDonnell-Douglas organize the performance of their airplane production contracts.

Complex public programs are also frequently coordinated in this fashion, when substantial program inputs are needed from organizations other than the lead agency. One example is the development of the Lakhish region in Israel, where the Settlement

Department of the Jewish Agency was named the lead agency because rural development, which was seen as the basic issue in this project, was its responsibility. Another is the Model Cities program in the U.S., for which the legislation gave HUD lead agency responsibilities in coordinating the inputs of other federal agencies, since HUD's own budget was to be the major source of funding for the program. We shall see how these organizations acquitted themselves of their coordination responsibilities in each of these cases.

The lead organization is a macro-model: it describes an overall framework of institutional relations between major participating organizations in the interorganizational system, rather than the detailed mechanics of organizational design through which concerted decision making is assured. As a result, we will find the lead agency model used in combination with other models at the meso-level.

In both private and public sectors, the lead organization enjoys its status as a result of contractual or mandated relationships.[10] These relationships are the product of high social awareness of interdependence (as expressed in legislation or regulations) or high mutual awareness of the benefits from participation in the relevant interorganizational system. Typically, the lead organization enjoys its status in relation to a particular issue, problem, program or project. If its position in the interorganizational system acquired broader connotations, and a degree of stability approaching permanence, the system would be an empire.[11]

Single Organization

The distinction between the lead organization model and the single organization may be a fine one, and depends on the degree to which the functional range of relevant activities has been internalized. The difference between the lead agency, like the local government housing authority, for example, and the single organization entrusted with the coordinated execution of a complex project or program, such as the British New Town Corporation, is a difference of this kind of degree.

It may seem anomalous to identify a single organization as an IOC model, but this is only if we forget the dynamic nature of the system we are looking at. Derthick recognizes this when she includes the creation of a new federal organization under her range of possible regional coordination models, which also includes the single coordinator and the interorganizational group (1974:195-206).

The arena of new communities' development in the U.S. provides a perfect illustration of this apparent paradox. It is an arena which combines national policy and legislation, resource allocation and implementation. Actors are the federal administration and its agencies; Congress with its legislative, budgeting, and review powers; state and local governments; landowners; developers; potential residents; and occupants of industrial and commercial space. This is an interorganizational system if ever there was one.

The New Communities program (described in more detail below) was a non-administered program. The offer of resources (hedged in, admittedly, by a thicket of regulations) was to be an incentive to mobilize relevant actors (private developers and lending institutions) to take the desired decisions which would stimulate the construction of planned new communities.

But thirty years earlier, a different administration—Roosevelt's "New Deal"— addressed the same problem, and the same interorganizational system, in a very different way. A new federal agency was created, as a subunit of the Resettlement Administration, to plan and build new towns to provide housing for rural migrants and employment for idle urban construction trades. This was the "Greenbelt Towns" program, conceived under the influence of the British garden cities movement and contemporary American planning ideologists, and until World War II brought the "New Deal" to a halt, it succeeded in planning and implementing three model new communities (Arnold, 1970). In fact, the coordination model adopted here was a pure form of the single organization.

Today, the same arena presents several examples of the single organization model of interorganizational coordination. These include Britain's New Towns Corporations and Stockholm's city administration in the development of its satellite suburbs (which are presented in more detail below), France's Etablissement Public d'Amenagement, and Malaysia's Federal Land Development Authority (Rubenstein 1978:88-89; Turner 1978:269-270). Another coordination arena where single organization models are popular is regional development. A trend-setting example is the U.S.A.'s Tennessee Valley Authority, established in the 1930's and still going strong (Derthick 1974:18-45). In the private sector single organizations may be formed as well, by merger or as corporate systems (Pfeffer 1972; Evan and Klemm 1980).

Comparative Case Analysis

These coordination models were designed to serve as a practical analytic tool. Below, their application is shown in a comparative analysis of fourteen cases of regional and urban development and neighborhood revitalization (see Table 2). A brief synopsis of each case follows.[12]

U.S.A.: The Appalachian Regional Commission (ARC)

The Appalachian Regional Commission was formed in 1965 with the passing, under the Johnson Administration, of the Appalachian Regional Development Act. This had been preceded by the Conference of Appalachian Governors in 1960, and PARC—the President's Appalachian Regional Commission—in 1963. ARC's charge was to promote the region's economic development and "serve as a focal point and coordinating unit for Appalachian programs."

Designed as an interorganizational group incorporating representatives from the states, and a federal representative as co-chairman, the ARC began with little authority and no resources. Thanks to a strong constituency and congressional base it lobbied successfully for additional appropriations for the region and gained control, in 1967, over earmarked Appalachian expenditures. During the same period it also transformed itself and effectively functioned as a coordinating unit with its own budget and staff.

A successful allocation process was developed which turned ARC into the major arena for coordinating multi-state planning and implementation, though ARC was less effective in coordinating other federal agencies such as OEO and EDA. It has been cost-effective in generating resources for the region, and ARC's performance has made it a model for regional development agencies.

TABLE 10-2: INTERORGANIZATIONAL COORDINATION CASES

ISSUE AREA	Regional Development	Urban Development –New Towns	Neighborhood Development and Revitalization
COUNTRY			
Great Britain	Regional Economic Planning Boards/Councils (REPB)	New Towns) (NTs)	General Improvement Area Program (GIA)
Israel	Lakhish Regional Development (LAKH) Coordinator of Government Activities in the Galilee (GAL)	Development Towns (DTs)	Authority for Clearance and Rebuilding of Rehabilitation Areas (AUT) "Project Renewal" (PR)
U.S.A	Appalachian Regional Commission (ARC)	New Communities Program (NCP)	Model Cities Program (MCP)
Others	Guyana Regional Development—Venezuela (CVG)	Vallingy & Farsta Satellite Towns– (VFS)	Standortsprotramme— Germany (STOP)

New Community Development in the U.S.A.

In 1968 the U.S. Congress passed Title IV of the Housing and Urban Development Act, which initiated the New Communities Development program. This consolidated prior elements assisting new community developers (insured mortgage loans for large-scale subdivisions) and added federal loan guarantees for approved projects and a variety of supplementary grants to developers. In 1970 the program was expanded from private developers to public agencies. The aim of the program was to provide alternatives to prevailing metropolitan sprawl, and to encourage the revitalization of depressed rural and inner-city areas.

After the program's phase-out in 1975, only six of the thirteen new communities financed under the program eventually got off the ground and after 2-7 years were housing populations of 1-6000. The federal government's investment in the program at its close amounted to nearly $300 million in loan guarantees, and $72 million in other assistance. This was a classic non-administered program, and its failure was attributed to several flaws: inadequate financing arrangements, lack of a broad constituency, expectation of a stable economy, and reliance on the private market to achieve redistributive social goals.

The program was a low-cost attempt to coordinate what was essentially a feudal network with only islands of interdependence on an intermittent basis, but in spite of the incentives it offered (which were too limited to be effective), the actors' essential autonomy and behavior remained largely unchanged. The private market actors (lenders and developers) used the program to reduce their risks and improve their profitability, and when economic circumstances changed they bailed out, leaving the government to hold the baby.

The U.S. Model Cities Program, 1968-1973

The model cities program was enacted in the Demonstration Cities and Metropolitan Development Act in December 1966. The program was designed to focus on deteriorated central city neighborhoods, and held out the promise of a streamlined funding process, earmarked funds from other programs, and coordinated federal efforts in the designated neighborhoods.

HUD was designated as the lead agency, but without authority over the other agencies it was supposed to coordinate. Interagency task forces which were set up at the federal level proved unsuccessful in effecting the promised redeployment of resources and coordination of action. At the local level, City Demonstration Agencies (CDAs) were set up to coordinate policy, planning and implementation in the model neighborhoods. These numbered 150 after 2 years, although the original intention had been to concentrate resources in only a few areas.

While some of the CDAs were successful at the local level, vertical coordination between federal and local levels was less than satisfactory, as evidenced by several rounds of restructuring the planning-approval and funding process. Under the Nixon administration, support for the program eroded, and it was frozen in the moratorium of 1973, to be killed with the passing of the Community Block Grant legislation in 1974. The program has been judged a failure, partly due to changes from its conception in the legislative process, and partly due to flaws in implementation. Among these are the failures of the various coordination models employed here, ranging from lead organization through inter-organizational group to coordinating unit.

Regional Development in Great Britain: The REPBs/REPCs

The Labor government which took office in October 1964, in its efforts to improve the coordination of regional development, placed this function under a new super-ministry, the Department of Economic Affairs (DEA) and divided the country into ten planning regions, each with its Regional Economic Planning Council (REPC) and Regional Economic Planning Board (REPB). The latter were advisory bodies made up of knowledgeable appointed individuals, while the former were made up of representatives of the relevant government departments. Together, these inter-organizational groups were supposed to coordinate public economic development activities in their regions.

In spite of several governmental reorganizations over the years, the efforts to decentralize and coordinate regional development at the local level were unsuccessful. The REPCs failed to affect the sectoral lines of communication and decision-making which linked the regional agencies with their respective headquarters in London, and only raised expectations which were disappointed. This failure was ascribed to the coordinating agencies' lack of statutory powers, and the low priority assigned to regional development coordination by the central government. As coordination mechanisms, the interorganizational groups were totally ineffective.

New Towns in Great Britain, 1945-1978
The 1946 New Towns Act initiated a program of new towns planning and construction which continued for over three decades, and has been responsible for the development of 28 new towns which are still growing. While the original stimulus was the need to cope with London's population surplus, later generations of new towns have been designed for other purposes, ranging from metropolitan decongestion to regional development.

A new organization type was designed to plan and implement the new towns: the New Town Corporation, a public corporation established with the designation of an area for new town development. Financed by the government, the corporation has at its disposal all the public powers for land acquisition and assembly, and is accountable to the minister and Parliament. It carries out all the planning and development functions, partly in-house and partly through purchase of services from contractors, and eventually recouping its front-end costs from the disposition of developed land and property. With the maturing of the first generation of new towns and their Corporations going out of business and transferring their administrative functions and services to local government, a National New Towns Commission was formed to own and manage the remaining public property.

The new towns program has been a striking success in terms of delivering the desired program outputs. In terms of its goals—economic growth, self-containment, and promotoing regional growth and employment—the record is more mixed, but still on balance positive, and the program has demonstrated its long-run financial viability. The coordination model employed, the single organization, can be credited in no small measure with the program's effectiveness.

Neighborhood Preservation in Great Britain: The GIA
In 1969, in response to criticism of its predominantly clearance orientation, and to the accumulation of a substantial volume of new public construction, Britain's urban renewal program was refocused to a greater emphasis on conservation and rehabilitation. The Housing Act of 1969 gave local authorities broad discretion to declare General Improvement Areas (GIAs) making them eligible for a variety of types of central government grant assistance.

The Local Authorities, for their part, committed themselves to coordinating their planning and services for the GIA's, and improving their infrastructure and environment. Government circulars directed establishment of a formal coordination apparatus for the GIAS at the local level; this took various forms. Most towns set up interdepartmental working parties; these interorganizational groups were usually ineffective. More successful were those authorities which appointed a "trouble-shooter" or coordinator, either a local government official or a consultant.

On the whole, the GIA program was unsuccessful. While exogenous factors also played an important part in its failure, part can be blamed on the failure to establish the local coordination mechanisms which were a vital ingredient of the policy. This failure is typical of the outcomes of multi-sectoral, coordinated, and comprehensive areawide planning and implementation in Britain, while successful programs, such as the massive Council Homes effort, have been accomplished largely on a sectoral basis.

The Lakhish Regional Development, Israel
In 1954 planning and development of the Lakhish region, an almost empty area of about 500 square kilometers east of the port of Ashkelon, began in response to the opportunities for settlement presented by the completion of the Yarkon-Negev pipeline, the need to absorb and integrate a growing immigrant population, and the threat of hostile infiltration. The Settlement Department of the Jewish Agency was designated as the lead agency, and planning was accomplished through several sectoral interagency committees.

For detailed planning and implementation, which began after less than a year, management of the project was transferred to a regional administration located in Kiriat Gat, the principal town of the region. The regional director enjoyed broad powers of command over other actors, enhanced by his "direct line" to the Prime Minister. Under him a Regional Directorate, made up of representatives of Jewish Agency departments and other participating agencies, became the arena for interorganizational coordination.

By mid-1956 the general planning process had been completed, and 26 new settlements had been established. The Regional Administration continued with implementation and development of the region over the following years, though there were significant departures from the original concept to adapt to changing circumstances and needs. In meeting the goals it set for itself, recent evaluations suggest that the project was a striking success, especially in its planning and implementation process.

Coordinator of Government Activities in the Galilee
Since the creation of Israel, the Galilee, the region in the North between Lake Galilee and the Mediterranean, has been beset with problems. Its natural characteristics limit its development potential, at the same time that development is essential for main-

taining the balance between the region's Jewish and Arab populations. Consequently, national policy in 1975 created an Interministerial Committee for Development of the Galilee, headed by the minister of commerce and industry. As its
executive arm a new post was established: coordinator of government activities in
the Galilee. The post has been filled by four incumbents (up to 1979), who either
resigned or transferred in frustration over their limited power to affect the behavior
and activities of the powerful government ministries which in fact determine
development patterns in the region.

The coordinator, with a skeleton staff, no discretionary resources, and no
authority over other public agencies, has been quite ineffective in fulfilling his
mission, and has had to limit his activities to informal interaction and information
exchange. In a few attempts to undertake planning, he has run the risk of domain
conflicts with another body in the area: the District Planning Commission. This
attempt at IOC has been a total failure.

New Towns in Israel, 1950-1975
Israel's development towns program began in 1950, to absorb the waves of immigrants flooding the country, disperse population pressures from the settled coastal
plain, and provide growth poles and central places for peripheral regions. This
national policy was expressed in the national physical plan of 1950, and subsequent
population dispersal plans drawn up by the Planning Bureau of the Ministry of the
Interior.

But these only indicated locations and approximate target populations of
new towns. They became guidelines for the Department of Housing in the Labor
Ministry—later the Ministry of Housing—which took over, almost exclusively,
the planning, development, and construction of the new settlements. In this
process, it also coordinated the activities of other responsible agencies, such as
the Ministries of Transportation, and Commerce and Industry. The Housing
Ministry's successful organizational imperialism rested on its claim to a dominant interest (housing being the major component of the new towns) and
government-coalitional politics.

While there has been valid criticism of the design and environmental quality of
many new towns, and they have often failed to meet their residents' social and
economic needs, the program succeeded in simple output terms. It created thirty new
settlements, providing housing, services, and much of their employment to over
400,000 people—nearly 15% of the country's population—and achieved its principal
goal: population dispersal.

The Urban Renewal Authority in Israel
In the early 1960's pressure was building up to address the growing problem of urban
slums and neighborhood deterioration, pressure which grew with the decline in
immigration which fueled the economy and especially construction. As a result, the

Law for the Building and Clearance of Rehabilitation Areas of 1965 established a national "urban renewal" authority, as an autonomous unit directed by a board incorporating representatives of central and local government, and chaired by the housing minister.

The Authority, however, received no implementation powers: coordination of the activities in the designated neighborhoods of the relevant agencies was to be effected by planning alone. The authority had the statutory power to proclaim an area a renewal neighborhood, after a specified survey, planning, and consultation process. Its budget was to come from its participating agencies, but in fact was funded by the Housing Ministry which, in a effect, captured the authority and turned it into a subsidiary.

After a national survey to identify potential renewal neighborhoods, the authority undertook detailed planning, proceeding to proclaim three areas. Lack of implementation powers, erosion of support in the Housing Ministry with a change in administration, and changes in the economic environment, combined to limit the dimensions of the neighborhood renewal program, and the Authority's eventual impact, until it received its administrative "kiss of death" in 1975, was negligible.

"Project Renewal" (Israel) 1978-1980

"Project Renewal" was conceived as a joint effort between the government and the Jewish Agency, who would together fund the comprehensive revitalization of deteriorated neighborhoods. The central coordinator of the program was the Interministerial Coordinating Committee (ICC), an interorganizational group jointly chaired by the deputy PM's representative and the head of the Jewish Agency's renewal team. The ICC was to review and approve plans submitted for funding, and allocate funds between neighborhoods, but the initiative for planning and program proposals was to come from the local level.

Each designated neighborhood set up a Local Steering Committee (LSC), also an interorganizational group made up primarily of local government officials. In the large cities, planning and implementation of neighborhood renewal was undertaken by the local Municipal-Governmental Development Corporations. These were more successful than the LSCs, generally, in accomplishing some tangible changes in their neighborhoods.

But on the whole, domain conflicts between public agencies dogged the project, the ICC's review and approval process proved unequal to its load, and implementation lagged. Finally, national fiscal exigencies eroded the government's capability to fund "Project Renewal," and by 1981 its continuation in its original form was in jeopardy.

The Guyana Regional Development Program—Venezuela

In the 1950's the resource potential of the Guyana region, in the lower Orinoco valley of Venezuela, was already recognized. After several predecessor organizations, the Corporacion Venezolana de Guyana (CVG) was established by the new Betancourt Administration in 1960, headed by an engineer, Alonzo Ravard, who had the confidence of the President.

The CVG enjoyed high government priority and wide political support, which it maintained by its technocratic administrative style, and by investing in technical development programs which reflected national priorities rather than narrower regional interests. The CVG planned and developed Ciudad Guyana as the region's capital and growth center, for a target population of 600,000 by 1980. In its regional development policy, the CVG focused on a few large industrial and infrastructure projects, filling the role of promoter and developer to recruit foreign investors and local capital.

In its task of enlisting and coordinating the activities of other public agencies, the CVG went through several phases. Until 1965 it internalized all essential functions, but with a growing population in the region it was forced to recognize its interdependence with other organizations. As a result the CVG adopted much more of an entrepreneurial and mediating role. Its basic developmental program was highly successful, putting the region onto the path of self-sustaining growth. We do not know how effective the CVG has been, in the long run, in its more interactive coordinating role.

The Satellite Towns of Stockholm, Sweden

A combination of land banking and a systematic public transportation policy formed the elements of the satellite town planning and development undertaken by the Stockholm municipality since 1940. The master plan of 1952 envisioned a ring of distinct medium-to-high density satellite suburbs, all linked to the central city by rapid transit. This plan was detailed out and implemented with the development of Vallingby and Farsta between 1950 and 1960, and other subsequent satellite suburbs.

The whole process was accomplished by the Stockholm munici- pality, which determined policy through a complex structure of committees made up of elected and appointed officials. Planning was done partly in-house, and detailed site planning was contracted out to consultants. The design and development of the civic-commercial centers were also contracted out, in Vallingby to a city-owned subsidiary, and in Farsta to a private consortium. Residential neighborhoods, too, were contracted out to cooperative and private developers, but the city retained tight control over design and construction.

As a delivery system, the process was highly successful, and Vallingby and Farsta are also model communities achieving most of their environmental, societal, and economic goals. Later settle- ments, however, conceived and executed under the pressure of an acute housing shortage, exhibit less sensitive planning and design, and show serious flaws in construction.

The Standortprogramme (STOP) in West Germany
The "Standortprogramme" was introduced in 1971 in North Rhine-Westphalia in response to perceived deficiencies in the planning process, both at the *Land* and the local levels. Its objectives were to coordinate local middle-and long-term planning and development processes, and to concentrate the *Land's* urban public investments in a few selected areas.

The *Land*-government guidelines prescribed the format and contents of STOP: a five-ten year development plan for a limited area, integrated into the municipality's comprehensive plan, and developed in an interactive process between the local authorities, the public, and relevant regional and public agencies. The bait was to be a simplified funding approval process for projects included in an approved STOP, while the submission of a STOP was to be a prerequisite for review of all funding applications by the *Land* government.

While these incentives recruited cities and towns to participate, many attempted to evade STOP's concentration requirements. This, combined with regional authorities' inexperience in reviewing plans, the *Land's* retreat from its proclaimed sanctions and incentives, and other economic factors, resulted in wholesale footdragging. By 1977, 80% of the local governments had only initiated the STOP process, and only five applications had been approved. The STOP program was totally ineffective in setting up the desired coordinative mechanisms, both at the local level and at the *Land* level, where each ministry continued to process funding applications in the traditional way.

Comparative Analysis
The fourteen cases presented above include a total of thirty-two instances of use of coordination models, and yield enough information about their implementation and effects to enable evaluation of their relative effectiveness. Such an evaluation could have taken the form of a dichotomous assessment: success or failure. This approach was rejected because of the information loss involved and the risk of a distorted picture of actual outcomes.

Accordingly, the measure adopted here is a five-point ordinal scale, ranging from "complete success" (1) through a neutral assessment (3) to "total failure" (5). Such a scale is sufficiently fine-grained, I believe, to reflect the qualitative assessments of the cases without too much abstraction. At the same time, it is not so detailed as to strain the judgment, or to project a spurious image of precision. An objection might be, however, that such a scale lends an aura of quantified and "scientific" objectivity to an evaluation which is still essentially qualitative and, at least to a degree, subjective.

Several considerations address these objections: 1) Comparative analysis is impossible on the basis of purely qualitative assessment; 2) the ordinal scale simply reflects differences in ranking, and does not imply any spurious quantification of findings; 3) Goal-related criteria of success have only been included in parentheses, as it were; each case of IOC has been assessed purely as a delivery system for the outputs it was designed to produce, and cases were chosen so that the evidence of this type of success or failure would be incontrovertible, so that the leeway for subjectivity is insignificant.

Table 3 presents the cases and their coordination models, with their evaluation according to this 5-point scale. Clearly, a wide range of effectiveness is displayed.

If the models are arranged to reflect their relative differences in effectiveness, we get the ordering shown in Table 4. This table makes apparent the variations in performance between the different coordination models, especially at the ends of the scale. Non-administered programs occupy only the lower third of the evaluation range while at the positive pole, the single organization model ranges only from 1 to 3, and four of the five observations of coordination units are clustered between 1-2 and 3.

How can we explain these variations? If there were one best coordination model, we should expect all cases where it was adopted to show highly positive evaluations. Alternatively, if all models can be clearly ranked on a scale of relative effectiveness, the assessments of each model's effectiveness should show quite a narrow range of variation. Neither of these possibilities is supported by our observations. The range of effectiveness of each model is quite wide, with the narrowest variance (excluding that for informal linkages, which is limited to a single observation) ranging from 3 to 4-5 (non-administered programs) and the broadest (coordinator, and interorganizational groups) extending over the whole gamut of evaluations from 1 to 5.

The explanation must be that there is some attribute of these coordination models, which is distributed so that its presence is most pronounced in the single organization, strong in the coordinating unit, gradually diminishing until in the inter- organizational group and non-administered program it is much weaker, and perhaps almost absent in informal linkages. I suggest that this characteristic is institutionalization.

Institutionalization has been defined as "... a process of crystallization of different types of norms, organizations, and frameworks which regulate the processes of exchange..." (Eisenstadt 1968:414-415). Attributes of institutionalization include permanence and stability (Ross 1979:29-30), and formalization of structure and interactions (Aldrich 1979: 273-274).

Formalization as an attribute of institutionalization can be expressed in various ways. It can be in the form of a formal framework, such as a contract, regulations, or legislation which established the structure and pattern of interaction. In this way, we can see that a coordination unit, such as OMB, which is established by statute, confirmed by executive orders and routinized in an exhaustive set of federal regulations is more formalized than an interorganizational group which several welfare agencies set up to implement a contractual agreement, which, in turn, is more formal than the informal arrangement by

TABLE 10-3: IOC CASES AND MODELS—EVALUATION

CASE		ICC MODEL	EFFECTIVENESS Ranking and Comments	
ARC:	APPALACHIAN REGIONAL COMMISSION (U.S.A.) Regional Development	Coordinating Unit Coordinator	2 —	not implemented
NCD:	NEW COMMUNITIES DEVELOPMENT PROGRAM (U.S.A.) New Towns	Non-Administered Program Coordinating Unit	4-5 4	macro meso
MCP:	MODEL CITIES PROGRAM (U.S.A.) Neighborhood Renewal	Lead Organization Interorganizational Group Non-Administered Program Coordinating Unit	4 4-5 4 3	macro-central meso-central macro-vertical local; evaluation averaged on a range from about 2 to 4
REP:	REGIONAL ECONOMIC PLANNING BOARDS/COUNCILS (Great Britain) Regional Development	Coordinating Unit Interorganizational Group	— 4-5	macro-vertical model inferred: sources provide no data for evaluation local
NTS:	NEW TOWNS (Great Britain) New Towns	Single Organization	1-2	macro-local
GIA:	GENERAL IMPROVEMENT AREAS (Great Britain) Neighborhood Renewal	Coordinating Unit Non-Administered Program Interorganizational Group Coordinator	— 3 4-5 2-3	meso-central-vertical unit inferred: sources provide no data for evaluation macro local local
LAK:	LAKHISH REGIONAL DEVELOPMENT (Israel) Regional Development	Lead Organization Coordinating Unit Interorganizational Group Coordinator	1-2 1-2 2 1	macro-central macro-local meso-central meso-local
GAL:	COORDINATOR OF GOVERNMENT ACTIVITIES—GALILEE (Israel) Regional Development	Lead Organization Interorganizational Group Coordinator	5 5 5	macro-central meso-central meso-local
DTP:	DEVELOPMENT TOWNS PROGRAM (Israel) New Towns	Single Organization Coordinating Unit	2 1-2	local-meso
URA:	URBAN RENEWAL AUTHORITY (Israel) Neighborhood Renewal	Coordinating Unit Interorganizational Group	— 4-5	macro; concept only, not implemented
PRN:	PROJECT RENEAL (Israel) Neighborhood Renewal	Interorganizational Group Interorganizational Group Single Organization	4 4 3	central; evaluation based on data 1978-1980 local: evaluation as above local: evaluation as above
CVG:	GUYANA REGIONAL DEVELOPMENT (Venezuela) Regional Development	Single Organization	2	
SAT:	STOCKHOLM SATELLITE TOWNS (Sweden) New Towns	Single Organization Interorganizational Group	1 1	macro meso
STP:	STANDORTSPROGRAMME-STOP (Germany—BRD) Neighborhood Renewal	Non-Administered Program Lead Organization Informal Linkages Coordinating Unit Interorganizational Group	4-5 5 5 — 4-5	macro central-macro central-meso central-vertical unit inferred; sources provide no data for evaluation local-meso

TABLE 10-4: MODELS BY EFFECTIVENESS

COORDINATION	HIGH			EFFECTIVENESS				LOW	
MODELS	1	1-2	2	2-3	3	4	4-5	5	TOTAL
Informal Linkages	0	0	0	0	0	0	0	1	1
Non-Administered Program	0	0	0	0	1	1	2	0	4
Interorganizational Group	1	0	1	0	0	2	5	1	10
Lead Organization	0	1	0	0	0	1	0	2	4
Coordinator	1	0	0	1	0	0	0	1	3
Coordinating Unit	0	2	1	0	1	1	0	0	5
Single Organization	1	1	2	0	1	0	0	0	5
TOTAL	3	4	4	1	3	5	7	5	32

which organizations appoint executive officers of their related agencies to their governing boards. Another manifestation of formalization is in the running of the coordination models themselves: to what degree have they developed standard operating procedures, rules, and formal (e.g. written) patterns of interaction. In these terms an information exchange by a telephone call between two officials is less formal than a memo, which in turn is a less formal pattern of interaction than the forwarding of a form that has been completed in accordance with a predetermined set of rules.

Stability and permanence are other recognizable attributes of institutionalization. The informal linkage of a short series of ad hoc meetings between officials of several organizations involved in a specific issue or problem of common concern is less institutionalized than the same group meeting as a task force to administer a contract that has a predetermined duration. Both of these, in turn, are not as institutionalized as the unit which a federation of organizations, such as, for example, the Petroleum Institute, sets up to coordinate the activities of its members for the duration of its organizational existence. When permanence, stability, and formalization of structure and interactions, therefore, are present to a high degree, a coordination model is highly institutionalized. Conversely, if they are largely absent or if only a few are weakly displayed, a model would rank low on the institutional scale.

Two important caveats must be noted here. One is that institutionalization does not necessarily equal power; it may or may not be positively related with the grants of authority or the control over resources on which other units are dependent which are usually associated with power. One may contrast the power of Britain's PESC with the impotence of the REPCs to be assured that coordination models—in this case, both interorganizational groups—at the same level of institutionalization do not need to enjoy the same degree of power. Comparing the administrator of the Lakhish region in Israel with the coordinator of government activities in the Galilee—both coordinators—teaches the same lesson.

The second caveat is that we are dealing with the intrinsic institutionalization of various coordination models, not with the actual institutionalization of specific cases. The latter may vary within quite a wide range, but I suggest that at the extremes of this range the variation in institutionalization will be accompanied by a qualitative change in the actual coordination model.

The intrinsic institutionalization associated with the various models, as shown in Figure 1 below, is an ordinal characteristic. In other words, this figure simply ranks the coordination models for their degree of institutionalization: it does not say how much more institutionalized the coordination unit, for example, is than the interorganization group. But to pursue this example, we can conceive of an interorganizational group which acquires a staff of its own, develops an identification of its members, and gains control of a budget to support its activities. At some stage in this process it would no longer be an interorganizational group, but would become a coordinating unit. This in fact, is what happened with the ARC.

Institutionalization and Effectiveness
In Figure 1, the coordination models are ordered by their relative degrees of intrinsic institutionalization. Informal links are obviously the least institutionalized, by definition. Of the macro-models, the non-administered program occupies a low place on the institutionalization scale, though it may be enshrined in legislation and implemented by a well-established and stable agency. But what is poorly institutionalized is the system of linkages between the delivery agency and the other participants in the program.

Higher on the scale of institutionalization is the interorganizational group. As factors associated with institutionalization grow stronger, the group becomes increasingly like a coordinating unit. The next highest macro-model on the institutionalization ranking is the lead organization. It is obviously more institutionalized than the interorganizational group: it is structured and formalized and enjoys organizational autonomy.

Close to the lead organization on the institutionalization scale is the coordinator: a meso-model often adopted together with this and other macro-models. The coordinator is more institutionalized than the interorganizational group, because he is clearly structured and has organizational autonomy in his role as coordinator. The coordinator is probably more "floating" than any other coordination model on the intrinsic institutionalization scale, because the variation between cases can be so large. The coordination unit is the first fully institutionalized coordination model we encounter. It enjoys all the attributes of a formal organization in its coordination role to which, by definition, it is limited.

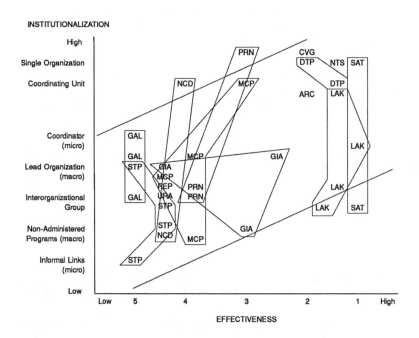

INSTITUTIONALIZATION

Figure 10-1   Institutionalization and Effectiveness

Finally, the single organization represents the highest level of institutionalization that a coordination model can attain. Here, most of the linkages between relevant organizational units are internalized and acquire the institutionalized characteristics —standardization, formalization, routinization—of interactions within a formal organization. Usually the remaining linkages with the environment become similarly formalized, as contracts or formal agreements to supply products or services which the organization cannot provide itself.

When our observations of coordination models are ranked by their relative institutionalization and distributed according to the evaluations of their effectiveness (see Figure 1) an association becomes apparent. Of the thirty-two coordination models which have been evaluated, twenty-seven lie in a broad band reflecting a positive relationship between institutionalization and effectiveness.

An explanation is also readily available for the exceptions: the five observations which fall outside the band—that is, those cases where the relation between institutionalization and effectiveness is other than the one predicted by the evidence of the other cases. The discrepancy may be related to the interaction between different coordination models which are adopted in the context of the same case.

Evaluations of success or failure were primarily of the effectiveness of the interorganizational system in each case as a program delivery system. In view of the relative presence or absence of tangible outputs, these evaluations were easily performed. Only secondary were the assessments of the effectiveness of each particular coordination model, in cases where multiple models (usually at the macro and meso scales) were deployed. Some interaction, then, is likely between the overall achievement of an interorganizational delivery system in a given case, and the performance of particular coordination models in that context.[13]

Our analysis readily presents examples of this interaction in both directions. The interorganizational groups, for instance, are all clustered between 4 and 5 on the evaluation scale, except those involved in the Lakhish regional development (LAK) and the Stockholm satellite towns project (SAT). Both these are conspicuously successful cases, employing other coordination models as well to better effect. Conversely, there is the example of the single organization model sometimes employed in the large cities in Israel's Project Renewal (PRN), which performs somewhat more poorly than seems warranted on the basis of the other single organization models observed. The coordinating unit (HUD's New Community Development Corporation) in the new communities' program offers a similar example in the American context.

With one exception,[14] then, the "deviant" observations can be explained on the basis of the interaction between these coordination models, and the performance of the whole interorganizational system deployed in each of these cases. The remaining observations exhibit quite a systematic decline in effectiveness as the institutionalization of the coordination models declines.

While the four single organizations are clustered between 1 and 2 of the evaluation scale, the four coordinating units range from 1-2 to 3. The coordinator model (which, indeed, is difficult to associate with a set level of intrinsic institutionalization) ranges across the entire scale, from the coordinator of government activities in the Galilee who was a total failure to the regional administrator in the Lakhish region who was a conspicuous success, and with the local "troubleshooter" in the GIA program occupying an intermediate position on the scale.

In the lower quadrant, we can observe even more marked clustering. With the exception of the Lakhish case (which exhibits the interaction effect discussed above) the three other lead organizations are located between 3 and 4 on the evaluation scale, as are all eight of the remaining interorganizational groups. The same is the case for the three remaining non-administered programs, and the single observation of informal linkages.

The contrast which emerges between the performance of what are highly institutionalized ("strong") coordination models, and models with much lower levels of institutionalization ("weak" models) is sharpened if we focus on these clusters. The "strong" cluster contains seven observations of single organizations and coordinating units. All have been rated successful or highly effective in achieving the goals of the coordination process. The "weak" cluster includes three of the four lead agencies, eight of the ten interorganizational groups, three of the four non-administered programs, and the single case of informal linkages. None of these achieved more than a relative degree of failure in delivering the outputs for which the coordination effort was undertaken in each case.

Findings and Qualifications

This comparative analysis of these coordination models applied in cases of regional, urban, and neighborhood development supports the conclusion that there is a relationship between the institutionalization of a model and its effectiveness in such cases of IOC. As suggested by the number of observations where coordination effectiveness varies from that which would be expected if this were a pronounced and monotonic relationship, the association is probably not a strong one. But it is sufficiently important in its implications to warrant pursuing its implications, even though our findings have to be hedged with several qualifications.

First, this investigation has been limited to cases in three closely related sectors. The number and range of observations probably enable us to generalize our conclusions to similar cases, i.e., coordinated interorganizational networks made up of a mixture of public and private sector organizations addressing problems of comprehensive area development. But these conclusions cannot be generalized to IOC in any circumstances.

It is quite possible that in different contexts such as intercorporate coordination in the private sector, for example, or cooperation between community organizations and voluntary groups, the prerequisites for successful coordination models may be different too. Some investigators have suggested that different bases for interaction—voluntary as against mandates exchanges—lead to different types of coordination behavior (Hall et al. 1977; Raelin 1980). A study of IOC in delivering services to the elderly in one metropolitan area, tentatively concluded that a combination of quite "weak" coordination models (informal linkages and interorganizational groups) was working quite effectively (Alexander 1983). A similar conclusion can be inferred from a study of six intergovernmental bodies dealing with human services networks (Agranoff and Lindsay 1983). Consequently, any transfer of the findings of this study to other functional sectors must make due allowances for probable differences in context.

Second, we should be cautious in embracing simple unidimensional explanations, both because of the complexity of the phenomenon under investigation,[15] and because of the relative weakness of the observed relationship. Clearly, the amount of unexplained variance in observed behavior and outcomes warrants a search for additional factors which may improve the quality of our account of the process at work in IOC.

Implications: Institutionalization and IOC - A Hypothesis

No obvious link presents itself to account for the association between institutionalization and IOC effectiveness unless we could say that institutionalization is related to better organizational performance; but this is not so. Often less institutionalized organizations have proved more effective (Burns and Stalker 1961), while highly institutionalized bodies, often bureaucracies, frequently prove disfunctional (Crozier 1964; Sofer 1972). There is no research that suggests any positive link between institutionalization and effectiveness, except in certain clearly identified contingencies. How then, are we to explain the finding of this analysis? In the absence of precedent research addressed specifically to this question, all we can do is to attempt a hypothesis.

The Costs of Institutionalization

In reviewing the coordination models observed in our cases, we distinguished between a cluster of highly institutionalized "strong" coordination efforts, employing the single organization and the coordinating agency models, and another group of "weak" attempts at coordination—generally less effective—which adopted much less institutionalized forms.

One distinction, made almost in passing, was the relative difference in "cost" in setting up coordinated efforts addressed to a common purpose between these two groups. By "cost" I do not mean exclusively cost in material (monetary and other) resources. Cost includes the mobilization of individual and organizational attention, the costs of incurring the traumas of change and reorganization, and the cost of deploying political power. Nor are costs limited to these start-up costs. In setting up a highly institutionalized coordination model, the responsible organizations, individuals, or political establishment are accepting a great increase in their vulnerability to failure. The new organization or coordinating unit becomes a visible symbol of program accomplishment, with all the associated risks.

All these costs are held down with the adoption of the "weaker" coordination models. Their lower level of institutionalization means that a lead organization, or an interorganizational group, can be set up and entrusted with coordination tasks with a relatively small investment of resources, authority, or power. Reorganization is temporary and minimal, and prevailing distributions of resources and authority can remain relatively undisturbed.

Many of our cases show this approach through mere legislative or executive fiat, identifying the common goal, establishing the arena in which coordination is to take place, and charging the appropriate officials with participation in the coordination effort. Such cases range from Germany's STOP program, through

Israel's attempt at coordinating government activities in the Galilee, to the GIA program in Britain.

The non-administered program, too, may be an intrinsically low-cost undertaking, depending on the resources (staff, authority, funds) allocated to it. While these were not lacking in the model cities program, for example, the legislative history shows that reorganization costs, which a reallocation of authority and resources from other line agencies would incur, were consciously avoided.

Costs and Commitment

In comparing the British and American new towns programs the connection between costs and commitment [16] suggested itself. Let us recall the contrast that emerges from the case analyses.

Britain was confronted with its post-war housing crisis, and saw the opportunity to realize the utopias which had captured the imagination of opinion-molders between the two world wars. To confront this problem, and realize these aspirations, the development of the new towns was undertaken, and to plan, develop and manage the new towns a new single organization was devised at the local level: the New Town Corporation. This demanded a massive allocation of funds, and called for a significant realignment of authority, involving a degree of decentralization almost unprecedented in British experience. Here, then, we see a high level of societal and political commitment.

The New Communities Development program, on the other hand, emerged as a limited response to the demands of a narrow constituency, and was hardly perceived as a solution to any pressing national or social problems. It enjoyed a fluctuating, and generally low, priority in its competition for support and resources, and was vulnerable to short-term changes in the political and economic environment. All these factors, reflecting low political commitment, were manifested in the "low-cost" coordination model adopted: the non-administered program.

For the assertion that differences in social ideology and political context are mainly responsible for the different models adopted to coordinate the delivery of two programs which are basically identical in their desired output (Corden 1977), the U.S. offers a control case. This is the federal "Greenbelt" program for constructing new communities in the 1930's, the TVA program for new communities to house their employees, and the AEC's new community construction during WWII. In these cases, when the federal government and the relevant agencies saw themselves confronted with an urgent problem, and were committed to giving its solution a high priority on their agenda, they did not resort to mobilizing the market through non-administered programs. They undertook the task directly through single organizations.

Our comparative analysis of cases of IOC now offers broader support for the suggestion that commitment might be the link between the institutionalization of IOC models and their relative effectiveness. Clearly, institutionalization is not the direct causal agent of more effective coordination, but it could be an expression of commitment.

Commitment may work in three ways. The first may be in creating a climate of expectation where commitment to achievement becomes a self-fulfilling prophecy. Looking back at some of our most successful cases, like the Stockholm satellite towns development, the Lakhish and Guyana regional developments, and the British and Israeli new towns programs, we can see this process in action.

In some of the cases where failure to achieve program objectives, or, indeed, to achieve anything at all, is as conspicuous as the success of the cases above, the reverse phenomenon is apparent. Often, such programs were hardly more than a token acknowledgment of some disfunction, or a politically convenient obeisance to a particular interest or pressure group. Examples of such cases are Britain's REPBs and its GIA program, the Galilee coordinator, and West Germany's STOP program.

The second way in which commitment may contribute to successful outcomes is in the array of "implicative acts" which are the symptoms of commitment. These will have a direct impact on program accomplishment, quite apart from the environment of expectations described above. Such acts include allocating ample funds for the achievement of important objectives, assigning individuals or organizational units conspicuous for their competence or talent to critical roles, and creating clear channels of authority, communication, and resource allocation to avoid any roadblocks which might inhibit successful achievement of program objectives. It is unnecessary to substantiate the efficacy of such actions with illustrations, and our cases provide examples in plenty.

The third way in which commitment works is by enabling the adjustments to the preexisting interorganizational network to take place without which, often, successful outcomes are impossible. Only when sufficient political, social, or ideological commitment is present, it seems, will the more institutionalized coordination models be adopted, which demand a willingness to incur the pain of reorganization, and to bear the costs of equipping the new coordination models with the tools of authority and control over resources adequate for performance of their tasks.

Conclusions

To understand IOC better, and to have a set of tools for learning from experience, a set of coordination models was proposed. Ranging from informal linkages to the single organization, these models enable us to articulate the process of IOC at the meso-and macro-scales, connecting the linkages and elements of IOC which have been identified at the micro-scale with the coordination strategies and contexts at the mega-scale.

These coordination models have been used in a comparative analysis of fourteen cases of IOC in regional, urban, and neighborhood development. We can draw the following conclusions from this study, at several levels of generalization.

Coordination Models in Areawide Development Programs
In the sector to which it was limited, namely regional, urban, and neighborhood development programs, the comparative case analysis suggests that there is no simple "secret for success"; no single coordination model can be identified as being more effective in all, or even most circumstances. But coordination models in this sector do vary systematically to some extent in their relative effectiveness; this variance seems to be associated with their relative degree of institutionalization.

In an attempt to explain the association between the institutionalization of coordination models and their relative effectiveness, the relationship was examined between institutionalization and commitment. Perhaps the initiators or sponsors of the coordination effort were only prepared to incur the costs of deploying a more institutionalized coordination model, such as a coordination unit or a new single organization, if they were highly committed to the goals which the program was designed to achieve, or if there was a strong consensus on the priority of the problems which the coordination effort was to address.

Some of our cases seem to provide support for this hypothesis. It also explains the relative success of the more institutionalized coordination models, which cannot be attributed only to institutionalization. But if institutionalization is just a symptom of a commitment which at once generates a positive climate of expectations and at the same time devotes the material, organizational and political resources needed for accomplishment, then the more successful results of the more institutionalized models are not so surprising.

The implications of these conclusions give cause for both optimism and pessimism. Optimism, because this study suggests that there is room for improving the effectiveness of interorganizational coordination, and that in areawide development the adoption of more institutionalized models could raise the chances of avoiding the pitfalls which have dogged so many coordination efforts in the past.

But this is not a novel prescription: it seems to be known or intuitively sensed whenever policy is developed in interorganizational systems for addressing problems or goals which transcend the capabilities of any one existing organization. When several organizations, or an issue-related network of institutions and interests, or a country's political establishment, are sufficiently committed to the realization of a program, they seem to know how to go about accomplishing their aim.

It is this realization which exposes the pessimistic implication of our conclusions. When coordination efforts do not succeed, perhaps it is less because the initiators did not know how to go about it, but because they did not want to succeed enough to accept the costs without which achievement is impossible. Instead they preferred to mount token programs which expressed little more than a symbolic commitment to their objectives.[17]

Coordination Models and IOC
The comparative case analysis demonstrates the coordination model as a tool for analyzing IOC to learn from previous experience. The substantive conclusions above are limited to the sector covered by the range of cases analyzed, but the utility of the coordination models as an analytic tool has been clearly demonstrated.

The same coordination models were also used in a pilot study in a different sector: human services delivery. This area, together with health services, has claimed the majority of IOC studies which have been carried out to date (Whetten 1982:6). In an examination of the interagency network which delivers services to the frail and incapacitated elderly in metropolitan Milwaukee, informal linkages and inter-organizational groups were found to be the prevailing coordination models. Coordinating units (e.g., staffed planning councils) were also observed, but their domains overlapped in this arena, each focusing on its parent funding agency's area of concern: poverty, or aging, etc. This system proved much more densely linked than one would suspect on cursory observation and, judging by the perceptions of service suppliers, works quite well (Alexander 1983). Coordination models can be a useful tool, then, in the analysis of IOC in a variety of areas, ranging from regional development to human services.

Implications: Planning for Power Sharing
The growing body of studies of IOC is contributing to an emerging consciousness that coordination among organizations involved in a program or project of common interest cannot be taken for granted. Assuredly, successful implementation is more easily accomplished the more the number of involved organizations can be limited—ideally to the one initiating organization (Pressman and Wildavsky 1973), but the complexity of many undertakings often makes that impossible. In situations where attainment of an objective requires the deployment of several, sometimes many, organizations, the recognition that power must be shared and distributed among the participants is essential.

This is where the set of coordination models presented here can make a useful contribution. Besides being an analytical tool, as demonstrated above, it can be a conceptual vocabulary for the interorganizational design[18] which must become an integral part of planning and program design. Early in the development of policy or in planning an undertaking which is likely to involve other organizations, the initiator's planners have to identify these and involve them as active participants in important decisions. One of these decisions, which may be critical for the project's success, is the design and adoption of an appropriate structure of interorganizational relationships to ensure that all participants will, in fact, carry out their assigned roles. As a design tool, the coordination models presented here offer a repertoire of available structures which can be adopted singly or in various combinations, through the different stages of a projected planning and implementation process.

Unfortunately, the conclusions of this study are too tentative, and too limited in their scope, to offer the normative guidelines that the "designers" of interorganizational structure will seek. We do not know yet which coordination models might be most effective in which situations; in the future, perhaps, additional research on these lines will offer more enlightenment. However, life goes on, and the argument for action even before "all the facts are in" is compelling when we review the relationship between theory and practice: "Disillusionment ... arises from a suspicion that being able to solve problems well depends hardly at all on being able to define problems well" (Nystrom and Starbuck 1977:4).

The experience of interorganizational coordination described above bears out Nystrom and Starbuck's pessimism. There are more stories of failure than success, and it is difficult to call the relationship between the outcomes and the factors involved in each of the cases much more than random. At the same time, this pessimism can reinforce our expectations of the potential usefulness of interorganizational design, because our expectations are so low. After all, with a record which is so poor, even a small improvement in coordination and implementation effectiveness can be a real contribution. This might become possible with more deliberate attention to and use of coordination models in policy development and planning and in interorganizational design.

Footnotes

1. This question, of course, raises a number of related issues, which can only be addressed here in passing: 1) What is effectiveness? For the purposes of this discussion we can adopt the "evolutionary" approach to organizational effectiveness (Zammuto 1982) which synthesizes the goal-oriented and systems-oriented approaches, but for the purposes of the case evaluations which follow a simpler, though admittedly very partial, criterion has been adopted: what was the output of the program, project, or interorganizational system? This is premised on the very pragmatic assumption that some concrete accomplishment is a necessary, though not a sufficient, condition for any positive evaluation. 2) Coordinate for whose benefit? Benson (1982) suggests that this question has been neglected; I have avoided it deliberately, however, in the conviction that we must first understand how to coordinate before we need to ask ourselves what we are coordinating for.

2. Much of this is reviewed in Mulford and Rogers (1982) and Rogers and Mulford (1982); other useful supplements are Lehman (1975) and Brickman (1979).

3. This is confirmed in empirical studies investigating type of interorganizational interaction; see, for example, Hall et al. (1977); Warren, Bergunder and Rose (1974); and Braito, Paulson and Klongton (1972).

4. Mintzberg (1979:165-168) describes the role of the coordinator in complex private sector organizations— businesses and corporations—whom he calls an "integrating manager" with formal authority to coordinate several line divisions. Wren (1967:80) proposes such a role, analogous to that of the "project manager" in

the aerospace industry, to address coordination problems in interstate power networks.

5. Analysis of this case (Alexander 1980) explains why this coordination model is seldom invoked alone.

6. An extensive literature attests to the impotence of planning agencies as coordinative units. For example, see Caiden and Wildavsky (1974) for national economic planning in developing countries, and Cohen (1976) for an evaluation of the French national planning system. For regional planning coordination in the U.S., see Derthick (1974:108-133), and in Europe, see Hayward and Watson (1975). For U.S. planning at the local level see Altschuler (1965) and Alexander and Beckley (1975), and in Israel, see Alterman and Hill (1978), and Alexander (1980). Naturally, there are exceptions too; for a view that British planning agencies are too powerful, see Levin (1976).

7. Such coordinating units are the "project offices" which have been established in the aerospace industry (Wren 1967:79).

8. For an analysis of PESCs role in coordinating British policy, see Heclo and Wildavsky (1974); NURDA's power in promoting regional development and new towns in Australia is limited by its need to arrive at binding agreements with State governments—see Neilsen (1978); the Israel example is elaborated in Alexander (1980).

9. Examples of non-administered programs where some failures were due to lack of federal enforcement capability, are the U.S. Community Development Block Grant (CDBG) and the Concentrated Employment and Training Act (CETA) programs (Williams 1980).

10. For a discussion of mandated coordination, see Raelin (1980, 1982).

11. Lehman (1975) describes hospital consortia "Empires."

12. These cases all have in common a geographically defined issue or area involving complex multisectoral problems; for the basis of their selection and a more extended presentation of the cases and their analysis, see Alexander (1980).

13. This interaction is indicated by the polygons in Fig. 1, each of which encloses the set of coordination models adopted in a particular case.

14. The non-administered program employed for the General Improvement Areas (GIA) in Britain performed rather better than our hypothesis leads us to expect; perhaps this can be accounted for, in part, by the tentative nature of the assessment of this model, on which our sources provide little information as they focused more on micro-scale coordination at the local scale. As a result, this model was evaluated as positively as possible in the light of the low overall assessments of the effectiveness of the program as a whole.

15. For a discussion of the problems of explaining complex systems and their implications, see Weaver (1948), Brewer (1974, 1975) and Winner (1975).

16. Commitment is used here in its usual connotations. It is related to the verb "to commit": "to engage or pledge by some implicative act (to a particular course)"

(OED:481). It is by the "implicative acts" related to a course of behavior intended to achieve a particular goal or address a problem, that we can gauge the level of commitment. Commitment itself, or the degree to which decision makers perceive themselves as bound by a resolve, is also a continuous phenomenon rather than a matter of "all-or-nothing," and is related to other decision characteristics, such as specificity (Levin, 1972:24-42).

17. For a discussion of coordination as a mere symbol of reform, see Weiss (1981).

18. Interorganizational design is defined by Aldrich (1979:23) and discussed in its relationship to IOC by Weiss (1981: 41-43). In interorganizational design, the coordination model is analogous to the "organizing mode" in Galbraith's model of organization design (1977:31).

References

Agranoff, Robert, and Valerie A. Lindsay. 1983. Intergovernmental management: Perspectives from human services problem solving at the local level. *Public Administration Review* 43(3): 227-237.

Aldrich, Howard. 1979. *Organizations and environments.* Englewood Cliffs, NJ: Prentice-Hall.

Aldrich, Howard, and David Whetten. 1981. "Organization sets, action-sets, and networks: Making the most of simplicity." In *Handbook of organizational design.* edited by Paul C. Nystrom and William H. Starbuck, 385-408. Oxford: Oxford University Press.

Alexander, Ernest R. 1980. "Slum rehabilitation in Israel: The administrative institutional context" (Working Papers 1-9). Haifa, Israel: Technion-Israel Institute of Technology, the S. Neaman Institute for Advanced Studies in Science & Technology.

_____. 1983. "Coordinating care services for the frail and incapacitated elderly." In *Health care research* edited by S.M. Smith and M. Venkatesan, 86-89. Provo, UT: Brigham Young University, Institute of Business Management.

Alexander, Ernest R., with Robert M. Beckley. 1975. *Going it alone? A case study of planning and implementation at the local level.* Washington, D.C.: USGPO.

Alterman, Rachelle, and Morris Hill. 1978. Implementation of urban land use plans. *Journal of the American Institute of Planners* 44(3): 274-285.

Altschuler, Alan. 1965. *The city planning process.* Ithaca, NY: Cornell University Press.

Arnold, Joseph L. 1971. *The New Deal in the suburbs: A history of the Greenbelt Town program 1935-1954.* Columbus, OH: Ohio State University Press.

Benson, J. Kenneth. 1982. "A framework for policy analysis." In Rogers, Whetten and Assocs., op. cit., 137-176.

Braito, Rita, Steve Paulson and Gerald Klongton. 1972. "Domain consensus: A key variable in interorganizational analysis." In *Complex organizations and their environments* edited by Merlin B. Brinkerhoff and Philip R. Kunz, 176-192. Dubuque, IA: William C. Brown.

Brewer, Garry D. 1974. "Systems analysis in the urban complex: Potential and limitations." In *Improving the quality of the urban environment* edited by Willis D. Hawley and David Rogers. Beverly Hills, CA: Sage.

_____. 1975. "Analysis of complex systems: An experiment and its implications for policymaking." In *Organized social complexity: Challenge to politics and policy* by Todd R. LaPorte. Princeton, NJ: Princeton University Press.

Brickman, Ronald. 1979. Comparative approaches to R&D policy coordination. *Policy Sciences* 11(1): 73-91.

Burns, Tom and G.M. Stalker. 1961. *The management of innovation.* London: Tavistock Pubs. Ltd.

Caiden, Naomi, and Aaron Wildavsky. 1974. *Planning and budgeting in poor countries.* New York: Wiley.

Clark, Burton R. 1965. Interorganizational patterns in education. *Administrative Sciences Quarterly* 10(2): 224-237.

Cohen, Stephen S. 1976. *Modern capitalist planning: The French model* (2nd Ed.). Berkeley, CA: University of California Press.

Corden, Carol. 1977. *Planned cities: New towns in Britain and America.* Beverly Hills, CA: Sage.

Crozier, Michael. 1964. *The bureaucratic phenomenon.* Chicago: University of Chicago Press.

Derthick, Martha. 1974. *Between state and nation: Regional organizations of the U.S.* Washington, D.C.: The Brookings Institute.

Dunshire, Andrew. 1978. *The execution process vol. 2: Control in a bureaucracy.* London: Martin Robertson.

Eisenstadt, Shmuel N. 1968. "Social institutions: The concept." In *International encyclopedia of the social sciences* edited by David L. Sills, 409-421. New York: Macmillan-Free Press.

Evan, William M., and R. Christopher Klemm. 1980. Interorganizational relations among hospitals: A strategy, structure and performance model. *Human Relations* 33(5): 315-337.

Galbraith, Jay R. 1977. *Organization design.* Reading, MA: Addison-Wesley.

Gillespie, David F., and Dennis S. Mileti. 1979. *Technostructures and interorganizational relations.* Lexington, MA: Heath.

Hage, Jerald. 1975. "A strategy for creating interdependent delivery systems to meet complex needs." In *Interorganization theory* edited by Anant R. Negandhi, 211-234. Kent, OH: Kent State University Press.

Hall, Richard H., John P. Clark, Peggy C.Giordano, Paul V. Johnson and Martha Van Rockel. 1977. Patterns of interorganizational relationships. *Administrative Sciences Quarterly* 22(3): 457-474.

Hayward, Jack, and Michael Watson, (Eds.). 1975. *Planning, politics, and public policy: The British, French and Italian experience.* London: Cambridge University Press.

Heclo, Hugh and Aaron Wildavsky. 1974. *The private government of public money: Community and policy in British political administration.* Berkeley, CA: University of California Press.

Hjern, Benny, and David O. Porter. 1981. Implementation structures: A new unit of administrative analysis. *Organization Studies* 2(3): 211-227.

Katz, Daniel, and Robert L. Kahn. 1966. *The social psychology of organizations.* New York: Wiley.

Kochen, Manfred, and Carl W. Deutsch. 1980. *Decentralization: Sketches toward a rational theory.* Cambridge, MA: Oelgeschlager, Gunn and Hain.

Lehman, Edward W. 1975. *Coordinating health care: explorations in interorganizational relations.* Beverly Hills, CA: Sage Pubs.

Levin, P. H. 1972. On decisions and decision making. *Public Administration* 50(Spring): 19-44.

Levin, P. H. 1976. *Government and the planning process.* London: Allen & Unwin.

Levine, Robert A. 1972. *Public planning: Failure and redirection.* New York: Basic Books.

Litwak, Eugene, and Henry J. Meyer. 1966. A balance theory of coordination between bureaucratic organizations and community primary groups. *Administrative Sciences Quarterly* 11(1): 31-58.

Mintzberg, Henry. 1973. *The nature of managerial work.* New York: Harper & Row.

_____. 1979. *The structuring of organizations: A synthesis of the research.* Englewood Cliffs, NJ: Prentice-Hall.

Mulford, Charles L., and David L. Rogers. 1982. "Definitions and Models." In Rogers, Whetten and Assocs., op. cit., 9-31.

Neilsen, Lyndsay. 1978. "New cities in Australia: The Australian government's growth center program. In *International Urban Policies: New Town Contributions* edited by Gideon Golany, 315-334. New York: Wiley.

Nystrom, Paul C., and William H. Starbuck. 1977. "Why prescription is prescribed." *In TIMS studies in the management sciences (VOL V): Prescriptive models of organizations* edited by ibid., 1-5. Amsterdam: North Holland Publishing Co.

Pfeffer, Jeffrey. 1972. Merger as a response to organizational interdependence. *Administrative Sciences Quarterly* 17(3): 383-394.

Pressman, Jeffrey L., and Aaron Wildavsky. 1973. *Implementation.* Berkeley CA: University of California Press.

Rabinowitz, Francine, Jeffrey Pressman and Martin Rein. 1976. Guidelines: A plethora of forms, authors and functions. *Policy Sciences* 7(4): 399-416.

Raelin, Joseph A. 1980. A mandated basis of interorganizational relations: The legal-political network. *Human Relations* 33(1): 23-39.

Raelin, Joseph A. 1982. A policy output model of IOR. *Organizational Studies* 3(3): 243-267.

Rogers, David L., and Charles L. Mulford. 1982. "Consequences." In Rogers, Whetten and Assocs., op. cit., 73-94.

Rogers, David L., David A. Whetten and Assocs. 1982. *Interorganizational coordination: Theory, research, and implementation.* Ames, IA: Iowa University Press.

Ross, G. Alexander. 1979. The emergence of organization sets in three ecumenical disaster recovery organizations: An empirical and theoretical exploration. *Human Relations* 33(1): 23-39.

Rubenstein, James. 1978. "French new towns policy." In Golany, ed. op. cit., 249-276.

Sofer, Cyril. 1972. *Organizations in theory and practice.* New York: Basic Books.

Turner, Alan. 1978. "New towns in the developing world: Three case studies." In Golany, ed. op. cit., 249-276.

Van de Ven, Andrew H., Dennis C. Emmet and Richard Koenig Jr. 1975. "Frameworks for interorganizational analysis." In *Interorganization Theory* edited by Anant R. Negandhi, 20-33. Kent, OH: Kent State University Press.

Warren, Roland L., Ann Bergunder and Stephen Rose. 1974. *The structure of urban reform.* Lexington, MA: D.C. Heath.

Weaver, Warren. 1948. Science and complexity. *American Scientist* 36:536-544.

Weiss, Janet A. 1981. Substance vs. symbol in administrative reform: The case of human services coordination. *Policy Analysis* 7(1): 21-45.

Whetten, David A. 1982. "Objectives and issues: Setting the stage." In Rogers, Whetten and Assocs. op. cit., 3-8.

Williams, Walter. 1975. Implementation analysis and assessment. *Policy Analysis* 1(3): 531-566.

Williams, Walter W. with Betty Jane Narver. 1980. *Government by agency: Lessons from the social program grants-in-aid experience.* New York: Academic Press.

Winner, Langdon. 1975. "Complexity and the limits of human understanding." In LaPorte, ed., op. cit., 40-56.

Wren, Daniel A. 1967. Interface & interorganizational coordination. *Academy of Management Journal* 10(1): 69-82.

Zammuto, Raymond F. 1982. *Assessing organizational effectiveness.* Albany, NY: State University of New York Press.

CHAPTER 11

Industrial Policy,
Full Employment Policy
and a Stakeholder Theory of the Firm

R. Edward Freeman and William M. Evan

Introduction

There has been much recent debate on the issues of industrial policy (IP) and full employment policy (FEP). A constant barrage of "new ideas" from the popular and scholarly press asks citizens to consider business-government-labor partnerships, job training programs, import barriers, domestic content legislation, plant closing prohibitions, employee bailouts of failing firms, incentives for high technology industries, incentives for low technology industries, smokestack subsidies, etc. The list of proposals seems endless. Most of these proposals accept the current state of the modern corporation as a constraint and argue that the power of government must be used either to direct corporate resources and decisions in one way or another, or to pay for the nonprudent decisions of the past.

We shall adopt a quite different line of argument in this paper. We shall suggest a revision of the currently received theory of managerial capitalism, and argue that if such a revision is implemented, the debate over industrial policy and full employment policy becomes much less interesting. By viewing the corporation as a marketplace for the voluntary exchanges among customers, suppliers, stockholders, employees and the local community, we can capture the intent and the effects of those who would reform the role of business and government in a democratic society.

It is first necessary to realize that the modern corporation has evolved to occupy a place of supreme economic and political importance in Western society. And it is the corporation that is the means of wealth production. Without the corporation there can be no question of industrial policy or any question of full employment policy. Rather than constrain the corporation to act in a certain fashion we must sustain the economic progress it has wrought. To do so we must revitalize the notion of managerial capitalism.

Managerial capitalism gives corporate managers a large degree of discretion to act in a manner which affects the interests of stockholders. However, these managerial actions also affect customers, suppliers, employees, and the local communities in which the firm operates. These groups may be said to have a stake in the firm and we shall call them "stakeholders." If we replace the notion that managers bear a fiduciary relationship to stockholders with the notion that managers bear a fiduciary relationship to stakeholders, the traditional shared-power problem among principals and agents is complicated enormously. However, the resulting form of capitalism, based on the principle of "respect for persons," which we call "Kantian Capitalism," is preferable to the current state of affairs. In a system of Kantian Capitalism, the concept of shared power is critical. The purpose of this essay is to examine the shared-power problems in a stakeholder theory of the firm, and to pay special attention to the issues of industrial policy and full employment policy. However, a number of preliminaries are necessary.

First, we shall sketch the argument for a stakeholder theory of the firm, or Kantian Capitalism. Second we shall show how a stakeholder theory leads to two related shared-power problems. Third we shall discuss three methods of "solving" the shared- power problems, relying on some concepts from bargaining and collective choice theory. Fourth, we shall argue that once we understand the stakeholder conception of the firm, the debate over full employment policy and industrial policy is reshaped, for these decisions can be made, in large part, *within the firm* through a network of stakeholders who share power and responsibility for the firm. The role of government is reduced drastically. Finally we shall sketch a program of further research.

From Stockholder to Stakeholder[1]

It has long been the gospel and conventional wisdom that management bears a fiduciary relationship to stockholders. In recent years managerial economists have affirmed this gospel in their argument that the corporation is a nexus of contracts among the owners of the factors of production and customers, with all other parties having residual claims (Coase 1937; Jensen and Meckling 1976; Cheung 1983). The theory of managerial capitalism claims that if management pursues the interests of stockholders to the fullest extent possible, then the public interest will be served. For managers to pursue stockholder interests, they must be free to act in the marketplace. The marketplace is conceptualized as a place where "there are voluntary exchanges among consenting adults." The law of corporations acknowledges the requirement for management to act in the interests of stockholders, and for directors to fulfill their duty of care to stockholders through exercising sound business judgment. In recent times there have been a number of challenges to the stockholder theory from the legal, economic, moral and political points of view. We shall briefly describe each challenge, having more fully articulated them in Evan and Freeman (1984).

While the law of corporations clearly states that the firm is to be run in the interests of stockholders, the legal system as a whole has evolved to take the interests of other parties into account.

Consumer protection has evolved through the products liability law, and administrative decisions of agencies such as the Federal Trade Commission and the Consumer Product Safety Commission. The supplier-firm-customer chain has been constrained by antitrust law and legislation such as the Foreign Corrupt Practices Act. Employees come under the aegis of the National Labor Relations Act, the civil rights acts, etc. The rights of stockholders are tacitly recognized in the securities law and the existence of the Securities and Exchange Commission. The rights of local communities have begun to be addressed by environmental law, and historic cases such as Marsh v. Alabama. While these changes in the legal system have taken a minimalist approach, they do raise the issue for managerial capitalism of "in whose interest ought the firm to be managed."[2]

The economic challenge to managerial capitalism rests on the concepts of externalities, moral hazards, and the avoidance of competitive behavior. In its perennial criticism of government intervention and regulation of the market-place, management espouses the "invisible hand" doctrine contending that, left to its own competitive devices, the marketplace will create the greatest good for the greatest number. However, the existence of the "tragedy of the commons" gives rise to the argument that markets sometimes fail when firms seek to internalize the benefits of their actions and externalize the costs. Thus, government is necessary to regulate the commons. Air and water pollution are the most common examples. Similarly, the existence of moral hazards distorts the "optimal" consumption and production patterns of certain goods and services. Finally, the existence of monopoly power suggests that firms seek to avoid competition, and to monopolize a "market niche." Thus, managerial capitalism has become an economic myth and constraints have emerged so that management cannot and does not act exclusively in the interests of stockholders.[3]

The corporation has also come under increased moral scrutiny for its actions. If corporate actions violate the rights of others, or harm and benefit some groups at the sole expense of other groups, then we must question the moral worth of the current form of corporate organization. It is morally impermissible to use corporate property to harm others or violate their rights, even if doing so is in the interests of stockholders. McMahon (1981) has argued that the marketplace contains some moral assumptions which must be squared with our notions about common morality (Donagan 1977).[4] Freeman and Evan (1987) have argued that any justification of managerial capitalism must address two principles:

1) *Principle of Corporate Effects*. The corporation and its managers are responsible for the effects of their actions on others.

2) *Principle of Corporate Rights*. The corporation and its managers may not violate the legitimate rights of others to determine their own futures.

While these principles can be seen as minimal, they give rise to the concept of "stakeholders," as a necessary revision of managerial capitalism.[5]

Politically the rise of the large corporation and the welfare state have raised questions about the ability of both firm and state to act in the interests of their constituencies. While there has always been an implicit assumption that government should shoulder the responsibility for the welfare of the diverse constituencies of the corporation, we are seeing increasing questions about the ability and the desirability of government's doing so. No longer can we be sure that the two principles articulated above will govern the workings of the modern corporation. Orwell (1946) has put the point succinctly:

> The real question is not whether the people who wipe their boots on us during the next fifty years are to be called managers, bureaucrats, or politicians: the question is whether capitalism, now obviously doomed, is to give way to oligarchy or to true democracy.

We believe that managerial capitalism can be revised in light of the notion that management bears a fiduciary responsibility to stakeholders (Evan 1976). Thus, we propose to acknowledge what has become increasingly obvious, that actions of the firm can significantly affect the current and future prospects of customers, suppliers, employees, stockholders, and the local community, and further, that the firm has some obligation, in accordance with the two principles articulated above, to act in the interests of these groups. Management of the firm then bears the obligation to act as fiduciary to stakeholders, rather than only to stockholders. Figure 1 depicts a "stakeholder model of the firm." There is obviously much more that needs to be said in support of this claim and much further research that needs to be done. However, we can begin to articulate some of the issues which any stakeholder theory must address.[6]

We propose two principles of "stakeholder management" to serve as guiding ideals in the revision of the theory of the firm. These principles are consistent with the Principle of Corporate Effects and the Principle of Corporate Rights.

Stakeholder Management Principles

(P1) The corporation should be managed for the benefit of its stakeholders, its customers, suppliers, owners, employees and local communities. The rights of these groups must be ensured, and further these groups must participate, in some sense, in decisions which substantially affect their welfare.

(P2) Management bears a fiduciary relationship to stakeholders and to the corporation as an abstract entity. It must act in the interests of "the stakeholders" as their agent, and it must act in the interest of "the corporation" to ensure the survival of the firm and the safety of the long-term stakes of each group.

P1 acknowledges the Principle of Corporate Effects and the Principle of Corporate Rights. It further ensures that groups will not be used as means to an end without their permission. P1 is ultimately derivable from some notion of Kantian morality, but it is a consistent prescription given the legal, economic, moral and political challenges to the stockholder view of the firm. It preserves the essential notions of capitalism, for markets must be allowed to operate in an unrestricted way if each group is to benefit from the actions of the firm.

P2 acknowledges the need for managerialism, if efficiency concerns of the large firm are to be retained. However, P2 requires that managers take a broader view of their constituency, again as required by the current challenges to the theory of the firm. By being responsive to stakeholders, management ensures the long term health and survival of the firm.

We intend these principles of stakeholder management to be both a positive description of the reforms now underway from a legal, economic, moral and political point of view, and normative to the extent that they represent a conception of the firm that is more consistent with notions of Jeffersonian democracy and Kant's principle of Respect for Persons. We envision a board of directors consisting of representatives of customers, suppliers, employees, stockholders, local community, and a director who represents "the long term health of the corporation." Given that P1 and P2 yield the general concept of a stakeholder theory of the firm, there are many different conceptions, or more concrete instantiations of the principles. We issue a plea for experiment rather than a call for structural change through government action. However, if these principles are to be meaningful, we must address the difficult shared-power problems which they raise.

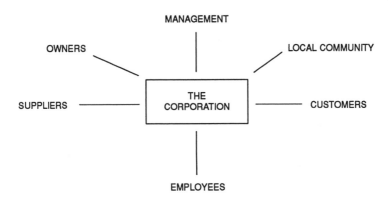

Figure 11-1   A Stakeholder Model of the Corporation

Shared Power and the Theory of the Firm

The stockholder theory of the firm yields at first glance a very simple shared-power problem known in the literature as "the principal-agent problem": how can management act in the interests of stockholders? (Ross 1973; Mitnick 1975; Jensen and Meckling 1976; Baiman 1982) This issue yields a number of questions: 1) How does the principal, P, design an incentive system for the agent, A, so that A represents P's interest? 2) How does P design a monitoring system so that P can receive accurate information to assess A's performance? 3) How does A act in P's interest while pursuing his own goals? and, 4) What is the role of the fiduciary norm? The principal-agent literature assumes that it is relatively clear, what is in the individual interest of P and what is in the individual interest of A. The problem comes in combining these interests in an efficient way, assuming that P is risk averse and that A is risk neutral. The principal-agent literature assumes that A will act in A's interest if there is no proper economic incentive for A to act in P's interest. It assumes that the fiduciary norm has little motivating force absent economic incentives. The stockholder theory implies that all other parties to the firm are either residual claimants (local communities and some employees) or express their power through a market relationship where prices reflect their level of power.

These difficult questions are compounded when we consider the requirements of P2 above. In essence there are "multiple-principals" for management, and hence multiple principal-agent problems. The interests of these principals do not necessarily coincide nor do they necessarily conflict. It is far from clear that the standard assumptions of the principal-agent literature hold, for not all of the principals may have the same risk functions, and further, there is little guarantee that an efficient outcome is even discoverable by management. In essence the multiple-principal

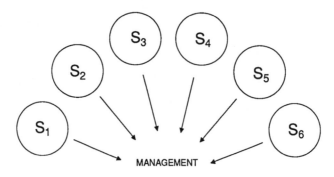

Figure 11-2 Management as Agent for Multiple Stakeholders

problem has two more fundamental aspects: 1) In whose interest does management act? and, 2) What is that interest? Thus, the principal-agent problem becomes a problem, in our view, of who shares power in the firm and how does power sharing occur. There are at least two ways to conceptualize the resulting shared-power issues.

Figure 2 depicts the schema whereby management is the agent of multiple principals. Power is shared through managerial action. Thus, management has an obligation to act in the interests of S1, an obligation to act in the interests of S2, etc. In most real problems the interests of these groups both coincide and conflict. A policy which benefits stockholders may not necessarily benefit customers or employees. On the other hand, a policy can benefit all stakeholders, but some more than others. If management is the agent for each then it is left with contradictory directives, or the need to determine how to balance the interests of all of the groups. Each of the principals is left with the problem of how to structure an incentive system for management to put the principal's interests first. Figure 2, in essence conceptualizes the shared-power problem as a more traditional principal-agent problem in economic terms, or as a problem of constituency representation in political terms.

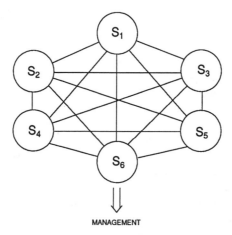

MANAGEMENT

Figure 11-3   Management as Agent for Collective Interest of Stakeholders

Figure 3 depicts the schema whereby management is the agent of the collective consisting of (S1, S2,...). While the fiduciary norm is clearer in this case: management must act in the interests of the collective; it is far from trivial how management is to determine that collective interest. Management is no longer torn among competing interests, it has the directive to act in the collective interest. Principals must resolve their conflict, so that it is possible for management to act in the collective interest. They share power by establishing governance mechanisms and procedures which guide management to act in their interest in areas where management has discretion.

With either interpretation we need some way of resolving conflicting interests, before we can begin to address the issue of incentive and monitoring systems. In the *individual interpretation* of Figure 2, management must resolve conflicts, but do so in a way that is true to the interests of each party. While in the *collective interpretation* of Figure 3, principals must resolve their conflicts and coordinate their interests, or else delegate to managment the right to do so.

Three Methods

The shared-power problem which we have described has been implicitly addressed in a large body of social science literature — most precisely in decision and game theory. Decision and game theory offer at least three methods for conceptualizing the generic problem of interdependent interests: 1) an underlying metric; 2) a collective choice mechanism; and, 3) a bargaining game. We shall discuss each in turn in hope of yielding some insight into the possibility for solution concepts.

An Underlying Metric

Let us suppose that management faces a set of alternative decisions for the firm, A, each of which has some "payoff" to the stakeholders in the firm. It would be a nice solution to our problem, if there were some way of measuring and comparing the payoffs to each group so that management could follow a simple decision rule, such as choosing that decision which had the largest possible payoff.

Is there some real-valued utility function, U, such that management can calculate U("Ai") for each "Ai" in A? Then we can define whether "Ai" is better than "Aj" simply by looking at the corresponding utilities.

The individual utilities to each stakeholder are not necessarily comparable, since we know that one person's heaven is another's hell. Indeed one of the strengths of modern utility theory since von Neumann and Morgenstern (1946) is the discrediting of the notion of interpersonal comparisons of utility. We need some underlying metric, or some transferrable commodity, if we are to make the needed interpersonal comparisons.

Corporate profits are an obvious candidate for the underlying metric, for if we could calculate the effects of a decision on the profit function of the corporation, and how that profit function affects each stakeholder in turn, then we could derive the needed utility function. Unfortunately such calculations are more artistic than scientific. It is far from trivial to calculate the effects of a particular decision, even an important strategic decision, on the profits of the firm, and even harder to calculate the effects of a particular level of profitability on a stakeholder group, such as the local community. We need some metric which translates corporate benefits into stakeholder benefits, and it appears as if that metric must be an unobtainable ideal for the present time.

Even if we had such a metric, note that it would give us a means to calculate a collective worth to particular alternatives. It would be a further feat to derive a decision rule which tells management which alternative to choose. It is not obvious that management should choose that alternative which maximizes the collective utility, except on the collective interpretation of Figure 3 above. If a particular alternative produces a greater return for several stakeholders at the expense of one group, then that decision rule is in violation of the principles of stakeholder management.[7] The fact is that government industrial policies implicitly assume an underlying metric. When industries become noncompetitive and government "forces" them to be more competitive, for whatever reason, it in essence makes wealth transfers from one group of stakeholders to another group of stakeholders. For example, the case of the Chrysler bailout can be viewed as government making stockholders of some banks the losers (among others) and stockholders of Chrysler the winners (among others).

A Collective Choice Mechanism

Is there a mechanism or process by which the principals, or management acting in their interest, can determine the best alternative given only information about the preferences of the principals? In short, is there a voting scheme which can be used to determine the best outcome?

Unfortunately, we are faced with the stunning result due to Arrow (1951) that there is no rational collective choice procedure which 1) always gives an answer; 2) yields Pareto efficient results; 3) is independent of the addition of irrelevant alternatives; 4) is nondictatorial; and 5) satisfies certain rationality constraints on the preferences of the principals. Thirty years of research has led to a deep understanding of the results in this area, yet there is little consensus on the interpretation or importance of the results.[8] Some work has emerged to the effect that if the preferences of the parties are "homogeneous" or if there are interpersonal comparisons of a certain sort then the result can be avoided (McClennen 1983; Riker 1982). However, we now have the problem of the underlying metric, or the problem of inducing homogeneity, precisely the issues which the spirit of Jeffersonian democracy is supposed to avoid.

One might well wonder why a theory of the firm is concerned with so abstract a result as Arrow's Theorem. Why ask more from the theory of the firm than we ask of democracy in general? Our answer is simple, for we are trying to articulate an alternative conception of the firm which overcomes the problem of agents being nonresponsive to their constituents. The ideal of nondictatorship is a crucial underpinning of our two principles. If our conception is to be preferable to the status quo, then we must minimize the ability of management to manipulate the collective choice mechanism, and the incentives of parties not to truly reveal their preferences. It is our reading of the Arrow literature that it warns us precisely of the dangers of "statism," namely, that it can be found in many guises, some of them democratic.

Given the results in the theory of collective choice, we are left with making the preferences of one group dictatorial,[9] or of adopting voting rules under which principals have incentives to manipulate, or a voting scheme which gives no action when there are intransitivities. Unfortunately, given our task, we must await further results.

A Bargaining Game

The third alternative comes from the theory of interdependent choice, known as the bargaining game. The bargaining game assumes that the players are in a situation where their interests both conflict and coincide, and further, each will do better by cooperating with the others than by not cooperating. Thus, if all agree to pursue their individual interests jointly, each is better off.[10]

The theory rests on the notion that there is a point of disagreement, or conflict, or threat, and that the payoffs to the individual players at the conflict point represent what each would obtain by not cooperating. Bargaining theory then gives conditions for the existence of an equilibrium solution.

The interpretation for a stakeholder theory of the firm seems quite natural, for it is precisely the issue of the conflicting interests and coincident interests of the claimants of the firm which led us to formulate such a view. Analogous to Hirschman's (1970) model of exit, voice and loyalty there is a point where the stakeholders will exit the firm. Hence there is a conflict point past which no stakeholder will be pushed, else it will act alone. This point is derivable from the stakes of each group and gives each its incentive to bargain.

Owners have some financial stake in the form of stocks, bonds, etc., and expect some kind of financial return. They have either given their money directly to the firm to be used, or have some historical claim made through a series of morally justified exchanges (Nozick 1975). The firm affects their livelihood, or if a substantial portion of their retirement income is in stocks or bonds, their ability to care for themselves when they can no longer work. Of course, the stakes of owners will differ by type of owner, preferences for money, moral preferences, etc., as well as by type of firm. The owners of AT&T are quite different from the owners of Ford Motor Co., with one being widely dispersed among 3 million stockholders, while the other is held by a small group of family, as well as a large group of public, stockholders. If the firm does not meet their underlying needs, then they will sell the stocks and bonds that they own.

Employees have their jobs and usually their livelihood at stake, for they have specialized skills for which there is usually no perfectly elastic market. In return for their labor, they expect some security, wages and benefits, and meaningful work. In return for their loyalty, the corporation is expected to provide for them and carry them through difficult times. Employees are expected to follow the instructions of management most of the time, to speak favorably about the company, and to be responsible citizens in the local communities in which the company operates. The evidence that such policies and values as described here lead to productive company-employee relationships is compelling. It is equally compelling to realize that the opportunities for "bad faith" on the part of both management and employees are enormous. "Mock participation" in quality circles, singing the company song and wearing the company uniform to please management, authoritarian supervisors — all lead to distrust and nonproductive work. When employees are no longer able to pursue their life projects through the firm they will leave, sell their skills elsewhere, obtain new skills or look for government and charity to help them pursue their projects.

Suppliers, interpreted in a stakeholder sense, are vital to the success of the firm, for raw materials will determine the final product quality, price, etc. In turn the firm is a customer of the supplier, and vital to the success and survival of the supplier. When the firm treats the supplier as a valued member of the stakeholder network, rather than a door-to-door salesperson, the supplier responds when the firm is in need. Chrysler traditionally had very close ties with its suppliers, even to the point of allegations of illegal payments. And, when Chrysler was on the brink of disaster, the suppliers responded with price cuts, accepting late payments, financing, etc. Supplier and company can rise and fall together. Of course, again, the particular supplier relationships will depend on a number of variables such as number of suppliers, whether the supplies are finished goods or raw materials, etc. When dealing with a firm becomes too costly, suppliers will search elsewhere for business opportunities.

Customers exchange resources for the products of the firm, and in return receive the benefits of the products. Customers provide the lifeblood for the firm in the form of revenue. Given the level of reinvestment of earnings in large corporations, customers indirectly pay for the development of new products and services. Peters and Waterman (1982) have argued that "being close to the customer" leads to success with other stakeholders, and that a distinguishing characteristic of some companies who have performed well is their emphasis on the customer. By paying attention to customers' needs, management automatically addresses the questions surrounding suppliers and owners, and it seems that the "ethic of customer service" carries over to the community. Almost without fail the "excellent companies" in Peters and Waterman's study have good reputations in the community. We would argue that Peters and Waterman have found multiple applications of Kant's dictum "Treat persons as ends unto themselves," and it should come as no surprise that persons respond to such treatment, be they customers, suppliers, owners, employees, or the local community. The real surprise is that the application of Kant's rule is so novel in a theory of what counts as good management practice. Obviously, customers can exit when the firm no longer meets its needs, and buy products and services elsewhere.

The local community grants the firm the right to build facilities and benefits from the tax base and economic and social contributions of the firm. In return for the provision of local services, the firm is expected to be a good citizen, as is any person be it "natural or artificial." The firm cannot expose the community to unreasonable hazards in the form of pollution, toxic waste, etc. If for some reason the firm must leave a local community it is expected to work with local leaders to make the transition as smooth as possible. Of course, the firm does not have perfect knowledge, but when it discovers some danger or runs afoul of new competition, it is expected to inform the local community and to work with the community to overcome any problem. When the firm mismanages its relationship with the local community, it is in the same position of a citizen who commits a crime. It has violated the implicit social contract with the community and should expect to be distrusted and ostracized. It should not be surprised when punitive measures are invoked.

We have argued that the bargaining game gives a natural interpretation to the problems: In whose interest is management to act and what is that interest? In essence we have claimed that management must act in the collective interest of the stake-holders, as determined by a fair bargaining process. Whether the stakeholders and their representatives actually engage in such a process or not is theoretically irrelevant as long as they have some monitoring system to ensure that management simulates the appropriate interests. However, in practice we would expect such bargaining processes to be both positive and normative for boards of directors in a "stakeholder firm." Note further that the bargaining model is consistent with P1 and P2, for stakeholders participate in bargaining for the future of the firm, and the firm is then managed according to the outcome of this process.

Of course, one might object that the bargaining model does not go far enough, for the outcomes depend on the exit points of each group. If a group has little to threaten, then it will not do well absolutely (though it will do well relative to its threat potential) in the resulting bargaining game. We have no answer to this objection, but simply claim that if a stakeholder theory is to be articulated that is at all descriptive, it must somewhere be anchored in the realistic bargaining power positions of stakeholder groups.

Full Employment Policy and Industrial Policy

With these rather lengthy preliminaries out of the way, we turn to the problem of Full Employment Policy (FEP) and Industrial Policy (IP) in a world where stakeholders share power. We shall first attempt to clarify the concepts of FEP and IP as they apply to the stockholder theory of the firm, and then show how a stakeholder theory of the firm obviates the need for government action on most issues of this type.

Do FEP and IP amount to the same thing? We shall look at the underlying reasoning for each and argue that in most interpretations FEP and IP are one and the same issue. Further we shall state the case in terms of the rights of parties to FEP and IP rather than in terms of harms and benefits to society. If a case can be made in terms of rights, then we are on stronger moral ground, for FEP and IP can be shown to be consistent with the liberal ideal of "autonomy of the person" (Goldman 1980). The rights of persons, at least the negative rights of persons, trump aggregations of utility, so that interventions by the government or the corporation must be justified in terms of the rights that they protect.

The liberal ideal of autonomy entails that every person has the right to pursue his or her own life projects in so far as they do not violate the legitimate rights of others. In most cases the pursuit of these projects requires work of some sort, so that we might frame the question of "right to a job" or "right to work." Note that this "right to a job" does not entail "right to a particular job," for such a right would violate the legitimate rights of others. Now there are two main arguments for FEP given this analysis of rights.

The first argument notes that in a free-enterprise society there will be temporary shifts in the work force due to the ebb and flow of the business cycles. Some industries prosper at a particular point in time, while others decline and fail. These cycles do not always coincide with a generation of employees. Hence, some employees will lose their jobs in such shifts and in many cases these employees will have gained specialized skills which are not readily transferable. In fact if an employee loses a job because of industry conditions, it is highly unlikely that a similar job with another company in the industry is forthcoming. Hence, employees who do lose their jobs, and who can find no other with their current skills, have their right to a job violated. Now it may be countered that the employee can always find a job doing something, so that even if he or she must take a huge decrease in income and wealth in moving from making steel to sweeping streets, still, there is some job. However, note that the right to a job is a derivative right. It comes from the ideal of autonomy. Given that I choose to pursue a set of projects, and that all conditions over which I have some control allow me to pursue those projects, my right to pursue them cannot be violated at the will of others (unless some more important rights are involved). This is especially true when I have made life decisions to specialize my labor to pursue these projects. Therefore, this argument concludes, government should guarantee, as far as possible, that employees do not lose their jobs because of an industry's life cycle. If employees do lose their jobs for that reason, then there must be available retraining programs, or the government must be willing to hire them or make transfer welfare payments to them.

The upshot of this argument is that FEP amounts to a government policy to protect declining industries. But, this is precisely what advocates of a "Sunset Industrial Policy" want. We must protect those industries such as steel and automobiles which are declining, simply because the massive employment dislocation would be disastrous, or more precisely, the resulting unemployment would violate the rights of employees to pursue their life projects.

The second major argument for FEP is more complicated. In a free enterprise society there will always be some people who are unemployed. Either they have no skills for which there is a market, or there is no growth in the economy, offering no opportunities for them to "latch onto" the system, even at the bottom rung. If they have no marketable skills, are "structurally unemployed," and cannot get any job, then their right to some job or other is violated. Hence, government must train them in some skills or hire them without skills and essentially make welfare payments to them. If there is no growth in the economy, and hence no place to "latch onto" the economic system, then government has the responsibility for creating or ensuring economic growth, by promoting "growth" industries (such as high technology industries), to cause them to grow faster by protecting them from foreign competition, giving favorable tax treatments, etc. On this argument, FEP amounts to an industrial policy for "sunrise" industries, or a call for training or welfare payments to those groups who are locked out of the economic system.

If we examine the other side of the coin we find two major arguments for IP. The first claims that some U.S. industries are no longer competitive in world markets. In a free enterprise system, when a firm is no longer competitive it goes out of business. But, when industries which are at the *core* of the U.S. economy go out of business, then the rights of many other "innocent" parties are violated. Many other industries depend on the steel and automobile industries in the U.S. Therefore, we need an industrial policy for sunset industries to be sure that they remain viable when attacked by foreign competition or at a later stage in their life cycle.

Why are the rights of "innocent" parties violated? There are only two possible reasons. Either some will lose their jobs, and not be free to pursue their life projects, or there are reasons of "national defense" whereby the particular industry is vital to the rights of all citizens. Thus, this argument for IP collapses into an argument for FEP or an argument for national defense, just as earlier arguments for FEP collapsed into arguments for IP or arguments for welfare payments and education/training.

The second argument for IP is again slightly more complicated. Some countries do not have a free enterprise system whereby there is a competitive economy, free trade, minimal government interference, etc. These countries and their firms do not "play by the same rules" as the U.S. When these countries, such as Japan, target a growth industry, such as high technology industries like computers and biotechnology, they can use national resources to make successful forays into world and U.S. markets. They will have competitive advantages over U.S. companies who will not be as successful as they would have been had every firm played by the same rules of free enterprise. The U.S. economy will not expand in a healthy manner since it will be difficult for growth industries to compete. Therefore, we need a sunrise industrial policy to protect growth industries.

But, once again we see that this argument works only if some rights are violated if growth is not as rapid as it could be. And, this is true only if some individuals have their right to pursue their own projects violated by not being able to find a job in times of slow growth. So we conclude that FEP and IP are equivalent except in cases where FEP leads to welfare and education policies, and cases where IP is justified based on national defense. It is interesting to note that this argument is really a restatement of the classical argument for the liberal state to have the functions of defending its citizens, allowing citizens to pursue their own projects, and redistributing income only to the extent that each can pursue his or her own autonomous life goals. We do not need, and indeed we eschew, any appeal to the greater good, the public interest, or other utilitarian notions.

Now there is one additional sense of IP which seems not to be captured by the above analysis, and that is the claim that the effects of government on the firm must be made consistent. We take this claim to be that government must not give contradictory incentives or imply that the firm perform a set of actions which cannot be implemented simply because they are contradictory. The argument is that we need an IP to eliminate these inconsistencies.

Laudatory as this notion is, it will not work, for there is no positive ground for choosing one action over another, other than the reasons given above. Suppose a set of policies in force by the government yield that a firm perform action "P" and that it not perform action "P." What is the reason for saying that performing action "P" takes precedence over not performing "P"? We claim that such a reason could only be because "P" promotes the liberal ideal of autonomy whereas the nonperformance of "P" does not. (Of course, there can be contradictions because the goals of welfare/education, national defense and jobs conflict, but it is clear that the principle of autonomy must be used to adjudicate these claims.)

What would happen to (FEP)/(IP) in a world where Kantian Capitalism is in force? There are three main issues: 1) jobs in sunset industries; 2) jobs in sunrise industries; and, 3) jobs for the disenfranchised. We assume that industries in between sunrise and sunset are thriving, in order to simplify the analysis.

It is easily seen that in existing industries, the "right to a job" is guaranteed. Since employees are a stakeholder with some bargaining power and who sit on the governing board of the firm, they would not agree to massive layoffs, etc. *unless there were some compensation from the other stakeholders.* Owners and customers may decide to buy out some employees' job rights by direct payments, job retraining programs (obviating the need for government action in this area), or other inducement. And, employees could decide to buy out the interests of owners through their pension funds or a leveraged buyout. Perhaps several firms would merge, form joint ventures, etc. (an analysis of the antitrust implications of our view will be postponed for now). Voluntary agreements could be reached, and there would be no need for government to undertake a sunset industrial policy. All effects of a government policy could be had voluntarily among stakeholders in a system where Kantian Capitalism prevailed.

Government could decide that a particular industry is necessary for the national defense. (Recall that this is an area where FEP and IP do not necessarily coincide.) It would do so by imposing constraints on stakeholders such that they could not shut down the industry, or it could willingly make non-optimal purchasing decisions to keep the industry "viable."

A policy for sunrise industries makes no sense in a system of Kantian Capitalism, since these industries will not arise by hiring the disenfranchised. Rather, they will emerge from healthy or declining industries in the form of entrepreneurs with better ideas. These businesses will acquire customers, suppliers, owners, local communities and employees, and within the professional ethics of Kantian Capitalism, managers will "manage the firm in the interests of stakeholders." If these firms encounter tough competition, they will have to resort to creativity and more research and development to stay ahead of the competition, for we must remember that under conditions of fierce competition, whether "fair" or "unfair," the consumer is the winner. Other stakeholders would bargain with the consumer representative on the board, and try to buy out the advantages he or she receives. However, we must note that we are not advocating our view only for U.S. firms. It is even doubtful in this day of far-flung multinationals, whether the locution "U.S. firms" makes any sense. Because our view is based on the liberal notion of rights to autonomy and Kant's principle of respect for persons, it knows no national boundary. If a price is to be paid for abiding by these principles, we can only say that such is the price of the moral point of view.

What about those people who have no jobs, who are not employees of some firms, would not they be disenfranchised under a system of Kantian Capitalism? Obviously not. They would be members of the local community and able to bring pressure to bear on the firm through their representatives. However, suppose that the disenfranchised comprise a minority of the local community. Can we be assured that they will have access to the system which allows them to fulfill their life projects?

To answer this question we must again return to the justification of Kantian Capitalism. It is based on the notion that we should not ever (morally) treat others as means to an end, and we respect others by virtue of their being persons. Rawls (1971) has eloquently translated this principle into a view of justice whereby social institutions are justified (in part) only in so far as they raise the level of the worst-off group (or class) in society. Given Rawls' arguments, we would claim that the corporation and its stakeholders have a moral obligation to raise the level of the least-well-off groups in a community. Such groups include the totally disenfranchised at the top of the list.

While such a system will not be perfect, we can easily imagine a simple system of giving 5% of profits to provide jobs over and above those provided by normal growth in the firm. Obligations would be fulfilled by seeking to train and employ the disenfranchised, rather than give to the charities whose benefits are enjoyed by those citizens who already are able to pursue their own life projects (such as the arts). We can make progress on this issue, again in a voluntaristic manner. In so far as corporations in a system of Kantian Capitalism raise the level of the least-well-off groups in society the need for welfare payments by government to these groups is lessened.

Thus, in the stakeholder view, governance mechanisms will be put in place to guarantee the right to a job for employees, without massive and cumbersome programs of redistribution. We argue that shared power among stakeholders is preferable to the need for government to exercise coercive power. Obviously the transition to Kantian Capitalism involves redesigning many features of our current system, and will require the firms who choose such a route to work closely with government officials. However our goal is to heed Orwell's warning by democratizing the corporation and dismantling the regulatory apparatus of government.

Future Research
Obviously much more work needs to be done to fully articulate a stakeholder theory of the firm. Aoki (1984; 1982; 1980) has begun to work out the theoretical economics of a theory of the firm based on the bargaining model articulated here as applied to customers, employees, suppliers, subcontractors, banks, and stockholders. We need to more fully specify the interests of each group, and to work through a number of "normal" cases of the bargaining game, in order to subject it to a more rigorous empirical test. Do stakeholders and firms make decisions that are consistent with the axioms that have been proposed?

Further theoretical analysis is necessary to explore the application of other models of shared power to the stakeholder problem, such as Saaty's analytical hierarchies process (Saaty 1980) and Riker's coalition theory (Riker 1962). Saaty's model has the advantage of not requiring an underlying metric, while Riker's coalition theory is pertinent since in an n-person situation his theory predicts the formation of minimum winning coalitions. Ideally, further theoretical analysis will be followed with empirical research including observational studies of corporate boardrooms, controlled experiments in a laboratory, and computer simulations.

The public policy implications of a stakeholder theory of the firm are pervasive. If the fiduciary norm proposed in P2 becomes institutionalized, then the public policy process will be less and less concerned with adjudicating the claims of conflicting interests in the firm, and can go about the more traditional tasks of government. If P2 is in force, and if the law evolves to reflect the norm of management's fiduciary duty to stakeholders, then the elaborate legal and administrative mechanisms of the last half century can begin to be dismantled. In particular we have argued that a system of Kantian Capitalism can ensure the right to a job which is derivative from the right to autonomy in the classical liberal conception of the human person.

Finally we issue a plea for experiment. We have argued that it makes "conceptual sense" to conceive of the firm as a network of stakeholder interactions. We have argued that managerial capitalism can be revised along the lines of P1 and P2. And, "Kantian Capitalism" will revitalize the corporation and make it a more productive social institution. Yet, we are far from confident that these revisions can be worked out in fact. The only test for them is experience, and managers and public policy makers alike must be willing to experiment.

Footnotes

1. A longer more complete version of this argument can be found in Evan and Freeman (1984).

2. See Breyer (1983) for a fuller account of the legal argument.

3. Less than perfect market conditions also arise in the interactions of the firm with other constituencies. For an analysis of the internal labor market of the firm, see Aoki 1984; 1982; 1980.

4. There has been a veritable explosion in the literature in business ethics. Two new scholarly journals, *Business and Professional Ethics* and *The Journal of Business Ethics* have been started in recent years. Business have hired moral philosophers, and a spate of studies on corporate values and ethics has been announced.

5. See Freeman (1984) for a history of the stakeholder concept. While the word "stakeholder" is relatively new, the concept goes back at least to the debate between Berle and Means (1932) and Dodd (1931/2). See Mitnick (1980) for the related literature in political science.

6. Again see Evan and Freeman (1984) for a fuller explanation.

7. By choosing the alternative which maximizes the collective utility, we automatically opt for some version of utilitarianism as a moral view. Such a position does not always guarantee the equal rights of the parties involved. See Rawls (1971) for a discussion.

8. See McClennen (1983) for a review of the literature and a substantial bibliography. He argues that the hope of recent research is progress on the issue of interpersonal comparisons.

9. An interesting twist to the managerial thesis is that managerialism emerges as a form of dictatorial collective choice. Figure 2 is equivalent to relaxing the nondictatorship condition.

10. See Luce and Raiffa (1957) and Rapaport (1970) for a general introduction to game theory and bargaining theory in particular.

References

Arrow, K. 1951. *Social choice and individual values.* New York and New Haven: John Wiley and Yale University Press. Second Edition, 1963.

Aoki, M. 1980. A model of the firm as a stockholder-employee cooperative game. *American Economic Review* 70:600-610.

_____. 1982. Equilibrium growth of the hierarchical firm: A cooperative game approach. *American Economic Review* 72:1097-1110.

_____. 1984. Managerialism revisited in the light of bargaining-game theory. International Journal of Industrial Organization 1(1): 1-21.

Baiman, S. 1982. Agency Research in Managerial Accounting: A Survey. *Journal of Accounting Literature* 1:154-213.

Berle, A. and G. Means. 1932. The modern corporation and private property. New York: Commerce Clearing House.

Breyer, S. 1983. *Regulation and its reform.* Cambridge, MA: Harvard University Press.

Cheung, S. 1983. The contractual nature of the firm. *Journal of Law and Economics* 27:(1)-21.

Coase, R. 1937. The nature of the firm. *Economica* 4:386-405.

Dodd, E. 1931/2. For whom are corporate managers trustees? *Harvard Law Review* 45:1145-1163.

Donagan, A. 1977. *The theory of morality.* Chicago: University of Chicago Press.

Evan, W. 1976. "Power, conflict and constitutionalism in organizations." In *Organization Theory* by W. Evan. New York: John Wiley and Sons.

Freeman, E. and W. Evan. 1987. "A stakeholder theory of the modern corporation: Kantian capitalism." In *Ethical Theory and Business*, edited by N. Bowie and T. Beauchamp. Fourth Edition. Englewood Cliffs, N.J.: Prentice Hall Inc.

Freeman, E. 1984. *Strategic management: A stakeholder approach.* Boston: Pitman Publishing Inc.

Goldman, A. 1980. *The moral foundations of professional ethics.* Towota, NJ: Rowman and Littlefield.

Harsanyi, J. 1956. Approaches to the bargaining problem before and after the theory of games. *Econometrica* 24: 144-156.

_____. 1977. *Rational behavior and bargaining equilibrium in games and social situations.* Cambridge: Cambridge University Press.

Hirschman, A. 1970. *Exit, voice and loyalty.* Cambridge: Harvard University Press.

Jensen, M. and W. Meckling. 1976. Theory of the firm: Managerial behavior, agency costs and ownership structure. *Journal of Financial Economics* 3:305-360.

Kalai, E. and M. Smorodinsky. 1975. Other solutions to Nash's bargaining problem. *Econometrica* 43(3): 513-518.

Keeny, R. and H. Raiffa. 1976. *Decisions with multiple objectives.* New York: John Wiley and Sons.

Luce, D. and H. Raiffa. 1957. *Games and decisions.* New York: John Wiley and Sons.

McClennen, E. 1983. Rational choice and public policy: A critical study. *Social Theory and Practice* 9(2-3): 335-379.

McMahon, C. 1981. Morality and the Invisible Hand. *Philosophy and Public Affairs* 10(3): 249-277.

Millstein, I. and S. Katsh. 1981. *The limits of corporate power.* New York: Macmillan.

Mitnick, B. 1975. "The theory of agency: The concept of fiduciary rationality and some consequences." Unpublished doctoral dissertation. Philadelphia: Department of Political Science, University of Pennsylvania.

_____. 1980. "The concept of constituency." Presented to the Academy of Management, Detroit. University of Pittsburgh Graduate School of Management Working Paper WP-376.

Nash, J. 1950. The bargaining problem. *Econometrica* 18:155-162.

Nash, J. 1953. Two person cooperative games. *Econometrica* 21:128-140.

Nydegger, R. and G. Owen. 1974. Two person bargaining: An experimental test. *International Journal of Game Theory* 3(4):239-249.

Orwell, G. 1946. "James Burnham and the managerial revolution. In *In front of your nose: Collected essays, journalism and letters of G. Orwell,* Vol. 4, edited by S. Orwell and I. Augus. New York: Harcourt, Brace and Jovanovich.

Peters, T. and R. Waterman. 1982. *In search of excellence.* New York: Harper and Row.

Raiffa, H. 1982. *The art and science of negotiation.* Cambridge, MA: Harvard University Press.

Rapoport, A. 1970. *N-person game theory.* Ann Arbor: University of Michigan Press.

Rawls, J. 1971. *A theory of justice.* Cambridge, MA: Harvard University Press.

Riker, W. 1962. *The theory of political coalitions.* New Haven, CT: Yale University Press.

Riker, W. 1982. *Liberalism against populism.* San Francisco, CA: W.H. Freeman and Sons.

Ross, S. 1973. The economic theory of agency. *American Economic Review* 62:134-139.

Saaty, Thomas L. 1980. *The analytic hierarchy process: planning, priority setting, resource allocation.* New York, London: McGraw-Hill.

Williamson, O. 1964. *The economics of discretionary behavior.* Englewood Cliffs, NJ: Prentice-Hall.

Zeuthen, F. 1930. *Problems of monopoly and economic warfare.* London: Routledge, Kegan and Paul.

CHAPTER 12

Macroeconomic Stabilization, Industrial Policy and Shared Power: A Preliminary Analysis

Gordon Richards

Introduction

Contemporary advanced industrial democracies conduct economic policy in several dimensions. At the macroeconomic level, monetary, fiscal and in some instances incomes policies are used in order to manage aggregate demand and stabilize real growth, inflation and unemployment. At the single industry level, what has been termed industrial policy has been used to achieve structural adjustment in a sector-specific context. The conduct of both macroeconomic stabilization and industrial policy provide milieus for power sharing. However, because of institutional and other differences in the ways in which these types of policies are conducted, the nature of the power sharing that takes place is likely to differ substantially. In order to gauge the degree to which power sharing takes place, political theory must develop a morphology of the socioeconomic groups involved in macroeconomic and industrial policy, and at the same time incorporate some notion of differences among the institutional centers of power through which policy is conducted. This paper aims at establishing the preliminary basis for a theoretical model of this nature.

At the outset, some basic definitions are in order. Macroeconomic policy is here defined mainly in terms of stabilization, i.e., monetary, fiscal and incomes policies. The institutional basis of alternative stabilization policy instruments, however, is dissimilar. Monetary policy is conducted through a central bank that frequently enjoys a measure of legal autonomy. Even in situations where the central bank is not legally independent, the conduct of monetary policy is usually relegated to a technocratic bureaucracy that may possess only weak linkages with established political parties and organized interest groups. Conversely, fiscal policy is normally conducted through an elected parliament, or by an elected executive of a particular political party, and is therefore more likely to reflect the objectives of political parties and the socioeconomic groupings aligned in their support. Finally, in situations where incomes policies have been employed as an adjunct to demand management, wage-price controls may be conducted either through independent bureaucracies or through governmentally mediated collective bargaining in conjunction with business and labor federations.

Industrial policy is more difficult to define if for no other reason than the usage of the term in the literature has tended to be exceedingly imprecise. The phrase "industrial policy" has been employed in reference to a plethora of different types of policies involving varying degrees of state interventionism in the economy, with the result that what has been connotatively understood as industrial policy frequently overlaps with other policy areas.

The objectives of industrial policy fall within a narrower range than those of stabilization policy. They have to do primarily with domestic industrial development, in the sense of sector-specific growth targets and sectoral allocation of resources. They also incorporate a nationalistic component in that industrial policy has frequently been aimed at protecting domestic industries from foreign competition or at enhancing exports. Further, the notion of industrial policy implies an element of strategic coordination by the government. Finally, industrial policy should be viewed as directed primarily at structural rather than cyclical issues in economic development.

Bearing this in mind, industrial policy can be defined as *systematic, coordinated government intervention in the economy aimed at structural adjustment through sector-specific policies.* It specifically excludes macroeconomic policies aimed at the management of aggregate demand and stabilization of the business cycle. While it may include components that also fall into other policy areas, such as tax exemptions and fiscal subsidies, these should be regarded as industrial policy only if they ostensibly incorporate industry-specific and structural adjustment goals.

Because of the constraint of space, extensive empirical research into the nature of power sharing in economic policy is precluded. Rather, the emphasis here is on the extent to which power-sharing arrangements conform more to macro-sociological models of the political process. Multiple elite pluralism, class cleavage and elite theories can be applied to stabilization policy; industrial policy can be analyzed in terms of established political models such as functional representation, and models of industrial organization such as regulatory capture. The rationale for preferring to look at power sharing in the context of larger theoretical frameworks has to do with the fact that since the policies under study here are economy-wide, the nature of the power-sharing arrangements characterizing them should also be analyzed through paradigms dealing with the nature of power at the aggregate level. In gauging the extent to which power is shared in the conduct of demand management and industrial policy, only highly aggregated models of political participation will suffice, and the issue therefore is whether existing political models constitute accurate representations of the nature of power sharing in the economic policy context, or whether alternative theories must be developed.

Macroeconomic Policy

During the last ten years there has been an outpouring of research on the political dimensions of macroeconomic policy. Largely because of an increased interest in inflation as a political and economic phenomenon. This literature is too extensive to be summarized here; a treatment is available in Alt and Chrystal (1983).

Elite Theories

Several branches of the literature on political economy posit that macroeconomic policy remains essentially an elite-dominated process. In this viewpoint, monetary and to a lesser extent fiscal policy are the exclusive preserve of independent bureaucracies. To the degree that demand management is subject to political influences, such influences must be understood within the context of institutional models of participation rather than more conventional representations of the political process.

In "pure" institutional models of stabilization, the degree to which outside political influences have any impact on monetary policy specifically is subject to the degree of legal autonomy enjoyed by the central bank. In countries where the central bank is subordinate to an elected parliament (Sweden, the Netherlands) or functions essentially as a branch of the treasury (Australia), monetary policy is likely to be subject to stronger political influences than in countries where the central bank is legally independent. The existing evidence, however, is hardly definitive as to whether the legal status of the central bank is a major factor, or even an important one, in the determination of monetary outcomes. Treatments of this issue are available in Beck (1983a, 1983b, 1984) and Woolley (1977, 1984); both attribute some influence over policy outcomes to the degree to which the central bank's institutional status insulates it from overt political pressures. Nevertheless, there is considerable evidence against the prognosis that legal status has been significant as a basic policy determinant. Numerous studies of monetary policy in the industrial countries (cited below) have found a role for non-institutional factors such as partisanship of government in countries where the central bank is legally independent.

From a strictly conceptual standpoint also, the notion of an independent central bank largely divorced from political influences and making policy according to purely technocratic considerations appears difficult to justify, inasmuch as legal autonomy does not imply complete independence. In this respect there are both formal and informal limits to the degree to which even a legally independent central bank can pursue monetary policies that directly conflict with the other macroeconomic objectives of the government in power. A series of channels exist through which elected governments can influence the conduct of monetary policy, even when the central bank is legally autonomous. Political leaders may control appointments to the central bank's directorate and may replace its officers. Political pressure can be brought against the central bank, either within the government or through the media. Even in the absence of an overt conflict between the government and the central bank, the normal interaction between the monetary authority and other branches of government should insure that there will be at least some degree of coordination between monetary and other macroeconomic policies. For this reason, irrespective of the legal status of the central bank, there are likely to be comparatively few instances of protracted divergences between the policies of the monetary authority and those of the elected political leadership, although this does not necessarily imply close coordination in the short term.

The hypothesis that institutional independence constitutes a policy determinant seems even weaker as applied to fiscal policy. Institutional explanations of fiscal policy have normally been limited to the issue of the secular growth of the public sector over time, rather than accounting for shorter term changes in demand management. In the institutional approach, the growth of the state over time is driven by bureaucratic pressures toward self-aggrandizement. The growth of the public sector here takes on the characteristics of an inertial process dominated by a trend toward secular expansion. Examples of this viewpoint are provided in Downs (1964), Niskanen (1971) and Wildavsky (1974). However, even in these works, the institutional model is not taken as a wholistic representation of the fiscal process, and other influences are acknowledged. Moreover, empirical tests have tended to disconfirm it. Analyses such as those of Cameron (1978) and Lowery and Berry (1983) find no evidence in support of institutional explanations, but considerably greater corroboration for sociological and economic determinist paradigms to explain fiscal expansion.

The degree to which elite models are applicable to incomes policies is also unclear but may be stronger in some instances than for fiscal and monetary actions. Incomes policies have frequently been imposed temporarily by governments in order to achieve short term stabilization objectives, and have been administered by bureaucracies responsible only to the government, which may not include representation from organized interest groups. The wage-price controls imposed in the United States in 1971-74, the United Kingdom in 1972-74 and Canada in 1975-78 are cases in point. In such instances, incomes policies have normally served as ways in which to achieve a more favorable short term Phillips tradeoff. Because wage-price cycles in the industrial countries exhibit structural inertia, causing the inflation rate to adjust to monetary impulses only with protracted lags, wage-price controls have periodically been used in order to brake the momentum of inflation and produce a more favorable mix of economic outcomes. To the degree that incomes policies of this type have been used, power sharing may be largely absent, and the actions of private sector organizations and other political parties will be limited to lobbying the price-controlling bureaucracies from outside. In several cases, because of the redistributive effects of controls, they have been systematically opposed by business or labor federations. It is in some measure due to the degree to which power is not shared in such instances, that direct lobbying has rarely been successful in altering wage-price targets, and that private sector resistance to incomes policy has generally involved recourse to non-institutional mechanisms such as black markets or strikes.

On other occasions, however, incomes policies have not involved short-lived government intervention in the economy, but longer-term governmental mediation in collective bargaining. This has been exceedingly common in small open economies where typically wage negotiations are conducted at the national level between business and labor federations, with participation by government representatives, rather than at the single-firm level.[1] Here, elite models are less applicable. Instead, it is more accurate to speak of a power-sharing situation in which business and labor organizations have an actual role in the determination of public policy, since their decisions are subject to formal ratification by the state. At the same time, models of regulatory capture are also probably inappropriate here inasmuch as in the conduct of incomes policies there is a countervailing element of greater political control over the economy. While state-sanctioned collective bargaining involves some access to political power by the private sector, the corresponding element of government participation may frequently subordinate wage-price decisions to political goals and influence factor income shares in ways that would not occur in a free market. In this manner, business and labor may actually sacrifice market power as the price of their access to political power. Examples are provided by unions in Austria, West Germany and Scandinavia which have agreed to wage restraint in return for other income benefits such as transfer payments, or even the more intangible political benefit of helping social-democratic parties remain in power.

On certain occasions, however, this tradeoff between market power and political power has been sufficiently unfavorable that private sector organizations have not been willing to make the economic sacrifices involved. Periodically labor unions have refused to accept wage restraint under social-democratic parties, and have made wage demands incommensurate with wage-price guidelines despite the fact that the stability of left wing government has been undermined as a result. The massive wage settlements engineered by unions in Sweden in 1974 and Australia in 1975 are cases in point. Similarly, the loss in the market power to set wages by private contracts by American unions during the Nixon Administration's 1971-74 controls program was evidently sufficiently distasteful that the AFL-CIO continued to oppose the controls, notwithstanding the fact that they actually shifted factor income shares in favor of wages.[2]

In sum, elite interpretations focusing on the alleged insularity of bureaucracies from outside political influences appear to provide comparatively little insight into the conduct of macroeconomic policy. At one level, of course, institutional interpretations are not lacking in validity: stabilization policy is formulated and implemented by autonomous bureaucracies, and in this sense technocratic factors clearly influence the administration of policy. However, what institutional interpretations fail to take into account is that macroeconomic targets are set in reference to political goals which are not determined by independent bureaucracies but by parties and interest groups. A better understanding of stabilization is therefore provided by analyses linking policy with political objectives of decision makers.

Political Models

The major political interpretations of macroeconomic policy date back less than a decade, originating in pioneering works by Nordhaus (1975), Frey and Schneider (1975) and Hibbs (1977). Of the various models that have been proposed, paradigms linking stabilization to socioeconomic cleavages are the most interesting for the analysis of power sharing, in addition to performing better empirically than competing interpretations.[3]

The most prominent paradigm linking macroeconomic policy to political cleavages is the partisanship interpretation. As initially formulated in Hibbs (1977), social-democratic and labor parties characteristically attach greater importance to the maintenance of full employment, while conservative parties typically accord higher priority to price stability. Expressed another way, the preferences of social-democratic parties are closer to the vertical region of the short-term Phillips Curve at points of confluence of higher output and inflation, while conservative parties will be more likely to bring the economy to the horizontal region of the near term trade-off, with greater degrees of price stability achieved at the expense of higher unemployment and output losses. The same interpretation is applied to fiscal policy by Cameron (1978) and applied to stabilization in open economies where the inflation rate is exogenously determined in Black (1979). There is substantial evidence in favor of the partisanship interpretation as a general model of demand management. Numerous econometric studies relying for the most part on estimation of reaction functions have documented changes in the parameters of macroeconomic policy coinciding with changes in government; historical works relying on qualitative techniques rather than time-series analysis have found comparable results for earlier periods.[4]

The partisanship interpretation relies essentially on the notion of a bilateral class-based cleavage. The policies favored by conservative parties are held to be determined primarily by the interest of the business sector and the middle classes in low rates of inflation and financial stability, while the preference of social-democratic parties for activist policies represents an expression of labor unions' priority for full employment. However, the bilateralism of the partisanship model has been criticized as excessively delimiting. An alternative approach is put forward by Beck (1984), who suggests that macroeconomic policy may more accurately reflect a form of multiple-elite pluralism. Here, while the left-right cleavage still exerts a considerable impact on policy outcomes, there may be sufficient division within or among parties that separate governments will evolve distinctive macroeconomic policies, based in part on differences in the constellation of interests underlying them.

The implications of these models for power sharing are fairly similar. Although the partisanship analysis incorporates more of a class cleavage interpretation than multiple elite pluralist models, it does not represent a model of class antagonism in the Marxian sense. Rather, it constitutes a model of conflict over factor income shares and political power within the context of an advanced capitalist welfare state. Election victories by conservative and social-democratic parties will push policy outcomes in the directions favored by business and labor respectively, but dominance will not be absolute. Because of institutional constraints on governmental power, and nonpolitical constraints operating in the private sector, changes in the balance of power between business and labor do not imply wholesale transformations of society as much as more limited changes in macroeconomic targets. Multiple elite pluralist models differ primarily in that they allow the balance of power to be determined more multilaterally than through a business-labor cleavage, and hypothesize more diverse types of coalitions, including business-labor alliances.

The issue of preferability of multiple-elite pluralist and bilateral cleavage models in macroeconomic policy may ultimately be resolvable as a function of which sectors of society benefit from and lobby for alternative stabilization targets. Stabilization policy, generically, is concerned with economy-wide targets—the rates of inflation, unemployment, real growth, and external targets such as the balance of payments and the exchange rate. For this reason, macroeconomic policy ought not to be analyzed through overly differentiated models focusing on single-interest constituencies rather than generalized models of cleavage that apply to the entire population. Paradigms linking policy to the interests of business and labor in price stability and high employment respectively may therefore possess greater merit than approaches linking policy outcomes with a diversity of specific interests.

While the multiple-elite pluralist and bilateral cleavage models originate in a common body of theory in political science, a wide gulf separates interpretations such as these from interest group theories of political economy originating in neoclassical economics.

In the neoclassical approach, policy outcomes are determined by competition from organized interests which attempt to maximize the benefits derived from public policy. Normally, this argument has been applied to the fiscal area. Here, interest groups demand various types of fiscal benefits—transfer payments, subsidies, tax exemptions, etc.—leading eventually to secular fiscal expansion and chronic deficits. The capture of fiscal benefits by interest groups then increasingly dominates the conduct of stabilization as a whole through monetary accommodation of fiscal deficits.[5] An alternative variant of this argument links monetary policy directly with interest group pressure in that organized labor may "demand" given levels of employment and wage-income growth, which can only be achieved through faster monetary expansion.[6]

From a strictly empirical standpoint, because much of the neoclassical literature has been explicitly polemical rather than analytic, the evidence alleged in its support has tended to be no more than equivocal; extensive theoretical and empirical critiques have been made of this approach in other sources.[7] From the perspective of the power-sharing issue, the neoclassical model appears suspect inasmuch as it links policies that are by definition economy-wide to competition among specific interests. In this model the state serves a function of political brokerage and policy outcomes are determined by an agglomerative process involving mediation among diverse demands. The conceptual difficulties involved in linking this process to monetary stabilization targets which are not directed at individual interest groups are self-evident.

On a subtler level, one of the major theoretical critiques that has been directed at the neoclassical approach has noted that this literature contains an implicit notion of power sharing and incorporates normative recommendations about the optimal distribution of political power that are substantially different from its formal interest group model. The neoclassical approach has normally taken the view that the appropriation of political power by interest groups is undesirable because the resulting state intervention in the economy leads to interference with market mechanisms; neoclassical writers have frequently concluded on this basis that market processes should be safeguarded through constitutional fiat. However, the interests that have been singled out as the most reprehensible in the destruction of free markets have been organized labor and low-income groups, which demand government intervention in the economy in order to maintain full employment and redistribute income. Furthermore, the implication of most of the constitutional measures endorsed in the neoclassical literature is that price stability should automatically be given priority over full employment, and that governments should be prohibited from practicing activist macroeconomic policies.

In this respect, the focus of the neoclassical attack can be seen as the sharing of power at the societal level by labor and low-income strata, the constitutionalist solutions advanced by the neoclassical school have frequently been aimed (whether ostensibly or in effect) at thwarting the political demands of these constituencies. A mandatory balanced budget, a major tenet of classical economic thinking, would prevent the government from undertaking countercyclical fiscal programs in order to restore full employment during recessions. It would also militate against the use of transfer payments in income redistribution. Similarly, constitutional amendments restoring the gold standard or constraining monetary aggregates to a constant growth rate rule would be associated with restrictive outcomes, or in the case of the classical gold standard, actual deflation. In this respect, the normative recommendations associated with the neoclassical school can be viewed as likely to result in the exclusion of organized labor and low-income groups from the determination of macroeconomic policy and the skewing of political power toward organized business and upper income brackets.

The Question of Linkage

Most of the sociological approaches of political economy represent broadly defined models of political behavior; they have not been closely concerned with the issue of linkages between policy-making elites and other sectors of society. The analysis of power sharing, however, requires a clearer notion of linkage than what has been put forward up to now. The hypothesis that macroeconomic policy is determined primarily by the ideological objectives of political parties is not invalid in itself, but it ignores the wider issue of the degree to which these ideologies reflect the interests of socioeconomic groups.

One common theory of linkage in political economy has had to do with the notion of mass support. As initially formulated by Frey and Schneider (1975), governments maximize a utility function based in part on their ideological objectives, but also subject to the necessity of keeping their popularity above a given threshold level commensurate with continuation in office. Tests in other works by the same authors, as well as a substantial literature on the effects of economic variables on public opinion, corroborate the hypothesis of a voter evaluation function based on economic outcomes.[8] Further, there is evidence in an extensive literature on economic voting that mass support is derived not from the evaluation of the electorate at large, but rather from voting constituencies based in socioeconomic classes that normally constitute the electoral base of political parties. In the partisanship interpretation, the finding of mass support for political parties based on economic outcomes is taken as evidence of a significant class-party linkage. In this viewpoint, parties are primarily the agents of a massed electorate divided along income class lines, and power sharing must also be interpreted as taking place on a class level.

An alternative hypothesis is that the critical linkage here is not that between parties and massed electorates, but rather between parties and organized interests. Although this type of approach is essentially closer to multiple-elite pluralist and interest group paradigms than to bilateral class cleavage models, it does not necessarily contravene the basic partisanship interpretation. Rather, it suggests that the policy programs of parties have to do more with organizational ties linking them with business and labor federations than with massed electorates. Here, parties are not so much the agents of income classes as interest organizations. Conservative parties are closely linked through finances and clientele with business federations. Social-democratic parties frequently have their organizational basis as well as their voting base directly in labor unions. This has been particularly the case in the United Kingdom, West Germany and Scandinavia, while even in countries where institutional ties are weaker, unions have often been politically affiliated with left-wing parties.

The interest group interpretation appears to be somewhat stronger as an explanation for policy inasmuch as the stability of electoral preferences toward macroeconomic targets is less clear than has sometimes been argued. Several studies have found evidence that the preferences of electoral constituencies toward inflation and unemployment exhibit considerable cyclical variation, making it difficult to link specific macroeconomic outcomes with the expressed interests of income classes over the business cycle. In this respect, excessive levels of inflation and unemployment may induce cross-over voting and transfers of party allegiance. For this reason, the notion that differences in macroeconomic policy between parties reflect changes in the balance of power between business and labor organizations is probably a more accurate representative of power-sharing relationships than electoral linkage models.

Industrial Policy

The type of power-sharing relationships involved in industrial policy exhibit substantial differences from those associated with stabilization. Because industrial policy is inherently sector-specific, power sharing is much more likely to consist of direct interactions among public sector officials, industrialists and labor unions at the microeconomic level. Furthermore, the distribution of power may be critically dependent on the nature of the institutions through which industrial policy is conducted. Consequently, the emphasis here is more on institutional factors than on broader sociological theories. The conduct of industrial policy has periodically involved central planning and the construction of a parastate sector of nationalized corporations or semi-public holding companies but may also be conducted on a less statist basis through tripartite commissions including representatives of business and labor. For this reason, the degree to which power sharing in industrial policy should be analyzed through generalized societal or more reified microeconomic models depends largely on the degree to which such policies involve central planning as opposed to decentralized intervention in specific industrial sectors.

The Interwar Corporate State

The major examples of peacetime centralized command economic systems in capitalist countries occurred in interwar Europe under the fascist regimes. The degree to which the fascist corporate state is comparable to contemporary industrial policies is unclear. On occasion, similarities have been noted between certain contemporary institutions and the corporatist systems of the interwar period, in that they have involved vertically integrated, sector-specific institutions supported by or licensed by the state.[9] Notwithstanding the common use of systematic intervention, however, the alleged similarities cannot be carried too far inasmuch as the objectives and institutions of interwar corporatism and postwar industrial policy are fundamentally dissimilar. Nevertheless, in order to evaluate power sharing in the context of state intervention on a comparative basis, some discussion of interwar corporatism is in order.

The relationship between public and private power under corporatism has been the object of a long-running debate. The hypothesis that fascist economies were "totalitarian" and involved the complete subjugation of the private sector by the state is now generally accepted as invalid. The suppression of private sector associations and their replacement with state-run organizations which effectively subjected their members to political control was largely confined to labor unions. While pre-existing unions were replaced by state-run syndicates, the business sector by and large escaped this degree of political control. Instead, studies of the fascist economic systems suggest that what took place under the corporate state was more typically penetration of coporatist bureaucracies by organized business and the expansion of private power. While corporate state systems operated with a battery of controls, the controls were frequently administered by representatives of industries ostensibly being regulated. Moreover, the formation of corporatist systems frequently led to the replication of pre-existing industrial associations within the state and their elevation to the status of government agencies with considerable legal power. The prevailing orientation of the literature on interwar corporatism therefore points in the direction of a regulatory capture interpretation.[10]

There were, however, limits to the expansion of private power, inasmuch as private sector groups could not control the macroeconomic policies and the foreign policies of the ruling fascist parties. Fascist regimes were committed to militarization, which entailed substantial costs for industries not involved in the rearmament effort, both in terms of access to credit and size of markets. The autarkic policies adopted as part of foreign policy strategies cut domestic industry off from external markets. Massive rearmament spending by the regimes led to diminutions of credit flows to the private sector and ultimately to inflationary pressures that were suppressed through controls, resulting in distortions and misallocations of resources. The limits of the regulatory capture interpretation under these circumstances is revealed in the fact that at the national level organized business had become subject to political revolutions that could not be controlled through the corporatist system.[11]

Industrial Policy: Central Planning
Among the advanced economies, there are two outstanding examples of countries that have adopted systematic central planning since the Second World War, France and Japan. These countries represent better cases for individual study despite the fact that most of the industrial countries have established cabinet-level ministries that are explicitly concerned with industrial and trade issues, because of the degree to which they have gone in the direction of full-scale planning.

The institutions and methods of industrial policy in France and Japan differ both in objectives and degree of centralization. Analyses of the Japanese planning system such as Johnson (1980) have stressed dualistic elements in which a series of cooperative arrangements between the government and business has coincided with a system of centralized control over the economy. The power sharing relationship underlying Japanese industrial policy has frequently been described as a government-business alliance that has operated through informal as well as formal mechanisms. Similarities in educational backgrounds and the career paths of political leaders, which typically originate in the bureaucracy, along with personalistic and clientelistic networks have all provided informal channels of interaction between the public and private sectors that have supplemented and reinforced the formal, institutional linkages. In this respect, the "Japanese model" has the quality of a coalition of business groups and political-technocratic forces which has been able to retain its cohesion throughout the postwar period through a commonly held set of ideals and values, and which has been able to perpetuate its political dominance through direct appeals to the electorate based on continuous economic growth.

The French planning system was conceived on the basis of substantially different economic premises from its Japanese counterpart. In France, the private sector up to the Second World War consisted of a mass of small firms that practiced anti-competitive cartelization, and was widely viewed as incapable of achieving the structural transformation of an economy which had seriously lagged in industrial development. As a result, French industrial policy was based on the systematic use of central planning, which aimed at diversification into heavy industry. The Planning Commission, established in 1946, was endowed with extensive regulatory and legal power, which in theory could have led to a virtual command economy in the sectors that were subject to targeting. Its regulatory capacities included the establishment of a complex system of price controls which were aimed less at suppressing inflation than at altering relative prices in order to achieve sectoral resource transfers. In practice, however, the degree to which these powers were used has varied, and France has in fact moved more in the direction of indicative planning from the early 1970s onward after the completion of initial industrialization goals. Nevertheless, up to the government of Giscard d'Estaing which substantially discontinued much of the planning process, the element of "dirigisme" (steering) that underlay French industrial policy has given it more of a centrally directed quality than the indicative planning practiced in Japan.

Notwithstanding the "dirigiste" thrust of French industrial policy, in terms of power sharing it cannot realistically be characterized as complete state control over the private sector. From the 1950s onward following the completion of postwar reconstruction, the Planning Commission has ostensibly attempted to achieve a consensus among business, labor and government technocrats in the development of plan targets, and as a result the actual policy outcomes have reflected a process of compromise among divergent interests. In this sense, the power sharing relationships underlying French industrial policy are better viewed in terms of a limited multiple-elite pluralism, with bargaining and competition taking place within planning agencies, rather than in terms of wholesale dominance by government technocrats. The results of the plans generally appear to have benefited industry at the expense of labor in terms of changes in factor income shares (leading to the temporary withdrawal of major unions from the planning process during the 1950s) and in terms of resulting increases in cartelization and concentration which were sanctioned by planning authorities. The second and third plans in particular appear to have been strongly influenced by the financial-industrial leadership. There are, however, limits to the extent to which a regulatory capture interpretation can be applied to French industrial policy, and in this respect the Planning Commission has frequently adopted targets which have been systematically opposed by the business sector; for instance, planning authorities have frequently aimed at growth rates and levels of employment incommensurate with price stability, in direct contravention of the preference of the industrialists for lower rates of inflation. In this sense, the ultimate implication of French industrial policy has been to concentrate greater power in the hands of independent technocrats than either business or organized labor in the determination of economic outcomes.[12]

Industrial Policy: Consultative Councils

Far more common than central planning in contemporary industrial policy has been the use of tripartite consultative commissions consisting of representatives from government, business and labor. The legal powers of these bodies have, however, varied from country to country.

In Austria and the Scandinavian countries, their power is extensive. In Austria the Economic Chambers operate as legally designated representatives of industry, labor and agriculture, with extensive research and consultative capacities. The chambers also interact with the Economic Advisory Council, which includes representatives of trade unions and independent technocrats.[13] Sweden, multipartite representation exists in the Councils for Economic Planning and Industrial Policy. In Norway, the Ministry of Industry incorporates sectoral councils including business and labor representation. In Finland, multipartite representation exists in the Economic Planning Center of the Council of State, which is responsible for forecasting, program evaluation and planning. In other countries, the roles of commissions are less pronounced. In the United Kingdom, tripartite representation has been used in the National Economic Development Council (NEDC) and single-industry EDCs, although these bodies have served primarily in a consultative capacity and have no political power. In Japan, MITI includes a series of councils with multipartite representation for given functional areas; partially because of the importance of informal contacts, however, the consultative process in Japan has accorded considerably greater weight to business and technocratic elements than to labor.

In the countries where the role of such councils has progressed furthest, they have acquired functions that were previously fulfilled by parliamentary committees and in this respect exert considerable influence over the policy-making process. To the degree that during the postwar period the power of parliamentary bodies has tended to decline relative to public bureaucracies, the business and labor groups that participate in consultative commissions have achieved greater importance in the policy-making process than political parties. The existence of functional representation has in this sense given interest groups a direct channel to policy making, and has reduced the degree to which interest groups have been subject to mediation by political parties in the policy determination process. Consultative commissions have in this sense served a linkage function establishing direct ties between policy-making authorities and the private sector, which have coexisted with and to some degree replaced more traditional parliamentary forms of representation.

One issue that has been raised in this context is whether consultative commissions have facilitated the formation of working agreements between business, labor and government, and in this sense provided the basis for stable interest group coalitions. In support of this argument it has been noted, particularly by advocates of industrial policy, that countries in which consultative councils have extensive power frequently have been characterized by high degrees of political stability and consensus. In Austria and the Scandinavian countries, a remarkable feature of economic policy in general has been the comparative absence of sharp differences between conservative and socialist governments. It would, however, be wrong to attribute this solely to the role of the consultative councils in minimizing class antagonism and facilitating compromise. While they have undoubtedly had this function, causality here has to some degree worked in the opposite direction, and consultative councils can be viewed as a reflection of consensus rather than a cause. In countries with successful industrial policies, high rates of growth during the postwar era enabled the successful resolution of distributional conflicts and led to the formation of explicit or implicit business-labor coalitions; the use of consultative councils facilitated but did not actually cause this process. Conversely, in countries when consensus has been minimal and politics has been dominated by class conflict such as the United Kingdom, the use of tripartite commissions has not led to greater political or industrial stability. Similarly, countries that have not relied heavily on consultative commissions or formal industrial policies such as Switzerland have been able to maintain high degrees of political stability and labor peace due to other factors.

The Parastate Sector

A final dimension of contemporary industrial policy has had to do with the parastate sector: publicly owned industries, or firms with joint public-private ownership. As with consultative councils, the role of the parastate sector has varied substantially across national boundaries. It has been particularly pervasive in Italy, where a substantial share of heavy industry has been owned by semi-public holding companies (IRI, ENI, etc.), in France where large numbers of firms were nationalized as part of postwar reconstruction efforts, and in the United Kingdom where the Labor Party made nationalizations a major component of its economic platform.

For the most part, however, the parastate sector has operated with considerable autonomy, and has not played a major role in economic planning. The management of the parastate corporations has been appointed by political authorities, but has normally been granted considerable leeway in microeconomic planning. In some instances, governments have actively supported the parastate sector through increases in credit allocation, liberalized depreciation allowances, or outright subsidies. In turn, the parastate sector has participated in the implementation of regional and sectoral growth targets. In Italy, the parastate conglomerates have been instrumental in channelling investment into depressed regions; in the United Kingdom, one of the major functions of the nationalized corporations has been to maintain employment and retain industries that would otherwise have failed. At the same time, in both Britain and Italy, the necessity of supporting loss-sustaining nationalized industries has entailed considerable costs to the central government. In this respect, the power-sharing relationships associated with the operation of the parastate sector in these countries may to some degree be subject to a regulatory capture interpretation. Conversely, in France nationalizations were for the most part aimed at bringing heavy industry under direct governmental control. Not only have the boards of nationalized industries been more heavily staffed with government technocrats, but the parastate sector has been more closely constrained to follow plan targets.

As with economic planning, power sharing in the parastate sector involves some form of alliance between government technocrats and private management. In situations where the existing management has been retained, nationalizations can be viewed as implying at least some degree of acquisition of public power by the private sector, inasmuch as heretofore private interests are able to obtain preferential treatment in such areas as access to government contracts, credit allocations and fiscal subsidies. This process is not necessarily limited only to administrative elements. Nationalizations may also permit labor unions to raise wages and shift factor income shares in their favor without risking job losses or endangering the survival of the firm. On the other hand, where the management of parastate sector has been taken over by government administrators, the result is not only an increase in the state's command over resources, but also greater appropriation of economic power and access to income gains by political and technocratic elements. For this reason, conventional notions of regulatory capture do not emerge as fully adequate to explain power-sharing relationships in the parastate sector. Instead, the flow of power appears to be reciprocal, and may involve simultaneous access to political authority by management and labor leaders, and increased control over the economy by technocrats.

Conclusions
Irrespective of whether macroeconomic stabilization and industrial policy share certain common objectives in promoting economic growth and high employment, they must be viewed as fundamentally separate policy areas. Both in view of differences in their implementation, the nature of power-sharing relationships in the types of economic targets associated with these policy areas, and institutional differences associated with macroeconomic and industrial policy are not comparable.

Macroeconomic policy can be viewed as an elite-dominated process only in the sense that it is formulated and implemented by a limited number of individuals in the treasury and the central bank, and directed by the governing executive. However, elite interpretations are inadequate to account for power-sharing relationships inasmuch as they cannot account for the content of macroeconomic policy. The result is that sociological interpretations such as the partisanship model appear to be preferable. While partisanship implies that the conduct of stabilization is proximately dependent on changes in parliamentary majorities, the final determinants of policy can be seen as depending either on the participation of income classes in the political process or on lobbying by organized interests. Given this ambivalence in the existing literature between mass support and interest group interpretations, what is needed primarily to flesh out the current sociological theories of political economy appears to be a better model of linkage. The power-sharing relationships that take place at the governmental level through coalitions between political parties may not always reflect broader societal cleavages, and in this respect contemporary sociological theory has yet to fully resolve the question of the types of linkages between political parties and the public at large that influence the policy determination process.

The types of generalized political theories applicable in the macroeconomic policy context are more difficult to apply to industrial policy. Moreover, in contrast to the substantial body of literature now available on the political economy of stabilization, the existing theory on the nature of power relationships in the industrial policy area is more limited. The regulatory capture interpretation, which is well established in the work on the economics of regulation, is clearly applicable in some instances of industrial policy. Another well-known sociological construct, the notion of functional representation at the institutional level, also provides some conceptual leverage in the understanding of the political implications of industrial policy. However, to the degree that functional representation and regulatory capture have been in evidence, it is difficult to characterize either of these processes as having dominated the conduct of industrial policy to provide a wholistic representation of the power-sharing process. Instead, some further concepts must be developed. The following does not constitute the basis for a general model, but may nonetheless point in the direction of more complete paradigms.

1. The nature of power sharing in industrial policy is critically dependent on institutional factors. Industrial policies involving central planning imply significantly different power-sharing relationships than in consultative councils or parastate corporations. Other possible industrial policy institutions not considered here imply corresponding differences. Consequently, no single process appears to characterize power relationships in industrial policy; instead, what is at stake here is a multiplicity of separate systems of power sharing which coexist with each other in different institutional contexts.

2. In different institutional environments, power-sharing relationships differ depending on factors such as degree of centralization. In economic planning, centralized direction imposed through legal controls is more likely to be associated with a concentration of power toward government technocrats at the expense of

business and labor, even when planning bodies are subject to penetration. Conversely, indicative planning has been more likely to be associated with alliances and cooperation between technocratic elements and the private sector, although it is possible to imagine scenarios in which this is not the case. Similarly, where industrial policy has involved the construction of a parastate sector, the degree to which regulatory capture or state control interpretations are preferable depend on the extent to which political authorities attempt to use the parastate in industrial targeting.

3. These two processes, expansion of private power through access to political authority and expansion of political control over resource allocations, should not necessarily be viewed as mutually exclusive. Rather, they appear to take place simultaneously, allowing for power-sharing relationships to develop on a reciprocal basis.

4. It is also clear even from a cursory review of industrial policy that the concept of power must be defined somewhat differently than in a purely political environment. Inasmuch as economic policy and industrial policy in particular determine factors such as the distribution of income and sectoral allocation of resources, the concept of power must be broadened to include these outcomes. A narrow definition of power phrased along the lines of political coercion will not suffice. Power in the industrial policy context appears to have more to do with command over resources and the allocation of income.

These points, of course, do not establish a full theory of power sharing, so much as set up a "cognitive track" for further analysis. The development of a more general model of the political economy of industrial policy, and of power sharing in industrial policy institutions awaits additional research.

Footnotes

1. For comparative studies of incomes policies in Western Europe, see Robert Flanagan, David Soskice and Lloyd Ullman, *Unionism, Economic Stabilization and Incomes Policies: European Experience.* Washington, D.C., The Brookings Institution, 1983. See also Nils Elvander, "The Role of the State in the Settlement of Labor Disputes in the Nordic Countries: A Comparative Analysis," *European Journal of Political Research*, Vol. 2, 1974: 363-383.

2. For the effects of the Nixon controls of factor income shares, see Robert J. Gordon, "Wage Price Controls and the Shifting Phillips Curve," *Brookings Papers on Economic Activity.* Vol. 2, No. 2, 1972: 385-422.

3. The main alternative viewpoint has been Nordhaus' notion of an "electoral cycle" in which an entrepreneurial government attempts to maximize its incumbency by the timing of business cycles around elections. Numerous critiques, both theoretical and empirical, have been made of this argument. From the standpoint of power sharing, the electoral cycle is merely a simplified elite model hypothesizing a government dominated by self-interest in vote-maximization, and ostensibly manipulative in its interaction with society at large. For references on the electoral cycle

concept, see James Alt and K. Alec Chrystal, *Political Economics*, Berkeley and Los Angeles, University of California Press, 1983.

4. See in particular the following works. In the United States, Nathaniel Beck, "Political Influences on Federal Reserve Policy in the 1970s." Paper presented at the annual meeting of the Public Choice Society, March 1981a; "Linkages Between Political Pressures and Economic Policy-Making in the Postwar United States." Paper presented at the annual meeting of the American Political Science Association, Sept. 1981b; "Parties, Administrations, American Macroeconomic Outcomes," in *American Political Science Review*. March 1982a, 76(1), pp. 83-93; "Presidential Influences on the Federal Reserve in the 1970s" in *American Journal of Political Science*, Aug. 1982c, 26(3), pp. 415-445; "Domestic Politics and Monetary Policy: A Comparative Perspective." Paper presented at the annual meeting of the American Political Science Association, Sept. 1983a; "Domestic Political Sources of American Monetary Policy: 1955-1982." Paper presented at the annual meeting of the Midwestern Political Science Association, Nov. 1983b. See also John T. Woolley, *The Federal Reserve and the Politics of Monetary Policy*. New York, Cambridge University Press, 1984. For bibliographical references on the monetary reaction function in the United States, see Richard Abrams, Richard Froyen and Roger Waud, "Monetary Policy Reaction Functions, Consistent Expectations, and the Burns Era," *Journal of Monetary Credit and Banking*, Feb. 1980, 12(1), pp. 30-42.

5. The major work in this category is James Buchanan and Richard Wagner, *Democracy in Deficit: The Political Legacy of Lord Keynes*. New York, Academic Press, 1977.

6. This point is made in particular in John Burton, "The Demand for Inflation in Liberal Democratic Societies," in *Models of Political Economy*, ed. Paul Whiteley, Pacific Palisades, Calif., Sage Publications, 1980. See also John Burton, Michael Hawkins and G.L. Hughes, "Is Liberal Democracy Especially Prone to Inflation? An Analytical Treatment," in *Contemporary Political Economy*, ed. Douglas A. Hibbs and Heino Fassbender. New York and Amsterdam, Elsevier-North Holland Co. 1981.

7. For critiques of the political implications of these arguments, see in particular Brian Barry, "Does Democracy Cause Inflation?" and David Cameron, "Does Government Cause Inflation?" both in *The Politics of Inflation and Economic Stagnation*, ed. Leon Lindberg and Charles S. Maier. Washington, D.C.; the Brookings Institution, 1985. See also Melvin Reder, "Chicago Economics: Permanence and Change," in *Journal of Economic Literature,* March 1982, 20(1), pp. 1-38.

8. Works by these writers include Bruno Frey, "The Political-Economic System: A Simulation Model," in *Kyklos*, 1974a, 27(2), pp. 227-254; Frey, "Politico-Economic Models and Cycles," in *Journal of Public Economics,* April 1978a, 9(2), pp. 203-220; Frey and Friedrich Schneider, "On the Modelling of Politico-Economic Interdependence," in *European Journal of Political Research*, Dec. 1975, 3(4), pp. 339-360; Frey and Schneider, "An Empirical Study of Politico-Economic Interaction

in the United States," in *Review of Economics and Statistics*, May, 1978a, 60(2), pp. 174-183; Frey and Schneider, "A Politico-Economic Model of the United Kingdom" in *Economic Journal*, June 1978b, 88(2), pp. 243-253; Frey and Schneider, "An Econometric Model with an Endogenous Government Sector," in *Public Choice*, 1979, 34(1), pp. 29-43; Frey and Schneider,

"Central Bank Behavior: A Positive Empirical Analysis," in *Journal of Monetary Economics*, May 1981, 7(3), pp. 291-316.

The literature on the impact of economic variables on public opinion is too extensive to be cited here. For a summary of this literature see Alt and Chrystal, *Political Economics*.

9. For an example, see Phillippe C. Schmitter, "Still the Century of Corporatism," in *Review of Politics*, Jan. 1974, 6(1), pp. 85-131.

10. For major studies of coporatism in Germany and Italy, see Arthur Schweitzer, *Big Business in the Third Reich*, Bloomington, Indiana University Press, 1964, and Roland Sarti, *Fascism and the Industrial Leadership in Italy*, Berkeley and Los Angeles, University of California Press, 1972.

11. This thesis is advanced in particular in Alan Milward, "Fascism and the Economy," in Walter Lacqueur, ed. *Fascism: A Reader's Guide*. Berkeley and Los Angeles, University of California Press, 1976.

12. Central planning in France was met with widespread resistance from the industrial leadership; particularly during the first plan, which was instituted by a left-wing government. Subsequently, however, during the 1950s, France's largest union, the Communist-led GLC (General Labor Confederation) announced its withdrawal from the Planning Commission's consultative process on the grounds that the economic results of planning were unfavorable to labor; it did not reenter until the third plan. Although the targets of the third and fourth plans reflected a greater influence by organized business, it is some measure of the continued opposition to planning by the industrial leadership that the substantial dilution of the planning process that occurred under Giscard d'Estaing was largely supported by French industry.

13. On industrial policy in Austria, see Sven W. Arndt, ed., *The Political Economy of Austria*, Washington D.C., the American Enterprise Institute, 1981.

References

Abrams, Richard K., Richard Froyen, and Roger N. Waud. 1980. Monetary policy reaction functions, consistent expectations, and the Burns Era. *Journal of Money, Credit and Banking* 12(1): 30-42.

Alt, James and K. Alex Chrystal. 1983. *Political economics*. Berkeley and Los Angeles: University of California Press.

Arndt, Sven, ed. 1981. *The political economy of Austria*. Washington D.C.: The American Enterprise Institute.

Barry, Brian. 1985. "Does democracy cause inflation?" In *The politics of inflation and economic stagnation*, edited by Leon Lindberg and Charles S. Maier. Washington, D.C.: The Brookings Institution.

Beck, Nathaniel. 1981a. "Political influences on federal reserve policy in the 1970s." Paper presented at the annual meeting of the Public Choice Society, March.

Beck, Nathaniel. 1981b. "Linkages between political pressures and economic policy-making in the postwar United States." Paper presented at the annual meeting of the American Political Science Association.

Beck, Nathaniel. 1982a. Parties, administrations, American macroeconomic outcomes. *American Political Science Review* 76(1): 83-93.

Beck, Nathaniel. 1982b. Presidential influences on the Federal Reserve in the 1970s. *American Journal of Political Science* 26(3): 415-445.

Beck, Nathaniel. 1983a. "Domestic politics and monetary Policy: A comparative perspective." Paper presented at the annual meeting of the American Political Science Association, Sept.

Beck, Nathaniel. 1984. "Presidents and monetary policy." Unpublished.

Black, Stanley. 1979. "The political assignment problem and the design of stabilization policies in open economies." In *Inflation and Employment in Open Economies*, edited by Assar Lindbeck. New York and Amsterdam: Elsevier-North Holland Co.

Buchanan, James and Richard Wagner. 1977. *Democracy in deficit: The political legacy of Lord Keynes*. New York: Academic Press.

Burton, John. 1980. "The demand for inflation in liberal democratic societies." In *Models of political economy*, edited by Paul Whiteley. Pacific Palisades, Calif.: Sage Publications.

Burton, John, Michael Hawkins, and G.L. Hughes. 1981. "Is liberal democracy especially prone to inflation? An analytical treatment." In *Contemporary political economy*, edited by Douglas A. Hibbs and Heino Fassbender. New York and Amsterdam: Elsevier-North Holland Co.

Cameron, David. 1978. The expansion of the public economy: A comparative analysis. *American Political Science Review* 72(4): 1242-1262.

Cameron, David. 1984. "Does government cause inflation?" In *The politics of inflation and economic stagnation*.

Downs, Anthony. 1964. *Inside Bureaucracy*. New York, Harper and Row.

Elvander, Nils. 1974. "The role of the State in the settlement of labor disputes in the Nordic countries: A comparative analysis. *European Journal of Political Research* 2: 363-383.

Flanagan, Robert, David Soskice, and Lloyd Ullman, eds. 1983. *Unionism, economic stabilization and incomes policies: European experience*. Washington, D.C.: The Brookings Institution.

Frey, Bruno. 1974a. The political-economic system: A simulation model. *Kyklos* 27(2): 227-254.

Frey, Bruno. 1978a. Politico-economic Models and cycles. *Journal of Public Economics* 9(2): 203-220.

Frey, Bruno and Friedrich Schneider. 1975. On the modelling of politico-economic interdependence. *European Journal of Political Research* 3(4): 339-360.

Frey, Bruno and Friedrich Schneider. 1978a. An empirical study of politico-economic interaction in the United States. *Review of Economics and Statistics* 60(2): 174-183.

Frey, Bruno and Friedrich Schneider. 1978a. A politico-economic model of the United Kingdom. *Economic Journal* 88(2): 243-253.

Frey, Bruno and Friedrich Schneider. 1979. An econometric model with an endogenous government sector. *Public Choice* 34(1): 29-43.

Frey, Bruno S. and Friedrich Schneider. 1981. Central bank behavior: A positive empirical analysis. *Journal of Monetary Economics* 7(3): 291-316.

Gordon, Robert J. 1972. "Wage price controls and the shifting Phillips curve." In Brookings Papers on Economic Activity 2(2): 385-422.

Hibbs, Douglas A. 1977. Political parties and macroeconomic policy. *American Political Science Review* 71(4): 1467-1487.

Holmes, Martin. 1980. *Political pressures and economic policy: British government 1970-74*. London: Butterworth.

Johnson, Chalmers. 1980. *MITI and the Japanese economic miracle*. Stanford, CA: Stanford University Press.

Lowery, David and William Berry. 1983. The growth of government in the United States: An empirical assessment of competing explanations. *American Journal of Political Science* 27(4): 665-694.

Milward, Alan. 1976. "Fascism and the economy." In *Fascism, A Reader's Guide*, edited by Walter Laqueur. Berkeley and Los Angeles: University of California Press.

Niskanen, William N. 1971. *Bureaucracy and representative government*. Chicago: Aldine.

Nordhaus, William G. 1975. The political business cycle. *Review of Economic Studies* 42(1): 169-190.

Reder, Melvin. 1982. Chicago economics: Permanence and change. *Journal of Economic Literature* 20(1): 1-38.

Sarti, Roland. 1972. *Fascism and the industrial leadership in Italy*. Berkeley and Los Angeles: University of California Press.

Schmitter, Phillippe. 1974. Still the century of corporatism? *Review of Politics* 36(1): 85-131.

Schweitzer, Arthur. 1964. *Big business in the Third Reich*. Bloomington: Indiana University Press.

Wildavsky, Aaron. 1974. *The politics of the budgetary process*. Boston: Little, Brown.

Woolley, John T. 1977. Monetary policy instruments and the relationship of central banks and government. *Annals of the American Academy of Political and Social Science* 434 (Nov.): 151-173.

Woolley, John T. 1984. *The Federal Reserve and the politics of monetary policy.* New York: Cambridge University Press.

CHAPTER 13

Sharing Power in the Federal System: The American States in World Affairs

John Kincaid

Authority to exercise power in international relations is customarily regarded as being the exclusive province of the general government of the United States. The constituent states of the union are not authorized either by the U.S. Constitution or by the traditions of international law to act as though they were nation-states.

Prohibitions placed upon the states by the U. S. Constitution and the lack of status of states in international law would seem to preclude any role, or at least any meaningful role, for the states in world affairs.

Yet in recent decades, most of the states have entered the international arena in some vigorous and unusual ways, from being direct parties to agreements with foreign governments to serving as public opinion forums on matters of world affairs. Although American federalism does not always conform to juristic theories of federalism—the presence of the states on the international scene is marked by four new and important dynamics.

First, a growing number of states regard themselves as having direct policy interests in world affairs. Second, states have expanded their international policy agendas over the last thirty years. Third, states have asserted an authority to act in the international arena somewhat independently of the United States government. Fourth, state contacts with foreign governments occur more often with subnational than national governments (e.g., states, *provinces, municipalities*).

There appear to be two principal reasons for this activity: reassertions of autonomy by the American states and deepening worldwide interdependence, especially economic interdependence. Indeed, economic concerns have stimulated much of the states' international activity. In certain respects, these state activities are similar to those of nongovernmental actors who have become increasingly involved in international affairs (Rosenau 1980). In a larger sense, however, the behavior of the American states resembles the behavior of subnational entities around the world which have asserted claims to autonomy and self-governance in recent decades, thereby challenging traditional views of national sovereignty.

Challenge to Sovereignty

Every era seems to generate contrary tendencies. The modern era has been no exception. Among the long-term trends characteristic of modernity, two stand out as being singularly important for contemporary life: 1) determined assertions of autonomy and self-rule on the part of peoples, nations, organizations, and individuals virtually everywhere, and 2) an inexorable deepening of global interdependence. Steps toward autonomy seem to introduce new elements of interdependence, while steps toward interdependence seem to evoke new concerns for autonomy. Just as the era of nationalism seemed to come into its own with the collapse of classical colonialism, most nation-states found their claims to sovereignty being challenged by internal autonomy movements and by external forces imposing demands for interdependency if not dependency.

Since World War II, there has been a proliferation of autonomy movements on the part of ethnic, racial, religious, linguistic, and territorial groups around the world. These movements have challenged national governments at a time when "parochial" loyalties were thought by many modernists to have been diminished by nationalism and national development as well as by rising incomes, urbanization, and secularization. Yet these "cosmopolitan" forces have often had opposite effects. Nationalism has stimulated forms of subnationalism, in part, because of fears that national development will erode traditional values, identities, and local liberties. Modernization has provided subnational groups with both reasons and technologies for reorganizing and maintaining cohesion (Young 1976). Thus, nearly every national government is confronted by one or more dissident autonomy movements seeking some measure of self-rule and/or some type of shared-power arrangement, if not outright secession.

At the same time, deepening interdependence is a rising threat to both national and subnational autonomy. The activities of the great world powers and the growth of strong national-central governments, plus rapid developments in communications and transportation, have served to penetrate and weaken virtually all boundaries that peoples, nations, organizations, and individuals have sought to erect around themselves in order to maintain autonomy or sovereignty. Interdependence introduces ideas and forces that may undermine the original goals of autonomy, thereby threatening certain values and power structures.

Growing interdependence is not merely a matter of external pressure, or of the effects of modern communications and technology, it also arises from internal desire. Rising expectations on the part of peoples everywhere for higher standards of living and qualities of life have stretched the resources of autonomous entities, thereby requiring the assistance and cooperation of outsiders. If a people chooses to pursue the insular course of an Albania, for example, then *de jure* sovereignty may equip the nation with formerly unavailable rights and powers essential for self-rule, but at great cost. Desires on the part of citizens for the goods associated with modernity, however, immediately introduce ever greater degrees of interdependence or dependence, which may make autonomy a receding reality. No nation possesses the resources needed to meet modern consumer demands alone. The alternative is to suppress demand, usually in some authoritarian manner, for the sake of autonomy.

In short, the long march toward autonomous spheres of influence, and especially national sovereignty, so characteristic of modernity, has been accompanied by internal and external challenges to particular claims of autonomy—with internal challenges arising from groups and individuals asserting their own claims for autonomy within and against larger spheres of influence, and external challenges arising from deepening interdependence. The sovereign authority of nation-states is being challenged, then, on one side by transnational organizations and linkages associated with interdependence and, on the other side, by subnational organizations and international linkages associated with autonomy movements. Perhaps the nation-state is becoming a "middleman" between transnational and subnational forces. In terms of the apparent preferences for some kind of localized autonomy on the part of so many peoples, modernity may not be moving, and perhaps should not move, toward a single, unified global power regime or even a small number of superpower regimes, but toward a larger number of smaller power regimes built around the preferences of the world's diverse peoples and linked in a complex manner by more or less voluntary networks of overlapping shared-power arrangements that respect the integrities of the world's minorities: an international e pluribus unum.

Power Sharing in American Federalism

As the first new nation of the modern era (Lipset 1963), the United States has fully reflected the tensions and pressures of autonomy and interdependence since its founding. The federal system, which James Madison described as a "compound republic" and others have referred to as a "republic of republics," is now a 200-year-old experiment in self-rule and shared rule involving peoples and polities virtually as diverse as those found throughout the world. While the United States is not necessarily an appropriate model for shared-power arrangements everywhere, the conflicts and achievements associated with those shared-power arrangements exemplify the range of forces and obstacles entailed in any approach to shared rule.

In principle, as a democratic polity, power in the United States is shared equally by all citizens. Sovereignty resides in the people. Through written constitutions, power is delegated to different governments and branches of government, all of which share in the governing authority. Essentially, there are two types of power sharing in the American system. Government bodies are given a share *of* power and a share *in* power. Both types characterize power relations within and between government bodies.

The distribution of powers among the United States government and the fifty state governments reflects the sharing *of* power. Each government is given a portion of the governing power by the people. This type of power sharing is territorially based and looks to the ends of government, namely, the kinds of functions appropriate to each government. Thus, the power to make war and conclude treaties is delegated to the general government, while such powers as education and policing are delegated primarily to the constituent governments. Because the assumption here is one of appropriate functions, not hierarchy, the government of the union of the states was often referred to, in the republic's early days, as the *general* government.

The separation of powers among the legislative, executive, and judicial branches of each government also reflects the sharing of power. Each branch is given authority to exercise a certain type of power within its nationwide or statewide arena. While the separation of powers may look like the opposite of power sharing, it is not because it serves to distribute power across many points rather than to concentrate power at a single point. Furthermore, the branches of government are regarded as generally co-equal, not subservient to one another. The historical tendency in empires and nations has been to centralize power whenever possible, not to divide it among co-equal bodies.

At the same time, the sharing *of* power is not an absolute division. Each government and branch of government is given a share in the overall governing power. In the separation of powers between branches, there are numerous checks and balances in which each branch exercises some legislative, executive, and judicial powers no matter what its primary role. The executive can veto legislation, the judiciary can invalidate legislation, and so on. The supremacy clause of the U.S. Constitution allows the general government to involve itself in state affairs. At the same time, the states share *in* the powers of general governance because they are the constituent elements of the general government. In foreign affairs, for example, treaties must be ratified by a two-thirds vote of the U.S. Senate, wherein each state has equal representation. On the other hand, voting is by individuals, not by state delegations.

The American system of power sharing, therefore, is complex. Neither centralization nor decentralization adequately characterizes that system. Implicit in the idea of decentralization as a form of power sharing is that power may be recentralized at any time by the sovereign center. Hence, the center still sets the rules and does not so much share power as parcel it out functionally and conditionally in a rather one-way manner. The American federal system might be characterized as one of non-centralization in which multiple centers exercise and share power by constitutional right and political force (Elazar 1984). A clear expression of this non-centralization is that there is no single American constitution. There is the United States Constitution plus fifty state constitutions. The authority and/or ability to establish a constitution is customarily associated with a self-governing polity having attributes of sovereign authority. State officials are elected or appointed by citizens of their respective states, not by national constituencies or officials. Thus, the coexistence of a general constitution of limited, delegated powers and fifty constituent constitutions implies neither centralization nor decentralization but rather a sharing of the attributes of sovereignty between and among fifty constituent polities and a general, nationwide polity in which "the people" hold the ultimate reins of sovereignty over both.

The U.S. Constitution acknowledges this non-centralized sharing of power in a number of ways. Most important is that the U.S. Constitution, which is the general framework for power sharing, cannot be amended unilaterally by the general government or by the constituent governments. Amendments can be made only by joint and extraordinary action by both parties (e.g., a two-thirds vote in the Congress and approval by three-fourths of the state legislatures). Similarly, the Fourteenth Amendment holds that Americans "are citizens of the United States and of the State wherein they reside." No state can be abolished or divided without its consent; representation in the Congress is based upon states; and the president is elected through the electoral college, which disperses majoritarianism among the states. Only the judiciary departs from this pattern, by design; however, appointments to the federal courts are made by joint action of the president and the Senate, and U.S. district courts, which handle the bulk of federal judicial business, all have boundaries that place them wholly within individual states. Appointments to the district benches are strongly influenced by senatorial courtesy and/or the preferences of members of the president's own party who reside in the district court's host state (e.g., Wechsler 1954). In short, at virtually every point, the states and the general government share in the action. This is one reason why Madison called the United States a "compound republic"—partly national and partly confederal.

At the same time, neither fragmentation nor sharp divisions of power adequately characterize the American system. Tendencies toward balkanization are present, and conflict is frequent; however, the structure of the system generally compels cooperation and coalition building among constituencies in order for any particular constituency to achieve its ends (Lindblom 1968). Even the formal separations of powers in the fifty-one American constitutions do not establish independent baskets of power but rather interrelated arenas of power, each having a certain autonomy of its own, even while being penetrated by the others. Similarly, dual federalism was more an idea of the U.S. Supreme Court during the late nineteenth century than a practical political reality. The general, state, and local governments have shared responsibility for many domestic policy functions from the very beginning of the republic (Elazar 1962).

The States in Foreign Affairs
Two policy areas, however, are generally held to involve more of a division than a sharing of powers, in which the general government is accorded clear supremacy:

1) interstate and foreign commerce and 2) foreign affairs and national defense. In these areas, the general government need not share power. It can simply prohibit or preempt state action. In the area of interstate and foreign commerce, however, the states are largely free to act where the general government chooses not to act; indeed, the Congress has frequently restrained the general government's reach or at least sought to accommodate state interests. In foreign affairs and national defense, the states are not so free to act, except in the case of actual invasion. There are specific constitutional limitations on state action, such as the prohibition of state treaty making (U.S. Constitution, Art. I, Sec. 10).

Foreign affairs is a hard case for power sharing, a litmus test perhaps for efforts to share power effectively in political systems. Sharing in this field cuts against the grain of modern theories of sovereignty which hold that a nation must act as an entity and speak internationally with a single authoritative voice. Other voices emanating from a nation must be regarded as non-authoritative. The U.S. Supreme Court has accepted this view of sovereignty by arguing, rather remarkably, that the general government's foreign affairs' powers derive not only from the U.S. Constitution but also from inherent powers of sovereignty in international relations, which lie outside the terms of the document (e.g., *U.S. v. Curtiss-Wright Export Corp.*, 1936).

The Logan Act, passed by the Congress in 1799, expresses the single-voice view by prohibiting private citizens from contacting foreign governments and attempting to influence their behavior "in relation to any disputes or controversies with the United States. Significantly, however, despite numerous private citizen initiatives in foreign relations, such as those of Jesse Jackson in 1984, no one has been successfully prosecuted for violating the act. Failure to utilize the Logan Act appears to be not so much a matter of lax enforcement but of federalist principle and First Amendment freedom, namely, that power is shared to some degree in foreign affairs and that the general government is reluctant to silence other voices, except under extreme circumstances.

Consequently, in spite of strong inclinations, coincident with tendencies toward centralization, to graft theories of unitary sovereignty onto American federalism, the republic's compound character continues to poke through the veil of national sovereignty. As former Texas Governor William P. Clements' special assistant for relations with Mexico and Latin America declared: "We don't have to ask the permission of Washington in order to talk to the Mexican government. We are a sovereign state" (Personal interview, 18 June 1980).

This attitude may be typically Texan; yet it reveals a continuing dynamic in American federalism as well as a renewed interest by the states in world affairs. To some extent, states have always had such interests and involvements. Mainly, they have sought to protect and develop their economic bases by having the general government erect barriers to foreign competition and intrusion, and by ensuring their own abilities to attract foreign capital and to export products. Immigration has also been a longstanding issue, both in terms of attracting foreign immigrants and curtailing their entry.

Before the Revolution, each colony pursued independent measures to promote its economic interests by dispatching agents abroad and circulating promotional literature. For nearly a decade, for example, Benjamin Franklin represented the mercantile interests of Pennsylvania and other colonies in London and Paris. Such interests did not end with the Revolution. Indeed, union exacerbated state concerns to some extent, insofar as the new general government could threaten state interests.

During the first fifty years of the union, states had a special interest in developing their economies by exporting resources and products and by attracting foreign capital to build manufacturing facilities and promote internal improvements. At the same time, there were occasional conflicts between states and the U.S. government over international obligations. In 1796, the U.S. Supreme Court voided a Virginia statute that would have cancelled a debt to a British subject owed by a Virginia citizen because the law violated the Treaty of Paris. Later, however, the general government was unable to enforce a U.S.-British commercial convention against South Carolina, which had imprisoned black British seamen under an 1823 state law. After other southern states took similar action, Great Britain opened consulates in the South and negotiated with state officials to gain the release of their seamen and obtain changes in the laws (Graves 1964).

The Panic of 1837-39, however, did much to reduce state roles in direct foreign relations as well as economic activity generally. American securities failed abroad, and many states lost considerable revenue on defunct public works projects. Furthermore, by the 1840s, the American economy was able to generate much more of its own capital, and private businesses were able to forge their own foreign connections. Rapid growth in population and expansion of the western frontier also reoriented state economies away from foreign markets and more toward their own growing domestic markets as well as those of the greater West. Additionally, the victory of the Union in the Civil War seemed to seal the case for U.S. supremacy.

Aside from their domestic "foreign relations" with American Indians, for which the general government assumed ever greater, though not total, responsibility (Taylor 1983), one continuing state interest was immigration. By the mid-nineteenth' century, most states had established immigration bureaus to attract foreign nationals. Frequently they sent "successful" immigrants back to their homelands as recruiting agents. Businesses also encouraged immigration. By 1883, for example, the Northern Pacific Railroad reportedly had 831 agents in Great Britain plus more on the continent (Billington 1979). By the end of the century, however, many states began to urge national controls and restrictions on immigration. Some states acted on their own, such as California's efforts in 1900-1905 to restrict Japanese immigration and alien land ownership and to segregate Orientals. California was instrumental in inserting restrictions on Japanese immigration in the Immigration Act of 1924. As a result, the states reduced their activities in this area.

On other foreign policy matters, the states continued to exercise some influence, primarily through their representatives in Congress and, secondarily, their leverage on the Presidency and periodic appeals to the U.S. Supreme Court. However, with the rise of the modern twentieth-century Presidency, the expanded use of executive agreements rather than treaties as a policy mechanism, the Supreme Court's willingness to interpret U.S. foreign affairs and commerce powers broadly, and the rise of a bipartisan foreign policy during World War II, the role of the states as states in foreign affairs became nearly invisible, except for periodic enactments of state "Buy American" regulations. On the whole, however, the hegemonic position of the American economy largely insulated the states from international turbulence.

Generally, states limited themselves to friendship and exchange programs, such as the Leader Exchange Program, many of which were conducted by or with U.S. agencies (Mettger 1955). When the states did assert their interests as states, they were often viewed as obstructionist, as in the controversies over the failure of the Senate to ratify the United Nations Genocide Convention. In 1955, the Southern Governors' Conference advocated restrictions on Japanese textile imports. A year later, South Carolina and Alabama enacted legislation to encourage consumer boycotts of Japanese textiles. The U.S. government sought to strike down these laws in the courts. During the litigation, however, the U.S. negotiated a resolution with Japan and the states whereby Japan voluntarily reduced its textile exports, and the states repealed their boycott laws (Palumbo 1969).

The decline of state interests in world affairs also reflected a general weakening of the states in the American system during the first half of the twentieth century. Among other things, industrialization and urbanization, the Great Depression, and the successful policy thrusts of the New Deal and Great Society seemed to render the states "obsolete" (Laski 1939), thereby shifting the federal system toward a more centralized power arrangement. The civil rights revolution of the 1950s and 1960s seemed to push centralization still further by pitting states' rights against individual rights and the authority of the general government to protect individual rights, and by diminishing the very legitimacy of the states as republics within the republic. Furthermore, the Cold War, the Korean War, and the Vietnam War—all of which coincided with the rise of the national media—fixed public attention firmly on the exercise of national power.

Fashioning New State Roles

However, just as it seemed that the states had withdrawn from foreign affairs, they gradually reasserted themselves with unusual, if largely unnoticed, vigor in the late 1950s. The National Governors' Conference adopted a number of foreign policy resolutions, and states began to send delegations abroad, often under gubernatorial leadership. The new turn toward foreign affairs can probably be marked at 1959 when Governor Luther Hodges of North Carolina led a state delegation to Europe to attract foreign investment to his state. Fifteen years later, North Carolina claimed to hold the record for 110 European firms having in-state branches or manufacturing facilities. Since then, many governors have led similar missions abroad. A 1979 study found that of forty-four states for which date were available, thirty-three governors had led eighty-four overseas missions, for an average of two trips per governor. The governors of Mississippi and South Carolina made seven trips each that year. In 1979, thirty-nine states hosted 265 foreign trade and business delegations (Committee on International Trade 1981). During the 1980s, the states have been sending more than a hundred other missions abroad annually.

Many factors distinguish the post-1950s state interest in world affairs: 1) The states are involving themselves as states in an increasingly organized and deliberate fashion. 2) States increasingly regard themselves as having vital interests in world affairs, especially international trade. 3) Governors, mayors, and other state and local officials are key participants, if not leaders, in state involvements abroad. 4) An increasingly close business-government partnership has developed around state international economic activity. 5) State foreign activities are less reactive and reactionary than they often were in the past. Instead, states are formulating long-term "foreign policies" and assuming more positive attitudes toward the solution of state and international problems. 6) States have expanded their international agendas, they are lobbying more intensively on foreign affairs, especially trade matters, and state officials are more vocal about foreign policy. 7) Citizens are using state and local mechanisms, especially referenda, as vehicles for expressing foreign policy concerns. 8) States are increasingly cooperating with each other in foreign affairs, although there is considerable competition as well, especially in efforts to attract foreign investment. 9) States are often acting independently of the general government; that is, governors are negotiating directly with foreign officials, especially their counterparts abroad, such as Mexican state governors and Canadian provincial premiers, and states are concluding compacts and agreements with foreign national and subnational governments in what one scholar has termed "micro-diplomacy" (Duchacek 1983). 10) These state activities have, to date, been marked primarily by amicable relations with the general government.

Under the Kennedy Administration, the U.S. Department of Commerce encouraged states to become more involved in the international economy. Commerce was then headed by former governor Luther Hodges of North Carolina. Presidents Johnson, Nixon, and Carter also encouraged the states to seek foreign investments and improve their export capacities. At the request of President Carter, who had visited ten nations as governor of Georgia (Porter 1981), the National Governors' Association (NGA) formed a new standing committee in 1978 on International Trade and Foreign Relations. The popularity of this committee is one indicator of the growing state interest in foreign affairs. Membership increased from twelve to twenty-three governors in one year. About three-fourths of the states now have identifiable policy interests in world affairs and some institutional mechanisms for handling foreign affairs. These mechanisms are mostly located in the executive branch, often its economic development arm, though state legislatures have also begun to add international relations to the jurisdictions of commerce and/or intergovernmental relations committees.

Why are the states developing "foreign policies?" For one, States have obvious interests in trade, investment, tourism, immigration, drug trafficking, and the like as well as in international activities that affect areas of traditional state authority, such as corporate chartering, crime control, public health and welfare, land use, labor relations, and the regulation of banking, insurance, professional activity, wildlife, and the environment. Also, there is no rigid separation between foreign and domestic affairs today. The two are intertwined in what has been called "intermestic" affairs (Manning 1977). As suggested earlier, the structure of the federal system and the persuasiveness of sharing within it virtually invite state intrusion into foreign relations (Palumbo 1969; Henkin 1972). At the same time, the general government cannot be equally and sufficiently attentive to all the discrete interests of particular states. Texas, New Mexico, Arizona, and California, for example, often criticize Washington for being inattentive to southern border problems and relations with Mexico, which are so important to these states. Consequently, state officials have acted jointly and individually to negotiate issues with Mexican officials.

Two major factors that appear to lie behind state activities abroad are those of interdependence and autonomy. Because of its dominant global position during the first sixty years of this century, the U.S. economy was relatively independent and protected against international perturbations. This is no longer true. The economic shocks of the 1970s, especially the oil crisis, have made it clear that the U.S. economy and, therefore, the fifty state economies are intimately linked to the global economy and increasingly locked into competition with other governments and enterprises. The challenge of the new interdependence is evident in the soaring U.S. trade deficit, which grew from $5.8 billion in 1976 to $123.3 billion in 1984. Former U.S. Commerce Secretary, Malcolm Baldrige, reported that each $1 billion increase in the deficit costs about 25,000 U.S. jobs (Associated Press 1984). In Texas, for example, about 285,500 jobs are linked to overseas export business.

Most states have now experienced the new interdependence. Competition from foreign auto makers has been felt strongly in Michigan. Shifts in worldwide mineral production have affected such states as Montana and Minnesota. Texas virtually dictated world oil prices and production from the 1930s to 1973. Now the state competes aggressively for business and investment in efforts to diversify its economy. The new economic interdependence reaches into virtually every sector of state life. As a rural representative remarked at a Texas state legislative hearing on international trade: "We don't raise many automobiles where I'm from, but we raise an awful lot of beef cattle that we have a lot of trouble selling in Japan. It seems to me we have the right to say we will let your manufactured products come into our country—but we expect the same for products we want to trade" (Kidd 1984).

In short, nearly every state has been drawn, willingly or not, into the international economic arena. Each state must, to some degree, fend for itself. Each state economy has its own unique problems and mix of imports and exports, which make it sensitive to particular international events, and the U.S. government cannot, in every instance, formulate general economic policies sensitive to the diversity of the fifty state economies (Kline 1983). At the same time, given the close ties between politics and economics, international economic interdependence has stimulated greater state interests in political developments abroad and, therefore, in American foreign policy more generally. To date, states have confined themselves largely to foreign policy matters of local interest, although the potential for expanding involvement is present.

Not surprisingly, interdependence has evoked new concerns for state autonomy and fiscal capacity. However, since autonomy concerns were already on state agendas because of the drift toward centralization in the American system, states have been able to respond more adroitly to international developments than would have been the case a generation ago. Since the 1950s, most states have strengthened and modernized their governments and tax systems so as to behave more like polities than beggars in the federal system (Elazar 1981; Kincaid 1984). Three-fourths of the states have either adopted new constitutions or amended their old ones to meet contemporary challenges. Significantly increased state and local employment, four-year gubernatorial terms, better staffed legislatures, unified courts, and new planning agencies are other indicators of state capacity building for self-governance. The fact that governors are now expected to leave their states to meet with other governors, lobby in Washington, and travel abroad marks a sea change in attitudes from the not-so-distant past when governors were often criticized for stepping outside their states for any reason (Sabato 1983). At the same time, the U.S. government has responded by encouraging many of these developments and by loosening its fiscal strings through such devices as block grants and general revenue sharing. Thus, most states now have the capacity to recognize and respond to the challenges of interdependence even if they lack the ability or authority to resolve all their problems alone. Hence, they have also cooperated with each other through regional and national associations and requested assistance from the general government in providing aid and formulating appropriate national policies.

New State Roles
Generally, the states have engaged the world arena in six ways: 1) partners in national policy formulation, 2) intergovernmental pressure points, 3) self-governing polities, 4) promoters of interests, 5) parties to agreements and exchanges, and 6) public opinion forums.

Partners. The states are necessarily partners in foreign policy formulation by virtue of their representation in the Congress. This is especially so with regard to treaty ratification by the U.S. Senate. Senators appear to have become more sensitive to the ways in which treaties may affect the interests of their states. Although many treaties have diminished state authority, "United States treaty practice, both multilateral and bilateral, continues to show reluctance to utilize the treaty power when the effect would be to displace private law shaped (often with substantial variations) by the states and when, moreover, the federation does not possess independent domestic lawmaking power" (Hay and Rotunda 1982). The states are also given substantial or concurrent authority to implement or enforce the terms of a number of treaties and statutes, such as those involving punishments for violations of the law of nations, the protection of aliens, and migratory bird conservation. States retain substantial taxing and regulatory authority over foreign firms doing business within state.

Pressure Points. For many reasons, though, congressional representation is not a sufficient guarantor of state interests. Consequently, state and local governments have increased their lobbying activities substantially, both individually and cooperatively through multi-state associations such as NGA, the National Association of State Development Agencies, and the National Conference of State Legislatures. Several recent cases illustrate this lobbying influence. In 1978, the states convinced the Senate not to ratify a U.S.-U.K. Tax Treaty, which was strongly supported by the Carter Administration and international business interests (Kline 1983). The states obtained important changes in reauthorization of the Export Administration Act in 1979 and in the Trade Procedures Simplification Act and the Refugee Act passed in 1980. In 1983 and 1984, the U.S. Supreme Court upheld the unitary tax methods used by some twenty-three states, which base taxation on a share of the worldwide income of corporations and their subsidiaries rather than on income earned by companies only in a particular state. The NGA lobbied vigorously for this outcome and convinced the U.S. to remain neutral in this litigation.

State lobbyists have also sought reductions in federal barriers to trade expansion, revisions in export policy, reorganization of export administration, greater attention to agricultural exports, more assistance for small business exporting, promotion and regulation of foreign investment in the U.S., improved federal trade adjustment assistance, changes in energy policy, revisions in immigration laws, changes in refugee relief and resettlement policies, better relations with Canada and Latin America, resolutions of cross-border environmental problems, expanded tourism, and reductions in obstacles to U.S. travel foreign business people and tourists in such areas as visas, passports, money exchange requirements, and foreign language translation. For example, Hawaii is concerned about the decline of its favored position as a place for filming Japanese television commercials because of U.S. visa requirements regarded as onerous by the Japanese.

Polities. As self-governing polities, the states have substantial authority over international and foreign policy matters impinging upon the states as well as over domestic activities having international ramifications. State "Buy American" laws and state treatment of aliens and minorities occasionally become sensitive foreign policy issues. Many state and local actions are simply irritants in international relations, as when the mayor of Miami, Florida, site of the 1984 Miss Universe pageant, announced: "We don't want any of those Commie girls walking around in bathing suits." The 1982 decision of Glen Cove, New York, to deny Soviet diplomats access to the town's beaches, golf course, and tennis courts is another example. In 1984, the U.S. House District appropriations subcommittee asked the District of Columbia Council to re-name a portion of the street in front of the Soviet embassy as Andrei Sakharov Avenue. The council refused because local law requires that streets be named only after persons who have been dead for at least two years. New York City, however, designated a street corner near the Soviet mission to the United Nations as the "Sakharov-Bonner Corner."

On the other hand, pressures to remove public funds from investments related to the Republic of South Africa have developed in a number of states and localities. Visits by South African officials often stir up local protests. Meanwhile, most of the states have resisted pressures from abroad to boycott Israel. Some 113 foreign trade zones have been established in the nation as authorized by the Foreign Trade Zone Act of 1934. State and local governments have primary responsibility for civil defense, and are also authorized by the U.S. to engage in mutual civil defense aid with neighboring countries. More important, states can regulate and tax foreign business and otherwise exercise their authority to protect public health, safety, and morals so as to create a climate that encourages and/or discourages a wide range of internationally related activity.

Promoters. States are increasingly becoming promoters of their interests as well, sometimes in competition with each other for foreign and domestic business (e.g., the conflict between Minnesota and South Dakota). Aside from gubernatorial and other state delegations sent abroad, at least twenty-seven states now have more than fifty-two offices abroad, mostly in Europe, though with increasing attention being given to Latin America, Asia, and the Middle East. (In 1970, only three states had overseas offices.) A number of state and interstate port authorities have foreign offices as well. Some states have invested heavily in foreign trade promotion. For example, Florida's promotion agency had a $3 million budget and thirty-three employees in 1983. Other states have been quite creative in promoting whatever they have, as in the case of New Mexico's adobe industry. Ironically, Middle Eastern countries have turned to New Mexico firms for advice and technical assistance in adobe construction. States are also encouraging nations to open consulates or other offices in their major cities. In June 1983, representatives of eleven U.S. cities met for the first National Conference on Consular Relations. Some states and cities now employ protocol officers and foreign affairs specialists. There has also been an increase in exchange programs, and with a new twist. Americans are increasingly interested in learning from their overseas counterparts. Even many sister city, and now sister state, programs have assumed a substantive importance beyond the cultural and ceremonial plane. For about fifteen years, Louisiana has hired as many as 300 teachers a year from Belgium, France, and Quebec to teach French in its public schools. In 1984, Georgia began a pilot program of hiring math teachers from West Germany.

Parties to Agreements. Direct relations with other nations may well be the most significant development. States are negotiating directly with foreign governments, especially comparable subnational governments, and state officials are involving themselves in business negotiations, in part, because many foreign enterprises are government owned, or regulated to a greater degree than American enterprises. Although the U.S. Constitution forbids states to make treaties and alliances, states can make agreements with foreign governments with and without congressional approval so long as they do not intrude upon the general government's prerogatives or give states the attributes of national sovereignty in international affairs.

Initially, states tended to request congressional approval. Thus, Congress approved Minnesota's entry into a highway agreement with the province of Manitoba in 1958. Wider agreements have also been approved, such as the Northeastern Interstate Forest Fire Protection Compact involving contiguous U.S. states and Canadian provinces. Now, many agreements do not entail congressional action, though when in doubt, state officials usually consult the U.S. Department of State or other relevant agencies.

Agreement making is most prevalent with Canadian provinces, which have somewhat greater freedom than American states to engage in such activity. The northern border states, Alaska, and several other states, such as Texas, are linked to Canadian provinces by more than 600 agreements of various types. Some agreements, such as the St. Lawrence Seaway Project, involve the U.S. government as a party along with the states. American governors and Canadian premiers have regularized consultations in the northeast, while other consultations are frequent elsewhere along the border.

Agreement making has developed more slowly along the southern border, in part, because Mexican states have less freedom than American states to engage in such activity and because, until recently, Mexico was not economically or politically important to the United States. Now, however, cross-border consultations are frequent between individual states. In 1980, governors of the four American and six Mexican states met for the first time to discuss mutual concerns, such as trade, industrial development, undocumented workers, drug trafficking, water, agriculture, pollution, energy, tourism, and cultural and educational exchanges. Cooperative projects have also been developed, such as the water treatment plant built by Nogales, Arizona, and Nogales, Sonora. In addition, for example, Texas has opened an office in Mexico City, engaged in a small foreign aid program, and returned Pancho Villa's death mask to Mexico. Governors William P. Clements and Mark White have met not only with Mexican governors but also with the presidents of Mexico. These are not, of course, formal diplomatic relations—states have no embassies—nor do these activities have the drama and visibility of such burning issues as arms reduction talks; but they do involve matters of importance to the states, matters which may, in some cases, be better managed locally than by Washington, Ottawa, or Mexico City.

Public Opinion Forums. States and localities have also begun to emerge as public opinion forums on foreign policy, especially since the Vietnam War when citizens began employing state and local referenda mechanisms to express dissent. As of January 1984, for example, sixty-one of sixty-six nuclear freeze propositions had been approved by voters in referendums around the country; thirty-six towns and cities had declared themselves "nuclear free zone;" and Cambridge, Massachusetts, had created a Commission on Nuclear Disarmament and Peace Education. In 1984 public health officials in Massachusetts produced a television commercial warning about the dangers of the "last epidemic," nuclear war. Some local referenda are hotly contested and attract outside support and opposition, as was the case in the June 1984 defeat of the Berkeley, California, Settlements Initiative which would have called upon the U.S. "to reduce its yearly aid to Israel by an amount equal to what it determines to be the most accurate approximation of what Israel spends annually on its settlements in the occupied territories of the West Bank, Gaza Strip and Golan Heights." Legislatures and city councils have also passed resolutions on a variety of foreign policy issues, while governors and mayors have become more outspoken. In December 1983, Wisconsin's governor startled his constituents by saying that mass demonstrations and even civil disobedience might be needed to boost the nuclear freeze movement. In 1985, the Texas legislature sent a resolution to the White House supporting President Reagan's "Star Wars" proposals.

Although these opinion expressions appear to have little, if any, immediate effect on U.S. foreign policy, they nevertheless suggest that interest groups have discovered state mechanisms as means for mobilizing and registering public opinion in ways that have the "official" character of a public vote or legislative resolution. The U.S. government has not sought to quash these opinion expressions, though the Nebraska Supreme Court ruled in 1984 that citizens could not use the petition process to place an initiative on the ballot to determine whether voters favored a bilateral nuclear freeze and opposed deployment of the MX missile in Nebraska. The Court, in a 4-3 decision, held that such an initiative "is nothing more than a non-binding expression of public opinion and not a proper subject for the initiative in Nebraska." It remains to be seen whether other state courts will follow suit.

Conclusion

Are the states about to become serious competitors or interlopers in U.S. foreign policy. Not at all. To date, both the general government and the state governments have acted with restraint and an attitude of negotiation. The states have confined themselves largely to "local" matters, while directing their efforts to influence national foreign policy through traditional intergovernmental channels and nonbinding opinion expressions. Furthermore, foreign policy issues rarely get to the top of any state's policy agenda, and most states devote less than 5 percent of their direct budgetary resources to "foreign affairs." Many trade promotion activities are partially supported by the private sector.

The significance of the states' activities lies instead in their very occurrence and recent expansion, and in the fact that the states are assuming roles for themselves in foreign affairs in ways which are important to their economies and to their self-governance. The states have always had a share in foreign policy making; now they are exercising a share of foreign policy making. The share claimed by the states deals primarily with matters vital to the interests of particular states and groups of states. These "local" interests may rank low on the general government's agenda, but rank high on a state's agenda. This suggests not only that states must sometimes act on their own behalf, but also that the general government may find it preferable to leave some foreign policy matters to the states rather than become embroiled in a host of local, business, housekeeping, and cultural negotiations which, with U.S. government involvement, could be more easily elevated to the level of major international issues.

The states' activities suggest that there is a place beneath the nuclear umbrella of superpower contention for subnational involvements in world affairs. These activities also suggest that power can be shared in the foreign policy field without demolishing the abilities of general or national governments to make policies that must affect all constituent units. A line between national and subnational policy making cannot be drawn with any precision or permanence, and there will be conflict, though conflict is often beneficial. Shared power, then, places a premium on consultation and negotiation. There is always the problem of dissident localities, such as Quebec in Canada, which may engage in bellicose foreign activities; however, these problems usually arise, not from foreign involvements, but from deeper domestic grievances, which give rise to these foreign activities in the first place, and which require a closer look at a nation's entire power system. A failure to share power may very well sharpen grievances insofar as localities may feel neglected by national authorities and constrained in their ability to address local problems effectively.

The obstacles to shared power, however, are severe. Those who already possess power are usually reluctant to share it, unless compelled to do so. There is also a tendency to view subnational governments as less competent, though after Vietnam, it is more difficult to sustain a case for superior U.S. competence in foreign policy making. Subnational interests also tend to be viewed as annoying and provincial rather than substantial and cosmopolitan. State "Buy American" laws, for example, are often viewed with derision, as being about what one would expect from locals, while U.S. tariffs and "Buy American" laws often escape such criticism. Advising a president on foreign affairs is prestigious; advising a governor is much less so.

Shared-power arrangements are rarely neat and simple. They require considerable negotiation and coordination; they call for sensitivity to due process; they admit more veto points than centralized arrangements; they imply nonhierarchical relationships; and they risk delayed decision making, factionalism, and fission. Some type of contractual or constitutional linkage is usually required in shared-power arrangements as well as a voluntary commitment to sustain the arrangement where contractual language is necessarily deficient (Elazar 1979). Shared power also implies mutual restraint and a tolerance of pluralism and diversity.

Perhaps the greatest obstacle, however, is the compelling idea of unitary sovereignty. So long as sovereignty is regarded as the essence of autonomy, even when it is a fiction in an interdependent world, neither shared power nor autonomy are likely to become general realities. What needs to be explored are the ways in which shared power or shared sovereignty actually enhances autonomy. This is a deeper implication of the states in world affairs. Because they are self-governing polities, the states can engage the world within limits. By doing so, they can enhance their autonomy in relation to outside forces. At the same time, they still need the general U.S. government and the common power represented by it. If each state were a sovereign nation, most of the states would have greater difficulty functioning in a truly self-governing manner.

References

Associated Press. 1984. "New U.S. foreign trade department urged." *Dallas Times Herald*, 22 February.

Billington, R.A. 1979. *Land of savagery, land of promise: The European image of the American frontier in the nineteenth century.* New York: W. W. Norton.

Committee on International Trade and Foreign Relations. 1981. *Export development and foreign investment: The role of the states and its linkage to federal action.* Washington, D. C.: National Governors' Association.

Duchacek, I.D. 1983. "Foreign relations of major non-capital cities: New York and Montreal, Geneva and Strasbourg—micro-actors in international politics." Paper presented at the annual meeting of the Study Group on Canada-U.S. Relations, New York State Political Science Association, New York City, 8-9 April.

Elazar, D.J. 1984. *American federalism: A view from the states.* 3d ed. New York: Harper & Row.

‗‗‗‗‗‗‗. 1981. States as polities in the federal system. National Civic Review 70, (February): 77-82.

‗‗‗‗‗‗‗. 1979. *Self rule/shared rule: Federal solutions to the Middle East conflict.* Ramat Gan, Israel: Turtledove.

‗‗‗‗‗‗‗. 1962. *The American partnership: Intergovernmental co-operation in the nineteenth-century United States.* Chicago : University of Chicago Press.

Graves, W.B. 1964. *American Intergovernmental Relations.* New York: Scribner's.

Hay, P. and R. D. Rotunda. 1982. *The United States federal system: Legal integration in the American experience.* New York: Oceana.

Henkin, L. 1972. *Foreign affairs and the constitution*. Mineola, N.Y.: Foundation Press.

Kidd, B. 1984. "World market plays role in Texas economy, expert says." *Denton Record-Chronicle*, 15 May .

Kincaid, J. 1984. Toward the third century of American federalism: New dynamics and new perspectives. *American Studies International* 22(Spring): 86-122.

Kline, J.M. 1983. *State government influence in U.S. international economic policy*. Lexington, Mass.: Lexington Books.

Laski, H.J. 1939. The obsolescence of federalism. *The New Republic* 98(May): 367-369.

Lindblom, C.E. 1968. *The policy-making process*. Englewood Cliffs, N.J.: Prentice-Hall.

Lipset, S.M. 1963. *The first new nation: The United States in historical and comparative perspective*. New York: Basic Books.

Manning, B. 1977. The congress, the executive, and intermestic affairs: Three proposals. *Foreign Affairs* 55(January): 306-324.

Mettger, H.P. 1955. Foreign relations at the state capital. *State Government* 28(October): 234-240.

Palumbo, D.J. 1969. "The states and the conduct of foreign relations." In *Cooperation and conflict: Readings in American federalism*, edited by D.J. Elazar, et al. Itasca, Ill.: F.E. Peacock.

Porter, S. 1981. Individual states assuming leadership roles in world trade. *Denton Record-Chronicle*, 10 February: 10A.

Rosenau, J. 1980. *The study of global interdependence: essays on the transnationalization of world affairs*. New York: Nicholas.

Sabato, L. 1983. *Goodbye to good-time Charlie: The American governorship transformed*. 2d ed. Washington, D. C.: CQ Press.

Taylor, T. W. 1983. *American Indian Policy*. Mt. Airy, Md.: Lomond.

United States v. Curtiss-Wright Export Corp., 299 U.S. 304 (1936).

Wechsler, H. 1954. The political safeguards of federalism: The role of the states in the composition and selection of the national government. *Columbia Law Review* 54 (April): 543-560.

Young, C. 1976. *The politics of cultural pluralism*. Madison, WI: University of Wisconsin Press.

CHAPTER 14

Some Aspects of Power Sharing in International Organizations

Lawrence S. Finkelstein

There is no power but shared power—and Easton is its prophet.[1]

Power in international arenas is ordinarily shared. It is rarely imposed.

That conclusion denies the inherited wisdom that power necessarily means "man's *control* over the minds and actions of other men"[2] and, by inference, since international politics involves the relations of states with each other, that power in international relations involves only the "control" states exercise over each other. It is, however, consonant with the basic principles of the international order. The international system is based on the sovereign equality of independent states (UN Charter 2/1). It is an almost pure model of a system in which no one is legitimately in charge. It lacks hierarchical sources of authority. Thus, except in rare instances of purely coercive outcomes of contested issues, dealing with the international agenda depends on the willing compliance of states.

The conclusion derives from a causative definition of power, namely that power is the ability to achieve preferred outcomes in competition with other relevant actors seeking to do the same Hart 1976, Baldwin 1979; Fox 1959). It stems from David Easton's definition of politics as the authoritative allocation of values for the society (Easton 1968, 1953, 1965). In international politics, therefore, power is the ability to dominate or, preferably, to determine the authoritative allocation of values at issue in international arenas. Control by actors over each other is thus an instrumental means to allocative ends.

Force, in this view, is one, but not the only, means of exercising power. As Schelling argued, even forceful power is only sometimes directly coercive. More frequently, the threat to use force is employed as an instrument of bargaining to achieve preferred outcomes, and this occurs even while war is under way (Schelling 1966, Halle 1984). Power, in this view, is ordinarily exercised in bargaining, with force one instrument among others. Other resources are relevant, such as money, raw materials, control over desired objects or means, diplomatic support including alliance, coalition or votes (Fox 1959). Power may also be expressed as influence, or the ability to persuade by information or propaganda, the force of reason or logic, or the projection of leadership. Power in international relations may be visualized as involving a spectrum as shown in Table 1.

TABLE 14-1: POWER IN INTERNATIONAL RELATIONS

	◄——— COERCIVE ———►	◄——— NONCOERCIVE ———►	
TYPE	Brute Force	Bargaining	Influence
MEANS	Military Force	Military threat	Ideas
		Material resources	Information
		Access/denial	"Psychological" factors
		Support	"Aura" of power
			Leadership/skill
		Dependence/autonomy	
		Negotiating freedom/constraint	

In this conception, power is not a generalizable quantity. It is not, in short, fungible. Far from being fungible, power is best understood as specific to individual situations, contexts and issues (Baldwin 1979). To understand power, it is always necessary to know what is the agenda, who are the actors, what relevant resources they bring to bear in the bargaining over the outcomes and what are the institutional settings and how they bear on the bargaining. In this context of specificity, the aura of expectation about influence which results from the widespread belief that power is fungible may paradoxically be a resource available to the actors (Mansbach 1981).

This approach to international power is compatible with a number of insights and developments of scholarship in recent years. It is entirely compatible with Robert Dahl's emphasis on the importance of context in considering power, even though he defines power as control of an actor by another (Dahl 1968, Baldwin 1979). That power is specific rather than general is a central theme of the leading study of interdependence (Keohane 1977). That theme structures the recent work on international regimes (Krasner 1982). It underlies recent suggestions that international politics can best be studied from a perspective of "issues" or "agendas" (Mansbach 1981, Coate 1982).

Understanding the role of power in the international system still requires first of all attention to the power relations of the states, which are the primary components of and actors in the international system. Such relations are acknowledged to be more complex than is implied by the simpler nostrums of simpler times—the strong prevail over the weak, big fish eat little fish, "the strong do what they can and the weak suffer what they must" (Hadas 1960). Alliances, for example, involve more than transitory coalitions of power to control adversaries in the short term. The sharing of power within alliances and coalitions does not coincide with obvious hypotheses about the dominance of the strong over the weak. The "big influence of small allies" (Keohane 1971) is a phenomenon which has had considerable scholarly attention. The best explanation appears to be the theory of collective or public goods (Olson 1971, 1970). Certainly, the assertion and sharing of power by states requires attention to the context of alliances and coalitions in which they participate.

Focusing first on the role of states in international relations does not, however, exhaust the questions about international power. The classical model of international relations involving nation states as actors no longer suffices. An implication of the specificity of power—that power is inseparable from the issues to which it applies— is that the politics of issues may involve interacting international and national dimensions. Neither the issues comprising contemporary political agendas nor the kinds of power relevant to determining and carrying out policies necessarily stop "at the water's edge." "It is highly arbitrary and misleading," says Coate, to assume that activities that cross national political-legal boundaries are analytically distinct from activities that do not cross such boundaries" (Coate 1982). By definition, transnational actors (Keohane and Nye 1971) are located in, draw their resources and power from and may have effect in both national and international milieux. Some issues which occupy prominent places in international agendas, human rights and ecological matters among them, involve the making of international policies with significant inputs from nongovernmental forces with national roots. They require national implementation for their effect. They engender political support and implementing action by actors within national societies (Puchala 1984, Forsythe 1984).

Moreover, in their relations with each other, states are influenced by international nongovernmental organizations (INGOs) as shown schematically in Figure 1.

That an arrow runs directly from INGOs to the international arena suggests that INGOs may have roles in directly shaping international agendas and giving impetus to policy development separable from the influence they may exert on governments via their national nongovernmental affiliates shown by the lower diagonal arrows.

Figure 14-1   The Interaction of States Influenced by INGOs

That seems to have been the case, for example, with respect to issues of the ecosystem in the 1970s (Puchala 1984).

Furthermore, intergovernmental organizations (IGOs) as entities distinguishable from the members which comprise them, and their staffs, are increasingly seen as actors in the international arena. They sometimes exert power other than that which represents the decisions of governments comprising the organizations. For example, a primary complaint voiced by the United States in support of the policy of withdrawing from UNESCO is that the power of the UNESCO Secretariat is too great and has displaced the role of governments in running the organization (Committee on Foreign Affairs 1984, Ascher 1983). More broadly, there is recognition that the executive heads of international agencies have become significant international actors.[3]

Understanding the sharing of international power requires attention to such nonstate actors. Moreover, to a degree, coalitions, blocs, or even "parties" have become features of the international system, as instruments of power magnification. Their internal dynamics are complex (Willetts 1978, Jackson 1983, Rothstein 1979, Mortimer 1984) but they are also, to an uncertain extent, themselves actors in the system.

From what has preceded, it should be apparent that the exercise of power occurs across a broad spectrum of international arenas. War is one end of the spectrum. It spans the "brute force" and "bargaining" zones of Figure 1. At the other end of the spectrum there is the European Community. Despite its current doldrums and fissures, the EC remains the world's most advanced international institutional framework for the sharing of powers between what may appropriately be called at least a quasi-government and the states which are its members, and among the latter. In between, there is a broad range of arenas for what are predominantly but, as has been explained above, by no means solely, state-to-state relations.

The arenas for peaceful state-to-state relations provide venues for the sharing of power through what are called in Figure 1 "bargaining" and "influence." They include bilateral relations, alliance-to-alliance relations, relations within alliances, and functional or issue-by-issue relations and general relations in regional or global conferences or continuing institutions. These categories are not discrete. Bilateral and alliance relations, for example, may operate within and have influence on the multilateral arenas.

The rest of the essay will lay out some questions about the sharing of power in continuing international institutions, or international organizations (IGOs).

Power Sharing In International Organizations

"Power sharing" in IGOs occurs in two different ways. One way is the formal, often constitutional, authorization of agencies to act. The second is the sharing of power which results from efforts to employ power in the struggle over authoritative allocation of values. The former has a static connotation although, as will be seen, formal allocations of power are by no means unchanging. The latter carries a more dynamic connotation. The sharing of power results from dynamic processes.

The main decision mode is voting, which rests on the principle of sovereign equality (UN Charter 2/1), hence the infamous predominant formula of "one nation—one vote."[4]

Formal Power Sharing

Authority is formally assigned and delimited in the international system in the constitutive instruments which empower the international agencies. These are often constitutions, such as the United Nations Charter and the Treaty of Rome, which founded the European Economic Community. Some are resolutions adopted by existing international organizations or by conferences they have convened. The basic constitutional arrangements are supplemented by rules of procedure, program resolutions and "action programs" adopted by major international conferences. Such instruments spell out and not infrequently alter the basic constitutional allocations. Insofar as such supplementary instruments allocate authorities to act, they may be considered to have constitutive functions.

It is necessary to say a few words about the connection between such allocations of authority and power. That they are linked is clear from the fact that the two words are often used interchangeably. That the concept "authority" involves great ambiguity is unfortunately true (Peabody 1968). One accepted meaning, however, is "institutionalized power," and closely related to that there is "formal power" (ibid.). "Authority" is used here in that sense. The "power" that constitutive authority conveys in the nonhierarchical international system is the power to deal with the allocated functions on the action agenda in accordance with the prescribed procedures for doing so. The legitimacy that attaches to the constitutive assignment of the formal right to consider acting on a matter is a source of potentially effective power. It authoritatively allocates the often contested value inherent in ensuring that an issue can be on the action agenda. It denies those who are opposed to having an item on the agenda a legitimate basis for resisting. It may or may not lead to effective authoritative allocation of the other values implicated in the issue (Keohane 1977, Pastor 1984).

Essentially, the formal allocation of authority in this way is of four types: a) allocation and delineation of powers between, on the one hand, the international organizations and, on the other, the members which comprise them; b) the creation and empowerment of international instrumentalities to deal with functions or tasks in the international system; c) a special form of the preceding, the allocation of responsibilities between universal and regional agencies, especially in the field of peace and security issues; and d) assignment of authority to organs within agencies, and delineation of responsibilities among them.

The first type of allocation of authority is exemplified by the UN Charter's drawing of boundaries between what the UN is entitled to do and the functions which, explicitly or by implication, remain vested in the member states. The organization is empowered, for example, to make "decisions" through the Security Council which the members are bound to carry out (Article 25). There is ambiguity as to the intended extent of that compulsory authority, as to whether, for example, it arises when the Security Council is authorized to "call upon" members to do something (Articles 33/2 and 40, for example) as well as when it is explicitly authorized to "decide" (Articles 39 and 41, for example) (Goodrich 1969). The procedures for action, especially the voting rules, are laid down (especially, for the veto power, Article 27/3). An important set of provisions authorizes the General Assembly to assess members their contributions to the organization's budget (Article 17/1 and 2). More broadly, by ratifying the Charter, which is a binding international treaty, members accept commitments to behave in specified ways (for example, Articles 2/2, 3 and 5, 25, 33/1, 43/1, 45, 48, 49, 56, 73, 74, 94/1) and to avoid certain prohibited behaviors, most notably to "refrain in their international relations from the threat or use of force against the territorial integrity or political independence of any state, or in any other manner inconsistent with the Purposes of the United Nations" (Article 2/4).

In addition to the restraints on members and the assertion of agencies' authority by which the members are bound, there are also limitations on agency authority which constitute protections of members' jurisdictions. Most notable among these is the so-called "domestic jurisdiction" clause of the UN Charter (Article 2/7), which protects the domain of members against "intervention" by the organization. A similar protection is incorporated in Article 1/3 of the UNESCO Constitution. In general, the fact that, with rare exceptions such as those referred to in the preceding paragraph, IGO authorities are limited to powers of discussion and recommendation, preparing draft treaties for adoption by members, and conducting studies implies that the members are as a rule protected against compulsion and that their consent is required for action affecting them. A good case in point is the functions given the UN Economic and Social Council in Chapter X of the UN Charter.

The meaning of such constitutive arrangements has depended on the changing political environments in which they have been given effect. The original empowerments of international agencies and the limitations upon them have both been altered as the context has changed over time. The supplementary constitutive instruments have assumed proportionately greater roles over the years. Ernst Haas once emphasized that "the UN system is hyperdependent on its environment" (Haas 1968). By and large that generalization applies equally to other international organizations. A consequence is that some of the powers constitutionally authorized have been unusable in practice. The binding authority given the UN Security Council does not in reality exist. The responsibility given the UN Secretary-General in Article 99 of the Charter to "bring to the attention of the Security Council any matter which in his opinion may threaten the maintenance of international peace and security" has been seldom fulfilled and has lapsed into near-desuetude[5], although resort to that authority by Secretary-General Kurt Waldheim in the case of the Iran-Iraq War suggests that it is not altogether dead (UN 1980).

In other respects, however, the original authorities have proven inadequate in the face of the changing political environment. Constitutive authorities have in some cases been broadened through what Farley has called the process of "mandated change" (Farley 1981, Rajan 1982). For example, the UN Charter does not specifically authorize what has been termed "peacekeeping," that is, UN intervention in the avoidance or suppression of hostilities, not by exercise of the Security Council's mandatory powers but with the consent of the interested parties. This certainly involves a different sharing of powers between the organization and the members than was originally contemplated (Haas 1983). Another form of growth in authority is what James termed "proselytism," that is "the organization seeking to act as an instrument of change. . . to rid the international society of situations which the majority regard as . . . 'sinful'" (James 1969). Another example is the growth of what is called the "operations" of the UN system, that is the entire apparatus of direct service and technical assistance to governments, especially insofar as that is related to the UN Development Program (UNDP). No provision of the UN Charter clearly serves as the authority for this function. The domestic jurisdiction of members has been narrowed as a result of changes in the balance of support for and resistance to intervention by the international agencies with respect to colonialism, human rights and related phenomena. Numerous further examples of such enlargement of agencies' authorities could be given. Two especially important ones are the assumption by the International Monetary Fund (IMF) of the authority to impose "conditionality" in connection with its lending (Cohen 1982) and the institutionalization of defense cooperation in NATO, including the creation of NATO's international secretariat and staff (Schaffer 1980).

A reasonable summation is that the original constitutive allocations of authorities have not held up notably well over time. The formal allocation of powers as between the international agencies and their members has been considerably altered by adaptation to changing circumstances, including the processes of struggle over the authority to allocate values in international arenas.

The second type of formal allocation of authority, that is, the distribution of functions among agencies in the system, was similarly originally achieved in the basic constitutional instruments establishing the agencies. In the UN system especially there was a sort of distribution pattern under which, for example, the UN itself was to deal with direct threats to peace and security and the settlement of international political disputes; the World Health Organization (WHO) health matters; the Food and Agriculture Organization (FAO) farm issues; the International Labor Organization (ILO) conditions of employment; the United Nations Educational, Scientific and Cultural Organization (UNESCO) education, science and culture; and the IMF the realm of international finance.

These original arrangements too have undergone considerable change over time. For one thing, precision in such allocations is inescapably difficult to achieve. There was a sort of overall design at the beginning. The constitutional actions were taken separately from each other, however, over an extended period of time in forums with different memberships and differing balances of intragovernmental representation. Complete consistency and clear delineations of exclusive jurisdictions were unattainable. Moreover, the United Nations itself was authorized to deal somehow with virtually any subject of international significance; however, the balance between its powers and those of the members was struck issue by issue. UNESCO mandates were also unusually broad. Inevitably, there was friction between and among the agencies over turf. Especially in the early years, for example, UNESCO was embroiled in boundary disputes with other agencies, particularly FAO, ILO, and WHO, arising largely out of UNESCO's interpretation of its mandate as requiring education in the subjects which were the primary concern of the other agencies. These early issues were by and large resolved through processes of friction and tension (Hill 1978). Frequently, however, frictions over authority pose difficulties because there is little coordinating or adjudicating authority in the system. Moreover, individual governments as a rule find it difficult to achieve that internal consistency of policies which is the indispensable prerequisite for effective agreement among governments to exercise control in the governing bodies throughout the system (Hill 1978, Smithers 1973, McLaren 1980, Meltzer 1983).

New issues continue to arise. There has been friction between GATT and UNCTAD (Hill 1978). In June 1984, to give another example, a dispute broke out during a meeting in Vienna of the UN's Committee on Peaceful Uses of Outer Space as to whether it was an appropriate forum for consideration of a moratorium on weapons testing and development in outer space. The United States was among governments which argued that the issue should be discussed only in the UN Conference on Disarmament. It had earlier announced that it would not participate in the committee's discussions of the militarization of space (UN 1984).

It is noteworthy that one of the complaints of the US Government about UNESCO, cited to justify the US decision to withdraw from the agency, was precisely that UNESCO dealt with some issues which the United States argued would be better left to other agencies. Particular emphasis was placed on UNESCO's work in disarmament education which US representatives said belongs to the UN itself (Committee on Foreign Affairs 1984). In this instance, the issue arose because of harmony between agencies in the system. UNESCO responded to a request in the Final Document on Disarmament adopted by the UN General Assembly's Tenth Special Session in 1978 that the specialized agencies give priority to public information about the dangers of the armaments race and, specifically, that UNESCO step up its efforts to develop disarmament education as a distinct field of study. Although UNESCO's assumption of authority in this instance was autonomous, since the agencies in the UN system are regarded as autonomous equals without authority over each other, it clearly acted cooperatively in response to the call of the UN General Assembly.

Such cooperation occurs frequently, often in response to the "action programs" of the major international conferences called in recent years to deal with emergent issues—the human environment, food, population, women, new and renewable sources of energy, water, desertification and so on. Agencies often cooperate in carrying out program responsibilities, jointly planning, funding and staffing missions, projects, and conferences of all descriptions. An outstanding example is the series of "cooperative arrangements" between the World Bank and FAO, UNESCO and WHO whereby the bank pays a large part of the costs of the staffs maintained by the three other agencies to provide the bank with pre-investment services in their respective fields (Mason 1973). While the bank retains its freedom as to the funding proposals which emerge from the pre-investment work, it does not carry out the preliminary processes itself. The three agencies welcome the opportunity to provide service in their fields of competence, and the funds and staff "slots" which accompany the role. The bank is spared the need to duplicate the technical resources in the other agencies. The arrangements have resulted in substantial bank funding of projects growing out of the relationship.

Other factors also inspire supplementary constitutive acts, altering the original allocations of authority. Over the years a veritable alphabet soup of new acronyms representing new international bodies has been created. In part, this reflects the need for new institutional capabilities to carry out newly identified international functions. NATO, OECD, the United Nations Environmental Program (UNEP), the United Nations Children's Fund (UNICEF), the General Agreement on Tariffs and Trade (GATT), the International Institute of Theoretical Physics, the Organization of African Unity (OAU), and the Asian Development Bank are examples of new bodies created in this way since the original allocations of authority occurred following World War II. None of them was contemplated in the original organizational design.

Some of the growth and diversification of authority is attributable to tensions over authority to allocate values internationally which will be dealt with in a later section. As the number of independent states comprising the international system grew with the ending of colonialism, the group of less developed countries (LDCs) became more assertive in its demands. Organized in the group of LDCs (G-77) and, with considerable overlapping, in the Non-Aligned Movement (NAM) (Willetts 1978, Jackson 1983, Rothstein 1979, Mortimer 1984), they pressed for and, in many cases, obtained the creation of new agencies. More agencies mean more budgets and staffs, as in the examples of the UN Special Fund which is now melded into the UNDP, itself a result of this process; the International Development Association (IDA) and International Finance Corporation (IFC) which have been added to the World Bank "family"; the United Nations Industrial Development Organization (UNIDO); the International Fund for Agricultural Development (IFAD); and several regional development banks. They also may mean additional means for the enunciation and programmatic development of LDC objectives. New membership and voting balances are also involved. In one case, a new organization—the United Nations Conference on Trade and Development (UNCTAD)—was created specifically as a "counter-organization" to an existing agency—GATT.

Thus, there has been a considerable proliferation of international organizations and what some consider duplication and redundancy. Certainly, proliferation of agencies has been accompanied by dispersion of authority. This development has incidentally given rise to new descriptions and conceptualizations of the workings of the international system, such as networks (Jacobson 1984, Jonsson 1984, Judge 1978) and issue regimes (Keohane 1977, Krasner 1982, Mansbach 1982, Coate 1982). Although they have different emphases, these new concepts share certain features. They assume that power is not general or fungible, but issue-specific (Cox 1973). They call for issue-by-issue examination of how the system works. They also look to the interconnections between IGOs and INGOs at the international level and between both of these and national governmental and non-governmental counterparts.

The third type of formal allocation of authority involves the distribution of responsibilities between IGOs of global scope, all of which except the UN itself have functionally delimited mandates, and regional IGOs (Nye 1971). In this respect too, the original constitutive allocations have been greatly changed under the pressures of changing circumstances over time. With respect to authority to deal with peace and security issues, there was considerable ambiguity at the beginning as to how responsibilities were intended to be divided between the UN and regional organizations (Claude 1964, Nye 1968, Bennett 1984). That makes it exceptionally difficult to know how much the practice as it has developed over the years represents conformity with or departure from the original expectations. Some things seem reasonably clear, however.

The most significant change from what was originally anticipated was the regionalization of security which stemmed from the Cold War and its effect on the UN's capacity to supply collective security. That led to emphasis on the second-best alternative, collective defense (Finkelstein 1966), through the systems of "regional" defense alliances which ring the globe. The Brussels Pact and the Western European Union, NATO, the Baghdad Pact and Central Treaty Organization, SEATO, ANZUS, the Rio Pact, the Warsaw Treaty Organization and a large number of bilateral defense alliances all manifest this development. This phenomenon involved a changed understanding of the character of the functions to be performed, rather than a new allocation of previously agreed upon functions.

Within the original framework of responsibilities for dealing with international disputes and handling threats to the peace, breaches of the peace or acts of aggression (UN Charter, Article 39), the dominant expectation that regional mechanisms would be subordinate to the UN Security Council has yielded to variable political exigencies. Claude once put it that "the Cold War has prevailed over the Charter" (Claude

1968). That referred to the departure by the United States in practice from its own original principle that the UN should dominate the regional mechanisms. Rather than invite intrusion by the USSR into affairs of the Americas by dealing with the latter in the Security Council, the US chose to turn to the Inter-American system where it dominated and the USSR was excluded.

Soviet-US relations were not, however, the only factors at play. Latin American countries sometimes chose to invoke the political balances of the UN, which differed from the intra-American balance, rather than submit to the prevalence of the Yanqui colossus within the OAS. They thus indulged in what might be called "forum shopping." That broader concept has a relevance beyond US-Latin American relations.

To begin with, a number of regional bodies have been created with authority to deal with disputes in the regions and with other issues affecting peace and security, in addition to the collective defense organizations referred to in a preceding paragraph which also exercise such functions.[6] States involved in contretemps with each other often shop for the forum in which they expect to find the friendliest, or least unfriendly, reception. Some international disputes find their way into both the UN and relevant regional bodies.[7] Since no compulsory jurisdiction exists, resort to the latent authority in the constitutions of regional agencies and the UN Charter depends on the choices made by states as to the mechanisms to which they wish to turn. The result has been a very mixed pattern. No very clear trend is visible as to the choices between the universal and regional agencies (Haas 1983).

Non-aligned countries often prefer to deal with their disputes in contexts which do not risk great power involvement. To mangle the well-known metaphor, the "grass" may turn to regional mechanisms for management of disputes to avoid trampling by the "elephants" in the UN (Obaseki 1981). Regional mechanisms are also preferred because they are better qualified by intimacy of interest and experienced knowledge than is the UN which is handicapped by its "effective distance," which implies less relevant understanding (ibid., 210; Burton 1972).

The only conclusion possible about the balance between the role of the UN and of regional agencies in the management of disputes is that they normally divide and occasionally share authority. One study of 138 disputes presented for settlement to the UN and to regional mechanisms from 1945-1981 shows that the UN handled 87 and the regional bodies 51 of them; 79 were not referred to settlement at all (Haas 1983).

There has been a remarkable growth in regional organizations to deal with functions other than security matters since the founding of the UN system. Whereas, by one definition, 63 such organizations were created with "potentially universal membership" between 1946 and 1980, 486 were created with "limited membership" during the same period (Jacobson 1984).[8] These figures do not reflect the regionalization which has occurred within the organizations of universal membership. The regional economic commissions under the UN's Economic and Social Council,

320

SHARED POWER

which were not anticipated when the UN was formed—Europe (ECE), Asia and the Pacific (ESCAP), Latin America (ECLA), Africa (ECA), and Western Asia (ECWA)—are examples of that. WHO has long emphasized regional decentralization of its program. Under pressures for reform, there is movement toward greater regional decentralization of the program administration of UNESCO (UNESCO 1983, 1984) and of the UN itself (Meltzer 1983, Renninger 1982). Unmistakably, there has been considerable constitutive dispersion of authority among universal and regional bodies. Some authority has devolved from the former to the latter.

The reasons for this development include those already given to explain the kinds of changes in authority discussed in preceding paragraphs. There is a natural urge to locate decisions about and administration of programs closer to those affected by them, closer to the "neighborhoods" as distinguished from the "distant" centers of global decision making. Regional foci enhance representation for regional states and are intended to enhance their influence. In some cases—the OAU is an example—regionalism is a deliberate defense against the entanglements of globalism. Regional organizations generally supplement universal ones, thus attracting additional resources for the functions they are created to perform. The regional development banks certainly were designed to do this and their creation reflects the demands of the G-77. Additional organizations expand the action opportunities for national bureaucracies and bureaucrats and, insofar as they involve bureaucracies of their own, provide additional employment opportunities. Finally, there have been the incentives to organize larger markets through regional schemes for economic integration which have given rise to the European Community and the small alphabet soup of attempts to apply its lessons regionally around the world. In the case of the EC, the logic of functionalism was harnessed to the goal of political unification as well.

Finally, there is the allocation of authority among organs within IGOs. Once again, original expectations have undergone considerable change in response to changing circumstances.

One example is especially interesting. The UN Charter, while it did not give exclusive jurisdiction in matters of peace and security to the Security Council, did give it "primary responsibility" (Article 24) and gave it the only clear action mandates and the only compulsory authority with respect to these matters. Several factors have led to change in the contemplated balance of jurisdictions between it and the General Assembly. One scholar refers to "the confusion of roles" between the Security Council and the General Assembly (Gordenker 1983).

One factor, evidently, was the conflict between the United States and the Soviet Union which in the early years immobilized the Security Council when the Soviet Union used or threatened to use its veto to block decisions. The United States responded by leading a voting majority in the UN to employ the General Assembly instead. The Uniting for Peace Resolution of 1950 emphasized the availability of the General Assembly as an agency to legitimize action which members were prepared to take voluntarily under US leadership. That resolution formally recognized the General Assembly's power to recommend action to preserve or restore peace when Security Council action was blocked by a veto. It was not really a constitutive act because it did not grant the General Assembly new powers. It rather highlighted, signalled intent to use, and eased resort to, powers of recommendation the General Assembly already had under the Charter (Articles 10, 11/2, 14). It did, however provide political endorsement for enlargement of the General Assembly's role when peace was threatened compared to that of an immobilized Security Council. It was the General Assembly, for instance, which was the main decision authority in the Suez (1956) and Congo (1960) cases, both of which involved substantial peacekeeping forces (UNEF and ONUC).

Great power stalemate also had a related effect. In part because the originally contemplated enforcement measures available to the Security Council could not be employed without the agreement of the five veto-capable powers, it became evident that the nominally binding authority of the Security Council had no reality. Thus, one important distinction in the empowerments of the two bodies vanished. If compliance with Security Council decisions depended on the voluntary action of member states, the Security Council's powers were in this respect indistinguishable from the recommendatory authority of the General Assembly. Moreover, the latter had the advantage in this respect of consisting of all members of the UN and could thus bring to bear whatever efficacy was to be found in the large numbers of votes necessary for adoption of recommendations.

Finally, there had always been dissatisfaction among the smaller powers with the emphasis given in the Charter to the limited membership Security Council, intended to be dominated by the great powers.

It should not have been surprising if, as their numbers grew, the smaller powers turned to the General Assembly to deal with political and security issues, especially when the Cold War induced stalement in the Security Council. The record, however, does not bear out this expectation. There has always, to be sure, been greater resort to the General Assembly than was originally anticipated or than the Charter's provisions gave grounds to expect. But, there has been no clear trend toward the General Assembly and away from the Security Council. Rather, the reverse seems to be more true, since the period in the 1950s when the US led in emphasis on resort to the General Assembly. Paradoxically, it seems that the greatest emphasis on the General Assembly over the Security Council resulted from the preference of one great power, the United States, rather than, as might have been expected, from the preference of the smaller powers wielding their voting strength. After the Soviet Union demonstrated its ability to offset US leadership during the crisis over financing of UN peacekeeping in 1964-1965, a swing back toward the Security Council was noticeable. Throughout the UN's history, there have been many cases in which both organs were involved. The following table summarizes the record, by decades:

TABLE 14-2

INVOLVEMENT OF THE GENERAL ASSEMBLY AND THE SECURITY COUNCIL
IN DISPUTES BEFORE THE UNITED NATIONS, BY DECADES (BENNETT 1984)

	Security Council		General Assembly		Total Cases
	#	%	#	%	#
1953–62	25	64	24	62	39
1963–72	31	94	6	18	33
1973–82	37	84	17	39	44

As to the rest of the functions performed by IGOs, the original constitutive allocations of authority within agencies have proven no more resistant to change than has been true in the field of peace and security. Fanning out from the major membership bodies of the UN itself, constellations of standing and ad hoc committees and commissions, "subsidiary organs" as authorized in the Charter (Art.22) and the other constitutional instruments in the system, centers, programs and funds have occupied the international firmament. One analysis attributes the phenomenon to "major transformations in the international system": the growth in membership and the consequent expression of new needs and demands; the effects of the Cold War; the replacement of East-West bipolarity by North-South bipolarity; increased concern with the operational aspects of economic and social development based on voluntary funding; reluctance by some countries to contemplate capital development within the UN framework; resistance to radical change in trade patterns; and opposition to the creation of additional specialized agencies (Elmandjra 1973). The result has been termed "segmentation" (ibid., 45). The broad category dealt with here is limited to new bodies which remain within the constitutional framework of the agencies which created them. It does not include autonomous bodies which have been created, although the United Nations Industrial Development Organization (UNIDO) has moved toward the latter category from the former. In at least one case, the World Food Program (WFP), a new body is organically connected to two sponsoring organizations, in this case the UN and FAO.

The authorized functions of these new bodies cover a considerable span. Many subsidiary and ad hoc bodies nominally have advisory roles in relation to the governing organs to which they report, for example, the UN General Assembly and Economic and Social Council, or the Executive Board of UNESCO. Some assist in the performance of management functions in the system, such as the Advisory Committee on Administrative and Budgetary Questions (ACABQ), the Committee on Contributions and the Panel of External Auditors. Others deal with the substantive agenda, such as the General Assembly's main committees and the regional and functional commissions of the Economic and Social Council. In addition, there are numerous bodies which perform substantial operational and operations-support functions. Among such bodies are: the United Nations Relief and Works Agency for

Palestine Refugees in the Near East (UNWRA); Office of the United Nations High Commissioner for Refugees (UNHCR); the United Nations Conference on Trade and Development (UNCTAD); UNIDO; UNDP; WFP; UNICEF; the United Nations Capital Development Fund (UNCDF); the United Nations Institute for Training and Research (UNITAR); and the Office of United Nations Disaster Relief Coordinator (UNDRO). Merely to list such agencies is to underscore the significance of the devolution of authority which has occurred. Several of the agencies are authorized to raise voluntary contributions and are predominantly funded in this way: UNDP, UNWRA, UNHCR, WFP, UNICEF, UNCDF, and UNITAR. As Elmandjra has underscored, control is arranged differently from case to case, with some authorized greater autonomy from the plenary organs than others (ibid., 37-114; Bennett 1984). What is clear is that, across the board, there is complex sharing of the power inhering in authority.

An aspect of this development has been the increase in the number of executive heads of international bodies. Inevitably, this has implied new authorities and thus new distributions of power among the heads of bodies in the system and, among and within, the bureaucracies they head. There is, as Cox noted, "a tendency . . . for bureaucracies to expand their functions" (Cox 1973). While the result is sometimes a growing "authority pie" to be shared, it is often the existing "authority pie" which is shared and the result is contest over how to do that. Since the issues of authority often are yoked to international controversy over the goals and nature of functions to be performed, the setting is one of "an intense, ingrown, and growing competition" (Meltzer 1983), especially in the UN system. In recent years, this problem has been a motivation for the movement toward UN "structural reform," one objective of which has been to introduce greater rationality to displace the chaos (ibid., passim). One important feature of that has been the attempt to vest authority in the newly designed position of UN director-general for development and international economic cooperation. The new post inevitably implies severe issues of sharing authority with the Secretary-General (ibid., 251-253).

Constitutive allocation of authority to executive heads has occurred in other ways as well. The normal method is a resolution requesting the executive head in question to assume new duties. An example is the "Programme of Action" which comprised part of the Final Act of the UN General Assembly Special Session on Disarmament in 1978. That document requested the Secretary-General to perform a number of functions, mainly having to do with disarmament studies (Weston 1980). In politically contentious cases, the membership body may decide only to authorize executive action without precise guidelines. This was true, for example, of the "leave it to Dag" period when Secretary-General Hammarskjold exercised broad discretionary authority to intervene in delicate political matters, in the interstices, so to speak, of agreement among the members (Bailey 1962, and inter alia Rovine 1970). More generally, the roles of the executive heads and their secretariats have been expanded in pace with the adoption of new programs by plenary bodies. When decisions have been made giving the agencies things to do, it has usually been the agencies' staffs, under the authority of their executive heads, which have become the doers.

It is particularly noteworthy that, in a system of sovereign states, the authority of executive heads has been expanded through processes of constitutional interpretation by the executive heads themselves. It is hard to know how often this has occurred. One recent example, however, was the apparent assumption by the director-general of UNESCO that he had the authority, contrary to the constitution, to revise the proposed budget before the organization's General Conference in 1983 after the Executive Board had approved it. There has also been explicit doctrinal interpretation, most notably Dag Hammarskjold's reading of the Charter as endowing the Secretary-General with "general authority" (Rovine 1970) not specifically derived from any particular provision of that instrument.

This interpretive method of extending the authority of executive heads of international agencies is only the most extended form of the broader phenomenon—the near-spectacular growth in the authority of executive heads. There are several reasons. Only one will be mentioned here. As the system of international agencies has grown larger and more complex, the executive role has become indispensable. In the international system, there is no substitute for permanent staffs and their leaders. Out of this necessity has accrued authority and, as will be seen hereinafter, effective power. The phenomenon may be likened to the tides of international authority lapping against the sands of national sovereignty. The beach owners are building seawalls, as the continuing crisis over UNESCO shows. It is too soon to know whether the tides or the walls will prevail. Likely there will be an altered shoreline.

Sharing Power in Practice

This section will sketch how power is shared in international organizations in the dynamic political processes by which actors seek to produce the results they prefer. The distinction between this topic and that of the preceding section—the "formal" sharing of power—is imperfect. The formal allocation of authority results from dynamic political processes and may itself be an objective sought by the actors. Moreover, "formal power" as it has been defined and considered in the preceding section is an "empty vessel." Formal power takes on its meaning when filled with the politics of value allocation.

A few words are necessary about the meaning of "value" as it is employed in this analysis. In a word, it is synonymous with "objective" or "goal." It is whatever the actors strive for. The objective may be sought either for its own sake, as an "end," or as a means or instrument toward ultimate objectives. It includes material ends, such as market shares, technology, capital or territory, and nonmaterial ones, such as prestige, status or enhanced power. Whether a value is ultimate or instrumental depends on the circumstances and intentions of the actors. Some values may be both.

This section will concentrate on the sharing of power between the international organizations and the states which comprise them, the first category of the four dealt with in the preceding section. When power to allocate values is exercised by the international organizations, that will be termed "centralized" to distinguish it from the decentralized character of the alternative, namely the continued veto power of each member state. The latter will be called the "unit veto" system. Since the exercise of centralized power rests finally on the mechanisms of majority decision, it will be categorized as "centralized majority decisions." The spectrum set forth in Figure 2 may be helpful.

Figure 14-2 U.N. System Politics of Vallue Allocation (Finkelstein 1984)

Disagreement over values is common in the politics of international arenas, including international organizations. Given the diversity of actors, that is not surprising. Sometimes, as when states converge on the necessity to deal with a commonly perceived problem or threat, there is agreement. Disaster relief and some kinds of humanitarian intervention are examples. More often, there is contention which involves some states, which either agree with each other *a l'outrance* or which come to agree through processes of bargaining among themselves, versus others which do not agree. Disagreements may be resolved in two ways. One is compromise in which the relevant actors trade concessions and mutually do not exercise their ability to obstruct. The second involves the stronger prevailing over the weaker. In international organizations, the ostensible measure of strength is votes. However, in a system which remains dominated by the reality of sovereignty—the ultimate ability of sovereign states not to do what they do not agree to do—a decision adopted by a majority against the resistance of a minority cannot be effective unless the minority agrees to the decision rule by which it may be bound without its explicit consent. For a decision to be effective in such circumstances, the minority has to be willing not to exercise its capacity to obstruct. There is a variant. Sometimes, there is a kind of "opting out" procedure under which the minority accepts the right of the majority to reach and act upon decisions which carry the cachet of legitimacy but without the minority's being bound by the decision. That is another form of minority concession of its capacity to obstruct. An example of this is the adoption of a decision by consensus, when the disagreement of some is not carried to the point of blocking the consensus but may take the form of stated "reservations."

The institutional implications of these considerations are relatively straightforward. Figure 3 intends to capture them. When there is agreement on values, decisions can be reached either under a centralized or unit veto rule. When there is not, a centralized decision rule enhances the power of the majority and a unit veto rule enhances the power of the minority. In some ways, the most interesting part of the spectrum shown in Figure 3 is the in-between zone, called "Intermediate Zone of Struggle over Authoritative Allocation." It is the battleground in which majorities seek and minorities resist the centralized allocation of values. It has been the battleground of North-South struggle especially since the G-77/NAM became the majority in the UN system.

As the section on formal powers made clear, the states relinquished little power when they established and joined international organizations. With exceptions which will be considered hereinafter, they planned an essentially unit veto system. Little power was shared between members and the organizations in the original constitutive arrangements. The states essentially held on to their power to refuse to do what they did not wish to do. Doctrinally, this conservation of their power by the states took the form of the assumptions of sovereignty and domestic jurisdiction to be found in Articles 2/1 and 2/7 of the UN Charter. The international agencies were endowed with little power to allocate values in the international system.

Exceptions to this generalization were important. There were from the beginning constitutive bases for centralized decision making which have proven important subsequently. Chief among these have been: limited powers to make binding decisions by majority procedures, usually on technical issues (Alexandrowicz 1973); the authority to set budgets and assess members, as in Article 17 of the UN Charter; the powers given agencies to regulate their own internal affairs; the power, whose significance was probably underestimated at the outset, to formulate recommendations to be addressed to members and to other international organizations; and the inherent power, which went largely unrecognized at the beginning, to make program decisions (Rucz 1983).

On the basis of such authorities, there has been movement from right to left in Figure 3, that is, toward centralized decision making. As was made clear in the preceding section, there has also been movement from left to right, that is from centralized toward unit veto modes. This has been true most notably in the realm of peace and security. As the previous section showed, there has been more than expected sharing of functions with respect to peace and security questions between the General Assembly, which lacks binding powers, and the Security Council, which has such power in theory (Goodrich 1969, Goodwin 1958). Within the Security Council, there has been a clear movement from the idea of binding authority toward the unit veto mode of acting.

There are numerous examples of behavior which clearly fall in these two categories, at opposite ends of the spectrum. There are also examples of mixed behaviors in which centralized and unit veto modes of reaching decisions mingle. UNDP, for example, makes its program decisions by majority procedures. It does so in response to the preferences of individual recipient countries. It depends for its resources on voluntary contributions of funds. There is intense interaction between the two modes, which complement each other. Program decisions which recipient countries do not carry out are useless if not harmful. Without funds, programs remain empty vessels. Thus, the centralized processes depend for their meaning on the voluntary ones. Conversely, the character of the centralized decisions about programs influences the national plans and requests of recipient countries and the willingness of the donors to volunteer funds.

Another example of mingling is the role of the international voting bodies in the treaty-making process. Majorities decide the content of the treaties which can become effective only through the voluntary acquiescence of states which remain free not to ratify them. In both cases, evidently, the right of nonparticipation is an important source of leverage in the majority decision processes. The reverse is also true. The weight of majority pressures can narrow the options available to states which resist the dominant preferences.

Much of the struggle in the intermediate zone has been concerned with the sharing of power, that is the attempt of the majority to establish the authority of majority decisions. By definition, authority in the intermediate zone is contested rather than established. There are gradations. Funding development programs ordinarily does not rely on the compulsory assessment authority in the agency constitutions; the unit veto rule unmistakably prevails in the face of majority pressures to extend decision authority. Susan Strange emphasized the point: "There is nothing resembling a world tax system to decide who should pay for public goods—whenever the slightest hint of any of these is breathed in diplomatic circles, state governments have all their defenses at the ready to reject even the most modest enroachment on what they regard as their national prerogatives" (Strange 1982). The majorities have every reason to be aware that the traffic will not bear an attempt to employ for broader purposes of public policy the compulsory assessment authority which applies to the "regular" budgets (Meagher 1983).

On the other hand, although the United States and other Western countries have not conceded binding authority to the majority seeking to establish it, for example, over racialism in South Africa, and such binding authority cannot be said to exist, nevertheless they appear to have acknowledged the appropriateness of majority assertion of principles to be applied. The power to vote a "rule" is denied. The power to vote a "principle" is not. This introduces considerable ambiguity in classifying such actions in terms of the spectrum of Figure 3. If "principles" adopted by majority votes are thought of as values contested by states, as indeed they are, then they probably deserve to be placed in the category of centralized decisions, even though, unlike rules, they are not in and of themselves binding. On many issues, majorities have established principles over the resistance of minorities. There are thus many cases of issues which have moved, so to speak, from the ambiguous zone of struggle over the question of authority into the zone of centralized decisions as a result of the assertion and final dominance of principles advocated by majorities.

The ambiguity is made more complex when implementation is considered. Some such principles probably take on the character of "concrete and imperative principles" (McWhinney 1981) or "public policy" (Zacklin 1969, Puchala 1984). Such principles may be said to have guiding, if not compulsory, effect, for those who have advocated them, or have come to accept them, but not for those who continue to resist. South Africa refuses to be bound by the delegitimization of apartheid which has been effected in principle by majority procedures over time. It remains, therefore, in the unit veto mode. The rest of the world, however, may be bound to accept the principle that apartheid is not legitimate and, by and large, states acknowledge that they are so bound. The result is a curious amalgam of what appears to be authoritative power to establish principles and the sovereign right not to be bound by them.

An important feature of the struggle over allocative authority in the intermediate zone has been the move in recent years to "restructure" the UN system. While the "restructuring" exercise has thus far involved more effort than effect, the processes continue. They represent a concerted campaign by the G-77 to alter in their favor the rules, procedures and organizational frameworks affecting allocative authority across the broad spectrum of economic and social functions in the UN system (Meltzer 1983, 1978, Renninger 1982).

Interestingly, a reaction has set in. The US decision to withdraw from UNESCO was said to be motivated in good part by dissatisfaction with the "tyranny of the majority"—the ways in which the majority seeks to employ the rules, procedures and framework of the organization in its effort to affect the allocation of contested values. In seeking to reform UNESCO, the United States advocated improvements in the procedures of the governing bodies and, notably, a new voting rule on appropriations whereby "no budget would pass without the affirmative support of members who together contribute at least 51% of the organization's funds." It also demanded, among other changes, improvement in UNESCO's consensus procedures and "creation of a mechanism to ensure that, in major matters, UNESCO decisions and programs enjoy the support of all geographic groups. . ." (United States Permanent Representative to UNESCO 1984). The last of these seems to endorse a new principle for distributing authority in the international system which Gottlieb has called "parity diplomacy" or "equality between groups of states" (Gottlieb 1982). In addition to these efforts to bring about constitutive change in UNESCO, to reconstitute the unit veto, or constitute a group veto, the United States and other countries have resorted to a policy of what has been labelled "nullification," that is a refusal to pay for decisions of which they do not approve (Finkelstein 1984).

Struggle in the intermediate zone has been concerned with authority. Power has been exerted to change the rules governing the exercise of power. Contestants have fought over the instrumental values of rules, membership and representation, procedures, structures and frameworks. They have fought over the claim of majorities that majority action can determine what is legitimate and what is not (Claude 1966). When the United States led the majority in the intense years of the Cold War, it led in the assertion of just such a claim. When the ascendancy of the G-77 was assured as a result of the surge of new members into the organization following the wave of decolonization, they did the same thing. With the reversal in numbers, the United States has reversed field and now leads the resistance to the majority's claim to command legitimacy by its voting power.

Legitimacy is a highly valued instrument in the international pursuit of valued ends, notably in the UN system. Majorities have been seeking the imprimatur of international agencies' endorsements of preferred policies, principles and rules as a source of legitimacy on a large range of international issues. To a considerable extent, this involves the attempt to employ parliamentary decisions, even when they are not intended to be binding in their own terms, as instruments of law creation. Resolutions, declarations and other instruments are employed as evidence of the developing customs of the international community, and custom is a source of law (Schacter 1983, McWhinney 1981). Such instruments are employed by their advocates as devices and perhaps as sources of authoritative power, in their campaigns to change rules in the system. Issues of legitimacy may also be particularized. Struggle over legitimacy has been at the heart of the issue of Israel as it has arisen in the UN system in recent years (Kirkpatrick 1983). In this case, preserving legitimacy in the UN system is an objective of Israeli policy and delegitimization seems an objective of the Arab rejectionists and their allies. UN legitimacy is itself an instrument in the broader struggle over security and survival in the Middle East. In this instance, as is often the case, legitimacy is both an end and a means. In sum, "the U.N. has become the foremost legitimizing authority in international affairs" (Schoenberg 1984, Gottlieb 1982).

The outcome of struggle over establishment of authority in the intermediate zone is issue specific. Such centralizing of decision power as has resulted from these processes has occurred unevenly across the system. Outcomes are affected by such variable factors as the salience of what is at stake to those whose concurrence or participation is most important, the ways in which issues are linked with each other in the complex bargaining within and between caucusing and voting groups in the system, and the domestic influences on national decisions, as well as the influence of the relevant rules and procedures of varied institutional settings. If the experience of the struggle over authority had to be summarized, the summary could only be—"indeterminate."

That does not mean, however, that there have been no significant substantive consequences of the struggle over authority. In many respects, there is stalemate. The attempt of the G-77 over more than a decade to employ voting pressure to produce significant change in the international economic and development order has not succeeded, although it has had some effect. In the realm of peace and security, resolution or amelioration of conflicts through the painstaking processes of unit veto diplomacy has been increasingly rare. All the same, the struggle to assert authority has produced a great many substantial consequences. Some of these are significant and many appear to be irreversible.

To begin with, the budgets of the international agencies have grown very substantially over the years through the grudging submission of the minority who bear most of the burden to the demands of the majorities expressed through the voting procedures. The regular budgets of the large UN agencies are now about thirty times what they were when they began. As has already been noted, these sums have been supplemented by the increase in the number of agencies commanding budgets and by the emphasis on voluntary funding arrangements. Reaction led by the United States has definitely set in. It is likely that the years ahead will see new formulas for sharing power over budget decisions. It does not, however, seem likely that the rate of growth in international funding will be notably slowed.

An important result of the struggle has been the creation of new agencies in response to majority demands. UNDP, IDA and the regional development banks are particularly important examples of this phenomenon because they dispose of relatively substantial resources for development of LDCs.

The majority has done relatively well also in enlarging its share of the places in the international system—memberships and elected offices in organs, commissions, conferences and committees to which the principle of proportionality has clearly come to apply and in staff positions and leadership. The majority has effectively asserted its power to claim its share of the values of this kind which are allocated in the system.

Perhaps of greatest significance has been the establishment through the voting processes of important international norms, which may even amount to rules. The right of colonies to self-determination has been established and colonialism has effectively been stripped of legitimacy. So have racialism and apartheid.

Finally, even with respect to the New International Economic Order (NIEO) in which the aspirations of the majority have been essentially blocked by the refusal of leading developed countries to cooperate in the achievement of the majority's objectives, there have been some concessions. One is the General System of Preferences (GSP) which is in effect a relaxation of the established rule, preferred by the United States, of reciprocity in tariff concessions. Another is debt relief for LDCs (Crane 1984). Another is the International Program for Commodities/Common Fund. A fourth is the creation of the special "facilities" in the IMF as additional sources of capital relief for LDCs in distress (Cohen 1982, Ruggie 1983, Crane 1984). The consensus is that these concessions to the G-77 have been more important in principle than in effect. Yet, the predominant reality in the relations between developed countries and LDCs has been the firm establishment of the development mission, which had no precedent before World War II.

Related to LDC power has been the growth in the role and influence of the executive heads and the staffs of international agencies. Jacobson has underlined the inadequacy of the simple reliance on the truth that, finally, secretariats are limited by the controlling power of governments (Jacobson 1984). In fact, the staffs have been to a great extent the beneficiaries of agency growth and of such transition of authority as has occurred from unit veto toward centralized authority modes and, indeed, in some cases have been important actors in the process of transition. As exercisers of authority, they have shared power both with member states and with the other organs in the agencies. The growth in the number of nationals of LDCs in the international secretariats has been one means by which the LDCs have shared in this transfer of influence.

Executive heads inherit functions which members desire them to exercise when the members cannot reach sufficient agreement to exert authority themselves. One example was, of course, the "leave it to Dag" phenomenon. The UN Secretary-General today is performing much the same function in playing a number of good offices roles in tense international conflict situations. The executive heads derive power from other kinds of indispensability. No one else can perform the tasks of administration which result from program decisions. They derive allocative power that way and gain different kinds of leverage over the decisions. They also have the resources of information and administrative control which only they can possess.

Moreover, in some cases at least, UNESCO being the most evident example, the power of the executive head and of the staff results from a symbiosis of interest with the G-77 which has resulted in the director-general becoming in effect the leader of the majority party in the organization (Finkelstein 1983). The UNESCO case makes clear that such executive power is one target of the reaction of the Western countries. Whether they can succeed in the long run in reining in the staffs is, however, uncertain. It is difficult to predict a significant diminution in their effective exercise of power in the future.

There remains the question of the result or effect of power sharing in international organizations. There is widespread belief that in the final analysis, the heaving and hauling over authority does not really matter. Since the collaboration of those with the capacity to make things happen is essential, things will happen if they collaborate, and if they do not, no exercise of apparent authority will change that.

Unfortunately, we can not evaluate such propositions empirically. To begin with, scholarship has been casual rather than rigorous about the criteria of judgment. What do we mean when we ask: "Does it work?"

Should we for instance want the UN to help stabilize or to help transform the international system? (Gregg 1984). Is the proper standard contribution to peace, or to "integration," task or function performance, agency benefit or growth, or satisfying the constituency (a criterion which is paid little attention, but which is a normal measure of the working of a domestic political system) (Finkelstein 1974)?

Usually, the implied standard is that of task performance—how well does the system do in getting done a job which has been assigned to it? Even when the evidence seems to be at hand, such as statistics on the incidence of war, there is what might be termed the correlational problem—that is, correlation is not synonymous with cause. It is very difficult to interpret results which seem to emerge from the institutional processes, or to have been affected by them, as having been caused by them (Jacobson 1984). For the most part, the international agencies are embedded in their environments. They are predominantly instrumental to the roles of the other actors involved, primarily the member states. It is possible to know that the agencies are implicated in the results, but rarely that they have caused them.

Moreover, when what is involved is the effect of programs undertaken by the international organizations, it is unhappily the case that scholarship is handicapped by inadequate tools for evaluation. One aspect of current reform efforts, in UNESCO and elsewhere, is to strengthen the evaluation functions. Such efforts confront a general paucity of information about results at the "consuming end" of the process, and severe political constraints in the international system of shared power which inhibit freedom to question whether the program decisions were the right ones or not. Evaluation is thus generally limited to assessing achievement of the goals of programs as they were adopted. By and large evaluation has for these reasons been concerned much more with efficiency of delivery than with efficacy of the program. The material and political costs of doing better are likely to impede doing so.

There is a certain cogency to the simple view that, since coercion is finally generally unavailable in the system of sovereign states, cooperation is the essential condition of effectiveness. The voluntarism that undergirds the UNDP procedures of authority is, in this view, a sensible model. The limited achievements of the effort to legislate system change as in the case of the NIEO constitute a cautionary reinforcement of the simple proposition that if it is to work, it has to be voluntary.

Yet this seemingly cogent moral is, finally, too simple. Of course, it is correct that states have the power to withhold the resources, the cooperation and the other forms of compliance on which successful international action normally depends. Of course, they must be willing to collaborate if there is to be successful international action. It is correct to deduce that power has to be shared at the decision-making stage if there is to be effective implementation of the decisions reached.

What this logic neglects, however, is the equally cogent truth that willingness to collaborate is not a constant. The time scale is an important consideration. States' perceptions of where their interests lie are, it has been often demonstrated, influenced by the pressures over time of majority interests upon minorities' resistance. Inducing the willing collaboration of minorities has been an important part of what the contentious political proceedings in the international organization system have been all about. The record is not void of successes.

Author's note: The author gratefully acknowledges the generosity of his colleague Martin David Dubin in critically reading an earlier version of this chapter.

Footnotes

1. Inscription found on a lavatory wall at the University of Chicago in the 1960s (apocryphal). Translation by the author: Which Chicago School do you follow?

2. Italics added. This is the famous definition by Hans Morgenthau (Morgenthau 1973: 9, 28). He clearly meant "control" to be synonymous with "rule," "govern," or at least "dominate," rather than the softer definition associated with the French word "*controler*" (ibid.: 28). Similarly, power is "command" to De Jouvenal (De Jouvenal 1952: 91-95).

3. One example was the key role of the director-general of IATA in the overturning of the US policy of withdrawing the exemption from US antitrust laws on which IATA's faresetting framework rested (Jonsson 1984).

4. Although there are weighted voting formulas, such as the requirement for concurring votes of the named members (the "veto") in the Security Council and the link with financial contributions in the World Bank and the International Monetary Fund.

5. An explanation is the fear that consensus might not exist to support such an initiative by the Secretary-General and that, in consequence, the latter would find himself in an untenable position (Nicol 1982:52).

6. Bennett lists the following as "multipurpose" regional organizations: Organization of American States (OAS), League of Arab States, Organization of African Unity (OAU), Commonwealth, Council of Europe, Organization of Central American States (ODECA), Common Afro-Mauritian (Sic! Read "Madagascan") Organization (OCAM), Andean Group; Association of Southeast Asian Nations (ASEAN), and Nordic Council. All but the OAS, the Commonwealth and the Arab League were created after the UN was founded (Bennett 1984:355).

7. Haas counted 20 between 1945 and 1981 out of a universe of 282 disputes studied in accordance with his special definition. He also identified three disputes dealt with by two regional agencies (Haas 1983:195).

8. Not all limited membership organizations are strictly speaking "regional," but most by far appear to be. Organizations appearing in Jacobson's Appendix were not counted if they were created before 1946, had fewer than three members, or dealt only with peace and security functions (Jacobson 1984:397-410).

9. The totals do not equal the sums of the preceding figures because many cases were dealt with by both organs. Bennett says 21% of all cases between 1946 and 1982 fall in this category (Bennett 1984:127).

References

Alexandrowicz, Charles Henry. 1973. *The law-making functions of the specialized agencies of the United Nations*. Sydney: Angus & Robertson.

Ascher, William. 1983. New development approaches and the adaptability of international agencies. *International Organization* 37(3): 415-439.

Bailey, Sydney D. 1962. *The secretariat of the United Nations*. New York: Carnegie Endowment for International Peace, 10.

Baldwin, David. 1979. Power analysis and world politics: New trends versus old tendencies. *World Politics* 31(2): 162, 165-184.

Bennett, Leroy. 1984. *International organization*, 3rd ed. Englewood Cliffs, N.J.: Prentice Hall, 105-112, 122-130, 351-355.

Burton, John W. 1972. *World society*. London: Cambridge University Press, 47.

Claude, Inis L., Jr. 1964. The OAS, the UN and the United States. *International Conciliation*, 547.

Claude, Inis L., Jr. 1966. Collective legitimization as a political function of the United Nations. *International Organization* 20(3): 367-379.

Coate, Roger A. 1982. *Global issue regimes*. New York: Praeger, 29.

Cohen, Benjamin J. 1982. Balance of payments financing: Evolution of a regime. In "International regimes", edited by Stephen D. Krasner, a special edition of *International Organization* 36(2): 457-478.

Committee on Foreign Affairs, US House of Representatives. 1984. Executive Summary of US/UNESCO Policy Review. *US withdrawal from UNESCO* (Appendix 6, Report of a Staff Study Mission, February 10-23, 1984): 101, 153-156.

Cox, Robert W. 1973. "The executive head: An essay on leadership in international organization." In *International Organization: Politics and Process*, edited by Leland M. Goodrich and David A. Kay. Madison, Wis: University of Wisconsin Press, 161.

Cox, Robert W., Harold K. Jacobson et al. 1973. *The anatomy of influence: Decision making in international organizations*. New Haven, Conn.: Yale University Press.

Crane, Barbara. 1984. Policy coordination by major western powers in bargaining with the Third World: Debt relief and the Common Fund. *International Organization* 36(3): 399-428.

Dahl, Robert A. 1968. Power. *International Encyclopedia of the Social Sciences*, Vol. 12. Macmillan & Free Press, 408.

De Jouvenal, Bertrand. 1952. *Power: The natural history of its growth*, translated by J. F. Huntington. London: Butterworth, 91-95.

Easton, David. 1953. *The political system: An inquiry into the state of political science*. New York: Knopf.

_____. 1965. *A framework for political analysis*. Englewood Cliffs, N.J.: Prentice-Hall.

1968. "Political science." *International Encyclopedia of the Social Sciences*. Vol. 12. Macmillan & Free Press, 286.

Elmandjra, Mahdi. 1973. *The United Nations system: An analysis*. London: Faber and Faber, 37-114, 222-292.

Farley, Lawrence T. 1981. *Change processes in international organizations*. Cambridge, Mass.: Schenkman, 130ff.

Finkelstein, Lawrence S. 1974. International organizations and change: The past as prologue. *International Studies Quarterly* 18(4): 505-515.

_____. 1983. "The politics of national governments and of international intergovernmental organizations: Are they comparable?" Paper prepared for presentation at the Annual Meeting of the International Studies Association, Mexico City, April: 30.

_____. 1984. "Forty years of the United Nations: From the multilateral diplomacy of sovereign equality toward the politics of value allocation." Paper prepared for the Workshop on the UN at 40, 25th Annual Convention of the International Studies Association, Atlanta, Georgia, March: 6-7, 15.

Finkelstein, Lawrence S. and Marina S., eds. 1966. *Collective security*. San Francisco: Chandler, 1-3.

Forsythe, David P. 1984. "The United Nations and human rights 1945-1985: Or, the reasons for schizophrenia." Paper presented to the Workshop on Forty Years of the UN, 25th Annual Convention of the International Studies Association, Atlanta, Georgia, March.

Fox, Annette Baker. 1959. *The power of small states: Diplomacy in World War II*. Chicago: University of Chicago Press, 2-3.

Goodrich, Leland M., Edvard Hambro and Anne Patricia Simons. 1969. *Charter of the United Nations: Commentary and documents*, 3rd and rev. ed. New York: Columbia University Press, 125, 208-209.

Goodwin, Geoffrey L. 1958. *Britain and the United Nations*. New York: Carnegie Endowment for International Peace, 246.

Gordenker, Leon. 1983. "Development of the UN system." In *The US, the UN, and the management of global change*, edited by Toby Trister Gati. New York: New York University Press, 15.

Gottlieb, Gidon. 1982. "Global bargaining: The legal and diplomatic framework." In *Lawmaking in the global community*, edited by Nicholas G. Onuf. Durham, N.C.: Carolina Academic Press, 109-110, 120, 123.

Gregg, Robert W. 1984. "International economic cooperation and development: The United Nations in search of a role." Draft discussion paper presented before the Workshop on the United Nations at Forty, Annual Convention of the International Studies Association, Atlanta, Georgia, March.

Haas, Ernst B. 1968. "Dynamic environment and static system: Revolutionary regimes in the United Nations." In *The United Nations System and its Functions*, edited by Robert W. Gregg and Michael Barkun. Princeton, N.J.: D. van Nostrand Company, 172.

_____. 1983. Regime decay: Conflict management and international organization 1945-1981. *International Organization* 37(2): 189-256.

Hadas, Moses. 1960. "The art and science of thucydides." In *Thucydides*, translated by Benjamin Jowett. New York: Bantam, 16.

Halle, Louis. 1984. *The elements of international strategy: A primer for the nuclear age*. New York: University Press of America, 84.

Hart, Jeffrey. 1976. Three approaches to the measurement of power in international relations. *International Organization* 30(2): 289-305.

Hill, Martin. 1978. *The United Nations system: Coordinating the economic and social work.* Cambridge: Cambridge University Press.

Jackson, Richard L. 1983. *The non-aligned, the UN and the superpowers.* New York: Praeger.

Jacobson, Harold K. 1984. *Networks of interdependence: International organizations and the global political system,* 2nd ed. New York: Knopf, 118-123, 198, 397-410.

James, Alan. 1969. *The politics of peacekeeping.* New York: Praeger, 9.

Jonsson, Christer. 1984. "Interorganization theory and international organization: An analytical framework and a case study." Paper presented at the 25th Annual Convention of the International Studies Association, Atlanta, Georgia, March.

Judge, Anthony J. N. 1978. "International organization networks: A complementary perspective." In *International Organisation: A Conceptual Approach,* edited by Paul Taylor and A.J.R. Groom. London: Frances Pinter, 381-413.

Keohane, Robert O. 1971. The big influence of small allies. *Foreign Policy* 1(2): 161-182.

Keohane, Robert O. and Joseph S. Nye, Jr., eds. 1971. "Transnational relations and world politics." *International Organization* 25(3).

Keohane, Robert O. and Joseph S. Nye. 1977. *Power and interdependence: World politics in transition.* Boston: Little, Brown.

Kirkpatrick, Jeane J. 1983. Statement of Ambassador Jeane J. Kirkpatrick, U.S. Permanent Representative to the United Nations. *The US role in the united nations.* Hearings before the Subcommittees on Human Rights and International Organizations, Committee on Foreign Affairs, House of Representatives, September 27 and October 3, 1983: 79-80.

Krasner, Stephen D., ed. 1982. "International Regimes," a special issue of *International Organization* 36(2).

Mansbach, Richard W. and John A. Vasquez. 1981. *In search of theory: A new paradigm for global politics.* New York: Columbia University Press, 213.

Mason, Edward S. and Robert L. Asher. 1973. *The World Bank since Bretton Woods.* Washington, D.C.: Brookings.

McLaren, Robert L. 1980. The UN system and its Quixotic quest for coordination." *International Organization* 34(1): 139-148.

McWhinney, Edward. 1981. *Conflict and compromise: International law and world order in a revolutionary age.* New York: Holmes & Meier, 18, 51.

Meagher, Robert F. 1983. "United States financing of the United Nations." In *The US, the UN, and the management of global change,* edited by Toby Trister Gati. New York: New York University Press: 111-114.

Meltzer, Ronald I. 1978. "Restructuring the United Nations system: Institutional reform efforts in the context of North-South relations." *International Organization* 32(4) Autumn: 993-1018.

Meltzer, Ronald I. 1983. "UN Structural Reform: Institutional Development in International Economic and Social Affairs." In *The US, the UN and the Management of Global Change*, edited by Toby Trister Gati. New York: New York University Press, 239-262.

Morgenthau, Hans J. 1973. *Politics among nations*, 5th ed. New York: Knopf, 9, 28.

Mortimer, Robert A. 1984. *The Third World coalition in international politics*, 2nd ed. Boulder, Colo.: Westview Press.

Newell, Hon. Gregory. 1983. On-the-record Briefing on US Withdrawal from UNESCO by Hon. Gregory Newell, assistant secretary of state, Bureau of International Organization Affairs, Thursday, December 29, 1983. *US Withdrawal from UNESCO* (Appendix 6, Report of a Staff Study Mission), Committee on Foreign Affairs, US House of Representatives, April 1984: 153-156.

Nicol, Davidson with Margaret Coke and Babatunde Adeniran. 1982. *The United Nations security council: Toward greater effectiveness*. New York: UNITAR, 52.

Nye, Joseph S., Jr. 1968. *International regionalism: Readings*. Boston: Little, Brown, 3-21.

Nye, J. S. 1971. *Peace in parts: Integration and conflict in regional organization.* Boston: Little, Brown, 6-8.

Obaseki, Nosa-Ola. 1981. "Conflict resolution in Africa: What role for international organizations?" In *The future of international organization*, edited by Rudiger Jutte and Annemarie Grosse-Jutte. New York: St. Martin's, 202, 209, 214.

Olson, Mancur, Jr. 1971. *The Logic of Collective Action.* New York: Schocken.

Olson, Mancur, Jr. and Richard Zeckhauser. 1970. "An Economic Theory of Alliances." In *Alliances: Latent war communities in the contemporary world*, ed. Francis A. Beer. New York: Holt, Rinehart and Winston: 120-140.

Pastor, Robert. 1984. "The International Debate on Puerto Rico: The Costs of Being an Agenda-Taker." *International Organization* 36(3): 575.

Peabody, Robert L. 1968. "Authority." *International Encyclopedia of the Social Sciences*. Vol. 1. Macmillan & Free Press: 473-474.

Puchala, Donald J. 1984. "The United Nations and ecosystem issues: A research note." Paper presented to the Workshop on Forty Years of the UN, 25th Annual Convention of the International Studies Association, Atlanta, Georgia, March.

Rajan, M. S. 1982. *The expanding jurisdiction of the United Nations*. Dobbs Ferry, N.Y.: Oceana.

Renninger, John P. 1982. "Restructuring the UN system." In *The emerging international economic order: Dynamic processes, constraints, and opportunities*, edited by Harold K. Jacobson and Dusan Sidjanski. Beverly Hills, Calif.: Sage, 260, 263, 266.

Rothstein, Robert. 1979. *Global bargaining: UNCTAD and the quest for a new international economic order.* Princeton, N.J.: Princeton University Press.

Rovine, Arthur W. 1970. *The first fifty years: The Secretary-General in world politics 1920-1970.* Leyden: A. J. Sijthoff, 279 ff., 330-340.

Rucz, Claude. 1983. *Le conseil economique et social de L'O.N.U. et la cooperation pour le developpement.* Paris: *Economica*, 154-209.

Ruggie, John Gerard. 1983. "Political structure and change in the international economic order: The North-South dimension." In *The antinomies of interdependence: National welfare and the international division of labor*, edited by John Gerard Ruggie. New York: Columbia University Press, 423-487.

Schachter, Oscar. 1983. "The nature and process of legal development in international society." In *The structure and process of international law*, edited by R. St. J. McDonald and D. M. Johnston. Boston: Nijhoff, 745-808.

Schaffer, Stephen M. and Lisa Robock Schaffer. 1980. *The politics of international cooperation: A comparison of US experience in space and in security.* Denver: University of Denver Graduate School of International Studies (Monograph Series in World Affairs, 17/4), 28.

Schelling, Thomas C. 1966. *Arms and influence.* New Haven, Conn.: Yale University Press, 1-34.

Schoenberg, Harris O. 1984. "Legitimizing the bad." Letter to the Editor, *New York Times*, March 20.

Smithers, Sir Peter. 1973. *Governmental control: A prerequisite for effective relations between the United Nations and non-United Nations regional organizations.* New York: UNITAR.

Strange, Susan. 1982. Cave! Hic Dragones: A Critique of Regime Analysis. In Stephen D. Krasner, ed., "International Regimes." *International Organization* 36(2): 487.

United Nations Department of Public Information. 1984. *Weekly News Summary* WS/1185, 22 June: 4.

UNESCO. 1984. Rapport Oral du Directeur-general sur l'Activite de l'Organization depuis la 118e Session (facsimile) before the 119th session of the Executive Board of UNESCO, May 9. Doc. 119 EX/INF 3 (prov.): 15-17.

UNESCO, General Conference, Twenty-second Session. 1983. *Draft programme and budget for 1984-1985* (22 C/5): 41-42.

United States Permanent Representative to the United Nations Educational, Scientific and Cultural Organization (UNESCO). 1984. Letter to the Director-General from Ambassador Jean Broward Shevlin Gerard, July 13 (Xerox): 2-3.

Weston, Burns H., Richard A. Falk and Anthony A. D'Amato. 1980. *Basic documents in international law and order.* St. Paul, Minn.: West, 150-155.

Willetts, Peter. 1978. *The non-aligned movement: The origins of a Third World alliance.* London: Frances Pinter.

Zacklin, Ralph. 1969. The challenge of Rhodesia: Toward an international public policy. *International Conciliation* 575(November).

CHAPTER 15

Power Sharing Regimes and Strategic Arms Control

P. Terrence Hopmann and John B. Harris

Introduction: Power Sharing Regimes in International Politics

Shared power is a concept that applies in situations where no one person, group, organization, institution, or nation-state is in charge. Rather, multiple actors share in influencing social decisions, with the influence of no single actor dominating. Interdependence exists in such relationships among actors, though the fact that power must be shared also implies the existence of independent actors whose goals are not completely synonymous. Therefore, shared power seems to apply to mixed motive situations, where the interests of actors are partially overlapping and partially in conflict. It also applies where the interdependence of their relationships requires joint decision making to coordinate common interests in the midst of conflicting ones.

Shared Power and the Concept of International Regimes

In the field of international politics, traditional conceptions have generally not paid great attention to power sharing. On the contrary, most so-called "realist" approaches to international politics have emphasized the autonomy of individual and sovereign nation-states, interacting in an anarchical international system. In so far as anarchy is limited in such a system, traditionally this was accomplished by the interactive consequence of each actor behaving in its own self interest. Or, in rare cases, prescient actors might recognize long-term interests in cooperation that would supersede short-run interests. For example, in the classical balance of power international system, self-interested behavior of individual nations was supposed to create a kind of self-enforcing equilibrium of power among the major states, preserving relative peace and the continued existence of the state system (Waltz 1979).

Recently, however, students of international politics have begun paying greater attention to these issues. The contemporary international system has been characterized by Robert Keohane and Joseph Nye (1977) as one of "complex interdependence." They define interdependent situations as those involving reciprocal effects among nation-states. These effects need not necessarily be perfectly symmetrical, but they must be at least bi-directional. Complex interdependence applies in situations where there are multiple actors interconnected across national boundaries, and where multiple issues may be aggregated to affect interdependence. Keohane and Nye define international regimes as governing relationships that affect interdependence. This concept of a regime seems to be quite appropriate for treating the issues of "shared power" at the international level.

In a recent work on regimes, Stephen Krasner (1983:2) has defined them as follows:

> Regimes can be defined as sets of implicit or explicit principles, norms, rules, and decision-making procedures around which actors' expectations converge in a given area of international relations. Principles are beliefs of fact, causation, and rectitude. Norms are standards of behavior defined in terms of rights and obligations. Rules are specific prescriptions or proscriptions for action. Decision-making procedures are prevailing practices for making and implementing collective choice.

Regimes are treated as intervening variables that link the power structure of the international system with specific behaviors, especially bargaining behaviors, among interdependent national actors. They thus reflect the fact of shared power, while also going beyond considerations of power alone. Above all, regimes depend not only on an appropriate configuration of power and interests, but also on a set of shared perceptions, understandings, and knowledge that govern joint behavior. As Ernst Haas (1983) has observed, regime analysis accepts the fact of power differentials and international hierarchy, while stressing that relations among nation-states are also governed by cognitive considerations. The emphasis is on how actors "perceive the need for collaboration...."

These joint understandings may be formalized in agreements, treaties, and institutions, though this is by no means essential. Indeed, some of the most prominent examples of successful regimes are based more on informal understandings of the "rules of the game" rather than on formal agreements or institutions. Alternatively regimes may be established through formal agreements, such as the Bretton Woods accords that established the postwar international monetary regime, or through formal treaties such as for the law of the seas regime. As Oran Young (1983) has suggested, "regimes are dependent upon the maintenance of convergent expectations among actors; formalization is not a necessary condition for the effective operation of regimes, and regimes are always created rather than discovered."

Political scientists have endeavored to define the structural relationships between nation-states which hold the potential for regime formation. Game theorists, for example, have extensively analyzed strategic relationships among nation-states in order to develop generalizable "rules" for international regime formation. Strategic relationships, sometimes called "strategic interactions," are those in which the outcome of one state's behavior depends upon the actions of at least one other state as well. Only certain types of strategic interactions provide the necessary conditions for regime creation.

For example, in purely cooperative relationships in which the interests of states coincide, joint decision making is unnecessary because each party can achieve its most preferred outcome by acting on its own without any necessity of coordination with the other party. In this instance, each actor's behavior will automatically converge with that of the other party without prior agreement. In purely conflictual relationships, on the other hand, cooperation is ruled out altogether. Because no area of mutual interest exists, there is no basis for the coordination of behavior which is essential for regime creation.

Therefore, international regimes, defined as coordinated or joint decision-making situations among nation-states, can only emerge from strategic interactions characterized by a mixture of mutual and conflicting interests among the relevant actors. Perhaps the most widely employed game-theoretic analogue to such "mixed-motive" situations in international relations is the "Prisoners' Dilemma" game, depicted in Figure 1.

		Actor B	
		B1— Cooperate	B2— Compete
Actor A	A1— Cooperate	3,3	1,4
	A2— Compete	4,1	2,2

Figure 15-1 The Prisoners' Dilemma Game

In this situation, individually rational behavior leaves actors with an equilibrium solution at A2, B2, which is less than Pareto optimal, in the sense that both actors could make a mutually beneficial improvement in their payoffs by agreeing at A1, B1. On the other hand, the superior solution of mutual coordination is not stable due to the temptation of each individual actor to defect from this agreement in order to try to maximize the actor's own payoff. Actor A clearly does best with A2, B1, whereas actor B prefers A1, B2; yet when each chooses the most preferred outcome, they both end up with A2, B2. Therefore, a mutually rewarding solution requires a coordinated agreement to settle at A1, B1, with some mutual expectations that neither actor will defect for individual gain. It is precisely in such situations where the creation of a regime may be appropriate. As Arthur Stein (1983) points out, in these situations regimes may help the individual actors to achieve common interests in order to overcome the "collective suboptimality that can emerge from individual behavior."

The Special Case of Security Regimes: The U.S.-Soviet Nuclear Arms Competition

Most analyses of regimes in international politics have focused on economic issues, where regimes have sought to achieve collaboration on mutually beneficial outcomes. However, security regimes may also exist in situations of avoidance of undesirable outcomes. In this domain states may establish regimes to coordinate behavior in order to control mutual conflict. Such cooperation is often complicated, as Robert Jervis (1983:174) has suggested, by the existence of a "security dilemma:"

> ...policies that are designed to increase a state's security automatically and inadvertently decrease the security of others. Security regimes are thus both especially valuable and especially difficult to achieve—valuable, because individualistic actions are not only costly but dangerous; difficult to achieve, because the fear that the other is violating or will violate the common understanding is a potent incentive for each state to strike out on its own even if it would prefer the regime to prosper.

A common example of the security dilemma is an arms race. Each state might generally prefer not to arm. However, seeing its potential enemy arming, it may feel that it must arm itself in response. Yet when the "enemy" responds according to the same logic, the result may be an arms race which may leave both sides less secure, due both to the larger quantity and improved quality of armaments, as well as to the hostilities engendered by the arms race. Each would find it advantageous to disarm if it could know with some certainty that its opponent was doing likewise, thus leaving both better off. However, in a system of anarchy, such a mutually beneficial agreement may be difficult to achieve and to enforce. Nowhere has this been demonstrated more clearly than in the joint effort by the United States and the Soviet Union to moderate and control their competition in strategic nuclear armaments.

Since the 1960s, the Soviet-American strategic balance has been characterized by a rough parity in the strategic nuclear capabilities of each country, in which neither the Soviet Union nor the United States has been able to exploit its strategic arsenal for the purposes of military attack or political intimidation. Mutual deterrence is based on each side's capacity to retaliate with devastating retribution following nuclear attack by the other (Harris 1986). In practice, this makes a first-strike a suicidal option for either country. In so doing, it also renders incredible the threat of such an attack for coercive diplomatic purposes.

Parity in this sense of mutual deterrence has existed since shortly after the Cuban Missile Crisis, when the Soviets deployed a large, survivable land-based missile force to match the existing American force of land-based and sea-based missiles, as well as heavy bombers (Berman and Baker 1982). In the ensuing period, the maintenance of an adequate retaliatory deterrent capability has become an absolute minimum requirement in each side's strategic nuclear weapons policy. (This does not necessarily mean that there are not other reasons for developing or deploying nuclear weapons [Gray 1974].) If either side were to lose this capacity, either through neglect or its inability to counter threats to its retaliatory force, it might become vulnerable both to attack and to political intimidation. In the absence of any arms control agreement restraining the other side's ability to develop offensive or defensive systems which threaten the survivability of retaliatory forces, therefore, each country has felt compelled to continue to acquire newer and better offensive nuclear weapons systems.

The outcome of this competition, however, has been simply the recreation of rough parity at higher overall levels of weaponry. Each country, in the face of uncertainty about its prospective opponent's strategic intentions and weapons programs, has tried, with notable but costly success, to maintain the adequacy of its retaliatory deterrent over time. At best, however, continued investment in offensive nuclear forces has paid no clear security dividend to either side. Indeed, it is probably more accurate to speak of a net diminution in each side's overall security since the mid-1960s. In the 1980s, each country faced a situation in which new weapons technologies, such as highly accurate ballistic missile guidance systems, had been developed to the point where they posed an increasingly serious threat to the survivability of land-based retaliatory forces, as well as the facilities for command, communications, and control necessary to carry out a retaliatory mission. If widely deployed, offensive ballistic missiles with pinpoint accuracy could increase the temptation for one side or the other to launch a preemptive attack in a future crisis, or to place its land-based missiles on a hair-trigger alert or "launch-on-warning" posture. Either of these developments would destabilize mutual deterrence in a crisis by increasing the risk of a nuclear war.

In addition, potential technical solutions to the heightened vulnerability of existing retaliatory forces threatened to make future arms control efforts more difficult. Taking again the case of vulnerable land-based missile silos, corrective steps like the deployment of less-vulnerable long-range cruise missiles or land-mobile ICBMs (two technologies available to both countries) posed the problem of seriously complicating the verification of future arms control agreements.

Finally, if one factors in a sound national economy and domestic social welfare as important components of national security, each country, in addition to exposing itself to an increased risk of nuclear war and complicating arms control negotiations, has also inflicted upon itself a significant economic burden as well in trying to re-establish mutual deterrence at higher and higher levels of weaponry.

Thus, despite the continued existence of U.S.-Soviet nuclear parity, the years of nuclear competition since the Cuban Missile Crisis have imposed heavy costs on both superpowers, both in economic terms and in terms of the increasing fragility of mutual deterrence. This competition has proceeded, moreover, despite the conclusion of the SALT I ABM Treaty and Interim Agreement on Offensive Weapons in 1972, and the SALT II Treaty in 1979. SALT, in fact, has had a largely imperceptible impact on the course of the superpower competition in offensive nuclear arms. The logical question that is often posed by critics of the nuclear arms race and the failure of SALT is the following: If mutual deterrence now exists and can be preserved without further competition, why don't the two countries stop competing and avoid the costs of future competition?

The answer to this question is largely suggested by the Prisoners' Dilemma game. Neither country can afford to risk a unilateral, unconditional halt to its own nuclear arms programs. It simply cannot trust the other party to reciprocate. For the United States, for example, the risk of trusting the Soviet Union to cease arming also, after the U.S. has unilaterally done so, is that American trust may be spurned, and the Soviets may keep arming. Over a short period of time, even a period of several months or a year, such a situation would not have grave consequences for U.S. security. (Indeed, some analysts have suggested that as a prelude to formal negotiations, the United States ought to suspend unilaterally the testing and deployment of certain strategic weapons, contingent on Soviet reciprocity, in order to lay the basis for more extensive limitations in a negotiated treaty.) Carried on too long, however, unilateral restraint, without reciprocity from the other side, could place the United States in a markedly inferior strategic position vis-a-vis the Soviet Union. In the worst scenario, unilateral U.S. restraint, coupled with vigorous Soviet efforts to reduce the effectiveness of current U.S. retaliatory forces, could make the United States vulnerable not only to nuclear blackmail but actual nuclear attack by the Soviet Union as well.

The Soviet Union harbors these same suspicions about U.S. intentions. Neither country, therefore, is likely to risk the dangers inherent in unilateral, unconditional strategic arms restraint. For most of the postwar period, in fact, and despite SALT, both Soviet and American leaders have accepted the costs and uncertainties of an open-ended nuclear arms competition, as a means to avoid the even more threatening uncertainties and risks of unilateral restraint.

In game theory terms, the preferences of Soviet and American leaders regarding the outcome of the superpower nuclear arms race can be ranked roughly as follows, where 4 represents the most preferred outcome and 1 the least preferred:

4) Possessing the capability to threaten credibly a nuclear attack on the other party, and thus to prevail over the other party in nuclear bargaining.

3) Avoiding the costs and uncertainties of unrestrained arms competition, while maintaining deterrence.

2) Paying the costs of unrestrained armed competition in order to maintain deterrence.

1) Possessing inferior capabilities relative to the other party, thus being vulnerable to nuclear attack or to diplomatic blackmail.

If each country, then, has two options for its policy, either to race or not to race, then one may obtain the following matrix of possible outcomes given in Figure 2.

		United States	
		B1— Do Not Race	B2— Race
Soviet Union	A1— Do Not Race	3,3	1,4
	A2— Race	4,1	2,2

Figure 15-2   The U.S. Soviet Strategic Arms Competition as a Prisoners' Dilemma

In this situation, each prefers the outcome when it races and the other does not (for the Soviet Union, this is outcome A2, B1, and for the United States it is A1, B2). Yet neither country achieves its most preferred outcome, superiority, precisely because the other side fears the consequences of inferiority, and so arms to avoid it. As each country arms, the short-sighted equilibrium outcome of A2, B2 is reached, and each party ends up at its second worst outcome. This solution will always be obtained in a single play of this game. Yet it creates a dilemma, because the outcome of 3,3 (solution A1, B1) is clearly preferred by both countries to their equilibrium outcome. In a single play, and in the absence of communication and cooperation, however, achieving this mutually beneficial outcome is ruled out by the Prisoner's Dilemma.

On the other hand, game theorists Brams and Whitman (1981), Brams and Hessel (1984), and Zagare (1983), recently have demonstrated a "nonmyopic" or long run solution to the dilemma when the Prisoners' Dilemma game is played repeatedly, as in the arms race. If both players can cooperate to reach the mutually beneficial equilibrium at A1, B1, then such a solution may be stable. Any threat by either player to move to the outcome which produces either player's most preferred outcome may be deterred by the threat of the other to defect also, thereby leaving them both at the inferior point of equilibrium. The problem remains, however, of how to reach the stable, mutually more beneficial outcome of A1, B1.

In this regard, arms control becomes a critical exercise in cooperative, joint decision making which can bring both countries to equal or greater security at lower cost than would be achieved through arming to protect its deterrent. An arms control regime would then serve two major, mutually beneficial objectives: it would reduce the risk of nuclear war and the economic burden that each country would bear. Obviously, the best overall solution would be mutual nuclear disarmament. Then neither country would have to worry about nuclear attack from the other, because nuclear weapons would no longer exist. Similarly, neither would have to invest any further in maintaining a nuclear deterrent, for there would no longer be any threat of attack to be deterred. In spite of the significant improvement of U.S.-Soviet relations in the late 1980s and a decision to seek a 50% reduction in the strategic nuclear forces of the two superpowers, it is still unlikely that Soviet-American ideological and other political differences will disappear completely in the near future. These residual conflicts are likely to prevent either country from completely divesting itself of nuclear weapons. Therefore, a U.S.-Soviet arms control regime might try to achieve the next best possible outcome. Given that both countries are likely to maintain at least a minimal nuclear force, maintaining the stability of deterrence will be a necessary objective of joint Soviet-U.S. strategic policy well into the future. This means that a security regime will still be necessary to minimize the risk that any remaining nuclear weapons will be used in war, and in a way that minimizes the cost to each country.

A U.S.-Soviet strategic arms control regime based on the concept of mutual "fundamental deterrence" would realize these two goals.[1] Under mutual "fundamental deterrence," each party would be allowed to possess a minimal, survivable stock of strategic nuclear weapons sufficient to maintain a convincing retaliatory capability against targets of high value to its potential adversary. (The exact number of weapons each country would require for this purpose is debatable, but it is surely far smaller than the number of presently deployed strategic weapons.) To minimize the need for replacement or modernization of fundamental deterrent forces, both countries would be prohibited from testing or deploying new weapons systems which might pose a threat to these forces. As an initial step towards fundamental nuclear deterrence, the two countries might agree to a set of strict qualitative weapons limitations such as a ban on the testing and further deployment of strategic weaponry. These limitations would effectively "freeze" the current rough parity in existing capabilities. Broader qualitative controls, perhaps extended to the actual production of weapons, and followed by phased reductions in existing forces down to a level compatible with fundamental deterrence (undoubtedly a good deal lower than the 50% reductions now contemplated in START), would in turn have the effect of drastically curtailing each side's need and ability to develop new weapons, thus reducing each country's cost of maintaining a deterrent.

In pursuing these mutual goals, each superpower would have to adhere to a set of national security policies compatible with the advancement of such a regime. First, each would have to adopt a nuclear strategy consistent with the regime's ultimate goal of mutual fundamental deterrence. In military terms, this means relegating strategic weapons to the sole role of deterring the other side's use or threatened use of strategic weapons. This further implies the necessity of abandoning the idea that nuclear weapons can be used to fight, limit, control, or win nuclear wars (Jervis, 1983). On a political level, this means eschewing a foreign policy of coercive diplomacy based on nuclear superiority, of the type advocated by Colin Gray and Keith Payne (1980), and accepting parity and the political neutralization of strategic forces as a long-term basis for U.S.-Soviet relations. In addition, it entails a long-term effort to avoid crises by agreeing to rules of mutual conduct outside of direct strategic relationships, as well as mechanisms for crisis management and resolution in the event that any such serious incidents do occur (Shulman, 1984; Allison and Ury, 1989).

Each country would also have to carry the concept of fundamental deterrence into its own weapons development, procurement, and deployment policies. In principle, this means being willing to forego weapons which are either superfluous to the mission of fundamental deterrence, or which undermine the basis of funda-mental deterrence by threatening the destruction of the other side's retaliatory forces. Finally, each country would be required to accede to whatever "cooperative" verification measures might be needed to assure compliance with the arms control regime (Miller 1984:70-74). The many innovations in Soviet arms control positions that Mikhail Gorbachev introduced after he assumed power in the Kremlin suggest that such conditions, once thought to be unrealistic, had become attainable by the end of the decade of the 1980s.

As alluded to above, however, success in achieving such a comprehensive strategic nuclear arms control regime remained an elusive goal for the Soviet Union and the United States by the beginning of the final decade of the 20th century. The U.S.-Soviet strategic arms negotiation process has fallen far short of producing the kinds of agreements that would be necessary to create and sustain a true regime in strategic nuclear arms control (Myrdal 1982 and Johansen 1979). The SALT I Interim Agreement on Offensive Weapons and the SALT II Treaty placed only the loosest of numerical restraints on offensive strategic arsenals, and they mostly failed to apply any significant qualitative controls on each side's arsenal. In so doing, they permitted costly and potentially destabilizing strategic weapons modernization and expansion programs to flourish on both sides. Meanwhile, the SALT I ABM Treaty and 1974 ABM Protocol, which limited each country to only one anti-ballistic missile interceptor and radar complex, were threatened after 1983 by the renewed momentum of ABM research and development imparted by the Reagan Administration's Strategic Defense Initiative and parallel Soviet efforts.

Yet the SALT negotiations did reflect, more than any effort before or since, a desire by the two superpowers to construct the foundations of a minimal security regime between themselves, based primarily on their common interest in avoiding nuclear war. Insofar as these negotiations failed to create a true nuclear arms control regime, an analysis of the reasons for this failure may help us to formulate a better theoretical understanding of the obstacles to security regime formation. A better understanding of these obstacles may in turn aid in identifying political strategies for overcoming them and, in so doing, increase the prospects for progress in international arms control negotiations, perhaps leading to the establishment of a more robust East-West regime, based on the concept of mutual rather than unilateral security.

As this analysis will demonstrate, obstacles to arms control and related joint security measures in East-West relations exist not only in international negotiations, but also in domestic policy making. That is to say, the international security regime "problematique" reflects conditions of shared power not only across national boundaries, but also within individual nation-states. The international impediments to a true Soviet-American strategic nuclear arms control regime have been extensively analyzed elsewhere (Newhouse 1973, Wolfe 1979, Smith 1980, and Talbott 1979, 1984). Among the most nettlesome of these issues, which have acted as brakes on the development of a more significant U.S.-Soviet SALT regime, have been: 1) asymmetries in U.S. and Soviet force postures, levels of technological development, geographical situations, and alliance relationships; 2) the tendency of policy makers, especially in the United States, to link SALT to a broader political accommodation with the Soviet Union on other issues, which has proven difficult to achieve; and 3) the persistent problem of arms control verification, an issue which took on even more importance in the 1980s amidst widespread allegations in the United States that the Soviets had violated various elements of the SALT I and SALT II agreements.

Here we intend to examine the relatively less well understood problem (Miller 1984, Allison and Morris 1976, and Steinbruner and Carter 1976) of how domestic political factors have impinged on the prospects for progress in strategic nuclear arms control negotiations at the international level. The final section of our paper therefore, will analyze central features of "the domestic politics of arms control" in the United States, how these have served to inhibit the advancement of a more significant strategic arms control regime, and how some of these domestic obstacles might better be overcome.

Shared Power in the Domestic Politics of U.S. Arms Control Policy Making

In order to achieve agreement on a regime to stabilize mutual deterrence, the domestic political leadership in both the United States and the Soviet Union must first recognize, and then be willing to act on the basis of, the common interests shared between the two superpowers. Political leaders must be prepared to override a series of domestic obstacles that tend to emphasize the competitive nature of East-West relations to achieve some measure of cooperation. Although there are undoubtedly many obstacles to such initiatives in the Soviet Union (Miller 1984: 68), many of these have been removed with Gorbachev's policies of perestroika at home and the presentation of many new and far-reaching proposals for arms control in the late 1980s. Therefore, this section will concentrate on U.S. domestic decision making in the arms control arena, due also to the more extensive information about how such decisions are made in the United States. We shall argue that international coordination of policy to create and maintain an arms control regime with the Soviet Union requires a number of domestic political groups to coalesce, and to share power in making difficult decisions. In this section, therefore, we shall explore some of the many agencies and individuals involved in such decisions, in order to elucidate some of the obstacles to power sharing in arms control policy.

The experience of American presidents in past arms control negotiations indicates that they have rarely been willing to trade off major opportunities to modernize the U.S. nuclear arsenal in order to create a more stable and less costly arms control regime. For example, the Nixon Administration decided relatively early on in its planning for the U.S.-Soviet SALT I negotiations that, although stringent controls should be applied to defensive anti-ballistic missile systems, a possible treaty on offensive nuclear systems should leave each country free to "modernize" (e.g., with multiple warheads) its existing offensive missile launchers once high numerical ceilings on these weapons had been set. Again in SALT II, the Carter Administration settled for relatively high numerical limits on various categories of offensive weapons systems, and only very modest restraints on each side's ability to improve the capabilities of its arsenal within these limits.

The SALT I and SALT II agreements were determined as much by the internal bargaining and politics which shaped American negotiating positions as they were by the formal discussions carried on between the two countries. American actions during these negotiations, and in particular the tendency to resist or neglect comprehensive, regime-oriented negotiating proposals, reflect the "shared" nature of the domestic U.S. arms control decision-making process and the political actors who dominate it. Over time these domestic forces have successfully opposed U.S. participation in a regime based on mutual fundamental deterrence. It is only when these domestic sources of past failures are well understood, moreover, that the prospects for future progress in Soviet-American nuclear arms control will brighten. As Steven Miller suggests (1984:70), success in future Soviet-American negotiations may well rest on the ability of arms controllers in the United States to "manage the political process in order to overcome or circumvent (domestic) political impediments" by building winning political coalitions in support of effective arms control.

Strategic nuclear policy making, and within this larger frame, the making of arms control policy, is in fact a highly political process. That military policy making does not conform to a stylized model of rational "means-ends" decision making is not a new idea, however. As early as 1961, Samuel Huntington (1961: 2,8) warned that military policy was only rarely based on "deductions from a clear statement of objectives." Policy, he argued, emerged from a process of political competition among varying attitudes about national defense, attitudes represented by individuals and groups in society." It is the result of politics, not logic, determined by "the power, interests, and attitudes of the public and private individuals and groups concerned with it and affected by it." In Huntington's view, diverging plural, national purposes had to be reconciled through a political process of competition, bargaining, and compromise before consensus on strategic policy could be achieved and implemented.

More recent analyses of U.S. arms control policy making bear out this conclusion. For example, Marshall Shulman (1982), a specialist on East-West issues in the Carter Administration, describes U.S. arms control policy making as an "irrational" process, one in which "random and parochial pressures" influence decision makers and in turn determine policy. According to Shulman, arms control decision making is a process of domestic bargaining in which these multiple, often conflicting, random pressures and interests must be reconciled.

In a similar fashion, Miller describes U.S. arms control decision making as a "game" of competition, bargaining, and compromise among various "players" whose parochial interests will be either enhanced or injured, depending on the outcome of the game. According to Miller (1984:80), the object of the game is simple and straight-forward: "Each of the (actors) involved will seek, within the limits of its influence and effectiveness in the politics of the situation to preserve its own interests or, at the least, to avoid having them badly violated."

The players in this game—those who, according to Huntington, concern themselves with arms control policy and who are affected by it—include the principal national security actors of the federal government (the president; the National Security Council; the departments of state, defense, and energy; and the uniformed military services), various quasi-governmental agencies whose work is tied to national defense like the national nuclear weapons laboratories, private corporate actors who do business with the Department of Defense, and Congress as well as the general public (Shulman 1982:35-36, and Miller 1984:80). Some of these have proven, over time, to have been more influential and critical to the determination of policy outcomes than others, and it is on these actors—their sources of political influence, their policy objectives, and specific examples of how they have affected policy—that this section will focus.

Four groups will thus be highlighted for the contribution that they have made to U.S. arms control policy: the President and his White House national security affairs staff, who set overall U.S. strategy and determine the role that arms control will play within that strategy; the military services and their political representatives, the Joint Chiefs of Staff, whose budgets, so-called "core missions," and overall "organizational health" can be vitally affected by both the general content of arms control policy and also by specific treaty limitations; the Congress, which must fund the procurement of military hardware, and especially the Senate, which must give its advice and consent prior to the legal ratification of arms control treaties; and finally the general public which, through the ability to elect or vote out of office national leaders, possesses the theoretical power to approve or reject the armament and arms control policies of the President and of individual representatives in Congress. Each of these groups will be examined in turn.

The President
As an effort to achieve greater national security through diplomatic means, arms control lies at the intersection of diplomacy and national defense policy. The constitutional authority for both the making of American arms control policy and the conduct of actual negotiations falls to the president of the United States. He and his executive national security advisors, primarily the National Security Council staff, play a central role in determining whether or not arms control is a major and substantively meaningful aspect of U.S. national security policy. Thus, presidential attitudes towards U.S.-Soviet arms control significantly condition the prospects for a true strategic nuclear arms control regime between the two countries. Four dimensions of presidential attitude have proven particularly important in determining the overall level of commitment in various postwar administrations.

First, and most important, is an administration's basic approach to U.S. nuclear strategy. If the president sanctions developments in U.S. military strategy which are at odds with a regime based on mutual fundamental deterrence, this will rule out meaningful progress in arms control. To back up a strategy of nuclear war fighting or nuclear war winning, for example, the United States would necessarily have to develop offensive capabilities that could threaten the survivability of Soviet deterrent forces, a policy incompatible with mutual deterrence (Jervis 1983 and Harris 1982).

Changes in U.S. nuclear strategy have in practice influenced the prospects for progress in U.S.-Soviet nuclear arms control. It was only after the United States had shifted away from the "damage limiting" strategy, oriented to nuclear war fighting of the early Kennedy administration, and to the "assured destruction" and "strategic sufficiency" policies of the Johnson and Nixon administrations, for example, that strategic "parity" based on the security of each side's deterrent forces became a viable basis for the SALT I talks, and for each side's renunciation of large-scale anti-ballistic missile deployments in the ABM Treaty of 1972. Developments in American nuclear strategy throughout this period, however, rendered the United States' commitment to further progress towards a true regime based on mutual fundamental deterrence increasingly problematic.

Indeed, throughout most of the period since the late 1960s the Strategic Integrated Operational Plan (SIOP) called for an ability to target the strategic forces of the Soviet Union. Whatever the doctrine may have been, U.S. operational plans consistently prepared for fighting a nuclear war. These realities were incorporated into strategic doctrine through a series of changes that at first appeared minor, but which cumulatively became significant. First, Nixon's Defense Secretary James Schlesinger announced a doctrine calling for possession by the U.S. of "limited nuclear options." Then, Carter's Defense Secretary Harold Brown released Presidential Directive 59 calling for a "countervailing strategy" directed against Soviet nuclear retaliatory forces. This process culminated in the 1980s, when the Reagan Administration adopted a strategy based on nuclear war fighting, abandoning any pretense of a policy of mutual assured destruction. Some analysts attributed the Reagan Administration's reluctance to endorse proposals for qualitative restrictions on U.S. and Soviet offensive nuclear forces (like the Nuclear Freeze) less to their concern about the "window of vulnerability" vis-*-vis the Soviets, than to the administration's chief strategists' desire to achieve outright nuclear superiority, based on the capacity to "prevail" over the Soviets in a protracted nuclear war (Harris 1982, 1986).

Second, presidential initiative can play an important role in moving the Washington arms control decision-making process forward, thus increasing the chances for progress in deliberations with Moscow. Richard Nixon, through his special assistant for national security affairs, Henry Kissinger, played a similarly instrumental role in the SALT I negotiations, both guiding the overall development of U.S. positions in Washington and in ironing out last-minute disagreements with the Soviets during the 1972 summit in Moscow. Jimmy Carter also immersed himself heavily in the process of formulating and adjusting American negotiating positions in SALT II (Miller 1984:83).

But if the level of presidential attention, commitment, and activity in the arms control area is a crucial variable, so too are the political and military rationales that lie behind a president's interest in arms control issues. Historically, presidents have tended not to pursue strategic nuclear arms control for the purely technical contributions it could make to a more stable and less costly U.S.-Soviet security environment. American leaders have sought negotiations with the Soviets for their political effects as well, and some analysts such as Colin Gray (1974) suggest that this has been the driving force behind U.S. arms control policy. While this may be an exaggeration, it seems clear that this was an important element, especially for President Nixon and Henry Kissinger.

In 1972, Nixon and Kissinger settled for less than ideal arms control agreements largely in order to enhance the process of East-West detente. They were satisfied with very high and purely numerical limits in the SALT I Interim Agreement on offensive nuclear missiles, with no restrictions on qualitative improvements of existing missile and bombers systems, and most importantly no limits on testing and deployment of multiple independent re-entry vehicles (MIRVs). These concessions to political difficulties, both domestically and across the negotiating table in Vienna and Helsinki, were accepted because of the salutary effects that SALT I was expected to have in contributing to the process of East-West detente.

However, when agreements are conceived largely in these terms, there is a risk that they may fail to achieve significant limitations on the arms race of the kinds required to assure stable mutual deterrence. The failure of SALT I to limit MIRVs meant that the number of warheads deployed by the superpowers grew significantly in the decade after the treaty was signed, even though the number of delivery vehicles was more or less frozen. Thus, when arms control efforts are primarily motivated by a thirst for concrete steps toward a U.S.-Soviet detente, without due regard being paid to the central problem of preserving stable mutual deterrence, they may leave loopholes that stimulate further arms competition and, over the long run, actually damage the dtente process as well.

In summary, the president's capacity to enhance prospects for a U.S.-Soviet arms control regime depends on more than just his willingness to participate actively in the policy-making process. It requires the president to restrict U.S. nuclear strategy to the role of fundamental deterrence, based on the ability to persuade any potential aggressors that their countries would receive more damage in retaliation than they could hope to gain from their own attacks. Equally important, the president must focus U.S. negotiating efforts on proposals that advance the objectives of the regime, seeking to achieve agreements that control destabilizing weapons technologies, close off "loopholes" for modernization that are unnecessary for the maintenance of a credible deterrent threat, and reduce existing levels of forces in a manner consistent with mutual deterrence.

The Joint Chiefs of Staff: Military Service Interests in Arms Control

Any president intent on accomplishing these arms control objectives always confronts the possibility of opposition from domestic actors whose political support is necessary to achieve an agreement. As Gray (1974) has suggested, over time the Soviet-American nuclear arms race has acquired a domestic constituency in each country that stands to benefit politically and/or economically from continuing competition. In reference to the American case, Graham Allison (1975:17) calls this the "Permanent Government" in national security policymaking, which he argues determines "which interests and perspectives are in fact introduced with what weights in the regular process of decision and action." Arms control, writes Miller (1984:81), "as an effort to interfere with defense policy processes, to constrain certain kinds of weapons, options, and practices for the larger goal of national security," represents a threat to these interests, and in so doing, attracts both the attention and opposition of this "Permanent Government." Depending on the level of political leverage the various elements of this constituency can gain over the president, its members can stymie an arms control-oriented foreign policy, inhibiting a president's desire for productive negotiations with the Soviet Union, and in so doing, protect their own parochial interests.

In theory, this constituency could include any member of society who benefits either directly or indirectly from continued investment by the United States in the development of new nuclear weapons systems. Thus, some have argued that defense contractors, insofar as their institutional and commercial health may depend on a continued flow of contracts for new weapons, are likely to pressure policy makers to oppose arms control agreements which could diminish that flow. Evidence for a direct relationship between corporate defense lobbyists and U.S. arms control policy making outcomes is thin, however (Aspin 1978:46; Cobb 1969, 1973; Frye 1975:12; Grey and Gregory 1968; and Moyer 1973). Support for the theory that intra-governmental interest groups have influenced the course of U.S. arms control policy, by contrast, is more robust.

By far the most influential of these intragovernmental (i.e., bureaucratic) actors have been the uniformed military services and their policy making representatives, the Joint Chiefs of Staff (JCS). Although nominally subordinate to the president and Department of Defense in the official chain of military command, the JCS frequently behave as independent political actors, who try to influence policy in order to defend the organizational interests of the services they represent (Luttwak, 1985). These organizational interests, in turn, have provided the basic motivation for the JCS's successful opposition over the last two decades to U.S.-Soviet arms control agreements which would seriously impinge on the United States' (as well as the Soviet Union's) ability to modernize its nuclear arsenal.

In general, the Army, Navy, and Air Force perceive their basic responsibility requires them to have the capability not only to deter nuclear war, but to fight one if necessary. In this sense, their basic operating assumptions and institutional interests are at odds with the goals of an arms control regime. Arms control, by sanctioning certain nuclear missions and capabilities (e.g., deterrence based on a survivable retaliatory capability) and branding as dangerous others (e.g., nuclear war fighting strategies, counterforce capabilities and strategic defenses), thus threatens important missions and capabilities of the military services. The one service that would probably be most threatened by the kind of arms control regime envisaged here is the Air Force, which has embraced counterforce as one of its core missions (Ford 1985; Kaplan 1983; Greenwood 1975). The counterforce mission has, in turn, provided the rationale for the major new weapons developed by the Air Force since the late 1960s, including MIRV'd warheads, the B-1 and B-2 bombers, and the MX missile. Interest in the Navy in counterforce weapons increased as well in the 1980s as it initiated development of a sea-based counterforce missile, the Trident II, and the Army gained a new role with the possible introduction of elaborate strategic defense systems. These weapons may give these two services an added stake in a U.S. nuclear strategy based on nuclear war fighting options, rather than on the concept of fundamental deterrence.

Even if, for any given issue, the strategic missions and interests of the services diverge (the Navy, for instance, is chiefly responsible for the "assured destruction" retaliatory mission of U.S. strategic forces), the JCS tend to act as a political mechanism for defending each service's individual core mission against the attempts by civilian policy makers to eliminate unnecessary, or to rationalize redundant, missions. This effect was particularly noticeable in SALT, when united military opposition to comprehensive arms control agreements was a persistent feature of the domestic politics of arms control in the United States. For example, one reason the

Nixon Administration resisted efforts to include limitations of MIRVs in the SALT I negotiations was its fear that such a limitation would result in the loss of JCS support for an eventual agreement limiting offensive strategic arms, which would be necessary to underwrite its passage through the congressional treaty ratification process. Gerard C. Smith (1980), chief SALT I negotiator for the United States, points out that the JCS also "made Administration support of a broad program of strategic modernization the fairly explicit condition of their support of the treaty." In his memoirs, Jimmy Carter (1982:239) relates the pressures he felt in trying to keep the Joint Chiefs "happy" with the American negotiating position in SALT II.

Congress and Arms Control Decision Making
When analyzing the power of private interests (bureaucratic or societal) to influence arms control policy, however, one must remember that they possess no autonomous source of political power. Bureaucrats like the Joint Chiefs of Staff, as heads of the military departments within the executive branch, have no constitutionally defined power or authority over the president. What they do possess, however, is the ability to appeal to other actors, the Congress, for example, who do retain such leverage over the chief executive.

In the areas of military and arms control policy, the potential power of the military services to employ these extra-executive sources of political leverage is large. Morton Halperin (1971, 1975) notes that the military services, and the Joint Chiefs of Staff in particular, are practically encouraged under law to outline their differences with presidential strategic and arms control policy before the Congress. Halperin also observes that senior military officers frequently avail themselves of this opportunity. The result has been that presidents have shunned policies which conflict with military interests (and which the military would publicly oppose before the Congress and in the press). It is the possibility of military opposition to comprehensive arms control treaties which will cause the president to account for military interests in making arms control policy, and nowhere has this been more glaringly demonstrated than in the development of American negotiating positions. Any treaty actually negotiated with the Soviets must pass through the domestic U.S. ratification process, which in effect means gaining the consent of a two-thirds majority in the U.S. Senate. To gain this consent, it is necessary for any treaty to obtain the blessings of the JCS. The Joint Chiefs, by virtue of their ability to withhold such support, are thus in a strong position to press for concessions or "safeguards," in the form of a presidential commitment to vigorous weapons modernization, in exchange for their willingness to testify before the Senate on behalf of arms control agreements negotiated with the Soviets. These "safeguards" were precisely the costs which Presidents Kennedy, Nixon, Carter and Reagan all had to pay to guarantee JCS and congressional support for the agreements they had negotiated, thus undermining the basic purposes of arms control (Seaborg 1981; Flanagan 1979; Talbott 1979; and Vance 1983).

The political make-up of Congress (and particularly the attitudes towards arms control of the Senate's 100 members) is, therefore, a third crucial variable in the domestic politics of arms control. If the president can count on the necessary backing for an arms control regime in the Senate, he is likely to worry less about potential JCS opposition to his arms control programs. If, on the other hand, the military services' political support in the Senate is sufficient to induce presidential doubts about a treaty's ability to gain ratification, the JCS will also retain the ability to limit the president's decision making latitude, and with that, the significance of arms control agreements which do survive the ratification process (Miller 1984:89; and Flanagan 1979).

The General Public and U.S. Arms Control Policy
The one group in society which possesses the capacity to create a political climate favorable to arms control in both the White House and the Congress is the general electorate. Congress—and most importantly the Senate—is account-able to the electorate, and for this reason sensitive to public opinion. But broad public interest in nuclear weapons issues, and concern about the lack of progress in U.S.-Soviet arms control in the early 1980s, was a relatively new phenomena in American politics. Prior to the burgeoning of the anti-nuclear war movement between 1981 and 1983, there was a distinct absence of a visible political constituency with a "national interest" point of view in regards to arms control (Shulman 1982). Historically, post-World War II public interest in arms control and disarmament issues has been characterized by sporadic, intense activity on issues linked with, but not central to, the dangers and costs of further U.S.-Soviet nuclear competition. Previous social movements against nuclear weapons and in support of arms limitation, for example, were hampered by their limited focus. Neither the public demonstrations in the late 1950s and early 1960s against atmospheric nuclear weapons tests, nor the protests against the deployment of a nation-wide anti-ballistic missile system in the late 1960s, had as their central focus the goal of reducing the risk of nuclear war and the costs of deterrence (Markusen and Harris 1984). In the former case, the primary impetus was concern about the health risks resulting from radioactive fallout produced by atmospheric testing. In the latter, it was the "bombs in the backyard" issue that was preeminent, namely the fear of deploying nuclear armed ABM interceptors in suburban neighborhoods surrounding major cities. In both cases the president was under considerable pressure from the Joint Chiefs of Staff and key senators not to sign an agreement which would preclude significant modernization of U.S. nuclear forces. The natural, and politically "safe," course to follow was that of appeasing the concerns of the public while at the same time ensuring that arms negotiations with the Soviets did not infringe on the interests of the military. As

pointed out earlier, for example, the SALT I agreements which severely restricted ABMs, still left each side free to modernize its offensive strategic forces. Viewed in this historical context, the increased political involvement and activity of movements such as the Nuclear Freeze Campaign during Reagan's first term in office, created a significant new factor in the domestic politics of arms control. To begin with, the Freeze was a broad-based citizens' movement whose support extended beyond the more traditional disarmament constituency in the United States (Blechman 1980). Secondly, the goals of the Freeze campaign—a negotiated, mutual, verifiable freeze on the testing, production, and deployment of U.S. and Soviet nuclear weapons systems, followed by reductions on each side—were consistent with the kinds of first steps that would be required to create an arms control regime. Third, the active participation of Freeze movement members in electoral politics created the possibility for influencing directly the attitudes and votes of national political leaders where a change of attitude was most needed: in the White House and in Congress. Finally, although the specific arms control policy objectives of the Freeze Campaign were not realized, and the political momentum of the anti-nuclear war movement as a whole slowed dramatically after 1983, the movement did experience some tangible, albeit smaller, political successes between 1981 and 1984. These achievements, though overshadowed by the failure to see the Freeze become an orienting goal of U.S. arms control policy, may nevertheless be viewed as examples of successful grass roots public intervention in the arms control policymaking process. They perhaps had a long-term effect in creating a climate more receptive to the arms control initiatives that began flowing from the Soviet Union by the end of the decade.

Conclusion

As the world entered the final decade of the 20th century, the prospects for the creation of a new regime in arms control and Soviet-American cooperation, embracing principles of power sharing between the superpowers in the quest for mutual security, appeared greater than at any time since the outbreak of the Cold War. The changes brought about in a period of three or four years by General Secretary Gorbachev seemed to suggest that the Cold War, as we knew it for more than four decades, had effectively drawn to a close. That did not mean that Soviet and American competition for influence in world affairs had come to an end, just that it had entered onto a new plain. No longer did premeditated nuclear war seem to be a real danger to most observers, although the risk of war by accident, miscalculation, or at the instigation of a third party still remained as an ominous threat to global security. However, the competition in Soviet-American relations would clearly move more towards the realm of economic and political competition, also taking place within an increasingly pluralistic world where the two superpowers, even together, no longer wielded the same influence that they had throughout the previous four decades.

Of course, no dramatic change in international affairs could remain certain, and the lessons of the lost detente of the 1970s remained as a reminder of possible reversal. Certainly the future direction of the changes initiated by Gorbachev within the Soviet Union in a time of revolutionary upheaval remained uncertain and indeterminate. The success or failure of the policy of perestroika, however, depended more on the performance of a sluggish Soviet economy and on the threat of discontent among minority nationalities within the USSR than it did on any international events. Even the most hardline observers of Soviet affairs in the West generally came to believe that significant changes within the Soviet Union, carrying profound implications for its foreign policy, were virtually irreversible regardless of the personal fate of General Secretary Gorbachev.

In the phraseology of Allison and Ury (1989), new "windows of opportunity" clearly opened up for the United States to create a new regime in arms control and in other important areas of the U.S.-Soviet relationship for the decade of the 1990s. The major obstacle to seizing these opportunities no longer came from the internal stagnation of Soviet policy, for that had been replaced by dramatic new policy initiatives; it no longer came from the inevitable hostility of the superpower relationship, for the change in the nature of this relationship was widely recognized by even the most skeptical observers; nor did it come from the reluctance of U.S. allies, who were uniformly eager to seize the opportunity to change the nature of the international regime dramatically; rather the major obstacle remained in the complex nature of the political and bureaucratic relationships among the many actors within the U.S. national security community.

Public attitudes towards arms control, which had wavered between skepticism at the time of the SALT II debate in 1979-80 to enthusiastic support for new arms control initiatives reflected in the Nuclear Freeze movement of 1981-83, seemed to settle on a more even keel by the end of the decade. As summarized by Yankelovich and Smoke (1988:1), the "American public is willing to experiment with winding down the cold war," but they also "insist upon proceeding cautiously, testing Soviet good faith at each step." Congress, readily susceptible to changes in the public mood, seemed to settle on a similar delicate balance between optimism about change and wariness. Rather the major problems seemed to derive from the complex nature of the relationships within the national security bureaucracy as the Bush Administration began to chart its course in foreign policy. Faced with a dramatic budget deficit as well as a strong campaign pledge not to raise taxes, the Bush Administration invariably had to look for ways to cut the defense budget. In this task, dramatic reductions of both nuclear and conventional armaments through negotiated arms control agreements with the Soviet Union were a necessity. Yet this created the natural reaction within the Defense Department and the military services, which saw their large share of the federal budget endangered. Along with relative budgetary decline, they also feared a decline in their power within the U.S. government. Clearly new relationships of shared power within the federal bureaucracy thus remained an essential requisite for new initiatives, and creative responses to dramatic Soviet overtures, to emerge from within the United States government. Creative management by the Bush Administration of these shared-power relationships within the federal bureaucracy could be critical to the rapidly changing future of the complex U.S.-Soviet relationship. If these internal relationships are managed successfully so that the United States is able to respond creatively to the "windows of opportunity" that opened up as we enter the 1990s, then the prospects are good that a new and viable mutual security regime, including major reductions and qualitative limitations in both nuclear and conventional armaments, can be achieved before the dawn of the 21st century.

Note
1. The idea of basing U.S.-Soviet arms control efforts on arsenals sufficiently only to provide each country with a secure and convinving retaliatory capability has been a basic element in arms control theory since the 1950s. The particular term "fundamental deterrence," which we use here in place of the frequently used terms "minimum" and "central" deterrence, originated with Dan Caldwell of Pepperdine University.

References
Allison, G. T. 1975. "Overview and findings and recommendations from defense and arms control cases." Commission on the organization of the government for the conduct of foreign policy, appendices, volume IV, appendix K: "Adequacy of current organization: defense and arms control." Washington: U.S.G.P.O.
Allison, G.T., and F.A. Morris. 1976. "Exploring the determinants of military weapons." In *Arms, defense policy, and arms control* edited by F.A. Long and G.W. Rathjens. New York: W.W. Norton.
Allison, G.T. and W.L. Ury, eds. 1989. *Windows of opportunity: From cold war to peaceful competition in U.S.-Soviet relations.* Cambridge, Mass.: Ballinger.
Aspin, L. 1978. "The Power of procedure." In *Congress and arms control* edited by A. Platt and L. D. Weiler. Boulder, Col.: Westview Press.
Berman, R.P., and J.C. Baker. 1982. *Soviet strategic forces: Requirements and responses.* Washington: Brookings Institution.
Blechman, B.M. 1980. Do negotiated arms limitations have a future? *Foreign Affairs*, 59(Fall): 102-125.
Brams, S.J., and D. Whitman. 1981. Nonmyopic equilibria in 2 x 2 games. *Conflict Management and Peace Science* 6(Fall): 39-62.
Brams, S.J., and M.P. Hessel. 1984. Threat power in sequential games. *International Studies Quarterly* 28(March): 23-44.
Carter, J. 1982. *Keeping faith: Memoirs of a president.* New York: Bantam Books.

Cobb, S.A. 1969. Defense spending and foreign policy in the House of Representatives. *Journal of Conflict Resolution* 13 (Summer): 358-369.

Cobb, S. 1973. "The United States Senate and the impact of defense spending concentrations." In *Testing the theory of the military-industrial complex* edited by S. Rosen. Lexington, Mass.: D.C. Heath and Company.

Flanagan, S.J. 1979. "Congress and the evolution of U.S. Strategic arms limitation policy: A study of the legislature's role in national security affairs, 1955-1979." Ph.D. dissertation, Tufts University.

Ford, D. 1985. *The button.* New York: Simon and Schuster.

Frye, A. 1975. *A responsible Congress: The politics of national security.* New York: McGraw-Hill.

Gray, C.S. 1974. The urge to compete: Rationales for arms racing. *World Politics* 26(January): 207-233.

Gray, C. S. and K. Payne. 1980. Victory is possible. *Foreign Policy,* 39, Summer: 14-27.

Grey, C.H. and G.W. Gregory. 1968. Military spending and Senate voting. *Journal of Peace Research* 5:44-54.

Greenwood, T. 1975. *Making the MIRV: A study of defense decision making.* Cambridge, Mass.: Ballinger.

Haas, E.B. 1983. "Words can hurt you; or, who said what to whom about regimes." In *International regimes* edited by S.A. Krasner. Ithaca, N.Y.: Cornell University Press.

Halperin, M. 1971. Why bureaucrats play games. *Foreign Policy* 2(Spring): 70-90.

Halperin, M.H. 1975. "The president and the military," In *Perspectives on the presidency* edited by A. Wildavsky. Boston: Little, Brown, and Co.

Harris, J.B. 1982. Nuclear war fighting as an issue for public education. *F.A.S. Countdown* 1(December): 1-6.

Harris, J.B. 1986. "Assessing the adequacy of U.S. strategic nuclear forces." In *Nuclear weapons and nuclear war: Critical issues,* edited by J. B. Harris and E. Markusen. San Diego: Harcourt, Brace, Jovanovich.

Huntington, S.H. 1961. *The Common defense.* New York: Columbia University Press.

Jervis, R. 1983. "Security regimes." In *International regimes* edited by S.D. Krasner. Ithaca, N.Y.: Cornell University Press.

Johansen, R.C. 1979. *SALT II: Illusion and reality.* New York: World Policy Institute.

Kaplan, F. 1983. *The wizards of armageddon.* New York: Simon and Schuster.

Keohane, R.0. and J.S. Nye, 1977. *Power and interdependence: World politics in transition.* Boston: Little, Brown, and Company.

Krasner, S.D. 1983. "Structural causes and regime consequences: regimes as intervening variables." In *International regimes* edited by S.D. Krasner. Ithaca, N.Y.: Cornell University Press.

Luttwak, E. 1985. *The Pentagon and the art of war*. New York: Simon and Schuster.

Markusen, E. and J.B. Harris. 1984. The role of education in preventing nuclear war. *Harvard Educational Review* 54(August): 282-303.

Miller, S. 1984. Politics over promise: Domestic impediments to arms control. *International Security* 8(Spring): 67-90.

Moyer, W. 1973. "House voting on defense: An ideological explanation." In *Military force and American society* edited by B.M. Russell and A. Stepan. New York: Harper and Row.

Myrdal, A. 1982. *The game of disarmament*. New York: Pantheon.

Newhouse, J. 1973. *Cold dawn: The story of SALT*. New York: Holt, Rinehart, and Winston.

Seaborg, G. T. 1981. *Kennedy, Khrushchev, and the test ban*. Berkeley, Cal.: University of California Press.

Shulman, M. 1982. "The Process of government policymaking in this area." In *The role of the academy in addressing the issues of nuclear war* edited by H.C. Dunathan. Geneva, N.Y.: Hobart and William Smith Colleges.

Shulman, M. 1984. "What the Russians really want." *Harper's Magazine* April: 63-71.

Smith, G.C. 1980. *Doubletalk: The story of the first strategic arms limitation talks*. Garden City, N.Y.: Doubleday and Company.

Stein, A.A. 1983. "Coordination and collaboration: regimes in an anarchic world," In *International regimes* edited by S.D. Krasner. Ithaca, N.Y.: Cornell University Press.

Steinbruner, J., and B. Carter. 1976. "Organizational and political dimensions of the strategic posture: the problem of reform." In *Arms, defense policy, and arms control*, edited by F.A. Long and G.W. Rathjens. New York: W. W. Norton.

Talbott, S. 1979. *Endgame: The inside story of SALT II*. New York: Harper-Colophon.

Talbott, S. 1984. *Deadly gambits*. New York: Simon and Schuster.

Waltz, K.N. 1979. *Theory of international politics*. Reading, Mass.: Addison-Wesley.

Wolfe, T.W. 1979. *The SALT experience*. Cambridge, Mass.: Ballinger.

Yankelovich, D. and R. Smoke. 1988. America's New Thinking. *Foreign Affairs* 67(Fall): 1-17.

Young, O.R. 1983. "Regime dynamics: The rise and fall of international regimes." In *International regimes* edited by S.D. Krasner. Ithaca, N.Y.: Cornell University Press.

Zagare, F.C. 1983. "Toward a reconciliation of game theory and the theory of mutual deterrence," mimeograph.

CHAPTER 16

Conclusions

Robert C. Einsweiler and John M. Bryson

A number of conclusions emerge from the preceding chapters. The principal conclusion is simply that a great deal of understanding can be gained by viewing the world through the lens of "shared power." As the world becomes increasingly interconnected, old distinctions blur, and the capacity to govern declines, a vast array of "shared power arrangements" have appeared to deal with these changing circumstances. A number of very important questions can be raised about the effectiveness and virtue of these arrangements, but the most important public issues of our time typically arise in settings where "no one is in charge," and in which organizations or institutions must share power in order to address these issues effectively. The extent of power sharing that occurs across levels and boundaries, and the power sharing commonalities across policy realms, have been obscured by our habits of focusing on separation and adversarial relationships, and on specific policy areas in isolation from other policy areas.

Note that we do *not* argue that power sharing is good in and of itself. We simply argue that the lens of shared power provides an extremely useful way of reexamining ideas about how the world works, and of thinking about ways to make the world work better. The term "shared power" labels an observed state of affairs in many different policy areas. The label prompts an exploration of the conditions that lead to shared power, along with the various shared power arrangements that organizations of many sorts use to cope with shared power situations.

A number of additional conclusions may be drawn, and will be discussed under the following headings: (1) growing interconnectedness and interdependence; (2) the idea and reality of separation; (3) what is shared and what is not; (4) organization for sharing; (5) new frameworks for analysis and design in shared power settings; and (6) planning and managing in shared power settings.

Growing Interconnectedness and Interdependence

A number of authors note that the world has become increasingly interconnected and interdependent, where interdependencies are defined as interactions that involve reciprocal effects on policy actors (Keohane and Nye 1977). These interactions and interdependencies are in part the results of tangible phenomena — such as new technologies for communications, information processing, transportation, and weapons. They are also the result of ideas. Perhaps the most basic ideas behind every chapter in the book are the concept of *systems* and the relation among subsystems or elements in systems.

Whether explicitly or not, every author describes a very complex *system* of interrelationships in which power is more or less shared with good or ill effects. Taken together, the chapters in this book argue for viewing the world of policy and planning problems as a more-or-less interconnected *system*. Wallerstein (1974, 1980) argues that such a system at the world scale began to take tangible shape in economic, social, and political spheres in the sixteenth century. The chapters in this book point out the extent to which further developments have involved increasingly elaborate articulations and interconnections of systems across all levels and policy areas with little regard for the traditional separations that bound our individual and collective "cognitive maps" (Hamden-Turner 1982; Eden et al. 1983). Regardless of our preconceptions, however, the world's *practice* is increasingly one of blurred distinctions and systemic interconnections at global and local levels in the economy, politics, environment, and other areas.

In embracing the system view, however, we face three related issues. One is the issue of what kind of system we confront; in particular, whether it is open or closed, and whether relations among subsystems are deterministic or not. The second issue concerns what we can know about large, complex systems. And third is the issue of what our traditional concepts—such as authority, accountability, and leadership—should mean when placed in an increasingly complex systems context.

Turning to the first of these—the open or closed, deterministic or non-deterministic—nature of systems, we find the dominant view of systems in the literature (based on physical science models) is that they are closed, hierarchical and embody causal (though often reciprocal) links (Laszlo 1972). There is a counter view, however, expressed earlier by such authors as James, von Bertalanffy, Boulding, and Koestler, and more recently, Battista, Beer, Churchman, Mitroff and Ulrich among others, who argue that systems can be quite open, hierarchical or non-hierarchical, and indeterminate. These systems views tend to be based on the life sciences or biological sciences. We use the terms open and closed, as do most of these latter authors, to mean that the system and its subsystems are open to and respond to their relevant external environments.

Koestler (1978), for example, drawing on von Bertalanffy, argues that the appropriate way to think of systems is as self-regulating, open, hierarchic orders (SOHO). In such systems, organizations are largely autonomous units which act in their own self-interest and in the interest of the larger system. They have one eye cocked upward or toward other lines of authority, advice or information, and adjust their internal actions in light of the external information or directive and their own preferences. Put another way, they balance self-assertive and integrative tendencies. Organizations in such systems are part of a "multi-holon" structure in which the systems functioning as wholes on one level function as parts on higher levels, and where the parts on higher levels operate as wholes on lower levels (Laszlo 1972: 51). A key point is that the nature and potential of "higher" levels in such systems is typically indeterminate and very much subject to alteration by interaction with the relatively autonomous parts and the external environment. That is, the nature and potential of the larger system is shaped through interaction with the constituent parts. The self-regulating nature of the system comes about through these interacting feed-forward and feed-back loops between the system and its subsystems. Shared-power systems seem to exhibit these characteristics.

The second issue concerns what we can know about large, complex systems. Obviously, there are limits on what we can know about such systems, particularly given their indeterminate nature. Still, a systems view provides some guidance on how to manage the complexity in the absence of complete knowledge. The first clue is provided by Luke (Chapter 2) in which he urges us to focus on the *interconnectedness* of the parts of a system. The linkages are what is critical—and also are what determine the actual level of complexity, uncertainty, and turbulence in a system. Luke argues that a focus primarily on the parts—rather than the interconnectedness of the parts—is likely to make a system seem more complex than it really is.

The second clue is that we can proceed in "chunks" (Peters 1987) within a system context; we do not have to know everything in advance in order to proceed. This is the way the Polaris submarine was constructed (Sapolsky 1972). The three main components of the system—the power plant, weapons system, and living space—were designed and developed simultaneously and fit together on completion. This fitting together could occur because there was agreement on a general space envelope, the locational relation of the three components, and careful management of the interfaces between the components as they evolved. Economic and political markets provide similar examples (Lindblom 1977). Individual units in such systems typically have much better local knowledge than system-wide knowledge, yet beneficial system-wide results can often result from the imperfect knowledge of individual actors interacting in a larger context. Further, the functioning of the whole can be improved by greater attention to information flows among the units.

The ability to chunk knowledge, yet still gain (at least potentially) major system-wide benefits, also points to the possibility of hierarchical or relatively non-hierarchical, open, indeterminate systems. Almost all systems theorists argue for hierarchy, since that is what is observed in Nature. However, they separate that from the nature of information flows among the levels or subsystems of the system. That is to say, hierarchy in current public affairs usage implies a top-down, central command organization. Most of Mother Nature's creatures and systems are hierarchically composed, but not with top-down, command type control systems. Rather, they are interacting hierarchical systems. Structurally, the implication of chunking is that the focus of attention should be on the interconnections among system elements and not on the detailed management of relations within elements. Processually, the focus of chunking is on the management of information flows or other resources across the links among system elements, and not so much on hierarchical authority relations. Most of the authors in this book seem to emphasize the importance of linkages, information, and resources, in contrast to hierarchical authority, when it comes to the design and management of shared power arrangements. That is consistent with systems and meta-systems theory (van Gigch 1987).

The third issue concerns what our traditional concepts—such as authority, accountability, and leadership—should mean in a shared-power systems context. Luke raises this issue most directly, and prompts serious speculation about the need for changed concept definitions. For example, it seems that in a shared-power systems context, authority is more a verb than a noun (Pondy 1977; Sonnett 1980). In situations where no one organization is "in charge," but many must be involved for effective action to occur, no pre-existing authority exists to act unilaterally—or if it does exist for some organization, it is relatively meaningless. Instead, the collective actions of the organizations involved "authorize" the creation and operation of shared power arrangements. Authorization and action are linked simultaneously in the same gesture, not linked sequentially with authority serving as a kind of platform from which action springs.

Similarly, accountability takes on something of a new meaning as Luke suggests. In situations where power must be shared among organizations to create desirable results, shared accountability for results seems to make sense. Holding each organization accountable for total results or a component of the results seems difficult when organizations cannot achieve the results individually, and when it is difficult for outsiders to disentangle individual contributions to collective outcomes.

Finally, leadership in shared-power arrangements clearly seems to highlight the importance of some form of *collective*, rather than individual, leadership. Most of the literature on leadership has focused on individuals operating in intra-organizational settings (Bass 1981). We really do not know a great deal about collective leadership in shared-power settings.

In summary, we conclude that behind each of the papers there is at least an implicit systems model and that, taken together, the papers imply it is increasingly useful to view the world of policy and planning problems as large, complex *systems* in which power is increasingly shared across levels and boundaries, across sectors, and within and across policy realms. The size and complexity of such systems (and of systems within systems) fortunately does not preclude effective knowledge and action. Attention to the design and management of linkages among elements and the appropriate "chunking" of elements can allow the emergence and management of relatively non-hierarchical, open, indeterminate systems that embody desirable means and achieve desirable ends. For this to happen, however, we may have to rethink many of the traditional concepts we have used to understand and govern our world.

Separation: Ideas and Reality

Four important conclusions emerge from the chapters concerning the ideas and reality of separation. First, the cultural roots that reinforce separation are deep. Second, the reality, however, is sharing, not separation. Third, we continuously confront the fundamental philosophical question of the one-and-the-many in shared-power situations. And finally, we probably need a new theory of policy intervention to guide decision making in shared-power situations. We discuss each of the first three conclusions in turn; the fourth is discussed later in the chapter.

Cultural Roots that Reinforce Separation

Luke points out that such concepts as individualism, autonomy, self-containment, self-sufficiency, and independence, for example, have become our Western legacy. This cultural legacy led to the separations-by-design in the U.S. Constitution, and in subsequent designs for state and local governments.

Governmental designs for the United States include three types of separation of powers—among the three branches of federal and state government, among functional agencies within any governmental level, and among governmental levels. All three of these separations were created on purpose. The separation of powers among branches of the federal and state government was to force shared responsibility in decision making rather than to vest it in a single office, and, as a consequence, to protect the liberty of the citizenry. This was a reaction against European monarchies. The reason for separated functional agencies was to create efficiencies based on concentrated expertise. The argument for the separation among the federal and state levels of government was expressly to preserve domains of autonomy and freedom—again as a reaction to highly centralized European governments. The glue holding these autonomous levels together was to be the electorate, the people who were the creators and electors of both systems.

The idea of separation clearly is strongly entrenched in the designs for government in the United States. One may question, however, the overall utility of these separations in a world where sharing—rather than separation—has taken on increased significance (Reich 1987). That question is prompted by our second conclusion; namely, that the reality typically is sharing, not separation.

The Reality Is Sharing

A number of authors—particularly Luke, Milward and Kincaid—point out how the presumed separation often is a myth; that the evolving path of the U.S.

governmental system typically has emphasized sharing as much as it has separation. Furthermore, the separations that do occur often are not the ones that were envisioned.

Milward, for example, traces the evolution of intergovernmental structure through the layer cake, marble cake, and picket fence models to his proposed policy network framework. The policy network is in fact a creation brought about through the sharing of funds collected at higher governmental levels for programs executed at lower levels. Milward notes this vertical "spine" of resource flows binds organizations and individuals across governmental levels together so strongly that the structural separations among horizontal levels of government (federal, state, and local) often are overridden, and the potentialities for general governance within a level are diminished. The program spine across levels has created cross-level sharing that was not envisioned, and made governance at any given level—where sharing was by design to be expected—more difficult.

Milward uses the Food Stamp program as an illustration. Congress allocated roles consistent with areas of expertise to various federal, state and local agencies and to private firms—banks and grocery stores. This created, in effect, an open, hierarchic order. The shared power lens and systems view also suggest operating improvements might be obtained by looking at the interrelations among these relatively autonomous actors.

The larger *world system* seems to be evolving along a path of sharing as well, although clearly important separations do—and are likely to continue to—remain. Kincaid, Finkelstein, and Hopmann and Harris, for example, all indicate the increased extent of sharing in international relations.

The One-And-The-Many In Shared-Power Situations
The third conclusion is that we continuously confront the fundamental philosophical question of the-one-and-the-many in shared power situations—a question that focuses on if, when, and how to "make whole" that which was separated. This ·question is posed, for example, by Kincaid as the tension between autonomy and interdependence, by Luke as the contrast between interconnectedness and separation, and by Freeman and Evan as a way of thinking about how things ought to be rather than how they are.

The chapters show that the philosophical question of the one-and-the-many has been resolved in a variety of ways, some surprising and others not. As many authors note, the rise of autonomy or individual action seems to lead inevitably to a societal or system response to assume that the actions of the individual person, government, or nation do not adversely affect the whole. These responses are the result of a perceived need to make whole that which has been separated structurally, because problems emerge that require a larger view if they are to be addressed successfully. This corresponds to the dual orientation—self-interested and integrative—of subsystems in general systems theory. The emergence of a vast array of shared power responses to problems that spill beyond organizational boundaries would not be surprising were it not for our cultural heritage's emphasis on separation.

On the other hand, complicating our capacity to act is an increasing pluralism. The empowerment of many partially autonomous entities is partly a consequence of our cultural heritage. It is also a consequence of economic growth that gives individuals and organizations the wherewithal to participate politically, and of new communications technologies that facilitate political participation. The pluralism is made real through, for example, non-governmental organizations (NGOs) in the international realm; interest group and political action committee activities at the national, state, and local levels; public-private partnerships; and the like. Unfortunately, the increased number of political actors has magnified the difficulty of arriving at consensus or majority positions on major political issues.

Said differently, as the interconnectedness of problems and actions increases, the boundaries of the "decision set" (Hickson et al. 1986) necessary to cope with the problems, required decisions, and actions increases. As the number of participants grows, the number of incompatible positions rises. The question then becomes, as Harlan Cleveland phrases it, "How can we get everyone in on the act and still get some action?" As a result of a kind of large-scale democracy among organizations, the very capacity for democratic action may be called into question (Olson 1971). Shared power may become shared impotence.

Another dangerous—and perhaps unexpected—consequence of increased pluralism is the emergence of a kind of "plural elitism" (McFarland 1979), as discussed by Milward, in which the few can defeat the many, if the benefits to the few are concentrated enough and the costs to the many are dispersed enough. Shared power in these situations may not indicate shared capacity for reasonably democratic action, either. Instead, it may simply mark a shared capacity among the "plural elites" to victimize the more plural masses. Shared power obviously does not necessarily lead to virtuous results. Whether it does or not depends very much on the situation and the actors involved.

In his chapter, Wood presents a potential consequence for education of "plural elitist" politics. He argues that we have a "protectionist" democracy (in contrast to a "participatory" democracy) that reduces citizenship to voting. He argues further that public education typically reinforces this strategy through emphasizing passive behavior and preparation for the workplace instead of preparation for active citizenship. Such an approach to education helps consolidate the hold of the elites on the power of the state. The one-and-the-many problem in this case is solved at the expense of the many.

Wood goes on to outline what education for democratic participation might look like—education, he argues, that would empower people to participate in our shared-power world. Wood therefore is one of the few authors in the book who outlines a potential shared-power *future* that is different from the present. He also emphasizes that people must *learn* how to participate in a shared power world, a position that places him in such diverse and esteemed company as John Dewey, Mao Tse-tung, and John Friedmann (Friedmann 1987). The difficulty with the Wood paper is that it also is an elitist position, since it would be implemented through elites in state education agencies, not through citizens and their elected officials. While we do not disagree with the concerns expressed, we do not believe any local school board, with broad citizen participation, would adopt Wood's agenda. In our view, many would see it as disbenefitting their children; such is the grip of competitive labor markets and no safety nets. The paper thus is weak on political action to achieve the objectives.

Freeman and Evan also outline a possible shared-power future quite different from the present. They propose a stakeholder— rather than stockholder—approach to corporate governance. Stakeholders would include all those affected by the actions of the corporation. The hypothesized effect is corporate decisions more acceptable to all interests, and in turn, reduction in the need for governmental intervention. The one-and-the-many problem in this case is solved by incorporating the many into the one. In effect, they argue in favor of socializing the major decisions of large corporations—much as Galbraith (1973) did earlier—in order to enhance their prospects for survival and effectiveness, and, not coincidentally, to reduce the size and scope of government. The fact that the argument is now made by two prominent business school professors—rather than by a left-of-center economist—perhaps is indicative of how far the shared-power practice—and supporting theory—of the world has come. On the other hand, left unsaid really is what should be done about the decisions of the large fraction of the economy represented by small businesses (O'Connor 1973). Also left unsaid is what happens to the individual firms who first assume these extra costs of operations and become non-competitive in the process. It may require power sharing with government to protect them in the process—an irony indeed!

In summary, we may conclude that it is critical to focus on the connections among elements in a system where divisions have occurred. For example, in the United States the separation between the executive and the legislative branches has long been at least partially overcome through so-called "iron triangle" arrangements—combinations of congressional committees, executive branch staffs, and interest groups, or more generally "issue networks of interested actors" (Heclo 1977). In parliamentary forms of government, the iron triangle is put together by design. The majority party or coalition in parliament dominates the legislative and executive process. What parliamentary governments have done by design to deal with "the whole" has occurred in the U.S. as a consequence of a void not addressed. The primary U.S. focus was on the separate authority and tasks of the elements rather than on the relationship between the branches. The form of the solution may not be appropriate, but the void virtually guaranteed that some bridging mechanism would emerge. Again, the power sharing perspective causes us to focus on relationships, linkages, and connections.

What is Shared and What Is Not?

We may conclude from the chapters that the preconditions for an organization to engage in shared-power relations have at bottom two attributes. First, there is a problem, a decision, or a project which the organization has the authority to act on, but which action, if taken alone, would not produce a result satisfactory to the organization. Second, there is enough self-interest involved for the organization to bear its share of the costs of a shared effort. The process of working out a shared-power arrangement, then, involves coming to grips with whether there is sufficient shared vision about a desirable process or outcome that the collaborative effort makes sense.

Given these preconditions, the following items are shared in the examples explored in the chapters:

1. Activity. The organizations engaged in a shared-power arrangement each contribute personnel or other resources so that joint activities may proceed aimed at achieving shared objectives or outcomes.

2. Trust. At least some measure of trust is involved in all of the examples, although the degree of trust varies. References to the prisoners' dilemma game appear in a number of the papers, and appropriately so, because the issue that lies behind the prisoners' dilemma is the question of what the involved parties can trust one another to do. The appropriate response to potential opportunism thus becomes highly problematic (Maitland, Bryson, and Van de Ven 1985).

3. Planning and Decision Making. The degree of sharing in the case of planning and decision making also varies, but there always appears to be at least some sharing in this area in all of the examples in the book.

4. Power. The power that is shared is the power to produce mutually desired results. What is not shared is authority (viewed as a noun), whether that authority be sovereign or organizationally-based authority. Rather, the participants in the shared-power arrangements use their authority in complementary fashion. Governments typically have constitutional or statutory limits on sharing or devolving authority and, thus, must seek other more limited means.

Organization for Sharing

It appears that in shared-power situations it is generally not possible to create a new structure or organization that "contains" the problem of interest and has all the necessary authority it needs to act. On the other hand, what does appear to be necessary in such situations is an arrangement that allows for, in Hirschman's (1970) words, both "voice" and "exit." Participating organizations need the opportunity to say their piece and be listened to, and also need the ability to withdraw if they do not like the results produced through shared activity, shared planning and decision making, and shared power. Exit presumably would not be a possibility if a new, encompassing, and authoritative organization were created to address the particular problem area.

Said somewhat differently, shared-power situations involve organizations with some authority to act on part of the focal problem or issue, but with not enough authority to produce satisfactory results for the organization through unilateral action. These organizations therefore come together to share power in order to tackle a problem, make a decision, or create a project. Further, it appears that these decisions to enter into shared-power arrangements are consciously made as a consequence of the organizations' realization that separate, uncoordinated actions are not acceptable alternatives.

In shared-power situations we thus are talking about the coming together of organizations in what several authors define variously as, for example, regimes, policy networks, interorganizational relations, or public-private partnerships. In such shared-power arrangements, as Whetten and Bozeman note, there is a need to be not too close and not too far—that is, close enough to get the job done, but not so close that the organizations' authority, sovereignty, or autonomy is threatened. Finkelstein, in his definition of regime, expresses this aspect of shared power arrangements as the "authoritative power to establish principles (by the majority) and the sovereign right not to be bound by them (for the minority)." Finkelstein then goes on to note that the real issue is not authority, but the collaboration of those essential to make something happen.

Hoppman and Harris, in their work on arms control, emphasize the important point that shared power arrangements almost always involve mixed-motive situations, in which the interests of the participating parties are partly in common and partly in conflict. In shared-power situations the parties actions have reciprocal (though not necessarily equal) effects on one another. The parties therefore strive for mutually beneficial outcomes at the same time that they seek to avoid mutually undesirable outcomes. They also reserve the right to withdraw—exit—from the arrangement when the results of shared-power actions are likely, in their estimate, to lead them to be worse off than if they acted alone.

These observations about organization for sharing bring us back to the first set of conclusions about systems. We emphasize that the view of systems implied by the chapters in this book does not involve completely understood, totally connected systems, nor is it one of completely autonomous and independent parts. Instead, there is organizational interdependence accompanied by an organizationally-retained right to take independent action. Shared-power arrangements therefore are in a middle ground between tightly-structured relationships and the very arms-length relationships of completely autonomous units. They have a degree of interdependence and a degree of independence. It appears that striking that balance is one of the important aspects of the design of shared-power arrangements. Put another way, it appears that shared power arrangements offer the benefits of joint activity by complementary organizations, a benefit that probably would be lost in a merged organization—where productive tensions would be submerged—and foregone when the organizations go it alone. Striking the balance that can produce the gain-gain from this complementary relationship is a key task.

New Frameworks for Analysis and Design in Shared Power Settings

The future of this field will draw on a variety of disciplines contributing a range of perspectives to our growing understanding. We noted the underlying sense of a system perspective in many of the papers. The early contributions of physical sciences to general systems theory—causally-linked command-type systems—and the more recent perspective provided by the biological sciences—open, interacting systems. Another aspect of the field is metasystem theory, or as van Gigch's book is titled "Decision Making about Decision Making" (1987). Put another way, these are frameworks for the study and design of systems.

Network analysis is another field contributing to the understanding of shared power settings. This field attempts to describe and analyze sets of units by focussing explicitly on their interrelationships. While most of the work to date is intraorganizational, the interorganizational aspect is increasing (Fombrun 1982). The field generally has drawn on organization theory from sociology, anthropology and political science.

Transactions cost analysis (see below) is another form of intra- and interorganizational analysis centered on the transactions between units in a network. It draws on strong roots in economics.

The focus on connections leads to the need for new theory of policy intervention. The country's initial attempts at policy intervention—particularly through the design of the United States Constitution—highlighted separations among governments and between politics and markets. Our subsequent approaches have not moved much beyond that.

Schultze (1977), for example, argues that our basic theory in practice has been to allow private sector markets to work until they fail. When they do fail we generally have not tried to get market *processes* to work better. Instead, we try to impose desired *outcomes* through replacing the market with public bureaucracies or through regulating the market. Recent emphasis on deregulation is essentially a reflection of this theory. In other words, much of the recent deregulation of, for example, airlines, railroads, truck transport, and telecommunications is based on the belief that public regulation does not work well—that, indeed, it is inferior to private sector markets because it causes more problems than it solves. Markets therefore should be reinstalled because they cause problems that are preferable to the ones regulation causes (Kingdon 1984).

Now, however, we have entered an era when interconnections and their management are increasingly important. Because of the growing importance of interconnections, it seems to us that we might consider taking actual or desired *transactions* as the basic unit of analysis, as proposed by advocates of transactions cost economics (Commons 1934, 1950; Ouchi 1981; Bryson 1984; Bryson and Ring 1988). We might then see markets, bureaucracies, taxes, subsidies, regulations, insurance schemes, information programs and self help, for example, as kinds of *transactions governance mechanisms* good for handling particular kinds of transactions in particular circumstances. The effectiveness of these transactions governance mechanisms would depend on the kind of transactions they sought to govern (Williamson 1985), as well as the criteria used to judge their performance. Bryson and Ring (1990), for example, propose efficiency, justice, and liberty as key criteria that should be used to evaluate the effectiveness of transactions governance mechanisms.

Such a new theory of policy intervention might allow us to design better, more targetted policy interventions less prone to unexpected or undesirable failures. The theory would help accomplish this purpose by focusing our attention on the kinds of transactions we wish to see—that is, the ends sought by a policy intervention— rather than on markets or bureaucracies—which are, or ought to be, means to an end. Our current theory, in other words, focuses our attention on means, not ends. Because of this inversion, it should come as no surprise that policy interventions often lead to surprising, or even destructive, results. Poorly designed policy interventions have been known to solve the wrong problems or even to create the problems they were supposed to solve (Bryson 1984).

A new theory of policy intervention that took the transaction as the basic unit of analysis also might allow us to manage the increasingly blurred distinctions between public and private, and to merge our concerns with both process and outcomes. Obviously a great deal of work will be necessary before such a theory can become fully operational.

In summary, we argue that while the cultural roots of separation are deep, the reality in the world of practice typically is sharing, not separation. In a world where much is divided and much is shared, the philosphical question of how best to handle the one-and-the-many arises constantly. A number of "solutions" to this problems have been worked out in practice, but not all are in the best interests of the majority of the people. Indeed, quite often the few gain at the expense of the many. In order to intervene more effectively in our shared-power world, a new theory of policy intervention probably is needed in which actual or desired transactions are the basic unit of analysis. The typical instruments of policy intervention in the U.S.—markets, bureaucracies, and regulations—then can be seen as particular kinds of transactions governance mechanisms suitable for governing particular kinds of transactions and prone to particular kinds of failure.

Planning and Management in Shared Power Settings

Finally, we come to the question of how to plan and manage in shared-power settings. Several conclusions seem to emerge from the chapters. First, planning and management should continue a trend already well underway; namely, to emphasize the management of the tensions and competing values embodied in a world of both increased autonomy and interdependence. Second, power sharing can be both a design tool and the object of design in a no-one-in-charge world. Third, planners and managers need to give increased attention to two capabilities. The first is the creation of a shared vision that can become an alternate to higher authority as a guiding force. Selected examples of new visions include those for new development projects (Frieden and Sagalyn: public-private), new schools (Wood: citizens, school boards; Kolderie: school administrators, teachers) new corporate cultures (Freeman and Evan: management and stakeholders), improved arms control (Hoppman and Harris: US-USSR), and improved international trade (Kincaid: federal, state). The second capability is the nature of, and skills necessary for, bargaining, negotiation, mediation and communication as a means to move toward desired shared visions or away from undesired ones. And finally, new theories of policy intervention designed for a shared-power world are likely to imply new roles for planners and managers.

The Need to Plan for and Manage Tensions and Competing Values

The fields of planning and management are increasingly aware of the need to *plan for* and *manage* the competing tensions and values presented by an increasingly interdependent world. Friedmann (1987), for example, describes what he believes are the four main traditions of *public planning thought* of the past two centuries. The four are: social reform, social learning, policy analysis, and social mobilization. (The different traditions would be identified with different writers. For example, social reform grew out of the work of Auguste Comte and Saint-Simon; social learning from the work of John Dewey and Mao Ze-dong; policy analysis from the early writings of C. West Churchman, Aaron Wildavsky, and others; and social mobilization from Marx and Lenin, as well as Mao.) He goes on to point out that each has something to offer in particular situations, and thus is contingently appropriate for use. There is no "one best way" to plan for all situations, but some ways that are better than others for particular situations (Bryson and Delbecq 1979; Christensen 1984; Alexander 1987).

In somewhat parallel fashion, Quinn (1988) argues that there are four main approaches to *management*, each of which also is contingently appropriate for use.

The approaches are the rational goal, hierarachical or internal process, developmental or open systems, and consensual or team approaches. The rational goal approach emphasizes achievement through logical, goal-oriented behavior within a firm or organization. The internal process perspective emphasizes security, stability, and control within organizational hierarchies. The open systems approach emphasizes growth, development, and change within very loosely-coupled organizations. Finally, the human relations model emphasizes affiliation, participation, and interpersonal concern expressed in teams. Quinn goes on to argue that *master managers* recognize the contingent appropriateness of all four approaches, and are able to employ each when needed. Since the organizational arrangements examined in shared power settings rarely have some one in charge, Quinn's latter two categories are likely to have more utility than the former two.

The chapters in the book represent varying blends of these eight schools of planning and management thought. On the planning side, for example, Kolderie's proposals for educational reform blend the social reform, social learning, and policy analysis traditions. Wood's arguments, on the other hand, emphasize social mobilization and social learning. On the management side, for example, Freeman and Evan argue in effect that corporations should move from more of a rational goal or internal process model toward more of an open systems or human relations model. Richards, on the other hand, would argue that corporations should not change from the rational goal or internal process model.

The point, however, is not to classify chapter authors according to some particular scheme. Instead, we wish to make the point that there does not appear to be any "one best way" to plan and manage in a shared-power world. Different approaches to the design and management of shared-power arrangements seem to be contingently appropriate depending on the particular circumstances at hand. Much more research and experience will be necessary, however, before we are able to say what sort of shared-power arrangements seem to work best to handle which sorts of tensions and competing values in which circumstances, and why.

Power Sharing As A Design Tool and Object Of Design

Organizational design is an important topic of research and discussion in the management literature. Unfortunately, most of the emphasis to date has been on *intra*organizational design and change, not *inter*organizational design and change; although most scholars clearly recognize the need to attend to the interorganizatinal dimensions of organizational design (Van de Ven and Ferry 1980). One can expect confidently that more attention will be devoted to interorganizational design and change as recognition of the importance and ubiquity of shared-power arrangements pervades the academic literature.

We hope in particular that increased attention will be focused on the design and management of shared-power arrangements—whether called regimes, policy networks, interorganizational relations or public-private partnerships. In a shared-power world in which actors maintain their rights to both voice and exit, shared-power arrangements become a principle mode of governance. Recall that regimes, as one example, involve "sets of implicit or explicit principles, norms, rules, and decision making procedures around which actors' expectations converge..." (Krasner 1983: 2). The design and management of regimes thus focuses particular attention on the construction and management of *lateral* relations, rather than *vertical* ones, a traditional object of attention in the *intra*organizational design and change literature (Van de Ven and Ferry 1980). Allocations of positions, offices, and authority are less important in regimes than are the design and management of interconnected lateral networks; lateral systems of information flows; and the "interpretive schemes" and precepts (Lindblom, 1977) that frame and shape actions within the regime.

The area of design of shared power arrangements, governance, and management would appear to be a very important and promising area of future inquiry. Fortunately, as the chapters in this book imply, there already have been important ground-breaking efforts, and not just in the area of international relations. Our focus on shared-power arrangements has helped clarify that much of the work on interorganizational relations, policy networks, and public-private partnerships, for example, is quite similar to the work done on regimes in the international relations field. The challenge for future research is to map further the similarities and differences among shared-power arrangements in different policy realms and to develop models that articulate the various contingencies governing the appropriateness of one set of arrangements versus another for particular purposes and circumstances.

New Management Skills

Planning and management in shared-power settings require skillful bargaining, negotiation, mediation and communication. These skills must be emphasized because shared-power situations involve mixed motives and lateral relations (or relations lacking coercive power). Unity of purpose and clear superior-subordinate relations cannot be assumed in such situations. Instead, agreements must be negotiated, politicked, hassled, and haggled out in a reasonably structured way.

Fortunately, much work has been done in the relatively recent past on how best to bargain, negotiate, mediate, and communicate. The work of Fisher and Ury (1980), Susskind and Cruikshank (1987), Fisher and Brown (1988) is representative of this developing literature. On the other hand, the use of information to enable subordinate units to act more fully in the larger interest as well as their own self interest is less studied than other facets. More work, of course, is still needed. Perhaps even more importantly, skill development in these areas should become a standard part of the education of professional leaders, managers, and planners who operate in shared-power settings. These skills can be learned, and even those people who already have the skills can become even more skillful through attention to the developing body of theory in these areas, use of skill-building exercises, and expert feedback (Whetten and Cameron 1984).

An important skill that must be singled out for particular attention is the need for leaders, planners, and managers to construct effective arguments in order to influence action in shared-power settings. One cannot bargain, negotiate, mediate, or communicate well without the ability to construct persuasive arguments. Indeed, some would argue that leadership (Burns 1978; Kouzes and Posner 1987), management (Daft and Lengel 1986), planning (Goldstein 1984) and policy analysis (Dunn 1979) are at least in part a kind of argumentation in which people are persuaded to do something they otherwise might not. Given the recent concern about the decline in Americans' ability to think, write, and talk (e.g., Bloom 1987), it would seem that special attention should be given to developing people's capacity to construct persuasive argumemts, since the ability to do so is crucial to effective action in shared-power settings.

Planning and Management Implications of a Transactions Approach to Policy Intervention

Some implications for planning and management seem to flow from discussion of policy intervention focused on the transaction as the basic unit of analysis. First, a great deal of work must address the question of how best to characterize transactions. What dimensions might best be used to typify transactions? Williamson (1975), Bryson and Ring (1988) and others have made a start, but more work obviously must be done. Second, planners and managers must become skilled at designing and managing transactions governance mechanisms suited for handling different kinds of transactions. Milward, Whetten and Bozeman, Frieden and Sagalyn, and Alexander, for example, at least implicity argue that effective planning and management in shared-power settings requires attention to the skillful manipulation of shared-power arrangements toward desired ends. Third, planners and managers must learn how to assess the utility of different governance mechanisms against many different criteria. Among chapter authors, Bolan, Kolderie, Wood, Freeman and Evan, Richards, and Hopmann and Harris perhaps emphasize most the need for shared-power arrangements to perform satisfactorily against multiple criteria if they are to be effective in some overall sense.

And finally, planners and managers must learn how to address failures in transactions governance mechanisms in such a way that the failures are neither glossed over nor aggravated. Among chapter authors, Whetten and Bozeman, Kolderie, Wood, Frieden and Sagalyn, Alexander, Freeman and Evan, and Kincaid probably emphasize most the need to clarify failures in shared-power arrangements and to fix these failures in such a way that more problems are not created than are solved.

Summary

Several conclusions may be drawn based on the chapters in this book. The most important one is simply that *a great deal can be learned by viewing the world through the lens of shared power*. Use of that lens helps clarify that many, if not most, of the most pressing issues we as people face arise in shared-power settings. Further, a variety of shared-power arrangements have been developed to address these issues. We need to explore further both the conditions that lead to shared-power arrangements and the relative effectiveness of those arrangements in different circumstances.

Second, *the world is characterized by growing interconnectedness and interdependence*. We confront an increasingly complex and articulated world system that must be both understood, planned for, governed, and managed if the most important problems we face are to be addressed in such a way that a large fraction of the world's peoples are better off. Taking a systems view, however, does not necessarily imply that a hierarachical, deterministic system is to be preferred. Indeed, quite the contrary. We hope that people will attempt to construct, govern, and manage open, hierarchical, indeterminate systems. In order to promote such systems, the design, governance, and management of shared-power arrangements should focus on the overall nature of the system and the linkages among the system parts, not on the detailed workings of the parts. Further, many of our traditional concepts may need to be redefined if they are to be suitable for use in a shared-power context.

Third, while our cultural roots emphasize separation, *the reality appears to be sharing*. In any system where divisions are important, the creation of a whole out of the separate parts is an enduring question that should be addressed in the design of any shared-power arrangements. Further, we probably need a new theory of policy intervention designed to focus on the creation and maintenance of desirable connections among system elements within the context of the larger system. A theory that takes the transaction as the basic unit of analysis, and views our "normal" tools of intervention (such as markets, bureaucracies, and regulations) as transaction governance mechanisms appears to hold some promise as one basis for such a new theory. Another related approach uses information, information flows, and information processing as key variables in explaining or designing effective organizations (Knight and McDaniel 1979).

Fourth, in all shared-power arrangements it appears that *what is shared is activity, trust, planning and decision making, and power*. What is not shared is authority; instead, authority is used in complementary fashion by the participants.

Fifth, shared-power arrangements do not involve creation of a new organization that "contains" the focal problem and has enough authority to act unilaterally. Instead, *shared-power arrangements involve organizations with some authority to act on part of the focal problem or issues, but not enough authority to produce satisfactory results for the organization through unilateral action*. These organizations come together to share power in order to tackle a problem, make a decision, or create a project. Further, these organizations come together conscious of the fact that they cannot achieve acceptable outcomes through unilateral action. The organizations reserve the right, however, to withdraw if unacceptable developments emerge through the sharing of power. The parties strive therefore for mutually beneficial outcomes at the same time they seek to avoid individually or mutually undesirable outcomes.

Finally, planning and management in shared-power settings involves different emphases than in more traditional settings. *In shared-power settings competing values and tensions must be both planned for and managed. Power sharing should be seen as both a design tool and object of design. Bargaining, negotiation, mediation, communication, and argumentation are crucial planning and management skills in shared-power settings. A focus on interconnections and their management implies that planning and management need to attend to: the characterization of transactions and transactions governance, including how to assess governance successes and failures according to many different criteria.* In these approaches, planning and management includes monitoring outputs for comparison with expectations as the basis for further adjustments. This output-oriented analysis is essential in non-deterministic settings, and contributes to solving the problem of accountability identified at the beginning of the book and emphasized by Luke.

Shared-power settings and shared-power arrangements are increasingly important. We hope that this book has helped illuminate what shared power is, how it works, and how it can be made to work better. Obviously, there is much more work to be done before we can truly understand what shared power is and how it can be used to improve our handling of the critical problems and issues that shared-power settings. Nonetheless, we believe the chapters in this book have made a start—and have prompted others to make their own contributions to this growing area of inquiry and practice.

References

Alexander, Ernest A. 1984. After rationality, what? A review of responses to paradigm breakdown. *Journal of the American Planning Association* 50(1): 62-69.

Battista, John R. 1977. The holistic paradigm and general systems theory. *General systems* 22:65-71.

Beer, Stafford. 1985. *Diagnosing the system for organizations.* New York: Wiley.

Bass, Bernard M. 1981. *Stogdill's handbook of leadership: A survey of theory and research.* New York: Free Press.

Bloom, Allan. 1985. *The closing of the American mind.* New York, NY: Simon and Schuster.

Boulding, Kenneth. 1968. "General systems theory: The skeleton of science." In *Modern systems research of the behavioral scientist*, edited by W. Buckley. Chicago: Aldine.

Bryson, John M. 1984. The policy process and organizational form. *Policy Studies Journal* 12(5): 445-463.

Bryson, John M. and Andre Delbecq. 1979. A contingency approach to strategy and tactics in project planning. *Journal of the American Planning Association* 45(2): 167-179.

Bryson, John M. and Peter Ring. 1990. "A transaction cost approach to policy intervention." *Policy Sciences* 23:205-229.

Burns, James McG. 1979. *Leadership*. New York, NY: Harper and Row.

Christenson, Karen S. 1985. Coping with uncertainty in planning. *Journal of the American Planning Association* 51(1): 63-73.

Churchman, C. West. 1968. *Challenge to reason*. New York: McGraw-Hill.

_____. 1971. *The design of inquiring systems*. New York: Basic Books.

Commons, John R. 1934. *Institutional economics*. Madison, WI: University of Wisconsin.

_____. 1950. *The economics of collective action*. Madison, WI: University of Wisconsin.

Daft, R.L. and R. H. Lengel. 1986. Organizational information requirements, media richness, and structured designs. *Management Science* 32(5): 554-571.

Dunn, William. 1981. *Public policy analysis*. Englewood Cliffs, NJ: Prentice Hall.

Eden, Colin, et al. 1983. *Messing about in problems: An informal structured approach to their identification and management*. New York: Pergamon Press.

Fisher, Roger and Scott Brown. 1988. *Getting together*. Boston, MA: Houghton, Mifflin.

Fisher, Roger and William Ury. 1981. *Getting to yes*. New York, NY: Penguin Books.

Friedmann, John. 1987. *Planning in the public domain: From knowledge to action*. Princeton, NJ: Princeton University Press.

Fombrun, C.J. 1982. Strategies for network research in organizations. *The Academy of Management Review*. 7:280-291.

Galbraith, Kenneth. 1973. *Economics and the public purpose*. New York: Houghton, Mifflin.

Goldstein, H.A. 1984. Planning as argumentation. *Environment and Planning B: Planning and Design* 11:297-312.

Hampden-Turner, Charles. 1982. *Maps of the mind*. London: MacMillan.

Hanken, A.F.G. 1981. *Cybernetics and society: An analysis of social systems*. Turnbridge Wells, Kent UK: Abacus Press.

Heclo, Hugh. 1978. "Issue networks and the executive establishment." In *The new political system*, edited by Anthony King. Washington, D.C.: American Enterprise Institute.

Hickson, David J. et al. 1986. *Top decisions: Strategic decision making in organizations.* San Francisco: Jossey- Bass Publishers.

Hirschman, Albert O. 1970. *Exit, voice and loyalty: Responses to decline in firms, organizations, and states.* Cambridge, MA: Harvard University Press.

Hopkins, Terence K. and Immanuel Wallerstein, ed. 1980. *Processes of the world-system.* Beverly Hills, CA: Sage.

James, William. 1975. *Pragmatism.* Cambridge, MA: Harvard University Press.

_____. 1979. *Some problems of philosophy.* Cambridge, MA: Harvard University Press.

Kingdon, John. 1984. *Agendas, alternatives and public policies.* Glenview, IL: Scott, Foresman.

Knight, Kenneth E. and Reuben R. McDaniel, Jr. 1979. *Organizations: An information systems perspective.* Belmont, CA: Wadsworth.

Koehane, Robert O. and Joseph S. Nye. 1977. *Power and interdependence: World politics in transition.* Boston: Little, Brown.

Koestler, Arthur. 1979. *Janus: A summing up.* New York: Vintage Books.

Kouzes, James M. and Barry Z. Posner. 1987. *The leadership challenge: How to get extraordinary things done in organizations.* San Francisco: Jossey-Bass.

Krasner, Stephen, ed. 1983. *International regimes.* Ithaca, NY: Cornell University Press.

Laszlo, E. 1972. *Introduction to systems philosophy: Toward a new paradigm of contemporary thought.* New York: Gordon and Breach, Science Publishers, Inc.

Lindblom, Charles. 1977. *Politics and markets.* New York: Basic Books.

_____. 1965. *The intelligence of democracy: Decision making through mutual adjustment.* New York: Free Press.

Maitland, Ian, John Bryson and Andrew Van de Ven. 1985. Sociologists, economists and opportunism. *Academy of Management Review* 10(1): 59-65.

Mitroff, Ian I. and Richard O. Mason. 1981. *Creating a dialectical social science: Concepts, methods and models.* Dordrecht, Holland: D. Reidel Publishing Co.

McFarland, Andrew S. 1979. "Recent social movements and theories of power in America." Paper presented at the 1979 American Political Science Association Meeting, Washington, D.C., August 31-September 3.

O'Connor, James. 1973. *Fiscal crisis of the state.* New York, NY: St. Martin's Press.

Olson, Mancur. 1971. *The logic of collective action: Public goods and the theory of groups.* Cambridge, MA: Harvard University Press.

Ouchi, William G. 1981. *Theory Z: How American business can meet the Japanese challenge.* Reading, MA: Addison-Wesley.

Peters, Thomas J. 1987. *Thriving on chaos: Handbook for a management revolution.* New York: Knopf.

Pondy, Louis K. 1977. "The other hand clapping: An information-processing approach to organizational power." In *Reward systems and power distribution,* edited by Tove Helland Hammer and Samuel B. Bacharach, 56-91. Ithaca, NY: Cornell University, New York School of Industrial and Labor Relations.

Quinn, Robert E. 1988. *Beyond rational management: Mastering the paradoxes of competing demands of high performance.* San Francisco: Jossey-Bass.

Reich, Robert B. 1987. *Tales of a new America.* New York: Times Books.

Sapolsky, Harvey M. 1972. *The Polaris system development: Bureaucratic and programmatic success in government.* Cambridge, MA: Harvard University Press.

Schultze, Charles. 1977. "The public uses of private interest." *Harpers* 254 (May): 43-62.

Sennett, Richard. 1980. *Authority.* New York: Knopf.

Susskind, Lawrence and Jeffrey Cruikshank. 1987. *Breaking the impasse: Consensual approaches to resolving public disputes.* New York: Basic Books.

Ulrich, Werner. 1983. *Critical heuristics of social planning: A new approach to practical philosophy.* Berne, Switzerland: Haupt.

Van de Ven, Andrew and Diane L. Ferry. 1980. *Measuring and assessing organizations.* New York: Wiley.

von Bertalanffy, Ludwig. 1969. *General system theory: Foundations, development, applications.* New York: G. Braziller.

van Gigch, John P., ed. 1987. *Decision making about decision making: Metamodels and metasystems.* Cambridge, MA: Abacus Press.

Wallerstern, Immanuel M. 1974. *The modern world-system.* New York: Academic Press.

Whetten, David A. and Kim S. Cameron. 1984. *Developing management skills.* Glenview, IL: Scott, Foresman and Co.

Williamson, Oliver. 1985. *The economic institution of capitalism.* New York: The Free Press.

Williamson, Oliver E. 1975. *Markets and hierarchies, analysis and antitrust implications: A study in the economics of internal organization.* New York: Free Press.

Index

by Eileen Quam and Theresa Wolner